DEVELOPMENT PERSPECTIVES
Problem, Strategy and Policies

Other Titles of Interest

SACHS, I.
Studies in Political Economy of Development
BALASSA, B.
Policy Reform in Developing Countries
SIMMONS, J.
The Education Dilemma: Policy Issues for Developing Countries in the 1980s
SINHA, R. and DRABEK, A.
The World Food Problem: Consensus and Conflict
GOLDSMITH, M. and KING, A.
Issues of Development: Towards a New Role for Science and Technology
GVISHIANI, J.
Trends and Perspectives in Development of Science and Technology and Their Impact on the Solution of Contemporary Problems
RADHAKRISHNA, S.
Views From the Developing Countries
URQUIDI, V.
Science and Technology in Development Planning
ADULBHAN, P. and SHARIF, N.
Systems Modelling in Developing Countries

DEVELOPMENT PERSPECTIVES
Problem, Strategy and Policies

by

V. V. BHATT

Development Economics Department, The World Bank

PERGAMON PRESS

OXFORD · NEW YORK · TORONTO · SYDNEY · PARIS · FRANKFURT

U.K.	Pergamon Press Ltd., Headington Hill Hall, Oxford OX3 0BW, England
U.S.A.	Pergamon Press Inc., Maxwell House, Fairview Park, Elmsford, New York 10523, U.S.A.
CANADA	Pergamon of Canada, Suite 104, 150 Consumers Road, Willowdale, Ontario M2J 1P9, Canada
AUSTRALIA	Pergamon Press (Aust.) Pty. Ltd., P.O. Box 544, Potts Point, N.S.W. 2011, Australia
FRANCE	Pergamon Press SARL, 24 rue des Ecoles, 75240 Paris, Cedex 05, France
FEDERAL REPUBLIC OF GERMANY	Pergamon Press GmbH, 6242 Kronberg-Taunus, Hammerweg 6, Federal Republic of Germany

First edition 1980

British Library Cataloguing in Publication Data
Bhatt, V. V.
Development perspectives.
1. Underdeveloped areas—Economic conditions
I. Title
330.9'172'4 HC59.7 79-42635

ISBN 0-08-025774-7

Printed and bound in Great Britain by
William Clowes (Beccles) Limited, Beccles and London

FOR PRAFULLA

व्यतिषजति पदार्थानान्तरः कोऽपि हेतु-
र्न खलु बहिरुपाधीन्प्रीतयः संश्रयन्ते

— उत्तररामचरित (६-१२)

"There is an immanent force that binds the universe together and makes of it a cosmos; this is love and it is not conditioned by external circumstances."

CONTENTS

PART III

Financial Structure and Policies

PART IV

Fiscal and Incomes Policies

PART V

International Aspects of Development Strategy

ACKNOWLEDGEMENTS

THE author is grateful to the editors and publishers who have kindly given their permission to reproduce in this book articles previously published in their books and journals, as follows:

Development Digest
Economic Theory and Planning
Economic and Political Weekly
Economic Development and Cultural Change
Economic Development in South Asia
Society and Change
The Bankers' Magazine
The Economic Journal
The Review of Income and Wealth
World Development

Chapters 1, 9 and 13 first appeared in the *World Bank Economic Development Institute Seminar Papers* series. Chapters 2, 3, 6, 8, 11, 12, 16 and 18 originally appeared in the *World Bank Domestic Finance Studies* series.

The views expressed in this book are solely those of the author and do not necessarily reflect the opinions or views of the World Bank and its affiliates.

Introduction

THIS book is primarily addressed to the general reader who considers the problem of development as a challenge to be faced with a creative response. Though written at different times and in different contexts, these interrelated papers have a certain common perspective—a leading thread that binds them together. The strengths and weaknesses of this book arise from this problem-oriented perspective, natural to one who has been an active participant in the development process as an adviser to policy makers. The other source of weakness or strength is the immaturity of orthodox economic theory and the author's conscious and deliberate "struggle to escape from habitual modes of thought and expression".[1] *

I

Mainstream orthodox economic doctrine provides quite useful analytic concepts and tools for understanding the short-run adaptive response of the economic system to marginal exogeneous changes in the objective environment. However, it sheds no light on the process of socio-economic evolution; its conceptual framework hence is not only inadequate but utterly misleading for understanding the vital issues related to development problems, strategies and policies. Such is the theme of Part I of this book. Because of its importance and since it recurs in different ways in the subsequent parts of this book, I would like to discuss briefly the central elements of this theme.

The basic limitation of the orthodox doctrine arises from a false perception or "vision"[2]—to use Schumpeter's expressive word—relating to the process of socio-economic change. This process is like the learning process; each act of learning increases the capacity to learn and hence leads to further learning. Similarly, socio-economic change in one direction leads to a further change in the same direction; change thus becomes self-reinforcing and cumulative. For example, a change in technology leads to a supportive adaptive change in institutions and ideology (attitudes, beliefs and motivation), which in turn leads to a further change in technology. This interaction among technological, institutional and ideological variables obviously takes place in historic time, any change in one leading sequentially to a change in the other is a sort of a chain reaction.[3] Thus a socio-economic system is always in a state of change or disequilibrium and its performance cannot be judged on the basis of static efficiency criteria, derived from an analytic framework that merely concentrates on passively adaptive equilibrating responses of the actors in the system to an external or exogenous change.[4]

A learning process inevitably involves error elimination as well as new perceptions, conjecture or expectations; it is thus creative as well as destructive.

* Notes, indicated by superior numbers, are at the end of each chapter.

Similarly, socio-economic change too is a process of "creative destruction";[5] institutions, ideologies and techniques that cannot adapt to change fade out and new ones take their place. The adaptation time lags and destruction involved in this evolutionary process make it both cumulative as well as cyclical.

Because of this circular and cumulative nature of the evolutionary process, differences between a socio-economic system changing in one direction and another experiencing a change in the opposite direction inevitably tend to widen. And more so if they are interrelated; as the "success" of the one inevitably limits the possibilities and tends to multiply the constraints and handicaps for the other.[6] Such polarization occurs also in the learning process; individuals and groups which learn tend to be learning at an accelerated pace, while those that do not tend to lag behind and stagnate.

The characteristics and mechanism of technological (including organizational) change strengthen and reinforce the cumulative nature of socio-economic processes. The economic process *as a matter of its inherent logic* induces technical change that is characterized by economies of scale, specialization and differentiation—thus leading to what economists call increasing returns to scale.[7]

How then is this process motivated and sustained? Human responses to a changing situation are generally motivated by the powerful instinct for security and survival on the one hand and on the other hand by an equally powerful passion for doing better than others—that is, envy, both individual and collective. It is this passion (envy) that causes both creative as well as destructive behaviour. These instincts by themselves would generate merely a competitive process but not necessarily a process of creative destruction. What sustains the latter is not the competitive yet passively adaptive response of individuals and groups but the creative response,[8] in Schumpeter's sense, of a few. In a very vital sense, the nature and structure of the evolution of a socio-economic system are determined by the extent to which individuals and groups with this capacity for creative response participate in the tasks and functions of the political economy. The competitive process, then, takes a different character; it is not competition in performing old and routine functions but a competitive behaviour that threatens the old ways of doing things by a *qualitatively* new and unexpected response that quickens the pace of innovative change in technology, institutions and ideologies.[9]

Time is of the essence in this cumulative process—time flowing irreversibly from the past through the present to the uncertain future. The irreversibility of history and the circular cumulative nature of the process of socio-economic change inexorably create different but interlinked patterns of change for different groups (countries) depending on their location in time and space; this leads to polarization of groups (countries)—success begetting success and failure heralding further failure. "For whosoever hath, to him shall be given, and he shall have more abundance: but whosoever hath not, from him shall be taken away even that which he hath."[10]

The groups which are victims of this polarization process (the inevitable complement of the cumulative process of change) try to counteract its effects through the political process. Once they become politically self-conscious and organized, they tend to demand, through political action, a new socio-economic order (a welfare state or a socialist–communist state) which can ensure them with a certain measure of equality of opportunity. At the international level, the backward countries' progressively insistent demand for a new international economic order has the same compulsive logic. Thus, at the present juncture, the gathering momentum of this counteracting and countervailing political process is in conflict with the logic of the economic process at the national as well as the international level. This conflict can be resolved through a *symbiosis* of these two processes—the political and the economic. But this is not possible unless the interests of the different groups can be reconciled through a consensus among themselves with regard to the political framework for decision-making and conflict resolution through consent rather than force. A large number of developing countries are still struggling to achieve such a national consensus—as are the different countries at the international level. Much depends on the nature and quality of the creative response of groups and countries, especially the privileged ones, to this world-wide challenge. Time is indeed "out of joint", while the orthodox doctrine concerns itself with ever more intellectual vigour and rigour, with Euclidean geometry in a non-Euclidean world,[11] trying to provide Platonic solutions to Socratic problems.

II

The symbiosis of the two processes (the political and the economic) is essential both at the national and the international level. The implications for such a symbiosis for development policy in poor countries are the theme of Part II to Part IV. The central propositions are stated simply and briefly in the following paragraphs; for elucidation of these propositions, the reader should turn to the individual chapters of these parts. Propositions 1 to 4 relate to Part II, while the rest relate to Parts III and IV.

1. The development problem essentially is a *human* problem and has to be formulated in human terms. Briefly the problem is: how to ensure a progressively rising *minimum* level of living to *each* individual and family—the minimum to be determined of necessity in the light of a specific context. It is neither possible nor desirable to ensure such a minimum without full employment (employment in productive tasks of each individual and family) at *progressively rising levels of productivity*. Without freedom, of course, the development process has no *rationale* in human terms. Physical security, employment and freedom—these have to be the basic objectives of development strategy and policies, once the problem is formulated not in ideological terms but as a human problem. In the present context, such an approach is not only a moral imperative but is also a political necessity and a technological possibility.

2. Once one starts from this *focal* point, there is no alternative but to understand the traditional structure (the initial structural characteristics and their dynamics in a specific context) and find out how it can be revolutionized from within. It is not possible to ensure full employment with a rising minimum level of living without a progressive increase in labour productivity in the traditional sector. The critical factors for the purpose are organization and technology. So the concrete task initially is to identify the possibilities of upgrading organization and technology and to induce, through a variety of policy instruments and

ideological change, such changes in them as are feasible and essential. Such identification and choice will also indicate the nature and structure of modern sector development that is essential for reinforcing and supplementing the growth in the traditional sector. The current approach to the problem begins at the wrong end—the modern sector, and hence of logical necessity, tends to supplant the traditional by the modern sector; this is simply impossible. For, wherever one wants to go, there is no alternative but to start from where one is.

3. It is because of this futile approach and endeavour that the problem of technology choice is not even perceived as a vital problem. The poor countries have one signal advantage of drawing on the accumulated and growing body of modern scientific and technological knowledge for the solution of their problems. But unless the questions can be formulated and posed, knowledge by itself cannot provide answers. "Seek and ye shall find." But to seek, search, select, adapt and improve presupposes a dynamic learning process. For upgrading traditional technology and creatively adapting modern technology, it is essential to formulate a technology policy that sets the learning process in motion.

4. The basic task or function relates to the identification of technology problems of specific projects or project complexes. And this precisely is the design-engineering function. Without such initial identification, one would not know how to search for possibilities of upgrading traditional technology and creatively adapting modern technology to a given problem situation. Thus design-engineering competence provides the link between Modern Technology and Technological Research Centres (TRCs)—wherever they are located—on the one hand and the Production System (PS) on the other. Hence my emphasis on the development of Technical Consultancy Service Centres (TCSCs) and Project Identification Centres (PICs).

5. In ultimate analysis, it is the Financial System (FS)—*including the government when it assumes the financing function*—that determines the choice of projects to be implemented. Its choice criteria should include as a vital part the technological dimension of projects or project complexes. Without such a dimension, however refined its selection criteria in terms of social cost-benefit analysis, they would be ineffective in inducing right technology choices. Thus the functions of the TCSCs and the FS are organically interrelated and one cannot function effectively without the other. Since the final choice is with the FS, it is the latter which has to take a leading catalytic role in formulating and implementing an appropriate technology policy; it has to identify and institutionalize the design-engineering tasks and functions and organically relate them to Modern Technology and TRCs on the one hand and the promoters of projects and project complexes on the other.

6. The development process is conditioned and shaped by, as in turn it conditions and shapes, the nature and characteristics of the FS. To the extent to which it induces pure savers to save in the form of financial instruments, it determines the magnitude of real saving—saving that releases real resources for productive investment. (It is not realized in the literature with sufficient clarity that saving which releases resources is only that part of total saving which is in the form of financial or paper instruments.) And both its historically determined philosophy or agenda and its criteria for choice (based on the nature and structure of its

expertise in judging projects and promoters) inevitably shape the pattern of resource allocation in favour of the modern sector of trade and industry. If it has to have a development orientation particularly with regard to the traditional sector, which it has ignored for historical reasons, it has to introduce such financial innovations that tend to reduce its own transaction costs (including risk) of lending to and borrowing from this sector, as well as the transaction costs borne by the traditional sector. Such changes in financial technology are essential if the system is to promote and facilitate the growth of the traditional sector.

7. Finance is the vital link between the present and the future and any weakness in this link heightens and aggravates uncertainty about the inevitably uncertain future. Monetary-financial stability is thus a pre-condition for orderly development. Inflation corrodes the development process from within, destabilizes the financial system and generally aggravates poverty and inequalities. Avoidance of inflation and inflationary expectations thus should be one of the major aims of all economic policies; and in particular fiscal and incomes policies need to reinforce the effectiveness of monetary-financial policies. For overall financial balance, it is essential to formulate policies within the framework of sound financial planning.

8. It is not possible to eliminate poverty, ensure full employment with rising minimum levels of living, avoid the disruptive effect of inflation and generate and sustain the development process without a progressive increase in land *as well as* labour productivity in the agricultural and, in particular, the food sector. Hence the task of upgrading organization and technology in agriculture is of critical significance.

9. Since output in the agricultural sector would continue to be vulnerable to the forces of nature that cannot be controlled, it is essential to insulate the socio-economic system and its development from the impact of fluctuations in agricultural output. In particular, buffer-stocks of food and other essential agricultural commodities or of foreign exchange are essential for off-setting the impact of output fluctuations on prices and incomes. But even such a buffer-stock policy may not serve the intended purpose, unless it is accompanied by and reinforced through a viable distribution system that ensures supplies to sectors that need them at reasonable prices.

III

The basic decisions about the development process have inevitably to be taken by the poor countries or the less developed countries (LDCs) as they are categorized in the literature. As the saying by Buddha goes: नाञ्ञो अञ्ञं विसोधये —none can purify another.[12] But the effectiveness of their strategy and policies critically depend on the international context within which they have to function; for, it is this context which has in fact created the problem and its salient characteristics as well as the possibility of its solution. This is the theme of the final part of this book (Part V), and its central propositions are the following:

1. Stability of the international currency and the international monetary system is an essential prerequisite for the sustained growth of the world economy.

But the question is: how does one measure the degree of stability of international currency? Obviously, it has to be related to some prices, and these should be prices of *basic* commodities that are produced through land—agricultural and mineral products. For, in the final analysis, the ultimate constraint on industrial and economic growth is the commodity constraint; the processing activity of the industrial sector depends upon the output of the land-based materials to be processed. The value, hence, of international currency should be linked in an essential way to the prices of commodities that are basic, in a fundamental sense, to the development process. The international monetary system would then have a firm and meaningful anchorage and international monetary policy would have a rationale and effectiveness which it lacks at present.[13]

There is another compelling reason, as argued by Kaldor, for linking the value of international currency with the prices of primary products. And this is related to the impact of fluctuations in terms of trade between the primary and the industrial sector on the growth of the world economy. Since industrial prices are "cost determined" and primary product prices are "market determined", any imbalance between the growth of the two sectors is corrected by changes in the prices of primary products. With the emergence of commodity surpluses, the terms of trade move against the primary sector but this does not lead to accelerated industrialization; for, its stimulating effect is more than offset by the decline in the demand for industrial products by the primary sector and the decline in investment in the primary sector by the industrial countries. Similarly, the emergence of shortages which should accelerate the growth of the availabilities of primary products through improvement in the terms of trade leads instead to an inflation of industrial prices which tends to offset the improvement in the terms of trade and, by its dampening effect on industrial activity, worsens the climate for new investment in both the primary and the industrial sectors.[14]

Thus, to provide stability to the international monetary system as well as to create conditions for the mutually reinforcing development of the primary and the industrial sectors, it is essential to link the management of international currency with the objective of stabilizing the prices of primary products. The mechanism for this purpose is discussed in Chapter 19. Though the context has changed since this was written, it is still relevant for providing the necessary link between SDR creation and the objectives of the UNCTAD proposal for a Common Fund for commodities.

2. For shaping the international monetary-financial-trade system in a manner that is consistent with their development strategy, the LDCs need to acquire enough strength to exert the required moral and economic pressure on the developed countries. They will not be able to do this unless they are willing to take such self-help concerted measures that are necessary for overcoming the balance-of-payments constraint on the expansion of their trade and production systems. Hence the concrete proposal in Chapter 20 for a universal payments union for trade creation among the LDCs as a group.

3. The process of socio-economic development has to be viewed as an integral part of the process of nation building as well as the building of an international community, within which conflicts of aims, objectives and methods are resolved by consent rather than by force. External assistance and in fact all types of other

mutual assistance in the field of ideas as well as techniques is a powerful instrument for accelerating these three interrelated processes. The time horizon for all these processes to work themselves out would be quite long—a generation or two—and if this time perspective is kept in mind, it has significant implications with regard to the nature, magnitude and forms of external assistance. Such is the main thesis of the final chapter.

. . . . .

Socio-economic processes have their own internal dynamic and inherent logic. The choice possibilities at a given stage of the process for conscious human action are inevitably limited. It is the function of intellectuals to try to tilt the balance of forces to the extent possible towards a course of action that can provide a sound material basis for upholding the sense of human dignity, expressed in the following felicitous lines from the Bangali poet Chandidas:[15]

सबार उपरे मानुष सत्य
ताहार उपरे नाहि।

Above all is Man; there is none above him.

NOTES

1. J. M. Keynes, *The General Theory of Employment, Interest and Money* (New York: Harcourt, Brace & World, Inc.: First Harbinger Edition, 1964), p. viii.
2. See J. A. Schumpeter, "Science and Ideology", in his *Essays*, edited by Richard V. Clemence (Cambridge, Mass.: Addison-Wesley Press, Inc., 1951), p. 272. To quote: "First, that perception of a set of related phenomena is a prescientific act. It must be performed in order to give to our minds something to do scientific work on—to indicate an object of research—but it is not scientific in itself. But though prescientific, it is not preanalytic. It does not simply consist in perceiving facts by one or more of our senses. These facts must be recognized as having some meaning or relevance that justifies our interest in them and they must be recognized as related—so that we might separate them from others—which involves some analytic work by our fancy or commonsense. This mixture of perceptions and prescientific analysis we shall call the research worker's Vision or Intuition" (p. 272).
3. See S. Kuznets, "Modern Economic Growth: Findings and Reflections", *American Economic Review* (vol. 63, no. 3, June 1973).
4. J. A. Schumpeter, *Capitalism, Socialism and Democracy* (New York: Harper & Row, 1975). To quote: "This fact bears upon our problem in two ways."

   "First since we are dealing with a process whose every element takes considerable time in revealing its true features and ultimate effects, there is no point in appraising the performance of that process *ex visu* of a given point of time; we must judge its performance over time, as it unfolds through decades or centuries. A system—any system, economic or other,—that *every* given point of time fully utilizes its possibilities to the best advantage may yet in the long run be inferior to a system that does so at *no* given point of time, because the latter's failure to do so may be a condition for the level or speed of long run performance" (p. 83).

   See also K. J. Arrow, *The Limits of Organisation* (New York: W. W. Norton & Co., 1974), chapter 3.
5. J. A. Schumpeter, *Capitalism, Socialism and Democracy, op. cit.*, pp. 82–5. To quote: "As we have seen in the preceding chapter, the contents of the labourer's budget, say from 1760 to 1940, did not simply grow on unchanging lines but they underwent a process of qualitative change. Similarly, the history of the productive apparatus of a typical farm, from the beginnings of the rationalisation of crop rotation, plowing and fattening to the mechanized thing of today—linking up with elevators and railroads—is a history of revolutions. So is the history of

the productive apparatus of the iron and steel industry from the charcoal furnace to our own type of furnace, or the history of the apparatus of power production from the overshot water wheel to the modern power plant, or the history of transportation from the mailcoach to the airplane. The opening up of new markets, foreign or domestic, and the organisational development from the craft shop and factory to such concerns as U.S. Steel illustrate the same process of industrial mutation—if I may use that biological term—that incessantly revolutionizes the economic structure *from within*, incessantly destroying the old one, incessantly creating a new one. This process of Creative Destruction is the essential fact about capitalism."

6. G. Myrdal, *Rich Lands and Poor* (New York: Harper & Brothers Publishers: 1957), chapter II.
7. N. Kaldor, "The Irrelevance of Equilibrium Economics", in *Further Essays in Economic Theory* (New York: Holmes & Meier Publishers, Inc., 1978), pp. 182–9.
8. See J. A. Schumpeter, "The Creative Response in Economic History", in *Essays*, edited by R. Clemence (Cambridge, Mass.: Addison-Wesley Press, Inc., 1951), pp. 217–18. To quote: "Creative response has at least three essential characteristics. First, from the standpoint of the observer who is in full possession of all relevant facts, it can always be understood *ex post*; but it can practically never be understood *ex ante*; that is to say, it cannot be predicted by applying the ordinary rules of inference from the pre-existing facts. . . . Secondly, creative response shapes the whole course of subsequent events and their 'long run' outcome. . . . Creative response changes social and economic situations for good, or, to put it differently, it creates situations from which there is no bridge to those situations that might have emerged in its absence. This is why creative response is an essential element in the historical process; no deterministic credo avails against this. Thirdly, creative response—the frequency of its occurrence in a group, its intensity and success or failure—has obviously something, be that much or little, to do (a) with quality of personnel available in a society, (b) with relative quality of personnel, that is, with quality available to a particular field of activity relative to quality available, at the same time, to others, and (c) with individual decisions, actions, and patterns of behaviour. Accordingly, a study of creative response in business becomes coterminus with a study of entrepreneurship" (pp. 217–18).
9. See J. A. Schumpeter, *Capitalism, Socialism and Democracy, op. cit.*, pp. 84–5. To quote: "The first thing to go is the traditional conception of the *modus operandi* of competition. Economists are at long last emerging from the stage in which price competition was all they saw. As soon as quality competition and sales effort are admitted into the sacred precincts of theory, the price variable is ousted from its dominant position. However, it is still competition within a rigid pattern of invariant conditions, methods of production and forms of industrial organization in particular, that practically monopolizes attention. But in capitalist reality as distinguished from its textbook picture, it is not that kind of competition which counts but the competition from the new commodity, the new technology, the new source of supply, the new type of organization (the largest-scale unit of control for instance)—competition which commands a decisive cost or quality advantage and which strikes not at the margins of the profits and the outputs of the existing firms but at their foundations and their very lives. This kind of competition is as much more effective than the other as a bombardment is in comparison with forcing a door, and so much more important that it becomes a matter of comparative indifference whether competition in the ordinary sense functions more or less promptly; the powerful lever that in the long run expands output and brings down prices is in any case made of other stuff. . . . It is hardly necessary to point out that competition of the kind we now have in mind acts not only when in being but also when it is merely an ever-present threat. It disciplines before it attacks" (pp. 84–5).
10. See the New Testament (St. Matthew 13: 12).
11. See J. M. Keynes, *op. cit.*, p. 16.
12. Dhammapada (Chapter 8, verse 9).
13. N. Kaldor, "Inflation and Recession in the World Economy", in *Further Essays on Economic Theory, op. cit.*, pp. 218–30.
14. *Ibid.*, pp. 220–1.
15. V. V. Bhatt, *Aspects of Development Strategy and Policies* (Bombay: Vora & Co., 1978), p. 181.

PART I. Economic Theory and Development Process

1. The Sterility of Equilibrium Economics: An Aspect of the Sociology of Science*

THE distinguishing characteristic of man is that he lives in two worlds—the world of reality and that of symbols. The world of symbols is his own intellectual creation in order to understand the real world in which he lives and has his being. The symbols which he creates are of two types: one type consists of a language—a set of symbols which helps him in analysing the aspect of reality in which he is interested; the other is intellectual recreation of reality with the help of language-type symbols. It is thus that he tries to understand and shape the world of reality.[1]

How then do we distinguish man's scientific activity from this general intellectual activity? His pursuit to understand reality becomes a scientific activity when he is prepared consciously to change and adapt his symbols to the emergent facts of physical or human existence. His intellectual creations suggest the facts that he should collect and his fact-finding suggests the way in which he should change and adapt his symbol systems to the emergent facts. This is an unending process of give and take between theory and observation as also of progressive discovery of objective reality.[2]

At any period of time, the state of scientific knowledge consists of theories—intellectual creations—that are not disproved by facts,[3] assuming of course that the fact-finding process generated by such theories has not meanwhile stopped and that "... scientists try to express their theories in such a form that they can be tested, i.e. refuted (or otherwise confirmed) by experience."[4]

When the processes of theorizing and fact-finding are not interrelated, scientific activity becomes sterile. Intellectual creations, in such a case, lose their instrumental value in understanding objective reality and fact-finding becomes a chaotic process without scientific significance.

This sterility of scientific effort seems to characterize the present state of economic science.

I

Explanatory Hypothesis

This sterility seems to be due to three factors: (*a*) a caste system that has developed among economists, (*b*) the fact that the sphere of the strictly provable is limited in economics, and (*c*) the presence of the inevitable ideological element in the scientific effort devoted to socio-economic phenomena.

There are three interrelated yet distinct phases of any scientific activity: the first is concerned with evolving an engine of analysis or an analytic apparatus suited

* Published in *Economic Theory and Planning*, editor: Ashok Mitra (Bombay: Oxford University Press, 1974).

for examining certain aspects of reality. This apparatus consists of a certain limited number of axioms or postulates, taken for granted on the basis of available facts, and the theorems derived from them on the basis of logically admissible scientific procedures. These theorems or propositions are logical in character and may or may not have any empirical content. Theory in this sense has only instrumental value in deriving propositions about empirical phenomena. The sole test of the relevance of this apparatus is its ability to generate explanatory hypotheses with regard to empirical reality.

Such explanatory hypotheses are suggested by facts—they are framed with an eye to observations made—and are formulated with the help of the analytic apparatus. In strict logic, the analytic apparatus as well as explanatory hypotheses are arbitrary intellectual creations. Their validity has to be judged on the basis of their consistency with additional facts and observations—the nature of which are suggested by them. Thus the fact-finding process generated by theoretical constructs is an integral part of scientific activity.

These three processes are interacting and interrelated and form the core of scientific activity in general.[5]

In economic science, these three processes have somehow remained by and large distinct with the result that we have few meaningful explanatory theories or propositions that are in harmony with empirical reality. There is no economic science in the meaningful sense of the term.

There can be two explanations of the evolution of this caste system in the pursuit of economic science. One is related to the complexity of the subject-matter itself. Economics has to deal with a unique historical process; this historical or evolutionary nature of the economic process unquestionably limits the scope of general concepts and of general relations between them that economists may be able to formulate.[6] Economic laws are much less stable than are the laws of any physical science; they work out differently in different institutional conditions. This complexity of the subject-matter indicates the inexorable necessity of specialization with regard to each phase of scientific effort till each one attains a degree of maturity for relating one phase to the other. In this sense, the present state of economic science mainly reflects its immaturity.

But there is, as a consequence, an additional barrier to communication. Each type of scientific effort tends to form a scientific school with more or less common outlook and perspective of approaching economic reality and more or less common scientific procedures or analytic techniques. Such perspectives and analytic techniques tend to get entrenched because of the association of scientific work with teaching and whatever changes take place in them are more as a reaction to the inherited perspectives and techniques rather than as a result of cross-fertilization with the other two schools.

The formation of such professional classes and their association with teaching is indeed a social mechanism for transmission of accumulated knowledge and for identifying areas for further scientific work. The bulk of scientific structure and knowledge is handed from generation to generation as a matter of course by a more or less definite group of professionals who teach the rising generations not only their methods and results but also their opinions about the direction and the means of further advance. In a majority of cases, competence in doing scientific work cannot be acquired, or can be acquired only by individuals of quite exceptional originality and force, from a source other than the teachings of recognized professionals.[7]

This social mechanism is not only favourable to the development of conceptual apparatus and to the accumulation of factual knowledge; it also supplies the most potent motive power of what is usually referred to as scientific progress. But there is the other side of the medal. Teaching in any established science stereotypes the mind of the scientific worker and may stunt such originality as he may have. Further, major changes in perspectives and techniques do get ignored or retarded because of the resistance that an existing scientific structure offers.

The fact that existing structures once established tend to persist accounts for the lack of communication among the three schools mentioned earlier. There is an additional fact to be taken into account. Professionals, who devote themselves to scientific work on any particular field, tend to become a sociological group. This means that they have other things in common besides interest in scientific work. In most cases they teach the science which they are trying to bring up and to make their living by teaching. Naturally, this tends to evolve a social and economic type. The group accepts or refuses to accept co-workers also for reasons other than their professional competence. The association of scientific work with teaching produces a profession in the full sense of the word and this profession tends to develop attitudes to social and political questions that are similar for reasons other than similar scientific views. This is closely associated with the phenomenon of scientific schools.[8]

This phenomenon of scientific schools is related to the problem of ideological bias in scientific work. Ideology or an intuitive perception of objective reality is an inevitable and integral part of any scientific work. Facts do not speak for themselves. To approach reality requires initially what Schumpeter calls a vision—a perception of a set of related phenomena.[9] This perception is pre-scientific but not pre-analytic. It does not consist in perceiving facts by one or more senses. These facts must be recognized as having some meaning or relevance that justifies an interest in them and they must be recognized as related—so that we may separate them from others—which involves some analytic work by our fancy or common sense. No scientific work is feasible without such vision or perception; it is a necessary and inevitable phase of the cognitive process.

Now this vision or intuition—whether explicit or implicit in scientific work—is socially conditioned; it is conditioned by the objective data of the social structure and in particular by the social location of a scientific worker that determines his outlook on reality and hence what he sees of it and how he sees it. This conditioning process relates not only to his social location but also to the manner in which he wants to see himself or his class or group and the opponents of his own class or group. This should be extended even to peculiarities of his outlook that are related to his personal tastes and conditions—again positively or negatively socially conditioned—and have no group connotation; there is even the ideology of the mathematical mind as well as an ideology of the mind that is allergic to mathematics.[10]

The source of ideology in this sense is the pre- and extra-scientific vision of the economic process; this is subjected to scientific treatment and would be either verified or destroyed by analysis and accumulated evidence and in either case, it should vanish as ideology. But this can happen only when the content of the vision is explicitly conceptualized—the fixing of its elements into precise concepts and in establishing relations between them—and reformulated in terms of the existing stock of facts as well as the new facts that the conceptual scheme requires to be collected and so on in an endless sequence till both the activities—formulation of the conceptual scheme and fact-finding—improve, deepen and correct the original vision and also each other's results. Of course, even such reformulated theories are provisional by nature and are always relative to the stock of facts we command.

Such a scientific procedure can progressively eliminate or reduce ideological bias; but in various lines of scientific work relating to economics and social sciences, the field of the strictly provable is limited in that there are always fringe ends of things that are matters of personal experience and impressions from which it is practically impossible to drive ideology, or for that matter conscious dishonesty completely.

But all these apply to explicitly formulated visions and not to those which are implicit in the scientific activity of the three schools. It is almost impossible to approach any set of interrelated phenomena particularly in economics and social sciences without having an implicit vision of the way in which economic and social processes work themselves out. And since each school has such a vision—explicit or implicit—this may pose a barrier to *inter se* communication; and even when such communication exists, it may promote such cross-fertilization that may lead to cross-sterility.

Some examples would illustrate what we mean.

Take equilibrium economics, for example, as has evolved on the Walrasian lines and forms the core of the analytic apparatus that has emerged as a result of two hundred years of scientific effort. The basic implicit vision of this school of analysis seems to regard the economic process as primarily a process of adjustment to change in data caused by other social processes. This adjustment mechanism ensures a smooth harmonious process as a result of the optimizing activity—in terms of each one's isolated preference functions taken as a psychological datum—of economic agents, each one of which takes the environment as given; it is not affected by nor does it attempt to affect the behaviour of other agents. A further crucial ingredient of the vision is that the cost of adjustment for each agent is an increasing function of the adjustment process itself. The main task of theory then is to derive the equilibrium properties of this process, which should come to an end unless disturbed by non-economic phenomena that may cause change in the data.[11]

Since the days of Walras, this analytic apparatus has been refined and the original theorems have been derived with progressively increasing rigour and elegance. However, there has been recognition of the fact that the adjustment mechanism may suffer periodically as a result of insufficiency or excess of over-all effective demand—a concession to Keynes that still remains an appendage rather than an integral part of equilibrium economics.[12] But then a convenient assumption is made that as a result of the benign activity of the State—again guided by its own given preference function—excess or insufficiency of over-all demand should not arise. Thus, in terms of the theoretical structure, these two types of analytic apparatus—the micro and the macro—co-exist without much cross-fertilization.

The implicit vision behind the Keynesian apparatus is still evolving. On the basis of the present evidence, it seems to regard economic change as an organic endogenous cumulative process, each historic stage determining the succeeding stage in a causal sequence. The problems of relative prices, actual choices made by economic agents and the nature of market structures are taken as of relatively minor significance, being conditioned by the inevitable necessities of the historic process of change. The process of accumulation and technical change holds the centre of the stage as also the activity of the State and the credit mechanism. There is also a hint that the actual process is one of disequilibrium; for without such a disequilibrium, the system would lose its motive power and stagnate and decay—a stationary equilibrium is just impossible.[13]

This type of vision comes close in essential respects to the explicitly formulated visions of Marx and Schumpeter;[14] however, its conceptualization is much more refined because of the specific quality of the Keynesian analytic apparatus.

The explanatory hypotheses formulated by econometricians assume that the past relationship between certain aggregates—whether causal or casual—is all that matters and that this should hold for the future too, unless other social processes tend to bring about structural changes in the system. Institutional changes are ignored, structural changes are regarded as impinging on the system from the outside and motivational factors seem to assume little or no significance. They take their analytic tools from the Keynesian theory of income determination and the Walras–Leontief input–output analysis.

The pure fact-finders like Kuznets,[15] the economic historian, base their analysis on both statistical tools as well as the Keynesian analytic structure and try to establish certain uniformities with regard to the economic process. This fact-finding process is extremely significant in the sense that such accumulation of facts is bound to affect the analytic structure of the other two schools; however, the implicit vision is a little simplistic and encompasses the entire social process of change without establishing organic links among the inter-dependent parts of the process and seems to imply that the observed regularities of the past worked themselves out in a similar way in different institutional and historic set-ups. Historians like Gerschenkron have gone a little further in suggesting a causal link between the degree of economic backwardness and the nature of the economic process—the supposed regularities of historic change—through mechanisms that are different in different institutional set-ups.[16]

Doubtless, the explicit or implicit vision with regard to the economic process plays a vital role in scientific effort through identification of the areas of analytic interest, and since these areas are different for the three schools, their perspectives and techniques also differ, with the result that while for genuine economic science there is need for a symbiosis of the three schools, in actual fact there is only peaceful coexistence, which at this stage adds only to the prevailing confusion. This confusion gets a sharp edge in view of the practical demands made on economists for suggesting and recommending appropriate economic policies for attaining the multiple objectives which the modern State strives to attain. In this sphere, confusion is worse confounded not only because of the peaceful co-existence of the three schools and the ideological bias inherent in each one of them, but also because of the different value judgements and preferences of the practitioners of each school. The latter are quite often clothed in analytic armour, which a layman or a politician may find difficult to pierce, but which he still may adopt for socio-psychological reasons to buttress his own value judgements and preferences—an integral part of the phenomenon of the competitive struggle for power among the contending group interests which tend to assert themselves in the political arena. Keynes was being extraordinarily relevant when he said that "... the ideas of economists and political philosophers, both when they are right and when they are wrong, are more powerful than is commonly understood. Indeed the world is ruled by little else. ... Madmen in authority, who hear voices in the air, are distilling their frenzy from some academic scribbler of a few years back. I am sure that the power of vested interests is vastly exaggerated compared with the gradual encroachment of ideas."[17] What Keynes did not mention are two patent socio-psychological facts: first, that "madmen in authority" seek power and that they like to clothe this quest for power in intellectual garments that would please those on whose support their power depends, and second, that intellectuals who help in this effort are conditioned by their past and their society and tend to see reality as they would like to see it. In individual and social behaviour, it is not the objective reality but the symbolic representation of that reality in human and social psyche that provides the motive power for action. Is it idea or illusion that rules men's minds?[18]

II

Irrelevance of the Basic Postulates

For the maturity of economic science, what is basic is the evolution of the analytic apparatus which has an instrumental role in formulating explanatory hypotheses with regard to economic reality and thus in promoting and motivating the fact-finding process. The sterility of economic science is thus basically due to the inadequacy of equilibrium economics *à la* Walras—the central core of economic theory. This sterility or irrelevance of equilibrium economics, as Kaldor has termed it,[19] is due largely to the irrelevance of the basic postulates of this theory.[20]

One of these basic postulates accepted as valid for the last two hundred years and more is that each individual entity—whether an individual or a firm—is motivated by self-interest and tends to maximize, given the environmental and other constraints, its satisfaction (represented by an index of utility or profits). Each economic entity has a given preference function—a sort of psychological datum—which is independent of such preference functions of the other entities.

These assumptions of maximization (or optimization) and independence have hardly any objective basis and represent a type of *naïveté* which is only explainable in terms of a metaphysical belief in the moral value of an individual entity.[21] The *naïveté* of this postulate is obvious when one tends to treat Robinson Crusoe on an equal footing with an individual who is an integral part of society. This is not only poor psychology but also reflects a complete lack of insight into the sociological foundation of what constitutes self-interest.

Man's own image about himself as well as his motivation and behaviour cannot be explained in terms which are independent of his relationship with others and with society in general. "Without relationship you are not; to be is to be related; to be related is existence, you exist only in relationship; otherwise you do not exist, existence has no meaning. It is not because you *think* you are that you come into existence. You exist because you are related. . . ."[22] Thus man's conception of his self-interest is not a psychological datum but is a sociological phenomenon—a thing which can be understood only in terms of his relationship with others in society.

Since man knows himself only through relationships, his effort at self-gratification or promoting his self-interest is not only conditioned by these relationships but is directed at using them for his own gratification. Thus the urge to dominate, to seek power, prestige and position, to feel secure in an insecure world, becomes the basic driving force of human behaviour. The desire to be something, to feel important in relationship, to be different from others or to be at least as important as others, is a form of envy in which self-interest is reflected. Self-interest thus is rooted in envy and one can even say that the motive-power for action is not some metaphysical concept of self-interest but envy.[23]

It is this envy that gives rise to the competitive process—a process in which each one wants to be different from the rest—and to be recognized as such by society.[24] Those who have the capacity to climb the ladder tend to become leaders. And those who have no such capacity tend to become followers; they satisfy their urge to power and security by belonging to a leader and thus experiencing reflected glory. Thus, the phenomena of leadership and group formation arise, the concrete forms and changes in them depending upon the objective situation and the competitive process, the driving force of which is envy—individual and collective.[25] And envy implies conflict—among individuals and among groups; hence for the stability for the social structure based on envy, each structure tends to evolve "rules of the game"—rules within which the game of envy can be played.[26]

If this statement of the motive power for action be true, it has several implications with regard to the basic postulates of economic theory—postulates relating to consumer behaviour and the behaviour of the firm:

1. Preference functions of economic entities are interdependent, interrelated and interacting and change over time as a result of the competitive process, which implies *differential* behaviour with regard to pace-setters (leaders) and imitators (followers). This would be particularly true in the context of a dynamic process which changes the nature and number of goods and services as well as the want-pattern of consumers. The consumption of unchanging goods and services is socially conditioned and the interdependent preference functions of consumers may hence show some degree of stability particularly when their consumption is of a recurring nature and has been subjected in part to the salutary rationalizing influence of social experience. But even in such cases, personal tastes account for less than is commonly assumed; the habit of coffee-drinking is socially conditioned but a consumer may prefer a certain brand of coffee as a result of his peculiar tastes![27]

2. There is no possibility of optimizing behaviour particularly in the context of

the competitive process. Whatever the decisions taken by the consumers at a point of time, they result in the building of tension because of the continuing change in the preference functions. Further, consumer behaviour has to be explained in terms of not an individual but a household; since a household comprises several individuals, conflict situations arise and have to be resolved through acceptable compromises.[28]

3. To posit given unchanging preference functions is a form of implicit or tautological theorizing;[29] consumer's decisions should be related directly to explanatory variables rather than to the *deus ex machina* of given preference functions.

4. Pareto's tastes thus cannot be taken as given data; hence all conclusions emanating from the Pareto optimality conditions are not objectively valid. The theorem that within the context of the given wealth- and income-distribution pattern, the competitive process would result in maximizing social utility or welfare is irrelevant for the purpose of analysing historic situations or for policy purposes.

5. The criteria for evaluating the performance of an economic system in terms of maximization of welfare have thus to be different from those provided by economic theory. These criteria have to be derived in terms of political, ethical or such other norms as may evolve at a given stage in the dynamic social process; however, as with an individual so also with a collective—whether a group or a state—these criteria cannot be described in terms of a given preference function as they emerge largely as a result of a compromise among conflicting interests within the collective as also within the decision-making entity. Thus it is incorrect to posit a social welfare function, maximization of which should be the objective of policy; the formulation of implications of hypothetical preference functions may however help the decision-making units in the process of making decisions.[30]

6. The competitive process and the differential behaviour of economic agents imply uncertainty and cannot be explained in terms of certainty-assumptions.

7. The flexibility of the economic system improves as a result of the phenomenon of changing preference functions.

With regard to the behaviour of the firm too, the implications of envy as the guiding principle of human behaviour are different from those posited by economic theory:

1. Competitive behaviour is insufficiently motivated in economic theory, while envy provides a principal motive for competition. Both equilibrium economics as well as the neo-Keynesian set-up fails to explain the existence of the inexorable motive for accumulation, which accounts for the evolutionary process.[31]

2. The decision rules of the firms cannot be derived from profit maximization behaviour; for profit maximization plays merely an instrumental role in the competitive process, the basic motivation of firms being either to do as well as the competitors or to do better in order to gain social recognition. Further, a firm does not consist of merely an individual; it consists of a group of individuals and hence the decision-making process involves compromises inevitable in a situation of conflict of wills. The nature of such compromises depends upon the quality of the leading personnel. This decision-making process cannot be understood without recognizing explicitly the factor of uncertainty.

3. The criteria for decision-making thus would be different for pacesetters (leaders) from those for adapters (imitators). In trying to set the pace, aspiring leaders have a powerful motive to introduce innovations in Schumpeter's sense of the term rather than to indulge in mere price-competition which can never give the expected results.[32] The main vehicle for competitive behaviour and in fact the essence of such behaviour is the progressive introduction of innovations including the exploitation of the objective opportunity for increasing returns to scale—a process which compels a certain adaptive response from the imitators.

4. Technical change and increasing returns to scale are not phenomena incidental to the competitive game; they are the essence of the process. It is the competitive process which provides the motivation as well as the means for the commercial use of available scientific and technological results as well as for sustaining and accelerating the process of such discoveries.[33]

5. The competitive process implies positive efforts by leader-type firms for the elimination of competition and hence for the emergence of what are recognized as monopoly elements in the system, but it is the essence of the process that such situations do not last. For competition that is relevant and effective, it is not essential that the number of firms in a given field be large; what is essential is the ever-present threat of the emergence of new commodities that would satisfy existing wants more effectively or the creation of new wants that may provide a substitute for existing wants. In fact, the competitive process implies the emergence of progressively larger-sized monopoly-type firms as Marx had foreseen; the existence of such firms, in fact, improves the competitive process and its results.

6. The competitive process creates and sustains tensions and disequilibrium-type situations as much as it promotes continuing adaptation to changing situations. By altering decision rules and behaviour and production and sale possibilities, it provides a mechanism for adaptation and selection, a mechanism which ensures the stability of the process—if one can use this term—by limiting it within ranges and bounds that prevent it from exploding in any one direction.

7. Again, it provides the men and the means and the motivation for changing the power structure and the rules of the game through the creation of countervailing power groups including government personnel and policies that impose limits on the process or redirect it along lines indicated by the emerging socio-political milieu.[34]

The main reason why the theoretical framework of economics has been based on postulates that are not consistent with reality is related to its exclusive concern with the problems of relative prices and resource-allocation. These problems are vitally related to the economic process and can be satisfactorily analysed only in the setting of a dynamic framework of analysis. In this context, our perspective on the dynamic process is of crucial significance: whether one regards it as endogenous and hence cumulatively self-reinforcing or merely as a process of adaptation to changes in exogenous factors—changes which compel a certain adaptive response on the part of the economic system—would determine the nature of problems that should be subjected to scientific analysis and inquiry.

If the dynamic process can be explained in terms of competitive behaviour, which not only creates the environment for exploiting meaningfully the available objective opportunities for increasing returns and technical change but also makes it possible to create such objective opportunities, the object of inquiry should in fact be the endogenous cumulative process. This is precisely what was realized by Marx and Schumpeter; the non-pursuit of this line of inquiry may probably have a sociological explanation.[35]

If it had been further pursued, it would have resulted in a meaningful accumulation of facts on the one hand and in a greater relevance of theory to practical problems of policy. Probably it was safer in the context in which economics evolved to concentrate attention on theorems and propositions that have no empirical validity; for neither an individual consumer nor an individual firm is much concerned with theorizing about his behaviour, and the governments, constituted as they were, liked to believe that their role was marginal in the process. Thus there were not many practical demands on economic theory, which, in the process, got immune from the salutary rationalizing influence of practical experience.

One of the basic weaknesses in theory came to be recognized only when the historical process reached a stage when employment became a political problem and government policy had to assume a critical role. The decisions to save and invest are two separate decisions and depend, in the short run, on different sets of factors; this patent fact had to await a Keynes before it was theoretically recognized. It was the insistent demand of the political situation that generated a theoretical framework suited to the analysis of real historic situations. Since then, it is recognized that economic theory has to take cognizance of the fact that there is no automatic process which ensures sufficiency of effective demand. But economic theory as it has evolved has still not integrated Keynesian macro-economics with equilibrium economics; they co-exist and one takes the other as valid in its own field. This is partly due to the absorption of both with short-run situations, which makes implicit theorizing possible.

But the neo-Keynesians have at least pinpointed the problems for relevant inquiry.[36] (*i*) the endogenous cumulative process of economic change; (*ii*) its vital link with the process of technical change and increasing returns to scale; (*iii*) the maintenance of adequate effective demand as a result of demand-induced innovative investment [the factor mentioned under (*ii*)], supply-induced stock-building of agricultural commodities and government policy relating to expansion of export markets; (*iv*) the permissive role of credit mechanism with regard to the investment process (Schumpeter regarded credit creation as an integral part of the evolutionary process and called it the monetary complement of the innovative process[37]); and (*v*) the dynamic process itself determining the evolutionary changes in resource-allocation and relative prices—problems which cannot be tackled without reference to the cumulative process.

III

Lack of Normative Significance

The question relating to the sterility of equilibrium economics has been posed with some intensity only recently as a result of the practical demands made on economics by government policy-makers, who have assumed the responsibility for maintenance of full employment with growth and welfare in the developed countries and for development with welfare in what are called developing countries.

Keynesian prescriptions have been found to be inadequate in this context.[38] How can governments assume responsibility for the maintenance of adequate investment growth without inquiring further into the pattern of investment, which is so much relevant for the nature and structure of growth and welfare? Can the decisions relating to the volume of investment be isolated from decisions relating to the pattern of investment? If the volume and the pattern of investment are interrelated, how are governments in a position to affect both without raising questions relating to objectives of economic policies and the political process through which these objectives are to be set? Again, can these objectives be formulated in terms of an objective welfare function of the government or the community?

Similar questions arise with regard to the problems facing the developing countries. One cannot attempt to answer such questions; for they are related in a vital manner with the nature and basis of the political process, conditioned by and conditioning the socio-economic structure. One can merely raise the question about the validity of the answers which are being suggested on the basis of equilibrium economics.

Without examining the relevance of the postulates and theorems of equilibrium economics, it has been suggested that economic policies be formulated in the light of such postulates and theorems. The principal theorem is that welfare would be maximized if economic agents take decisions on the basis of the shadow prices as would be generated by a model of "competitive behaviour". Equilibrium economics may not be relevant for the analysis and understanding of the past but is relevant for decision-making now for maximizing welfare—so runs the argument.

Now these prices can be derived only in terms of a given social welfare function. Does such a function exist? Is the competitive process in politics any different from such a process in the economic field? It is the essence of the competitive process in politics that those who wield power would like to maintain it and those who seek power would have to create a following adequate enough to overthrow those who are in power. In the process, both have to seek popular support. In this struggle for power, both have to seek such compromises as would appeal to various groups with diverse interests. The nature of compromises thus would change as a result of the political process. These compromises and their shifting nature and structure, conditioned by the socio-political process and the contending interests in the government itself, rule out the possibility of any objective social welfare function. To disregard the nature of the political process amounts to the same intellectual *naïveté* as reflected in the utilitarian philosophy.[39]

If there is no possibility of formulating a stable objective welfare function, how does one derive shadow prices?

Any way, the problem as it is posed does not seem to be a relevant one. The major problems arise in the fields of socio-political structure, legal framework, and economic institutions—structural problems that cannot be wished away by the implicit harmony of interests suggested by the search for an objective welfare function. This structural change has to be such as would sufficiently motivate the process of economic change along lines that could make it possible for such workable compromises with regard to objectives of economic policy as are required at different stages of the process of change.

Along with the other instruments of policy, pricing policy has certainly to be used as an instrument to motivate and induce structural change along desired directions; but one cannot solve this problem through the price system. The so-called distortions in the price structure are the result of either institutional factors or government policies. In either case, such distortions reflect economic reality which cannot be changed by fixing such decision rules that ignore this objective reality and ignore, in fact, the dynamics of decision-making which is much more complex than that suggested by theory.[40]

A variant of the shadow-price policy for decision-making is the suggested use of international prices.[41] This again is inspired by the perfect competition model of theory which posits that once all economic agents take prices as given, welfare is automatically maximized.[42] But what about the preference function? If that does not exist, how does one measure the impact of world prices as decision rules on welfare? The principal problems that are posed are those relating to efficiency and maximization of results in terms of foreign exchange; world prices if they can be identified, of actually tradeable goods and services[43] are certainly helpful in these spheres. But efficiency aspects that need to be emphasized are the long-run aspects and again relating to the dynamic process of development as a whole,[44] separate projects or project complexes have to be viewed in the context of the whole dynamic process and not as isolated entities. Further, for the long-run efficiency of the process, all projects cannot be judged on the basis of uniform criteria; it may indeed be necessary to use different sets of criteria for different types of projects—sets of criteria which become relevant for the different objectives that emerge at each specific stage of the process. Once the possibility of an objective social welfare function is eliminated, it would indeed be rational to try to attain each set of objectives by the selection of such projects or project complexes as are relevant for that set. For example, certain projects or project complexes may be selected on the basis of criteria related to improving the saving capacity of the system, while some others may be selected on the basis of criteria related to income distribution objectives or balance of payments objectives. Given the nature of the political process and the complexity of the decision-making process, it is only rational to identify and select projects or project complexes on the basis of different sets of criteria—each set being relevant for a specific objective. These different sets of projects or project complexes can be integrated and effectively co-ordinated only with the help of over-all planning, the success of which has to be judged on the basis of its impact on the development process. But the major problems are not in these fields;[45] they relate to the process of accumulation and technical change, the formation of scientific and technological skills, the building of appropriate institutions that can motivate as well as facilitate change and the creation of politico-social mechanisms for facilitating the formulation of workable compromises relating to the nature, content and structure of objectives as seem appropriate at each stage of the process of socio-economic change. These are much more vital problems that cannot be solved by arbitrary decision rules which have no objective basis. And if these problems are solved, relevant decision rules would emerge as an integral part of the process of change.

NOTES

1. See J. Krishnamurti, *The First and Last Freedom* (London, 1964), pp. 9–12.
2. See J. A. Schumpeter, *History of Economic Analysis* (London, 1954), pp. 42–7.
3. See K. A. Popper, *The Open Society and its Enemies*, vol. ii, p. 205, quoted by Joan Robinson, *Economic Philosophy* (London, 1962), pp. 22–3.
4. *Ibid.*, p. 205.
5. See J. A. Schumpeter, *op.cit.*, pp. 14–20 and 45–7.
6. *Ibid.*, p. 34.
7. *Ibid.*, pp. 45–7.
8. *Ibid.*, p. 47.
9. "Science and Ideology", *Essays of J. A. Schumpeter*, edited by R. V. Clemence (Cambridge, U.S.A., 1951), pp. 272–5.
10. *Ibid.*, p. 275.
11. *Ibid.*, pp. 159–60, "Preface to the Japanese Edition of Theory of Economic Development".
12. J. Kornai, *Anti-Equilibrium* (London, 1971), pp. 331–2.
13. N. Kaldor, "The Irrelevance of Equilibrium Economics", *Economic Journal*, December 1972. See also J. Knapp, "Economics or Political Economy", *Lloyds Bank Review* (Jan. 1973).
14. See J. A. Schumpeter, *Capitalism, Socialism and Democracy* (New York, 1950).
15. S. Kuznets, *Modern Economic Growth* (London, 1966). This approach originated with Mitchell; see in this connection "Mitchell's Business Cycles", by J. A. Schumpeter in *Essays, op.cit.*
16. A. Gerschenkron, *Economic Backwardness in Historical Perspective* (Cambridge, U.S.A., 1962).
17. J. M. Keynes, *The General Theory of Employment, Interest and Money* (New York, 1965), pp. 383–4.
18. See, in this connection, J. A. Schumpeter, *Capitalism, Socialism and Democracy, op.cit.*, pp. 256–64, particularly the following passage: "This subject belongs to a chapter of social psychology that might be entitled Human Nature in Politics. . . . During the second half of the last century, the idea of the human personality that is a homogeneous unit and the idea of a definite will that is the prime mover of action have been steadily fading—even before the times of Theodule Ribot and Sigmund Freud. In particular, these ideas have been increasingly discounted in the field of social sciences where the importance of the extra-rational and irrational element in our behaviour has been receiving more and more attention, witness Pareto's Mind and Society" (p. 256).
19. See N. Kaldor, *op.cit.*
20. "The classical theorists resemble Euclidean geometers in a non-Euclidean world who, discovering that in experience straight lines apparently parallel often meet, rebuke the lines for not keeping straight—as the only remedy for the unfortunate collisions which are occurring. Yet, in truth, there is no remedy except to throw out the axiom of parallels and to work out a non-Euclidean geometry. Something similar is required today in economics." J. M. Keynes, *General Theory*, pp. 16–17; see also pp. 1, 32–3.
21. "Before going any further, we must sadly observe that all the modern refinements of this concept (utility) have not freed it from metaphysics. We are told nowadays that since utility cannot be measured it is not an operational concept, and that 'revealed preference' should be put in its place. Observable market behaviour will show what an individual chooses. Preference is just what the individual under discussion prefers; there is no value-judgement involved. Yet, as the argument goes on, it is clear that it is a Good Thing for the individual to have what he prefers. This, it may be held, is not a question of satisfaction but freedom—we want him to have what he prefers so as to avoid having to restrain his behaviour." J. Robinson, *Economic Philosophy* (London, 1962), p. 49.
22. J. Krishnamurti, *op.cit.*, p. 104.
23. "So we must begin near, that is, we must concern ourselves with our daily existence, with our daily thoughts and feelings and actions which are revealed in the manner of earning our liveli-

hood and in our relationship with ideas or beliefs. This is our daily existence, is it not? We are concerned with livelihood, getting jobs, earning money, we are concerned with the relationship with our family or with our neighbours, and we are concerned with ideas and with beliefs. Now, if you examine our occupation, it is fundamentally based on envy, it is not just a means of earning a livelihood. Society is so constructed that it is a process of constant conflict, constant becoming; it is based on greed, on envy, envy of your superior; the clerk wanting to become the manager, which shows that he is not just concerned with earning a livelihood, a means of subsistence, but with acquiring position and prestige . . . envy indicates the desire for power, for position, and it ultimately leads to politics; both are closely related." J. Krishnamurti, *op.cit.*, pp. 36–7. The following passage from J. Krishnamurti, *Commentaries on Living*, 3rd series, edited by D. Rajgopal (London, 1965), pp. 258–60, may also be compared: "But why this urge to possess? And what do we mean by possessing? In possessing, in feeling that you own, there is pride, a certain sense of power and prestige, is there not? There is pleasure in knowing that something is yours, be it a house, a piece of cloth, or a rare picture. The possession of capacity, talent, the ability to achieve, and the recognition that it brings—these also give you a sense of importance, a secure outlook on life. As far as people are concerned, to possess and to be possessed is often a mutually satisfactory relationship. There is also possession in terms of beliefs, ideas, ideologies, is there not? . . . But possession implies all this. You may want to possess people, another may possess a whole series of ideas, while someone else may be satisfied with owning a few acres of land; but however much the objects may vary, all possession is essentially the same, and each will defend what he owns—or in the very yielding of it, will possess something else at another level. . . . At all costs, you must possess. . . . We possess because in ourselves we are nothing, and in possessing we feel we have become somebody . . . the label gives us a sense of importance, so we defend it with the sword and with the cunning mind. We are nothing but what we possess—the label, the bank account, the ideology, the person—and this identification breeds enmity and endless strife."

24. With regard to the significance of social recognition and prestige—the most subtle of all economic goods, Social Distance—as the propeller of action, as belonging "to the logic of life within our social group", see J. A. Schumpeter, *Capitalism, Socialism and Democracy*, pp. 207–9.
25. "Why do you seek power? Having power over one, or over thousands, gives an intense possessive pleasure, does it not? There's a pleasurable feeling of self-importance, of being in a position of authority. . . . Why do we seek and try to maintain this exciting sense of power? . . . why do we want to be leaders? There must be recognition in order to feel important; if we are not recognized as such, importance has no meaning. Recognition is part of the whole process of leadership. Not only does the leader acquire importance, but also the followers. By asserting that he belongs to such-and-such movement, led by so-and-so, the follower becomes somebody. . . . As with the followers, so with the leader. Being insufficient in ourselves, empty, we proceed to fill that emptiness with a sense of possession, power position, or with knowledge, gratifying ideologies, and so on; we crowd it with things of the mind. This process of filling, of escaping, of becoming, whether it be conscious or otherwise, is the net of the self; it is the ego, the 'me', the entity that has identified itself with an ideology, with reform, with a certain pattern of action." J. Krishnamurti, *Commentaries, op.cit.*, pp. 232–2.
26. See J. Robinson, *op.cit.*, pp. 4–6.
27. See, in this connection, J. S. Duesenberry, *Income, Saving and the Theory of Consumer Behaviour* (New York, 1967); also J. A. Schumpeter, *Essays, op.cit.*, pp. 305–6; and J. Kornai, *op.cit.*, chapters 10 and 11.
28. J. Kornai, *op.cit.*, chapter 11.
29. W. Leontief, "Implicit Theorising: A Methodological Criticism of the Neo-Cambridge School", *Quarterly Journal of Economics* (Feb. 1937).
30. See the illuminating discussion of the political process in J. A. Schumpeter, *Capitalism, Socialism and Democracy*, chapters 21 and 22.
31. *Ibid.*, p. 160.
32. *Ibid.*, chapters 7 and 8.
33. *Ibid.*, chapters 11.
34. See J. K. Galbraith, *American Capitalism* (Cambridge, U.S.A., 1957).
35. Compare Keynes's comments on Ricardo in *General Theory, op.cit.*, pp. 32–3: "The completeness of Ricardian victory is something of a curiosity and a mystery. It must have been due to a

complex of suitabilities in the doctrine to the environment into which it was projected. That it reached conclusions quite different from what the ordinary uninstructed person would expect, added, I suppose, to its intellectual prestige. That its teaching, translated into practice, was austere and often unpalatable, lent it virtue. That it was adapted to carry a vast and consistent logical superstructure, gave it beauty. That it could explain such social injustice and apparent cruelty as an inevitable incident in the scheme of progress, and the attempt to change such things as likely on the whole to do more harm than good, commended it to authority. That it afforded a measure of justification to the free activities of the individual capitalist, attracted to it the support of the dominant social force behind authority."

36. See N. Kaldor, *op.cit.*
37. J. A. Schumpeter, *Business Cycles*, vol. i (New York, 1939), pp. 109–12.
38. J. Robinson, *op.cit.*, chapter 4.
39. For an illuminating discussion of the classical doctrine of democracy, see J. A. Schumpeter, *Capitalism, Socialism and Democracy, op.cit.*, chapter 21.
40. On the complexity of the motivation pattern and the decision-making process, see J. Kornai, *op.cit.*, chapters 7, 11 and 13.
41. See Organization for Economic Co-operation and Development, Development Centre, *Manual of Industrial Project Analysis*, vol. ii, by I. M. D. Little and J. A.Mirrlees (Paris, 1967).
42. "Modern economic systems . . . are controlled by a complex control sphere, and the market is only one regulator of it. The GE school suggests that planning is a superfluous luxury, that an 'optimal price system' could be found which in itself is sufficient for control. . . . The task of science is not to see the 'optimal' simple regulator of an unrealistic Walras-world but to describe, explain and improve the complex control system of the real economy . . . we cannot arrange the control system of an economy in a way that does not reckon with the real motivations of human activities, the finite limits of human intellect and capacity, the complexity and intricacy of the system, and so on. Therefore, before putting forward normative proposals, careful descriptive explanatory analysis is needed." J. Kornai, *op.cit.*, pp. 342–3. "As a matter of fact, price is a variable of the control sphere. We cannot draw valid conclusions for prices from a model which considers prices outside their natural medium, independently of other types of information and from the functioning of the control sphere." J. Kornai, *op.cit.*, p. 353.
43. How to find out what is tradeable in a given context is a problem by itself. See A. K. Sen, "Control Areas and Accounting Prices: An Approach to Economic Evaluation", *Economic Journal* (Mar. 1972) (Supplement).
44. In this connection, the concept of the leading sector has been historically very important; it is relevant for the choice of development strategy as well as of projects and project complexes. See W. W. Rostow, "The Beginnings of Modern Growth in Europe: An Essay in Synthesis", *Journal of Economic History* (Sept. 1973).
45. J. Robinson, *op.cit.*, chapter 5.

2. Economic Development: An Analytic-Historical Approach*

THE MOST important change which has occurred in the developed as well as the developing countries since the Second World War is in the role of the State. Previously, the State had played an active role in facilitating economic development in the various developed countries,[1] but development had not been the supreme objective of economic and social policy. Now the State has assumed direct responsibility for promoting development as well as other social objectives. But a government's development policy cannot be rationally determined without some idea about the process of development itself; only then can the spheres in which the State should be active be identified.

This is not a simple subject. It is a vast and complex problem related to the whole process of social change. Social and historical processes cannot be understood without some historical sense and command over historical facts and material together with an insight into present given social conjuncture. It is because of the complexity of the subject that we do not have any generally accepted and verified theory of economic change or development. There have been some powerful insights and hypotheses about this social process; but these hypotheses remain largely speculative, influenced by the humours of the times, the ideological bias of the proponents and their value judgements.

This chapter seeks to present some of the tentative hypotheses—conjectures—that have been discussed in the literature on the historical process of economic development. In section 1, the nature and limitations of economic science are discussed, while section 2 indicates the framework that has been evolved so far for analysing the logic of the economic process. Some theories of economic evolution are presented in section 3. The final section attempts to indicate the relevance of the entrepreneurial role of the State for the developing countries.

1. Nature and Limitations of Economic Science

Economic theory as far as it has developed is indeed helpful in understanding some issues of policy; but, by and large, it is silent when it comes to the relative significance of different causal factors influencing the process of economic development. And this is not so much a reflection on the state of economic science as on its subject matter.

Economics has to deal with a unique historical process; the historical or evolutionary nature of the economic process unquestionably limits the scope of general concepts, and of the general relations between them (economic laws) that economists may be able to formulate. Economic laws are much less stable than

*Published in *World Development,* vol. 4, no. 7, 1976.

are the laws of any physical science; they work out differently in different institutional conditions. There is a further problem; economics is not a matter of theory. Doubtless, economic theory, as an instrument of analysis or, in Mrs. Robinson's felicitous phrase, a box of tools, is essential for understanding complex phenomena. However, it has only an instrumental role to play; and it is useful in economic analysis only where the analyst has a good command over historical and contemporary facts and material, statistics and economic sociology. Even to mention these requirements is to underscore the complexity of economic analysis.[2]

There is a further characteristic of economics and all social sciences, which makes scientific effort much more difficult in these fields than say in physics. The subject matter of economics is an irreversible process; this being so, it is difficult to devise laws which are not bound by place and time. Further, economics lacks the benefit that physics derives from laboratory experiments. Again, in economics and social sciences, scientific effort is much more socially conditioned than in mathematics or physics.

This social conditioning gives rise to an ideological bias which arises, as Marx first realized, from the dependence of social science upon social structure, and in particular upon the social situation of practitioners in the field, which determines their outlook on reality—and hence what they say of it and how they see it. Of course, this ideological bias affects mathematics and physics also. But in their cases, the influence of ideological bias does not extend beyond the choice of problems and approaches; that is to say, the sociological interpretation does not challenge the "objective truth" of the findings. This "objective truth" may be, and currently is being, challenged on other grounds but not on the ground that a given proposition is true only with reference to the social situation of the men who formulated it. To some extent at least, this favourable situation may be accounted for by the fact that logic, mathematics, physics and so on deal with experience that is largely invariant to the observer's social situation and practically invariant to historical change: for capitalist and proletarian, a falling stone looks the same. The social sciences do not share this advantage.

Now, this ideological bias is an inescapable curse, and it permeates economics to its core. For ideologies are not simple lies; they are truthful statements about what a man thinks he sees. Just as the medieval knight saw himself as he wished to see himself; just as the modern bureaucrat does the same; and just as both failed and fail to see whatever may be adduced against their perception of themselves as defenders of the weak and innocent, and sponsors of the Common Good, so every other social group develops a protective ideology which is nothing if not sincere. *Ex hypothesi,* we are not aware of our rationalizations. One can find such ideological elements in the great works of Adam Smith, Marx and Keynes.[3]

There is another source of confusion, another barrier to advance in economics. Most economists, not content with their scientific task, yield to the call of public duty, and to their desire to serve their country and their age; in doing so, however, they bring into their work their individual schemes of values and all their beliefs and opinions—the whole of their moral personalities including their spiritual ambitions. It thus becomes necessary to try to separate the value judgements of economists from their scientific work. Doubtless this can be done, but it requires much greater awareness, in both economists and the laymen, of the ways in which value judgements affect scientific conclusions. The nineteenth-century alliance of classical economy with political liberalism illustrates the point.[4]

It is for these reasons that the growth of economic science has not been as spectacular as it could have been, and that scientific analysis in economics has not been a progressive discovery of an objective reality. Rather, it has been "progressing", if at all, in a criss-cross fashion, not in a logical way but rather as the impact of new ideas, observations or needs, and also as the bent and temperaments of new men, dictate.[5] To give an example from the field of central banking: the concept of a managed currency was formulated quite early in the seventeenth century by John Law,[6] and in fact a complete theory was formulated by Thornton by the middle of the nineteenth century, as is shown admirably by Schumpeter and Hicks.[7] However, it took almost a century for the principles of currency and credit regulation to be accepted and recognized—largely through the analysis of John Maynard Keynes.

2. Logic of the Economic Process: Static Framework

A similar situation pertains with regard to the theory of economic evolution. In spite of the powerful analytic insights into this process provided by Marx and Schumpeter, and more recently by Kaldor and Gerschenkron, a pure theory of economic change still remains to be developed; moreover, these insights have been generally ignored in the recent development of dynamic analysis. But more of this, a little later.

An observer from Mars might reasonably think that the human mind, inspired by experience, would start analysis with the relatively concrete and then, as more subtle relations reveal themselves, proceed to the relatively abstract, that is to say, to start from dynamic relations and then move on to work out the static ones. But this has not been the case in any field of scientific endeavour whatsoever. In mechanics, for example, static relations were worked out first, dynamic ones later; and it was only Lagrange who conceived of statics as a special case of dynamics. Always, static theory has historically preceded dynamic theory and the reasons for this seem to be as obvious as they are sound—static theory is much simpler to work out; its propositions are easier to prove; and it seems closer to logical essentials. The history of economic analysis is no exception.[8] But compared to the other sciences, the static method took longer to mature in economics and it took an even longer time to change over to dynamic theorems—a development which has taken place only after Keynes.

It was this static framework of economic analysis that economists were busy perfecting since the days of Cantillon. The history of analytic effort is the history of a growing awareness, partial at first, more general later on, of the presence of a logically coherent economic process, an awareness first consciously formulated in the works of such men as Cantillon, Quesnay, Smith, Say and Ricardo. But it was only during the latter half of the nineteenth century that the conception of an economic cosmos made up of a system of interdependent quantities with all its problems, if not quite satisfactorily solved, at least clearly arrayed, together with the idea of general equilibrium between these quantities, was clearly established in the centre of pure theory. This was due to Marshall and more particularly due to Walras.[9] The controversies of that age testify strongly to the revolution that occurred in economic theory. "We may smile at Gossen's boast of having accomplished a Copernican feat", says Schumpeter. "But this boast was less unreasonable than it may seem at first sight. The replacement of the geocentric by the heliocentric system and the replacement of the 'classic' by the marginal utility system were performances", adds Schumpeter, "of the same kind; they were both essentially simplifying and unifying reconstructions".[10] The only significant advance that has been made since is that of perfecting this static system, of making it quantitative and numerical through the contribution of Leontief, and recently of dynamizing it. The dynamic theory, however, has since Keynes largely taken the form of macro-dynamics rather than the form developed by Walras. Macro-dynamics has served a useful purpose in clarifying our minds about some aspects of dynamic change, but it suffers from a basic limitation: economic evolution takes place through sectional or sectoral changes rather than through social aggregates of the Keynesian type and this fact is ignored in macro-dynamics. Further, it lacks a sound empirical basis.

Sharper, more powerful methods of formal reasoning which have developed since Keynes—particularly due to the use of advanced calculus, higher algebra and mathematical statistics—will certainly permit us to extract from each bit of factual evidence the very last drop of possible logical conclusions that can be drawn from it. But since economics is an empirical science, these formal methods are not a substitute for systematic observation of the phenomena which are to be explained. The greatly perfected engine of economic theory is already using up the available factual information much more quickly than the limited resources devoted to collection and organization of basic contemporary and historical data can now replenish it. As Leontief observes: "In the tone of some of the contemporary theoretical discussions (on growth models), one can discern the high pitched sound of an engine revolving faster and faster in idling run. What is required for the growth of economic science and its ability to explain historical processes of development is a massive flow of historical and contemporary data. Our ability to ensure such factual research will determine whether economic science will advance as a viable inquiry, aimed at effective systematic understanding of the structure, function and development of real economic systems, or will settle into a loose albeit peaceful co-existence of mathematical exercises and casual empiricism with conventional (or unconventional as the case may be) wisdom. Imagine where modern physics would be if an attempt were made, say, from the time of Maxwell on, to develop it as a purely mathematical discipline, without or with only a limited recourse to systematic factual observation."[11]

Thus, then, all that economics has done so far is to formulate the logic of the economic process, which is largely independent of time and place. What economists have developed is an engine of economic analysis, consisting of logical propositions or theorems which are analytical tools for the understanding of economic reality. This truth that economic theory is nothing but an engine of analysis has been little understood; and the theorists themselves, now as before, have obscured it by dilettantish excursions into the realm of practical questions. But it was emphasized by Marshall, who in his inaugural lecture at Cambridge in

1885 coined the famous phrase that economic theory is not universal truth but "machinery of universal application in the discovery of a certain class of truths".[12] This truth again was clearly perceived by Keynes when he said: "The theory of Economics does not furnish a body of settled conclusions immediately applicable to policy. It is a method rather than a doctrine, an apparatus of the mind, a technique of thinking. . . ."[13]

Much of the hostility of the layman and policy-maker to economics is due to their ignorance of the scientific process of isolation and abstraction. Doubtless, this hostility was fed by the policy recommendations of economists who barely perceived the impact of ideology and value judgements on their analysis. The classic expression of this hostility is found in Carlyle's characterization of economics as a "dismal science". "Completely incapable of understanding the meaning of a theorem, overlooking the fact that all science is 'dismal' to an artist, he thought he had got hold of the right boy to whip".[14] Carlyle influenced Ruskin who was one of the creative interpreters of art and whose interpretations are themselves works of art. His comments on economics, however, consist of wrathful and dilettantish criticism of the sins of capitalism. "The judgment I pass on him—and he stands for so many—is exactly the same that he himself would have passed on any writer who undertook, for example, to criticize Turner's paintings without having previously acquired, by morally neutral study, an adequate mastery of the relevant facts and techniques".[15]

3. Theories of Economic Evolution

The foregoing discussion of the nature and limitations of economic science as it has developed so far suggests that we have no valid theory of economic evolution or economic development. However, we do have a number of what Schumpeter calls "visions" or "intuitions" about the process of economic evolution. A vision, in this sense, is the result of perceptions and pre-scientific analysis on the part of research workers. Of course, this pre-scientific cognitive process is the source of all scientific discoveries. But until this vision has been analytically and empirically substantiated, it does not have the status of a scientific truth. Moreover, some visions regarding the process of economic development are simply invalid, because the perceptions or insights of the researchers are not penetrating enough.

One such vision is that of Smith–Ricardo–Mill–Marshall.[16] Briefly, it may be stated like this: economic growth is a function of increase in numbers and saving. This induces a "widening of markets", which in turn, increases division of labour and thus increases "productivity". With Smith, division of labour is a catch-all for changes in methods of production of all kinds, but with Mill, and more explicitly with Marshall, the idea of "induced inventions" appears as a distinct factor in the growth process, whereas inventions which are not induced by a previous increase in production remain outside the theoretical framework—they just happen, as manna might fall from heaven—and break the line of growth, establishing a new one. Growth is, therefore, reduced in substance to increases in the quantities of means of production on the one hand, and increases in effective demand for this potential output on the other. The characteristic feature of this process is its impersonal automatism; human beings merely adapt themselves to changing objective data but they do not actively respond to the challenges of their environment. One need not waste time pointing out how clearly invalid this vision is in the light of available historical data. It is obvious to students of history that the process of evolution is neither smooth nor impersonal. The world would look very different if people, apart from having their economic life changed by natural events and changing it themselves by extra-economic action, had done nothing else except multiply and save. In fact, economic evolution is the result of the introduction of innovations—improvements in productive and commercial methods, changes in production techniques, conquest of new markets, development of new commodities, etc. Without this creative response by man to his environment, no evolution could take place. In the words of Schumpeter, "Add as many mail-coaches as you please, you will never get a railroad by so doing".[17]

Marx saw this process of industrial change more clearly and realized its pivotal importance more fully than any other economist of his time. Much more important is the fact that he tried, though unsuccessfully, to implement his vision analytically and empirically. "He was the first economist of top rank to see, and to teach systematically, how economic theory may be turned into historical analysis and how the historical narrative may be turned into *histoire raisonné*. Marx's economic theory tries to complement his sociological framework. It does not succeed; but in failing, it establishes both a goal and a method."[18]

Marx, unlike the classical and modern economists, had a deep insight into the workings of the economic evolution of capitalism. For him, capitalism is a process characterized by constant revolutions of production; stationary capitalism—the idea of Ricardo–Mill–Marshall—would be a *contradictio in adjecto*. In the Communist Manifesto, he writes, "constant revolutionizing of production, uninterrupted disturbance of all social conditons, everlasting uncertainty and agitation distinguish the bourgeois epoch from all earlier ones".[19] Innovations are thus inherent in the process of economic evolution. They are the vehicle for the process of capital accumulation.

And he came very near to saying that this process of innovation was the result of the creative response of entrepreneurs to their environment. After having blocked out the historical background of capitalist development in a few strong strokes that are substantially correct, Marx launched a panegyric upon bourgeois achievement that has no equal in economic literature.[20] The bourgeoisie "has been the first to show what man's activity can bring about. It has accomplished wonders far surpassing Egyptian pyramids, Roman aqueducts, and Gothic Cathedrals", and "by the rapid improvement of all instruments of production . . . draws all nations, even the most barbarian, into civilization . . . it has created more massive and more colossal productive forces than have all preceding generations together", and so forth.[21] No reputable "bourgeois" economist of that or any other time—certainly not Adam Smith or J. S. Mill—ever said as much as this. Observe in particular the emphasis on the creative role of the businessmen, and of the business class as such, that the majority of "bourgeois" economists so persistently overlooked. But even having got this far, most of us would have made two mistakes: on the one hand, adding into the picture non-bourgeois contributions to the success of the bourgeoisie—the contributions of non-bourgeois bureaucracies for instance; and, on the other hand, listing science and technology as independent factors. Marx's sociology enabled him to see that these factors, as well as "progress" in such fields as education and hygiene, were just as much products of the bourgeois class culture—and hence ultimately of the business class itself—as was business performance narrowly defined.

However, Marx's ideology prevented him from observing that innovations were the result of entrepreneurial ability—the ability to perceive new opportunities which cannot be proved at the moment at which action has to be taken, and the willpower to break down the resistance that the social environment offers to change. He attributed innovations to the bourgeois urge to accumulate. "'Accumulate, accumulate', that is Moses and all prophets", he wrote.[22] However, this is a *non sequitur*. Marx did not satisfactorily establish that compulsion to accumulate which is essential to his argument. Marx's failure in this respect was due to the fact, as Schumpeter observes, "that he had no adequate theory of enterprise";[23] he failed to recognize entrepreneurship as a distinct function—the function of creatively responding to objective opportunity. For him, the whole process of economic change was an automatic process—and is this not still the view of modern planners?—resolving itself into the mere mechanics of amassing capital. He perceived the process of economic change more clearly than anybody else during his time, but failed to provide an adequate motivating force for it.

Entrepreneurial activity and innovations form the very cornerstone of Schumpeter's theory of economic development. Like Marx, he realized that . . . "innovation is the outstanding fact in the economic history of capitalist society".[24] However, unlike Marx, he has an adequate theory of its motive power. He emphasizes that the carrying out of innovations is a function *sui generis*,[25] and that this function is performed by the entrepreneur. Motivated by non-hedonist considerations—the dream and the will to find a private kingdom, the will to conquer, the joy of creating—the entrepreneur–innovator becomes the *primum mobile* of economic change in Schumpeter's theory. Pecuniary gain for its own sake is not of much significance to him. He strives for it because in an acquisitive society, it is an objective symbol of success largely independent of the opinion of others.

Let us observe that Schumpeter, like Marx, had a complete command of the *available* historical and statistical facts and of economic sociology, quite apart from his pre-eminence in economic theory. Let us also observe that he was keenly aware of the distorting role of ideological bias and value judgements in economic analysis. Marx was aware of this problem, too, but in others and not in himself.

The entrepreneurial function, according to Schumpeter, need not be embodied in a physical person and certainly not in a particular individual. Every social environment has its own ways of filling the entrepreneurial function. For instance, the practice of farmers in the USA has been revolutionized again and again by the introduction of methods worked out in the Department of Agriculture, and by the Department's success in teaching these methods. In this case, then, it was the Department of Agriculture that acted as an entrepreneur. Again, the entrepreneurial function may be and often is filled cooperatively. With the development of large corporations, this has become of major importance: aptitudes that no single individual combines can be built into a corporate personality.[26]

The role of corporate entrepreneurship has been demonstrated by Gerschenkron in his research into the process of development of relatively backward states during the nineteenth century. He has analysed how the banks filled the role of the entrepreneur in France and Germany during this period, and how the State played this role in a relatively more backward state—Tsarist Russia between 1880 and 1900.[27]

If the nineteenth-century European countries are grouped in terms of their relative economic backwardness at the time of their respective industrial spurts, it is clear that France was more backward than the United Kindom, Germany more backward than France, and Hungary and Russia more backward than Germany. With respect to capital supply, entrepreneurship and ideology, Gerschenkron found that countries could be grouped in three types or stages of development. In advanced countries, private entrepreneurs are able to provide the necessary capital and no radical ideology motivates either the State or the entrepreneur (UK). In a relatively backward country (France and Germany), banks provide both capital and entrepreneurial guidance, and a radical ideology (St. Simonian ideology and nationalism) is a motivating factor. In a still more backward country (Hungary and Tsarist Russia) the State provides capital and entrepreneurial guidance, and the motivating ideology is still more radical (surprisingly, Marxism). In his analysis, there are no set prerequisites for industrialization; what seem to be prerequisites in an advanced country are generally lacking in a backward country. The fact that the latter nevertheless did industrialize suggests how indigenous elements may substitute for apparently absent prerequisites.

Gerschenkron draws attention to another historical fact. In a backward country, if the State does not actively play real entrepreneurial role, industrialization opportunities get missed. For example in Italy (1886–96) the State's role was perfunctory and in fact created obstacles to the growth process. This was partly the result of the absence of a powerful ideology of industrialization. Further, egalitarian ideas dominated the labour unions before the industrialization process was completed and this led to industrial and social strife. Another instance is Bulgaria during the latter part of the nineteenth century. There, the State was more interested in playing the game of high diplomacy under peculiarly unstable political conditions than in the industrialization process; further, its policies were affected by agricultural vested interests which prevented the pursuit of any active industrialization policy through the promotion of railroad building. Thus, both Italy and Bulgaria "missed" the opportunity of industrialization largely due to inadequate State policies.

There is a popular school of thought at present which relates the emergence of entrepreneurs to a certain value system (witness the debate about achieving and non-achieving societies and the like). Gerschenkron has found from his historical researches that there is no clear relationship of this kind. Further, entrepreneurs did emerge even in a social climate inimical to them (Russia before 1914). It is thus not possible to explain the emergence of entrepreneurs in terms of value systems. Historically, the experience has been that unless a certain social value system gets formalized in the shape of government policy, it has little influence on the entrepreneurial class.

It may be mentioned that Keynes accepted Schumpeter's theory of economic evolution. In his "A Treatise on Money" he wrote, "Professor Schumpeter's explanation . . . may be unreservedly accepted".[28] Observe the word "unreservedly". Then Keynes approvingly summarizes Schumpeter's main thesis.

Nevertheless, it is worth noting that Keynes talked of the euthanasia of the rentier, and of saturation of capital due to vanishing investment opportunities. This vision, born of purely English experience, is quite similar to the vision of a stationary state of Ricardo–Mill. Imagine Ricardo–Mill visualizing the immediate advent of a stationary state at a time when Great Britain was at the height of her "industrial revolution", and Keynes visualizing saturation of capital just when the world economy was on the threshold of a "scientific explosion". These examples show how invalid the visions of theorists can be when they lack historical sense. It is worth emphasizing with Schumpeter that nobody can hope to understand the economic phenomena of any age, including this one, without an adequate command of historical facts and an adequate amount of historical sense, or what may be described as historical experience.[29] Even the analytic methods of Ricardo and Keynes were similar; both were guilty of what Leontief calls "implicit theorizing" or what Schumpeter calls "Ricardian Vice" and hence deduced their propositions tautologically.[30]

Modern economists who have dealt with this subject have found that the Schumpeter–Gerschenkron analysis with regard to the role of the creative response of people to objective opportunities is substantially sound. Robert Solow has shown that 87.5 per cent of the growth in GNP per capita in the United States during 1909–45 cannot be explained by quantitative increases in labour and capital inputs.[31] Obviously what he calls "the residual factor" is the innovation factor which produces scientific and educational advances. But some, like Schultz,[32] have emphasized only the factor of educational advance not realizing that educational advance is itself a result of the innovation process and that if mere skills *of the workers* were important, the craft-guild system should have led to economic evolution. Like the nineteenth-century economists, Schultz has missed the significance of enterprise and innovation and of their impact on the entire social structure, including science and technology and educational systems.

With greater command over stylized facts and with a better analytic apparatus, Kaldor has attributed development to what he calls technical dynamism of the economy or the strength of entrepreneurial impulses. To quote Kaldor: "And Schumpeter's hero, the innovating entrepreneur, whom we dismissed so summarily and rather contemptuously at the beginning, is found after all, to have an honorable place, or even a key role, in the drama. He is a promoter, a speculator, a gambler, the purveyor of economic expansion generally and not just of the 'new' techniques of production."[33]

What tentative conclusion can we come to on the basis of this research discussed so far about the process of economic development? One fact which stands out, and which can be perceived by any observer who is prepared to set aside ideological biases and do a doctrinally neutral study of available material, is that economic evolution is not just a matter of capital accumulation and saving, but is vitally related to the process of innovation. And to ignite and further this process is a function *sui generis* in a social system—a function that is performed by the entrepreneur, be it an individual, a group or a State, who must be able to perceive opportunities in fields where results cannot be firmly ascertained, and who must have the energy and willpower to innovate in the face of the resistance which all social environments offer to change. Thus, the human factor, or to put it another way, the quality of human material generally and particularly its relative strength in the economic sphere, is essential for change; for evolution is the result of the creative response—which is *ex ante* indeterminate—of this material to objective economic reality which itself gets modified and changed in the process. Of course, the pace and pattern of growth are conditioned by the opportunities offered by the objective environment, like natural resources and other historical factors. However, the full exploitation of the objective opportunities depends upon the strength of the entrepreneurial impulses in a society.

4. Role of the State in Developing Countries

As Gerschenkron has shown, in the present developing countries, the entrepreneurial role of the State needs to be even greater than in the developing economies of the nineteenth century. The practical question that arises in this context is: in what spheres should the State play an entrepreneurial role?

Even if the State is quite powerful, it does not automatically follow that it would show entrepreneurial impulses; it could obstruct the process as it did in France during 1815–50 and in Italy and Bulgaria during the latter part of the nineteenth century.

The value of the role of the State in economic development depends upon the quality of the people involved in political and administrative tasks, and the extent of the State's basic interest in economic development. Two further conditions need to be fulfilled. First the effective range of purely political decisions should not be extended too far. Otherwise, strictly technical questions might become political battlefields, leading to contradictory and inconsistent policy decisions and legislative and executive aberrations. This does not mean restriction of the role of the State. Almost any matter can come within the sphere of the State, but still not become subject to the competitive struggle for political leadership. This is the logic behind the innovation of statutory public corporations. Of course, broad social and economic objectives have inevitably to be decided through the political process.

The second condition is that a government in a modern society must be able to command, throughout the public sector—large or small—the services of a well-trained bureaucracy of good standing and tradition, endowed with a strong sense of duty and an equally strong *esprit de corps*. Such a bureaucracy is the best answer to the argument about government by amateurs. It is not enough that the bureaucracy should be efficient in current administration and competent to give advice. It must also be strong enough to guide and, if need be, to instruct the politicians who head the ministries. To do this it must be able to evolve principles of its own, and be sufficiently independent to assert them. It must be a power in its own right.[34]

The actual fields of State economic development activity will depend on the insight that the administration has about the problems of a given country, and its ability and willpower to implement these insights. However, on the basis of historical and current experience, certain fields can be broadly indicated.

The State should not, through its actions and policies, obstruct the process of innovation; more positively it should create a climate favourable for the emergence and functioning of entrepreneurial talent in both the private and the public sectors. This it can do by undertaking infrastructure development designed to create new opportunities for entrepreneurial exploitation, and by trying to improve the human material in the economic field so as to strengthen its capacity to respond creatively to the new opportunities created in the economy. Infrastructure needs in the fields of transport, power and financial institutions will probably be clear; let us, therefore, consider how to elicit a creative response from people to the changing social and economic environment.

The developing countries at present have an enormous opportunity in their ability to borrow already well-developed technology. But to adapt this technology to the needs of development requires entrepreneurial decision. Such adaptation is not possible without complete mastery of the kind of technology relevant for each developing country. *And such mastery can come only by developing local talent in this field.* This indicates an appropriate science and technology policy.[35] Initially, this policy would have to cover fields of applied science and technology relevant for each country; but, as the OECD studies in science policy have shown, a country cannot acquire adequate scientific awareness without developing the ability to do fundamental research.[36]

Now science and technology are a vast complex field, and it is not possible for a given country with limited resources to cultivate the whole area. The initial vital decision, hence, would have to be one about which aspects of scientific and technological research are potentially relevant to a given country in the light of its objective situation.

Thus, science and technology policy cannot be evolved in a vacuum. It has to be integrated with the social and economic objectives of a given country. This has only recently been realized in the OECD countries, but this point is even more relevant for the developing countries. For the training of scientists and technologists in fields unrelated to economic growth would merely lead to a brain drain, and to social discontent and frustration. A vital link thus needs to be forged between science and technological research and agricultural—industrial development.

On the other hand, no science and technology policy can be evolved without an adequate educational system which could provide both the requisite number of researchers and teachers for the system and the required technical personnel for industry, agriculture and administration. Thus, as the OECD studies show,[37] the development of scientific and technological research and of the educational system must go hand in hand with economic growth. An educational system which outruns the concrete needs in other sectors leads to waste and social discontent. To give an example in the field of primary education, compulsory primary education without a balanced plan of farm modernization would merely lead to migration from rural areas to urban areas and thus to open unemployment. On the other hand, if primary education lags behind the needs of the modernization of the farm sector, agricultural development would be impeded. Much of the "student problem" in all parts of the world at present is due to the rigidity and incapacity of educational systems to respond to the changing needs of countries' economies with regard to student enrolment, curricula, equipment and the needs and aspirations of society generally.

In the field of education, the question is not merely one of the quantitative expansion of the system. Again to borrow from the OECD studies, what is much more significant is the quality of education. In the OECD countries, it was found that the curriculum for science and mathematics at a secondary school stage included material which was about fifty years old. Such obsolete instruction obviously has no value. As a result of the efforts of the OECD Committee for Scientific and Technical Personnel, the teaching in science and mathematics in the OECD countries is being revolutionized. Educational planning in the context of economic development is a vast field; the system needs to build into itself the capacity to innovate so as to meet creatively the needs of social and economic development.[38]

The other field where entrepreneurial action by the State is required to create a favourable climate for innovation is that of management training. The good manager is a scarce factor in a developing economy. This is not surprising. This factor is scarce even in some developed countries like the UK. The USA has realized the key role of this factor for growth, and has provided adequate management training institutes for the purpose. The results of scientific and technological research and of an expanded programme for educational development can bear fruit in terms of social and economic development only if managers–administrators in both the public and private sectors are energetic and imaginative enough to make use of them. Initially, to the extent to which this talent is limited, it may be necessary to utilize it most effectively by concentrating it at suitable strategic places like development banks, large public corporations, government planning departments and the like. This very limitation of entrepreneurial talent and of private resources might lead, in some contexts—where the State could attract the limited talent to public sector institutions—to the development by the State of certain vital industries in addition to the infrastructure which the State would have to build in any case.

Obviously, development in all these fields cannot be properly coordinated and integrated without appropriate planning. Further, such planning is also necessary to identify the optimum external assistance requirements and to use that assistance effectively for social and economic development.

The experience of Japan is of interest with regard to the entrepreneurial role of government during that country's initial phase of development in the last quarter of the nineteenth century.[39] Japan was poor in natural resources—particularly coal and iron ore—and was completely isolated from other countries. During the rapid and controlled modernization of the nation following the Meiji Restoration, the Japanese Government took the leading role in the introduction and promotion of science and technology. Partly because of the sudden fashion in which Japan—after two and a half centuries of isolation—was thrust into the contemporary world, the nation had a recognizable science policy from the beginning of this era, principally with respect to the development of trained manpower. The role of the government, of course, has varied with the time and circumstances—for example in the establishment of national industries which were turned over to private enterprise, later nationalized, and after the Second World War again denationalized. Yet, whatever the particular events at a given time, it remains true that government has been the principal sponsor of science and often the principal advocate of innovation.

Again, it was the Japanese Government which introduced compulsory primary education even before the UK did so. It is also of interest to note that the first attempt at national economic planning was undertaken in Japan in 1884, when the objective opportunities and required policies were formulated in the shape of a plan for economic development.

After the Second World War, the miracle of Japanese reconstruction and development was again due to the continuity of public administration, a long history of universal compulsory education, close cooperation between leaders of government and industry, increasing investment in scientific and technological research in both the private and public sectors, and planning of a type suited to the country's requirements.

NOTES

1. V. V. Bhatt, *Employment and Capital Formation in Underdeveloped Economies* (Bombay: Orient Longmans, 1960), chapter vi.
2. J. A. Schumpeter, *History of Economic Analysis* (London: Oxford University Press, 1959), pp. 12–13.
3. J. A. Schumpeter, *Science and Ideology, Essays of J. A. Schumpeter,* edited by R. V. Clemence (Cambridge, Mass.: Addison-Wesley Press, Inc., 1951).
4. J. A. Schumpeter, *History of Economic Analysis, op.cit.*, pp. 19–20.
5. *Ibid.*, p. 4.
6. *Ibid.*, pp. 321–2.
7. *Ibid.*, pp. 717–25; and J. Hicks, *Critical Essays in Monetary Theory* (London: Oxford University Press, 1967), chapter 10.
8. J. A. Schumpeter, *History of Economic Analysis, op.cit.*, p. 964.
9. *Ibid.*, p. 918.
10. *Ibid.*, p. 919.
11. W. Leontief, *The New Outlook in Economics*, paper presented at the Indian Economic Conference, Madras (1967). See also, V. V. Bhatt, "The Sterility of Equilibrium Economics", in Ashok Mitra (ed.), *Economic Theory and Planning* (Oxford University Press, 1974).
12. J. A. Schumpeter, *History of Economic Analysis, op.cit.*, p. 954, footnote 2.
13. J. M. Keynes, *Introduction to the Cambridge Economic Handbooks*; for example, see Hubert Henderson, *Supply and Demand* (Cambridge University Press, 1921).
14. J. A. Schumpeter, *History of Economic Analysis, op.cit.*, p. 410.
15. *Ibid.*, p. 411.
16. J. A. Schumpeter, "Theoretical Problems of Economic Growth", in *Essays, op.cit.*
17. J. A. Schumpeter, *op.cit.*
18. *Ibid.*
19. *A Handbook of Marxism* (New York: Random House, 1935), p. 26.
20. J. A. Schumpeter, "The Communist Manifesto in Sociology and Economics", in *Essays, op.cit.*, pp. 292–3.
21. *Ibid.*
22. K. Marx, *Das Kapital* (Everyman edition), vol. i, p. 654.
23. J. A. Schumpeter, *Ten Great Economists* (Oxford University Press, 1951), p. 40.

24. J. A. Schumpeter, *Business Cycles*, vol. i (New York: McGraw-Hill Book Company, 1939), p. 86.
25. *Ibid.*, pp. 103–4.
26. J. A. Schumpeter, "Economic Theory and Entrepreneurial History", in *Essays, op.cit.*
27. A. Gerschenkron, *Economic Backwardness in Historical Perspective* (Cambridge: Harvard University Press, 1962).
28. J. M. Keynes, *A Treatise on Money,* vol. ii (London: Macmillan & Co., 1950), pp. 95–6.
29. J. A. Schumpeter, *History of Economic Analysis, op.cit.*, pp. 12–13.
30. *Ibid.*, pp. 472–3; see also Wassily Leontief, "Implicit Theorizing: A Methodological Criticism of the neo-Cambridge School", in R. V. Clemence (ed.), *Readings in Economic Analysis*, vol. i (Cambridge, Mass: Addison-Wesley Press Inc., 1950).
31. R. Solow, "Technical Change and the Aggregate Production Function", *Review of Economics and Statistics*, vol. xxxix, no. 3 (Aug. 1957).
32. T. W. Schultz, "Reflections on Agricultural Production, Output and Supply", *Journal of Farm Economics*, vol. 38 (Aug. 1956) and "The Education of Farm People: An Economic Perspective", in P. Foster and J. R. Sheffield (eds.), *Education and Rural Development*, World Year Book of Education (London: Evans Brothers, 1973).
33. N. Kaldor, "The Relation of Economic Growth and Cyclical Fluctuations", in his *Essays on Economic Stability and Growth* (London: Gerald Duckworth & Co., Ltd., 1960).
34. J. A. Schumpeter, *Capitalism, Socialism and Democracy* (New York: Harper & Row Publishers, 1962), pp. 291–3.
35. V. V. Bhatt, "On Technology Policy and its Institutional Frame", *World Development*, vol. 3, no. 9 (Sept. 1975).
36. OECD, *Science and Development* (Paris, 1968).
37. OECD, *Social Objectives in Educational Planning* (Paris, 1967).
38. OECD, *Financing of Education for Economic Growth* (Paris, 1960).
39. W. W. Lockwood, *Economic Development of Japan—Growth and Structural Change* (Princeton University Press, 1954). See also K. Ohkawa and H. Rosovsky, *Japanese Economic Growth* (Stanford University Press, 1973).

3. Some Notes on Balanced and Unbalanced Growth*

RECENTLY, the controversy with regard to balanced and unbalanced growth has been revived by Lipton[1] and Nath.[2] Lipton, however, does not seem to have grasped the basic idea behind either balanced growth or unbalanced growth.[3] Nath has made out a lucid and for the first time a fairly integrated case for balanced growth.[4] However, for him growth problem seems to be as simple as any maximizing problem in mathematics; further, he does not seem to be aware of the motivation problem, posed by the protagonists of unbalanced growth.

The purpose of this chapter is to clarify the issues involved in this controversy and to suggest that the conflict between these two seemingly different prescriptions for growth is more apparent than real; unbalanced growth has justification only in the perspective of balanced growth, and the movement of the economy towards balanced growth is not inconsistent with, and may actually be facilitated by, a strategy of unbalanced growth. Further, it is shown how both these concepts are *operationally meaningful* in formulating as well as implementing development programmes. In both these tasks the role of the State is considered to be basic, but there can be no sovereign rule about the actual extent of its active participation in both these activities.

The controversy regarding balanced and unbalanced growth seems to have been carried on at cross purposes, as the protagonists of neither have brought out clearly the implications of their respective theories. The problem of balanced as well as unbalanced growth involves five interrelated but analytically distinct problems, which have not been so far specified clearly:

(*a*) The problem of objectives in relation to constraints or conditioning factors, such as, for example, the initial condition of an economy, its existing as well as prospective technical relations, demand relations, propensity to save, foreign-exchange availability (depending on prospects with regard to exports and external capital inflow) and the growth rate of population.

(*b*) The choice of volume of investment in the light of (*a*).

(*c*) The choice of investment or output pattern in the light of (*a*) and (*b*).

(*d*) The choice of production techniques in the light of (*a*), (*b*) and (*c*).

(*e*) The problem of internal consistency of a development programme.

For balanced as well as unbalanced growth, what is necessary is a *simultaneous* and *mutually consistent* solution of all these problems.

As these five analytically distinct problems have not been clearly stated, the discussion on balanced and unbalanced growth shifts from one related problem to the other and the protagonists and the critics argue at cross purposes on different planes of discourse.

* Published in *The Economic Journal*, vol. lxxv, no. 297 (Mar. 1965).

A. The Problem of Objectives

With regard to the problem of objectives, none of the protagonists has presented the issues clearly. It appears from the discussion, however, that the attainment of the maximum possible rate of growth within *a certain finite time horizon* is the objective of all.[5] The advocates of unbalanced growth, however, assert a certain relationship between the rate of growth and unbalance such that the creation of unbalance itself ensures the maximum rate of growth; thus unbalanced growth, itself, becomes the proximate objective.[6]

The basic difference between the two schools of thought relates to the constraints. Balanced-growth discussion implies more or less perfect knowledge of the constraints or conditioning factors such as technical and demand relations, propensity to save, possibilities relating to foreign trade and assistance and the growth rate of the labour force.[7] Further, the protagonists of balanced growth take these constraints as given data or independent variables of the model. A balanced growth model is then like the Von Neumann model[8] or any one of its recent variants, of which there is a large number.

Unbalanced growth does not imply perfect knowledge of these constraints; it holds that the exact nature and intensity of the constraints can be known only during a growth process. Unless, therefore, the economy keeps bumping against the Hicksian ceiling,[9] it is not possible to know the full possibilities of growth even under *existing* constraints. Further, and here lies the basic distinguishing feature of unbalanced growth, the basic constraints are assumed to be amenable to change, of course within certain limits. These limits are not known *a priori* during a growth process and it is, in fact, the *raison d'être* of unbalanced growth to modify the conditioning factors or the "external frame" of the economy so as to raise the growth rate higher than can be attained otherwise.[10] Technical change or innovational activity is as much conditioned by the nature of the growth process as is the latter by the former. Or to use Harrod's terminology, the natural rate of growth is not independent of the warranted rate; the more the latter tends to exceed the former, the more it will shape the natural rate in its own mould.

Unbalanced growth provides the inducement mechanism for breaking through the constraints, overcoming the conditioning factors and bursting through the pre-existing external frame of the economy by means of innovations, to use the phrase in Schumpeter's sense. Because of imperfect knowledge as well as the possibilities of changing the nature and intensity of the basic constraints by the nature of the growth process itself, it is not possible to specify *a priori* the exact course of the growth process by the working out of a neat model with given data and a clear-cut solution. The actual growth process as well as the growth rate will depend upon the nature and intensity of unbalances and the elasticity of response (not known *a priori*) in each of the elements of the basic constraints.[11]

To repeat, balanced growth discussion takes the "fundamental conditions" determining the natural rate of growth, to use Harrod's terminology, as given data or independent variables; it is the basic assumption[12] of unbalanced growth that these conditions are pliable, within wide limits, by the endogenous forces of the economic system. In Schumpeter's terms, balanced growth would represent only "growth", while unbalanced growth would represent "economic evolution".[13]

B. Choice of Volume of Investment

This difference with regard to the objectives explains the difference in the approach of the two theories to the problem of the choice of the volume of investment over a finite time horizon. For balanced growth, the volume of investment can be decided *a priori* on the basis of the objectives and the data with respect to the constraints mentioned earlier. Unbalanced growth, on the other hand, assumes a certain relationship between the volume of investment and the nature and intensity of imbalance such that the volume of investment is an increasing function, *within certain* limits, of certain types of imbalance.

C. Choice of Investment Pattern

The crucial choice thus from the point of view of unbalanced growth is the choice of investment or output pattern. For balanced growth, the rate of growth will be maximized, given perfect knowledge about the initial conditions, existing as well as prospective demand and technical relations, propensity to save, foreign-exchange availability and the population growth rate, by choosing such an investment or output pattern that, at each stage, in all the sectors the available production capacity is fully utilized and no surplus capacity or shortages and bottlenecks arise.

However, balanced growth at this stage recognizes the need for the creation of surplus capacity with regard to social overheads for maximizing the rate of growth, in view of technological factors and a certain functional relationship between social overheads and other direct investment.[14] The creation of social overheads involves a long gestation period, and if bottlenecks arise in this sector the rate of growth will be adversely affected, as these overheads cannot be imported and their creation would take considerable time.[15] Further, the process of creating social overheads as well as their existence *induces* investment in a large number of sectors, and this *inducement effect* is pervasive and is capable of generating a cumulative process of investment. Moreover, because of technological reasons and in the light of prospective demand, it may be cheaper to create temporary surplus capacity in this sector to attain the maximum growth rate. Of course, the extent of temporary surplus capacity that can be created in this sector will depend on the time path with regard to the volume of investment.

The argument for an unbalanced investment pattern where social overheads are concerned can be extended to some other vital sectors which also involve long gestation periods and similar technological requirements, though, unlike social overheads, their products in principle are importable. For example, investment in the steel industry has a long gestation period, and from the technological point of view it is cheaper to expand the capacity of a given steel plant than to set up a new plant; this means that the basic lay-out of a steel plant should be such that its productive capacity can be easily expanded. The total capital costs as well as production costs per ton of steel decline with the increase in size of the plant. Because of these technological factors, it may be advantageous to create some surplus capacity in steel output.[16] Of course, this argument about steel applies only to those countries for whom it is possible and advantageous to develop a steel industry in the light of their resources-endowment.

It may be argued that steel is an importable commodity, and hence even if a shortage of steel developed it would not create a bottleneck. However, the gestation period for steel is quite long, and so if a shortage of steel developed, it would have to be imported during this long gestation period; this would commit the limited foreign exchange available to the import of steel, and thus would mean less of other imports. If the growth rate is not to be adversely affected it seems desirable to create surplus capacity for products which have a long gestation period, even if they are, in principle, importable and let imports soften the impact of shortages of domestically produced goods which have a fairly small gestation period.

Hirschman, too, recognizes the need for development by means of excess capacity in social overhead capital during the initial stages of the growth process.[17] He, however, fails to recognize the need for such excess capacity at later stages also. Further, there is a type of dichotomy in the arguments which he advances against excess capacity in the social overhead capital in Chapter 5 and the arguments for concentrating on projects with the highest combined forward and backward linkage effects in Chapter 6. Railroad transport, for example, has both linkage effects; it directly stimulates industries such as iron and steel, coal and other related industries, and indirectly, through the opening up of new areas to trade, it has a trade-creating effect which results in profit opportunities for trade and industry, and thus provides exactly the type of inducement mechanism which Hirschman advocates. His quantification of the linkage effects of various industries is misleading for two reasons: first, his data relate to advanced countries, in which the development of basic facilities, including transport, has already reached a high level and, second, as he recognizes, his linkages are calculated only on the basis of current input requirements and not also on the basis of capital requirements.[18] The value of linkages in the case of basic facilities like transport is therefore low in his calculations. If his quantification of the linkage effects of basic facilities was done appropriately it may have contradicted his arguments against excess capacity creation in social overhead capital. And, finally, the unpredictable but none the less massive inducement effects through trade creation of the development of basic facilities have been ignored by him completely.

Balanced growth recognizes that the creation of surplus capacity in some vital sectors is necessary for accelerating the pace of development; however, it does not recognize that a deliberate creation of shortages in some lagging sectors may be equally necessary for inducing the process of overcoming bottlenecks.

And it is in this respect that unbalanced growth differs basically from balanced growth. The former asserts a certain relationship between shortages of certain types of products and the inducement to break these shortages; this inducement takes the form not only of market incentives by raising prices and hence profits in the relevant sectors, but also of non-market pressures, compulsions and tensions, inducing either the State or private agencies to expand the lagging sectors by an appropriate change in their attitudes, institutions and policies.[19] This inducement mechanism, working through the creation of shortages as a result of a deliberate strategy of unbalanced growth, would generate a much faster rate of growth in the lagging sectors than the growth which would result from a strategy of balanced growth.

The basic contribution of unbalanced growth then is to suggest that the nature and intensity of the basic constraints, including production techniques, should not be taken as given data or independent variables for the purpose of growth strategy; explicit recognition should be given to the possibilities of modifying these constraints within limits provided that an appropriate inducement mechanism is set in motion by the deliberate creation of a *certain* type of imbalance in the investment or the output pattern. Lagging sectors can be induced through price-rises and the resulting profit opportunities to expand their output by improving their organizational and technical efficiency; there will thus be an inducement to adopt innovations appropriate for expanding output. Further, the sectors using the scarce products or services will also be induced to substitute other products and services for the scarce ones. Price-rises and profit increases in the lagging sectors will also lead to a change in the distribution pattern in favour of profits, whose share in national income would increase as a result of successful innovational activity, and this would raise the rate of saving and investment and accelerate the pace of growth. Moreover, if these market incentives did not prove adequate for the purpose, non-market incentives and compulsions would induce the State to take adequate policy measures to generate a process of correcting the imbalances.[20] Thus,[21] the economy can break through the known technical and demand constraints to some extent and realize a growth rate higher than would be possible with a strategy of balanced growth. Balanced growth objective, in the absence of a strategy of unbalanced growth, would mean a growth rate more or less equal to the growth rate of the lagging sectors.

It must be emphasized, however, that the objective to be attained through a deliberate policy of creating imbalances is to induce a *movement* towards a balance; this balance may not be reached, but the objective would be to set in motion, each time that a deliberate imbalance is created, a corrective process.[22] This may result in a cyclical growth path around a rising trend; this policy, however, would be desirable if it resulted in a trend rate of growth higher than would otherwise be attained. This in fact is the Schumpeterian growth path.

But then there are limits within which imbalances can generate a corrective process. Imbalances beyond a point could lead to an explosive situation, both from the economic as well as the social point of view. Hence in deciding about the type and extent of imbalances to be created, it would be necessary to ensure that their intensity was such as to generate a corrective process; these limits can be determined, as I have shown elsewhere, only on the basis of informed judgement about the working of the economy.[23]

Further, even when imbalances are deliberately created, it is necessary to have an idea about the nature of the balance that it is sought to attain thereby; otherwise, a deliberate policy of creating imbalances would merely mean a leap in the dark. *In operational terms*, this implies two types of balanced growth paths, one type based on *given known* constraints and the other based on informed judgement (for no *a priori* knowledge in this matter is possible) about the ability of the economy to break through the known constraints through a process of unbalanced growth. The objective, then, should be to attain a balanced growth pattern of the latter type. This would inevitably result in imbalances; but these imbalances would provide the necessary motivation for generating a corrective process such that the resulting growth rate would be higher than would have been attained on the basis of the first type of balanced growth pattern.

Unbalanced growth, then, as a strategy, has justification only in the perspective of balanced growth;[24] balanced growth by itself, to use Schumpeter's phrase, is *insufficiently motivated* and it is the purpose of unbalanced growth strategy to provide the necessary motivation for the purpose. Unbalanced growth strategy is not inconsistent with the objective of balanced growth; it provides the latter with the element of motivation which it lacks.

Of course, unbalanced growth strategy would not succeed in its aim if, as mentioned earlier, the nature and intensity of imbalances are such as to result in an explosive situation or if they result in creating and supporting sectors, which may have vested interests in perpetuating them.[25]

D. *Choice of Production Techniques*

Except for Lewis and Hirschman, the protagonists of neither balanced nor unbalanced growth have devoted any attention to the problem of choice of production techniques. And even the treatment of the problem by Lewis and Hirschman is inadequate. Lewis discusses this problem in relation to the over-populated underdeveloped economies and mentions that since the social opportunity cost of labour is zero, it would be advantageous for these countries to adopt labour-intensive techniques wherever feasible.[26] However, he does not seem to be aware of the time dimension in the process; he does not mention the conflict, which I have pointed out elsewhere, between the two criteria—output maximization and the maximization of the rate of growth *over a specified period of time*—with regard to the choice of techniques, once it is assumed that the social cost of additional labour employment is positive; nor does he discuss the need for choosing production techniques, where fixed and durable capital goods are involved, in the light of not only the present but the prospective social labour cost during a specified time horizon.[27]

Hirschman, too, ignores this time dimension; he, however, introduces one significant additional factor that has been generally ignored in the discussion of this problem, that is the quality of labour available in the underdeveloped countries. He suggests that the choice of production techniques should depend on the nature and type of labour available. It is in this context that he favours the adoption of process-centred industries rather than the product-centred ones.[28] At this stage, however, he confuses two analytically distinct problems: the problem of choice of production techniques and that of choice of industries. Of course, this confusion, as I indicate in the next chapter, has crept into a major part of the discussion about production techniques.[29]

The choice of production techniques would have to be related to the initial conditions and objectives as well as to the choice of the volume and the pattern of investment.

E. *Internal Consistency*

The final problem of internal consistency of a production programme or a plan has been explicitly mentioned by the balanced growth theorists and particularly Lewis.[30] However, the unbalanced growth advocates have not even mentioned this problem. Balanced growth in fact is so defined as to result in internal consistency of the plan or production programme. However, this problem is as much relevant for unbalanced growth as for balanced growth. A strategy of unbalanced growth cannot succeed unless the unbalanced growth pattern is internally consistent in such a way as to result in the desired imbalances. This aspect of the unbalanced growth strategy has been ignored in the discussions on the subject.

II. The Role of the State and Planning

Both balanced and unbalanced growth, whether as a strategy or as an objective, are related to the objectives and goals of the community as a whole, and involve decisions by a collective agency with adequate policy instruments at its disposal to affect the growth process in the desired direction. Such a collective agency, in fact, is the State. Since the objectives relate to the community as a whole, and since the growth process has to be initiated in a certain way, and since it has to be ensured that it follows a certain pattern, it follows that this responsibility has inevitably to be borne by the State. This is explicitly recognized by Lewis, Streeten and Nath,[31] Hirschman[32] is a little ambiguous in this matter and Nurske just does not recognize the need for State action.[33]

Further, for balanced as well as unbalanced growth, it is necessary for the State to work out the full implications for the growth process in order to find out whether it follows the desired direction and to be able to take appropriate policy measures if it does not. Planning or programming thus is an integral part of both balanced and unbalanced growth. This is realized by Lewis, Streeten and Nath,[34] but Hirschman and Nurkse[35] have failed to recognize this aspect of their respective theories.

Since Hirschman associates planning or programming with balanced growth, he fails to realize its significance for his own theory. He holds that economic "backwardness is due to insufficient number and speed of development decisions";[36] if so, then planning should have become an integral part of his theory, as planning would, as Nath[37] argues, make it easier for the State as well as the private sector to take decisions. Since the plan would indicate the pace and pattern of growth, it would provide all the basic information necessary for taking decisions and thus facilitate the most economical use of the scarce factor, decision-making ability.

This, however, does not mean that a development plan or programme should be necessarily formulated and implemented by the State. All that is necessary is that the State should have such a plan or a programme formulated by it, or, if formulated by other agencies, it should be acceptable to it. Further, the State need not implement the plan or programme itself; it should have adequate sanctions and policy instruments to effect its implementation in the desired way, whether the implementing agency or agencies are the State or private individuals or groups.

Thus, the nature and extent of the role of the State in the planned process of development in terms of either balanced or unbalanced growth will vary from country to country, depending on the nature, ability and efficiency of the State, as well as of the private sector, and the policy instruments at the disposal of the State and its ability in wielding these instruments. In some countries overall development programming, together with appropriate monetary-fiscal policies, may suffice, while in others some physical controls as well as direct implementation of some plan projects may be necessary. There can be no sovereign rule in this matter.

NOTES

1. M. Lipton, "Balanced and Unbalanced Growth in Underdeveloped Countries", *Economic Journal* (Sept. 1962).
2. S. K. Nath, "The Theory of Balanced Growth", *Oxford Economic Papers* (June 1962).
3. Who would take Lipton seriously when he says that balanced growth implies that all sectors, including the inefficient ones, should expand or that income-elasticity of demand has to be taken in static terms, or that everything is top priority or development should be autarchic? See M. Lipton, *op.cit.*, pp. 654–5. See in this connection W. A. Lewis, *The Theory of Economic Growth* (London, 1955), chapters iii, 5(a); v, 3(b); vi, 2(a); and vii, 1(b). See also "Equilibrium and Growth in the World Economy", *Economic Essays*, by R. Nurkse, edited by G. Haberler, 1961, pp. 316–22 and pp. 250–9.
4. Most of Nath's arguments for balanced growth would be found in Lewis with proper qualifications. See W. A. Lewis, *op.cit.*, chapters ii, 3(b); vi, 2(a); and vii, 1(b). Just as Nath has misrepresented Streeten (see P. Streeten, "Unbalanced Growth: A Reply", *Oxford Economic Papers* (Mar. 1963)) with regard to the role of the State, he also not properly and adequately represented Lewis's case for balanced growth.
5. See W. A. Lewis, *op.cit.*, pp. 383–92; A. O. Hirschman, *The Strategy of Economic Development* (New Haven, 1958), p. 140; R. Nurkse, *op. cit.*, pp. 248 and 316.
6. A. O. Hirschman, *op.cit.*, p. 140.
7. Lewis, of course, recognizes that demand and output relations are apt to alter in unforeseeable ways. See W. A. Lewis, *op.cit.*, p. 389.
8. See *Review of Economic Studies*, 1945–6; originally prepared for a Princeton mathematical seminar in 1932.
9. See J. R. Hicks, *A Contribution to Theory of the Trade Cycle* (Oxford, 1950).
10. A. O. Hirschman, *op.cit.*, chapter iv.
11. See for a similar view N. Kaldor, "Economic Growth and Cyclical Fluctuations", *Economic Journal* (Mar. 1954), reprinted in his *Essays on Economic Stability and Growth* (London, 1960), pp. 229–32; and "Characteristics of Economic Development", in his *Essays*, pp. 253–7. Kaldor observes, "Once the planning of production gets under the control of men who are actuated by the desire to expand, progress tends to become self-generating; higher rates of capital accumulation and a higher rate of population growth are called forth in response to the requirements of expansion. The stronger the urge to expand . . . the greater are the stresses and strains to which the economy becomes exposed; and the greater are the incentives to overcome physical limitations on production by the introduction of new techniques . . . however strong the urge to expand, the actual rate of economic progress could never exceed a certain maximum, determined either by a maximum attainable rate of saving, or a maximum attainable rate of population growth, or a maximum attainable flow of new ideas (or some combination of these). But the point is that the *actual* values of these variables, in any given society or at any given age, are not determined by their theoretical maximum values, but are capable of being slowed down or accelerated in accordance with the push or pull exerted by entrepreneurial behaviour. There is an elasticity of response in each of these elements, which means that the postulate of some supply curves gives a truer representation of their character than the usual postulate of an independent constant." See his *Essays*, pp. 236–7.
12. R. F. Harood, *Towards a Dynamic Economics* (London, 1949).

13. J. A. Schumpeter, *Business Cycles*, vol. i (London, 1939), pp. 82–7. Growth, as defined by Schumpeter, is the result of changes in population and capital accumulation; economic evolution is the result of innovations. Unbalanced growth has great similarity with Schumpeter's model; in both, the outcome is not known *a priori* and the actual result depends on the nature and the intensity of innovating activity. In Schumpeter's model, however, entrepreneurial activity is insufficiently motivated as he starts from perfect equilibrium conditions. His model in fact requires some visible stresses and strains to induce entrepreneurial activity. Of course, he recognizes that "For a given innovation to become possible, there must always be some 'objective needs' to be satisfied and certain 'objective conditions'; but they rarely, if ever, uniquely determine what kind of innovation will satisfy them, and as a rule, they can be satisfied in many different ways." See his *Business Cycles*, p. 85, footnote.
14. R. Nurkse, *op.cit.*, pp. 267–74.
15. In the case of India, particularly since 1957–8, industrial development is being held back because of shortages of power, transport and steel. Steel, of course, has been imported, but then this has been responsible for aggravating the foreign-exchange crisis. See Reserve Bank of India, *Report on Currency and Finance* (Bombay: 1958–9; 1959–60; 1960–1; 1961–2).
16. Cf. M. N. Dastur and R. D. Lalkaka, "Lay-out of Large Integrated Steel-works", *International Symposium on Recent Developments in Iron and Steel Making with Special Reference to Indian Conditions* (London: The Iron and Steel Institute, 1963).
17. A. O. Hirschman, *op.cit.*, p. 94.
18. A. O. Hirschman, *op.cit.*, chapter vi. See also, for historical experience in this matter, W. W. Rostow, *The Stages of Economic Growth* (Cambridge, 1960), pp. 55–7.
19. A. O. Hirschmann, *op.cit.*, chapter iv, and P. Streeten, "Unbalanced Growth", *Oxford Economic Papers* (June 1959).
20. Nath fails to recognize that the State could be ignorant as well as weak and would require inducements to act. See S. K. Nath, *op.cit.*; on this point see also P. Streeten, "Unbalanced Growth: A Reply", *op.cit.*
21. In a democracy, as Galbraith once observed, no major unpleasant decisions can be taken by the State unless an atmosphere of minor crisis is deliberately created. In India the emphasis on agricultural development and export promotion during the Third Plan was largely due to the food and foreign-exchange crises which arose during the Second Plan period; the emphasis on steel during the Second Plan period, similarly, was the result of acute shortage which developed in the latter years of the First Plan period. See V. V. Bhatt, "A Decade of Planned Development: The Indian Experience", *Economia Internazione* (May 1962).
22. A. O. Hirschman, *op.cit.*, chapter iv and p. 93; P. Streeten, "Unbalanced Growth", *op.cit.*, pp. 169–71; H. W. Singer, "The Concept of Balanced Growth in Economic Development—Theory and Practice", *Malayan Economic Review* (Oct. 1958), p. 11; W. A. Lewis, *op.cit.*, p. 147.
23. V. V. Bhatt, "Deficit Financing, Inflationary Pressures and Economic Development", *The Economic Weekly* (Special Number—June 1960).
24. The use by Hirschman of the input–output tables for calculating his linkage effects, in fact, points to the importance which he attaches to balance.
25. See P. Streeten, "Unbalanced Growth: A Reply", *op.cit.*
26. W. A. Lewis, *op.cit.*, pp. 351–2 and pp. 385–7. Of course, Lewis does pose the problem rightly; he says, "the methods used in carrying out projects must be those which economize the scarce resources", p. 385.
27. See V. V. Bhatt, *Employment and Capital Formation in Underdeveloped Economies* (Bombay, 1960), chapter v; also "Techniques, Employment and Rate of Growth", *Economic Journal* (June 1958). See also A. K. Sen, *Choice of Techniques* (Oxford, 1960), M. Dobb, *An Essay on Economic Growth and Planning* (London, 1960), and D. R. Khatkhate, "Investment Pattern, Techniques and Growth", *Economia Internazionale* (Feb. 1961).
28. A. O. Hirschman, *op.cit.*, pp. 150–2.
29. See V. V. Bhatt, "Techniques, Employment and Rate of Growth", *op.cit.*
30. W. A. Lewis, *op.cit.*, pp. 383–92.
31. W. A. Lewis, *op.cit.*, pp. 348–50, and chapter vii; P. Streeten, "Unbalanced Growth: A Reply", *op.cit.*; S. K. Nath, *op.cit.*; see also M. Lipton, *op.cit.*

32. Hirschman, in the earlier part of his discussion, favours only some initial action by the State, but in his final chapter he seems to recognize the need for subsequent state action too. See pp. 60–5 and 202–3.
33. R. Nurkse, *op.cit.*, pp. 249–50. He, however, does recognize the need for state action for anticipatory overhead investment and in lagging sectors such as agriculture. See pp. 270–5 and 315–17.
34. W. A. Lewis, *op.cit.*, chapter vii; P. Streeten, "Unbalanced Growth: A Reply", *op.cit.*; R. Nath, *op.cit.*
35. A. O. Hirschman, *op.cit.*, pp. 50–7; R. Nurkse, *op.cit.*, pp. 249–50.
36. A. O. Hirschman, *op.cit.*, pp. 24–6.
37. S. K. Nath, *op.cit.*

4 Techniques, Employment and Rate of Growth*

Our object is to present the problem regarding the choice of techniques for an underdeveloped economy with considerable underemployment of labour. Our contention is that because of a possible divergence between the private and social cost of labour, even on the maximization of rate-of-return criterion, the techniques chosen for the various industries of such an economy should be more labour intensive than those indicated by the prevailing real wage-rate. Further, for such an economy, there exists an alternative criterion for the choice of techniques: it could choose such techniques as would maximize its income and employment in the short run. Which of these two criteria or an admixture of the two it would adopt would depend upon its economic objectives.

Assumptions

The following assumptions are made:

1. There is considerable underemployment of labour in agriculture such that with appropriate agrarian reorganization involving little capital expenditure the agricultural output would not be affected if the underemployed labour were taken away from agriculture.
2. When the surplus labour from the agricultural sector is removed and employed in the industrial sector the *per capita* output in the former sector would increase.
3. The *per capita* consumption, however, in the agricultural sector would not increase as much as the increase in the *per capita* output.
4. The cost of labour in terms of wage goods in the industrial sector, therefore, would be less than that measured by the given real wage-rate.
5. All profits are saved and invested, and all wages in the industrial sector are consumed.
6. There exists a choice for each firm between techniques of varying degrees of labour intensity.
7. The problem regarding the choice of industries or investment pattern is already solved in the light of the existing natural resources and the desired time-pattern of growth.

Rate-of-return Criterion

The problem to be solved now is: What techniques or input combinations to adopt for the various industries. The private firms obviously would adopt such techniques as would maximize their respective rates of profit, given the relative prices of various inputs. However, since the real wage-rate for labour is higher

* First published in *The Economic Journal*, vol. lxviii, no. 271 (Sept. 1958).

than the real social cost of labour (Assumption 4), the techniques so chosen by private firms would not maximize the rate of social surplus (profits). For maximizing the rate of return over cost from the social point of view, therefore, the techniques for various industries will have to be more labour intensive than those based on the prevailing real wage-rate.

It is easy to see that the techniques so chosen would also maximize the rate of growth of investment, income and employment, because of Assumption 5.

Maximization of Income and Employment Criterion

There exists, however, an alternative criterion for the choice of techniques. Since the marginal productivity of the underemployed labour in agriculture is zero or near zero, such an economy could maximize its income and employment in the short run by choosing the most labour-intensive techniques for its industries, from among all the available economically feasible techniques. This could be seen from the diagram on page 42.

In the industrial sector the *available wage goods value of capital* is measured along the *X* axis in terms of wage units and is represented by *OA*, while the available labour is measured along the *Y* axis and is represented by *OB*. There are two industries *V* and *W*, and two techniques are available for each of these two industries. Techniques I and II as shown with reference to the origin *O* represent the two techniques for the industry *V* and techniques I and II as shown with reference to the origin *Q* represent the two techniques for the industry *W*. OL_1 represents a certain output of *V* with technique II and OM_2 represents the same level of output with technique I; different points on the line L_1M_1 represent identical levels of output of *V* but with different combinations of techniques I and II. The lines LM_s are thus equal output lines for *V*. The level of output of *V* is shown by the distance of each such line *LM* from the origin *O*, such that the greater is this distance, the larger is the output. *ST*s similarly are equal output lines for the industry *W* and are drawn with reference to the origin *Q*.

Now let us assume that at the given real social cost of labour, only technique I for each of the two industries is profitable. Suppose that on the basis of the maximization of the rate-of-return criterion, only technique I for each of the two industries is chosen and QS_1 output for *W* and OM_1 output for *V* are produced, leaving *CD* amount of labour unemployed.

However, if techniques or the combination of techniques for each of the two industries were so chosen as to fully employ both available labour and capital it could be easily seen that outputs for both *V* and *W* could be larger than in the previous case.

By choosing, for example, technique I for *V* and technique II for *W*, full employment of both available labour and capital could be attained at point T_2, where the output for *V* would be OT_2 and the output for *W* would be QS_2; outputs of both the industries, thus, would be larger than in the previous case. Similar would be the case if a combination of both the techniques for each of the two industries were chosen so as to attain full employment of both capital and labour. For example, at point *P*, where the equal output lines L_2M_2 and S_2T_2 intersect, there would be full employment of both the inputs and larger outputs

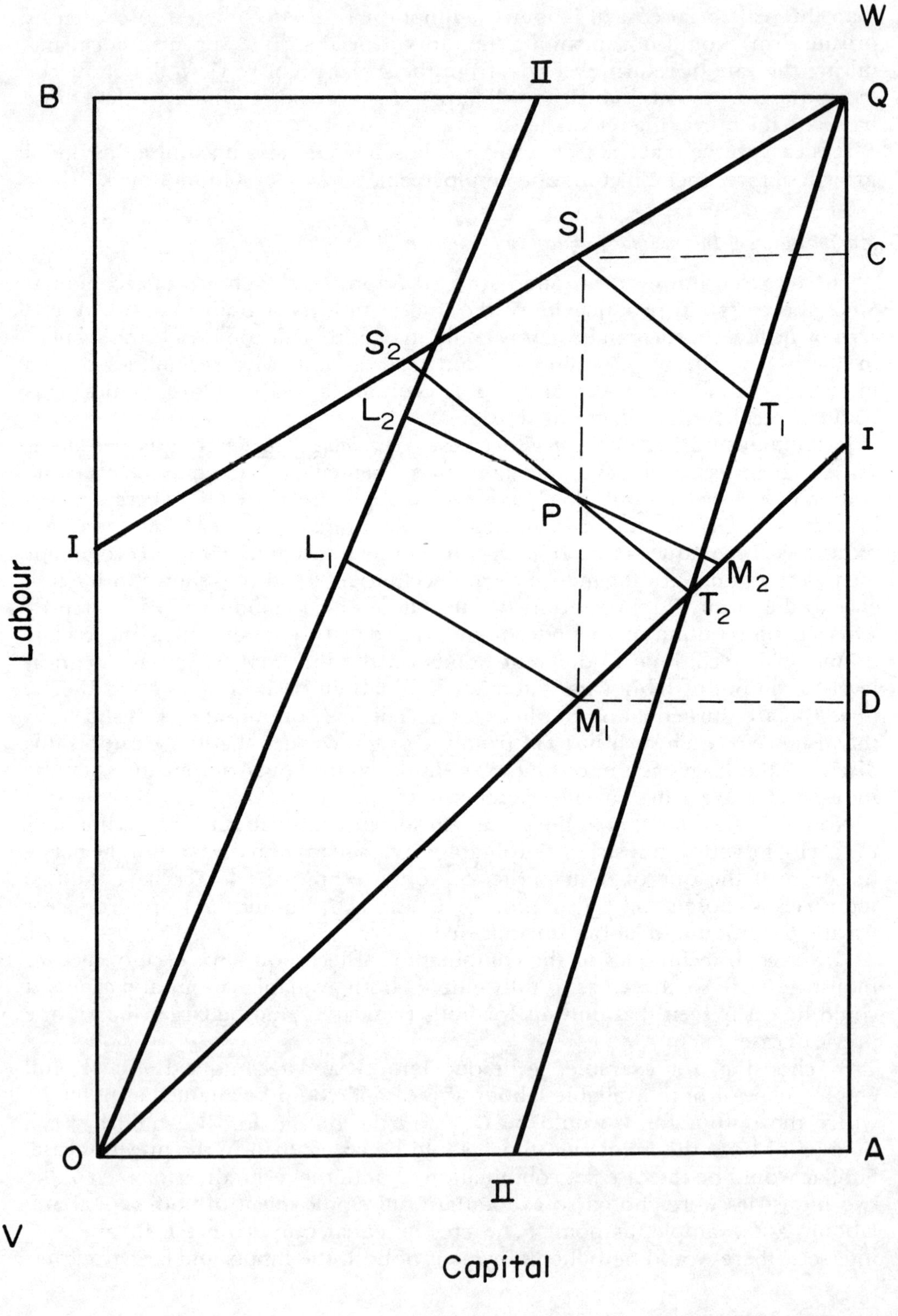
W
II
B
Q
S1
C
S2
L2
T1
I
P
I
L1
M2
T2
Labour
D
M1
O
A
II
V
Capital

of both V and W. Output of V would be now OM_2 instead of OM_1, and the output of W would be QS_2 instead of QS_1.

Inadequacy of food output could put a limit to this process of attaining full-employment level of income immediately. It is assumed, however, that food output can be increased in such an economy by introducing minor innovations in agriculture involving an insignificant amount of additional capital.

Choice between these Two Criteria

Thus an underdeveloped economy has also a problem of choosing between the two criteria for the choice of techniques: (*a*) Maximization of the rate of return over cost, and (*b*) Maximization of income and employment in the short-run.

If the first criterion is adopted, the rate of growth also is maximized. With the second criterion, though full-employment level of income would be attained almost immediately, the rate of growth thereafter would be smaller than what would be with the first criterion, because of a lower rate of profits and hence of capital accumulation (Assumption 5).

The choice of techniques thus would depend upon *the desired time-pattern of growth.* The following diagram shows the time-pattern of growth on the basis of the two criteria mentioned above.

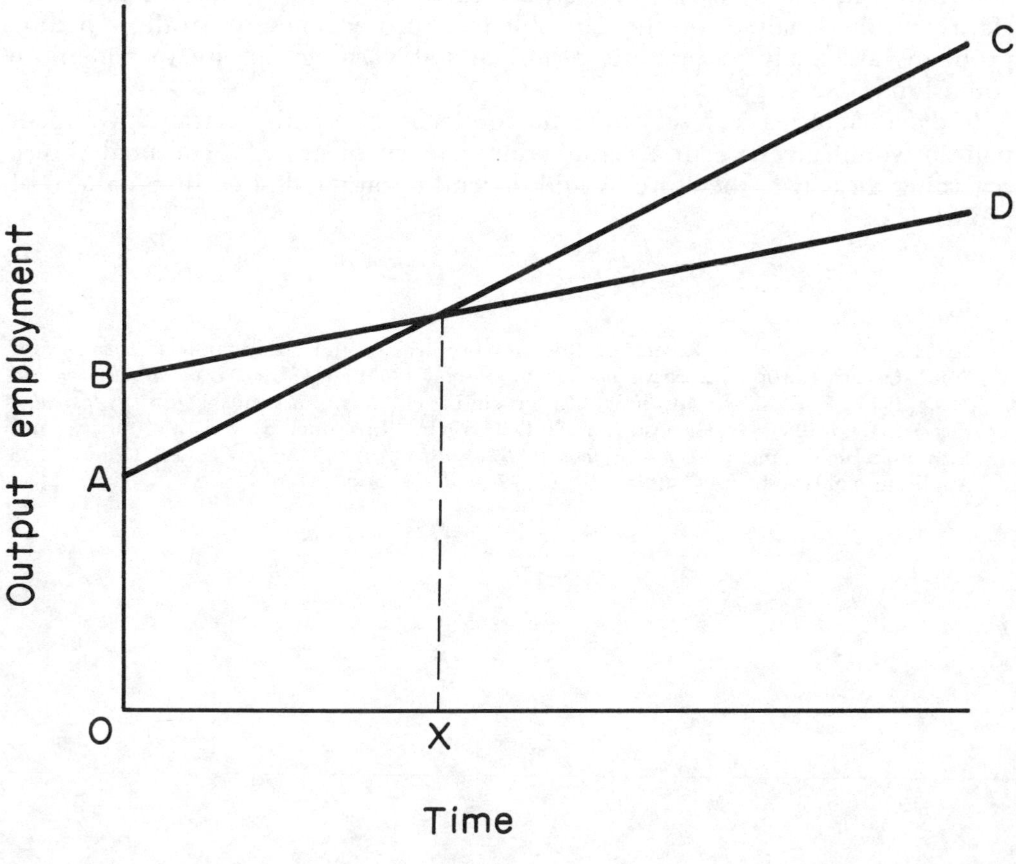

Time is measured along the *X* axis, and output and employment on the *Y* axis. *OA* gives the initial output and employment. *AC* shows the time-pattern of growth with the maximization of rate of return over cost criterion. With the maximization of income and employment criterion, full-employment level of output is immediately obtained so that there is a sort of a jump from *A* to *B*; thereafter *BD* shows the time-pattern of growth. Maximization of income and employment criterion gives a higher average rate of growth than the other criterion for the period *OX*; but thereafter the average rate of growth would be smaller than under the maximization of the rate-of-return criterion. The choice of techniques would depend upon which of these two time-patterns of growth or what combination of these two patterns is desired by an underdeveloped economy.

Concluding Remarks

In the economic literature on the subject[1] it is not sufficiently emphasized that the underemployment of labour affects directly only the choice of techniques and has no direct relevance for the choice of investment pattern. In fact, it is not realized that the problem of the choice of techniques and the problem of the choice of investment pattern, though interrelated, are analytically distinct. This failure to distinguish analytically between these two problems has led to lack of clarity in the analysis of these problems. Further, these basically dynamic problems are analysed in static terms, and this has given rise to still more confusion.

In dynamic terms each set of production techniques with a certain investment pattern would give rise to a certain time-pattern of growth. The final choice regarding these two, therefore, would depend upon the desired time-pattern of growth.[1]

NOTE

1. See, for example, P. N. Rosenstein-Rodan, "Problem of Industrialisation of Eastern and South-Eastern Europe", *Economic Journal* (June–Sept. 1943); A. J. Brown, *Industrialisation and Trade* (1943); K. E. Kahn, "Investment Criteria in Development Programs", *Quarterly Journal of Economics* (Feb. 1951); W. Galenson and H. Leibenstein, "Investment Criteria, Productivity and Economic Development", *Quarterly Journal of Economics* (Aug. 1955); B. Chenery Hollis, "The Application of Investment Criteria", *Quarterly Journal of Economics* (Feb. 1953).

PART II. Development Problem, Strategy and Technology Choice

5. On Development Problem and Strategy*

It is only since the nineteenth century and, more particularly, since the Second World War that development has become an objective of state policy. This has been the result of the growing recognition and awareness of interdependence and interaction among various socio-political groups (countries in which human society is divided) and among different socio-economic groups within a country—groups which have become self-conscious only because of this interaction and interdependence brought about by the impact of the revolutionary growth in scientific and technological knowledge.

This development problem has given rise to various conflicting ideologies of development—theories that seek to solve this problem. As often happens in human affairs, these theories have become more important than the problem itself and in this confusion between ends and means, the problem of ideologies is erroneously identified as the problem of development. Ideologies and systems assume greater significance than the *human* problem; the problem is dehumanized into an abstract problem without relationship with the man in society.[1]

The problem of development is *a concrete human problem* and has to be posed and understood as such if we are to succeed in responding to the myriad complex challenges that the problem in its dynamic perspective represents. It is not possible to indicate the solution of this problem or a strategy of development without understanding it; and no solution can be valid in all contexts and at all times as any attempt to solve it changes the nature and structure of the problem. Since the future is unknown and unknowable, the problem can be understood only in the context of the concrete present; no ideologies or theories or utopias which promise a solution for the future generations hence can be valid. We are concerned only with the present generation and possibly the next and the solution has to be valid only in this context.[2]

And even in this context, no solution can be perfect. For, we cannot know the problem completely; its character changes with each attempted solution. So in a sense we move from problem to problem. Hence, what becomes of crucial significance is only our *approach* to the problem—our method of approaching, understanding and solving the problem *here and now* as it faces us. Our response to the problems as they arise would be adequate only if we are free to learn. Hence the categorical imperative of establishing such social institutions and traditions that not only protect but also foster this freedom for *each* individual.

Such is the broad theme of this chapter. In section I we deal with the nature of the development problem and in the light of this discussion, an attempt is made to indicate in broad terms the overall strategy of development. The problem of social change or evolution is discussed in the final section.

* First published in *Society and Change*, editors: K. S. Krishnaswamy *et al.* (Banking: Oxford University Press, 1977).

I. Nature of the Development Problem

We have been discussing the problem of development policy for at least twenty-five years and one wonders whether we have even posed the problem correctly in *human* terms. What, then, is the problem?

In concrete terms, the problem is that of providing physical security to each individual family—a certain *minimum* of food, clothing, shelter, education and health facilities—in an environment free from crime and violence. What this minimum should be has to be determined in the specific context of each country and even within the country, each specific region. The content and quality of this minimum should improve progressively with time. The initial task of development policy, thus, should be to determine this minimum and ensure its provision to each individual family. If the problem is viewed in human terms, this has to be the *focus* and *the starting-point* of a good development policy.[3] As the Chinese proverb has it: "A long journey starts with a single step." If the intention and direction are right, the rest follow.

The second basic element of the problem is employment. Each able-bodied adult member of a society should have a right as well as a duty to work. Quite often in literature, a question of trade-off between full employment and growth is raised and it is argued that growth should have primacy over the objective of full employment, provided the unemployed can be ensured a minimum living standard.

This argument is a good instance of an ideology of development that has no human content and of an assumption about human nature that is not valid. An individual loses self-respect if he can have his living without work and again loses an opportunity for self-expression and development without work. It is a matter of common observation that to work is as much a biological-psychological necessity as to eat.[4] Apart from an individual's need to work, habit of work or a tradition that nobody has a right to eat without contributing through work to the process of development is a social necessity. "In the sweat of thy brow thou shalt eat thine bread" expresses both an individual as well as a social need to work.

The third basic element is freedom. Minimum level of living and employment have no significance unless an individual has the freedom to arrange his life himself in so far as this is compatible with the *equal* rights of others. This implies freedom of intellectual and spiritual inquiry and freedom to be happy or unhappy as he chooses to be. This freedom, again, is a social necessity. Since nobody knows the problem of existence and each one is fallible, it is only through inter-personal discussion and criticism of tradition, and actual empirical and, if possible, experimental tests of bold and imaginative formulation of problems and their solutions that human knowledge can grow and human understanding of ignorance improve. Search for truth and knowledge is a social process and no individual and no tradition, ancient *or* modern, can be accepted as authoritative: for there is no authority save truth (which is unknowable) and no method of reaching nearer truth save the method of negating that which is false through critical reasoning and testing.[5]

The human problem of development, thus, is the problem of ensuring to each individual physical security, employment and freedom. This problem cannot be tackled without collective action; for without collective action, the strong would destroy all the three for the weak and in the process corrupt themselves as well as inter-personal relationships.

There has, thus, to be a government with coercive powers as a final sanction that can ensure the required collective action. Though a government can and should provide a regulative framework for the social process of development, it can itself become tyrannical and destroy security and freedom. And this is the problem of power. Power corrupts. Hence the need for an impersonal rule of law that ensures the minimum misrule. That is the argument for democracy: an institutional provision for changing the rulers peacefully, and individual and social vigilance to prevent even with direct—and, if need be, violent—action the destruction of the rule of law by the powerful or even Plato's guardians or the majority.[6] The problem of power is not the question of who should rule; it is the question of *minimizing* misrule.

Just as the problem of power is quite often formulated incorrectly in terms of who should rule, the problem of development is posed equally falsely in terms of what economists call welfare maximization. Implicit in this naive formulation of the problem is the utilitarian pleasure–pain calculus and social philosophy. This raises several metaphysical and philosophical problems.

What is welfare? Does it imply the individual sensation of pleasure? If so, can the individual demand for pleasure be ever satisfied? As Gandhi said: "Mind is a restless bird; the more it has, the more it wants." In that case, can the marginal utility of income over time ever diminish?[7] Apart from this, how do we know—can anybody know—whether an individual is actually deriving pleasure from whatever choices he has made? What then does welfare mean? Does it merely imply individual freedom of choice? Why, then, not say so?

The idea of social welfare is even more metaphysical. A social welfare function represents either the preferences and prejudices of the rulers or of the individual intellectual who formulates it. How do they know that these would not change with time—can anybody know how they will change? Can and should they be imposed on society? If the expressed individual preferences are the criterion, can they be aggregated without the possibility of paradox? Even if they can, how does one know whether they will not change over time? Anyway, this approach is bound to lead to tyranny or stagnation: for, social evolutionary processes involve learning from mistakes.

The basic objection to this type of approach, however, is different and it is related to the theory of knowledge and its growth. We do not know that which is true in any field of life for there is no criterion of truth; had there been one, we would know what truth is. The world in which we live is complex—infinitely complex—and the future is unknown. Even if the future were knowable in some objective sense, we cannot know it for the simple reason that we can know the world only in the way it relates to us. We cannot know the world as it *objectively* is. Since the future is unknown and unknowable, truth is ever unknown and unknowable. Truth is beyond human authority.

But we can know that which is false through critical inquiry and reasoning and, if possible, through empirical tests. We can refute our expectations, our theories through which we try to discover the regularities in nature and in human societies. Thus all our knowledge is inevitably tentative and it grows only through discovery of errors—through falsification of our theories, frames of references, expectations. Search for truth, thus, is the search for error.[8]

So our theory of development policy too has inevitably to be based on a *negative* approach to individual and social good. We cannot know the good but we do know the concrete evils; they are matters of everyday human experience—if not ours, of people with whom we come in contact. So there is a possibility of agreement with regard to social evils though there cannot be an agreement with regard to that which is good. We can approach the good through the elimination of the concrete social evils just as we can approach truth through the elimination of errors. So the principle of social policy has to be: *minimize pain and avoidable suffering, and share equally the suffering and pain that are unavoidable.* This principle is the basis of formulating the development problem in terms of the problems of physical security, employment and freedom.

Approaching truth through the negation of the false is a theory of knowledge as old as the Upanishads (Yagnavalkya: नेति, नेति—not this, not this), Buddha,[9] Xenophanes and Socrates; contemporary rediscovery of this theory by Popper[10] and Krishnamurti[11] confirms the validity of an old tradition of critical rationalism.[12] Gandhi[13] and Mao[14] have applied it as the basis for generating socio-political change.

II. Problem of Development Strategy

This negative approach to the development problem draws attention to real issues and indicates in concrete terms the action to be taken. It is possible to recognize physical pain and suffering where they exist.

> Human suffering makes a direct moral appeal, namely, the appeal for help, while there is no similar call to increase the happiness of a man who is doing well anyway . . . from the moral point of view, pain cannot be outweighed by pleasure, and especially not one man's pain by another man's pleasure. . . . Such an approach . . . leads to a perpetual stream of demands for immediate action to remedy *identifiable* wrongs. And such action is of a kind most likely to secure widespread agreement, and result in manifest improvement.[15]

Given a concrete problem, its solution lies in understanding it. The starting-point hence has inevitably to be the question: how is it that the traditional sectors, where a large number of people are employed and from which they derive their livelihood, have failed to generate the type of change required for responding to the development problem? This means an inquiry into the structural-organizational characteristics of the traditional occupations, its technological base, the constraints under which it suffers, the economic potential that it fails to actualize and its relationship with the modern sectors within the country and outside the country. *Wherever one wants to go, there is no alternative but to start from where one is.* The approach to the problem, thus, has to be from the traditional sectors: traditional occupations and skills, and knowledge. How can this traditional sector be transformed, revolutionized so as to secure full employment and a progressively growing minimum living standard?—*this is the relevant question.* Once the question is posed thus (and there is no other way of posing it), the direction and content of an action programme would become obvious.

The action programme would relate to the identification of (*a*) households, (*b*) natural resources, (*c*) structural-institutional context, (*d*) traditional skills and (*e*) traditional technological base. Given the households, traditional skills and technological base, and natural resources, the question to be examined would be: What are the structural-institutional changes that are required to improve progressively the technological basis of the traditional sector so as to maintain full employment and at the same time a rising minimum living standard? The next question would be: How and in what manner should the "modern" sector grow for the purpose of transforming the traditional sector? The action programme, thus, would be *focused* on the traditional sector and the modern sector growth would be planned with a view to supplementing and complementing the traditional sector development; there would be an organic fusion of the two sectors, each reinforcing the other.[16] Such has been the logic of Gandhi's idea about rural industrialization based on power and the Chinese strategy of "walking on two legs".[17]

This strategy cannot be based merely on existing knowledge and technology—whether traditional or modern. It involves *an active search* for improving traditional technology on the one hand and for creative adaptation of modern technology on the other. Thus, there has to be *an active learning process* which can ensure the growth of the necessary scientific and technological competence to identify and solve the technological problems as they arise. Simultaneously, the learning process should relate to the identification and solution of the structural-institutional problems.

This, thus, becomes a dynamic strategy of attempting to refute the current solutions to problems and finding out new, more viable and effective solutions. To be effective, this strategy has to institutionalize the process of "conjectures and refutations", the critical rational search for problems and their tentative solutions. This process, because of its inherent nature, cannot be captured once and for all in a blueprint or a model of development for the whole country; for, we are dealing with a process of learning from mistakes and this cannot be known *a priori*. The planning process has thus to be decentralized—each region with its own planning mechanism with the centre's function being that of coordinating and reinforcing the regional processes. "In this structure", as Gandhi said, ". . . life will not be a pyramid with the apex sustained by the bottom. But it will be an oceanic circle whose centre would be the individual. . . . The outermost circumference will not wield power to crush the inner circle but will give strength to all within and derive its own strength from it."[18]

The development strategies pursued so far (excepting possibly in China) have failed to generate a viable development process because of two reasons. Firstly, they represent possible solutions to either pseudo-problems or non-problems; they are not based on the perception of the *human* problem of development. Secondly, they have been *imitative* with regard to both norms and standards as well as institutional-technological means; as a result, they are resulting not in the creative transformation of the traditional sector but in the destruction of the traditional by the organically unrelated modern sector, which is largely an appendage—the outer fringe of the modern sectors in the developed countries. The poor countries, thus, are engaged not in generating a process of creative destruction; they are actually generating *a process of destructive creation*—creation of a Frankenstein's monster.

This attempted solution of pseudo or non-problems is reflected inevitably in the direction of research in the socio-economic as well as technological fields. Most of this research—the activity of the intellectual élite—is irrelevant and expensive; it is not focused on the development problem. It is based on the problems facing the developed countries or problems created by the respective scientific traditions—again based on the problems of the developed countries.

Let us take, as an illustration, the vast amount of resources devoted to empirical research. What are the problems of this research? For instance, one research project has shown that the poor countries are not as poor as one would make out on the basis of international comparisons of national income converted on a comparable basis through the use of official exchange rates. Or, take the resources devoted to various types of rural and urban surveys: what are the results? They show that the poor spend most of their income on food, their saving is negligible and their employment is uncertain. Or they show that saving depends on income and asset holdings and probably on educational levels. Or there is the revealing truth that those who are economically better-off get the maximum out of government policies to ameliorate the conditions of the poor.

With all these resources devoted to research, we still do not know the socio-economic basis of traditional crafts, industries and skills, traditional financial and distribution mechanisms, traditional educational, medical and health systems, traditional food habits and the nutritive content of this food, traditional modes of behaviour and cultural patterns and even the traditional means of communication.

Or consider theoretical research. What are the problems which it attempts to solve? Problems of allocation of *given* resources among competing uses. What are the solutions offered? Individuals behave rationally but the allocation is inefficient and sub-optimal in terms of a social welfare function. Now, what is this social welfare function? And what are social costs and benefits? These are either the analysts' own creation or the *declared* objectives of a power group. What meaning has this social welfare function on the basis of which we have a large number of multi-sector planning models? Or the solution offered is that we should have "right prices" so that allocation of resources is "rational". What do we mean by "right prices"? Or the theory that problems do not exist and cannot be tackled (like the problem of poverty) before we can provide a *quantitative* index of their dimension!

In fact, most of these solutions are not related to actual problems. They are related to a theoretical model which recognizes neither history nor an actual world of unequal individuals, collectives and countries. The truth of the matter is that it does not recognize that a human being is a social creature to the inmost centre of his being; that he is society and its past, that he is conditioned by the social context in which he lives and has his being, that all processes of change are social processes and that the present is not only shaped by the past but also by social theories—expectations of the future—which by definition is unknown and unknowable. Hence, there is no place in this theory either for cultural patterns and traditions, which bind society together, or for the processes of learning which are the crux of all human evolutions.[19]

This sort of theoretical research arises not out of actual problems but out of a pedantic scholastic tradition of a professional élite, which constitutes a social (parasitic?) class, which is divorced from reality and yet which is supported by society as it did earlier and still does a priestly class—a repository and transmission agent for the sacred lore.[20] The only difference between the two is that while the priestly class represents an authentic element of tradition, the new professional élite *in the developing countries* is an alien element from another tradition, to which it wants to belong and yet cannot do so. It is unfortunate but true that in the present international historical context, the power élite and the intellectual élite reinforce each other, while both are divorced from the poor of the land, whose policies of development they tend to shape in terms of the norms and standards derived from their intellectual and material tutelage to the rich countries. It is this fact which produces poverty and inequality on the one hand and totalitarian socio-political systems on the other.

III. Problem of Social Change

The problem of development essentially is the problem of social change and more particularly the problem of establishing a tradition of critical examination of the framework of social traditions. It is this framework which is out of tune with changing reality and thus needs to be transformed from within to respond effectively to the challenge of development.

The problem, then, is: How to change tradition? One answer has been to destroy tradition by cleaning the canvas thoroughly as Plato suggested. But that would amount to destroying society including the revolutionaries and their Utopias. For, we are the product of tradition, the accumulated past, and rejecting this past is logically impossible. Man is himself and society is what it is only because of his relationship with other men and with the world of material things and the world of cultural tradition—both of which are objectively given to him. One knows oneself to exist only because of this relationship. Without tradition, no social life is possible; for there can be no human relationship without order, without a sort of framework of expectations or theories about human behaviour and relationships—which constitute society.[21]

But these traditions are man-made though they are independent of any one individual. They get formed as a result of human interaction and relationships out of the necessity for order and regularities in social intercourse. But since they are man-made, they can be changed. And the only way they can be changed is through a critical attitude towards the whole framework of traditions. But one can criticize one tradition only in terms of another; there can be no criticism without something to criticize and something to criticize with. It is through self-criticism and social criticism that one can find that which is false in the realm of tradition and standards as in the realm of science. Science is not truth, nor does the tradition of justice represent perfect justice; truth and justice and goodness are regulative ideas and human beings cannot know them, though they can get nearer to them only by a negative critical approach—by discarding that which is false, unjust and evil.

But to know what is wrong with tradition, it is essential to understand it. One cannot understand it if one is evaluating it—either by condemning it or praising it. One can understand it and have a perception of its strong and weak points only by loving it. And it is only then that tradition can be transformed and revolutionized.[22] Such was the approach of Gandhi and of Mao. Gandhi was as much a revolutionary as Mao. Common elements in both have been: understanding and pride in traditional values, traditional language and idiom, fearless critical attitude towards tradition and a striving for a social environment of individual freedom of inquiry and search.[23]

The pride in tradition and at the same time a critical attitude towards tradition is not possible without minimizing the role of privilege and power and violence; for they destroy the environment of freedom, without which no tradition of critical inquiry can flourish. The poor societies have been élitist societies—it is the élites who have power born of education and privileged positions in the social hierarchies. In a world in which rich societies coexist with the poor and still are interrelated in a variety of ways, the élites of poor societies are inevitably conditioned by the norms and standards of the rich countries not only in the field of consumption behaviour and technology, but also in the fields of intellectual inquiry. It is this imitative élite that is interpreting the problem of development as the problem of entrenching its privileged position—of developing the modern sector by attempting to destroy the traditional.

This élitist attitude and orientation cannot be transformed without establishing impersonal institutions and traditions of dignity of physical labour and self-reliance, equality of status of intellectual and manual workers and organic interaction between the cadres and the masses, the managers and the workers, the rulers and the ruled. It was for such reasons that Gandhi urged the educated and the intellectuals to learn from the peasants, do bread labour and work for ways to improve village life through what he called his constructive programme. Mao's attack on the mandarin attitude, his periodical cultural revolutions, his exhortation to the intellectuals to learn from and work with the peasants are of the same nature and are motivated by the desire to minimize status differences and direct attention towards the essential tasks and problems of development.[24]

Both refused to be swept off their feet[25] by the intellectual and cultural currents and tidal waves originating from the rich countries; hence Gandhi's law of Swadeshi and Mao's insistence on things Chinese,[26] his discovery of "the ancient dialectics"—the unity of the opposites. Yet both insist on creative learning from the rich countries in matters of culture as well as technology; both believe in the freedom to learn without accepting any authority—whether of tradition or of modernity. *The problem of development is the problem of learning; the process of development, of living is the process of learning from mistakes.* There can be no end to the process; all men are equal as each one is fallible and yet each one has the capacity to learn. Human fallibility and human reason are the bonds that unite mankind and make each one the equal of another. This unity and this equality can be real only when each one tries to generate "Light without Heat".[27]

NOTES

1. See J. Krishnamurti, *The First and Last Freedom* (London: Victor Gollancz Ltd., 1964), pp. 23–4.
2. See K. R. Popper, *Conjectures and Refutations* (New York: Harper & Row, 1963), p. 362.
3. See N. K. Bose, *Selections from Gandhi* (Ahmedabad: Navjivan Publishing House, 1957), pp. 46–8. Gandhi writes: "True to his poetical instinct, the poet lives for the morrow and would have us do likewise. . . . But I have had the pain of watching birds who for want of strength could not be coaxed even into a flutter of their wings. The human bird under the Indian sky gets up weaker than when he pretended to retire. For millions it is an eternal vigil or an eternal trance. . . . The hungry millions ask for one poem—invigorating food. They cannot be given it. They must earn it and they can earn only by the sweat of their brow."

   See also V. V. Bhatt, "The New Ideology of Development", *Imprint* (Bombay, July 1970). To quote: "The practical point then is: if the several benefits I mentioned are not measurable precisely by the usual yardsticks, how to make an optimum choice from among the various objectives of planned development? In this context I think it is appropriate to quote the criterion which Gandhiji indicated. He said: 'Whenever you are in doubt, or when the self becomes too much with you, apply the following test. Recall the face of the poorest and the weakest man whom you may have seen, and ask yourself if the step you contemplate is going to be of any use to him. Will he gain anything by it? Will it restore him . . . control over his own life and destiny? In other words, will it lead to Swaraj for the hungry and spiritually starving millions? Then you will find your doubts and . . . self melting away.' "
4. *Ibid.*, p. 47. Again to quote Gandhi: "Imagine, therefore, what a calamity it must be to have 300 millions unemployed, several millions becoming degraded every day for want of employment, devoid of self-respect, devoid of faith in God. . . . I can take before them a message of God only by taking the message of sacred work before them. . . . My ahimsa would not tolerate the idea of giving a free meal to a healthy person who has not worked for it in some honest way, and if I had the power I would stop every *sadavrat* where free meals are given. It has degraded the nation and it has encouraged laziness, idleness, hypocrisy and even crime. . . . Do not say you will maintain the poor on a charity."
5. See K. R. Popper, *op. cit.*, pp. 27–9.
6. *Ibid.*, pp. 350–2.
7. See J. M. Keynes, *Economic Possibilities for Our Grandchildren*. He writes: "Now it is true that the needs of human beings may seem to be insatiable. But they fall into two classes—those needs which are absolute in the sense that we feel them whatever the situation of our fellow human beings may be, and those which are relative in the sense that we feel them only if their satisfaction lifts us above, makes us feel superior to our fellows. Needs of the second class, those which satisfy the desire for superiority, may indeed be insatiable, for the higher the general level, the higher still are they. But this is not true of the absolute needs . . . ", quoted in J. Robinson, *Freedom and Necessity* (New York: Vintage Books, 1971), p. 117.
8. See K. R. Popper, *op. cit.*, pp. 27–9.
9. See E. Fromm, D. T. Suzuki and R. De Martino, *Zen Buddhism and Psychoanalysis* (New York: Harper & Row, 1960), pp. 166–7.
10. See K. R. Popper, *op. cit.*, pp. 13–14 and 152–3. To quote Xenophanes:

    The Gods did not reveal, from the beginning
    All things to us; but in the course of time,
    Through seeking, men find that which is the better . . .
    But as for certain truth, no man has known it,
    Nor will he know it . . .
    And even if by chance he were to utter
    The final truth, he would himself not know it:
    For all is but a woven web of guesses

11. J. Krishnamurti, *The Awakening of Intelligence* (New York: Harper & Row, 1973). To quote: "You know, to find out what is, one must deny, put aside totally what is not. Through negation come to the positive; do not seek the positive, but come to it by understanding what it is not. That is, if I want to find out what truth is, not knowing what it is, I must be able to see what is false. If I

do not have the capacity to perceive what is false, I cannot see what truth is. So I must find out what is false" (p. 358).

12. B. Magee, *Karl Popper* (New York: The Viking Press, 1973).
13. Gandhi writes: "Evolution is always experimental. All progress is gained through mistakes and their rectification. No good comes fully fashioned, out of God's hand, but has to be carved out through repeated experiments and repeated failures by ourselves. This is the law of individual growth. The same law controls social and political evolution also. The right to err, which means the freedom to try experiments, is the universal condition of all progress." N. K. Bose, *op. cit.*, p. 36.
14. See his doctrine of unity of opposites—"The dialectics of ancient times"—"Mistakes will inevitably be committed. It is impossible not to commit them. The commission of mistakes is a necessary condition for the formation of a correct line. The correct line is formulated with reference to the erroneous line, the two constitute a unity of opposites. The correct line is formed in the struggle with the incorrect line" (p. 113). "No man can be without error" (p. 193). Quoted in *Chairman Mao Talks to the People,* edited by S. Schram (New York: Pantheon Books, 1974). See also the Editor's introduction.
15. B. Magee, *Karl Popper, op. cit.*, p. 82.
16. See V. V. Bhatt, "On Technology Policy and Its Institutional Frame", *World Development,* vol. 3, no. 9 (Sept. 1975).
17. See G. Woodcock, *Mohandas Gandhi* (New York: The Viking Press, 1971), chapter 7 and *Chairman Mao Talks to the People, op. cit.*
18. *Ibid.*, p. 94.
19. The seminal idea of Walrasian theory is that the actual outcome of economic activities is determined by interaction among individuals and is independent of individual wills and desires. In an unchanging static context, this outcome may be determinate and stable. However, in a dynamic context, neither individual preferences nor techniques can be taken as given. Further, inequality relating to capacity to adapt to change has to be recognized as much as the uncertainty with regard to the future. So one would be left with a social process of change—or a process of learning from mistakes. The outcome of necessity has to be indeterminate and the "stability" of the process of change would depend on the way in which social traditions change and power relations among individuals, groups and countries alter.

    It was a great insight of Marx—and Schumpeter—to have drawn attention to this process of evolution. However, Marx had no theory of enterprise, and scientific and technical change, nor had he a theory of the process of class formation. Further, he suffered from a wrong view about science as did Kant; he failed to realize that science is not truth but a process of discovering errors.

    For all these, see (i) K. R. Popper, *op. cit.*, (ii) K. R. Popper, *The Open Society and Its Enemies,* vol. ii (Princeton: Princeton University Press, 1966), (iii) J. A. Schumpeter, *Imperialism and Social Classes* (New York: Augustus M. Kelley, Inc., 1951), (iv) V. V. Bhatt, "The Sterility of Equilibrium Economics", *Economic Theory and Planning,* edited by A. Mitra (Bombay: Oxford University Press, 1974), and (v) K. J. Arrow, *The Limits of Organization* (New York: W. W. Norton & Co., 1974).
20. What Popper says about philosophy is probably true also about social sciences. He says about philosophy: "Genuine philosophical problems are always rooted in urgent problems outside philosophy, and they die if these roots decay. In their efforts to solve them, philosophers are liable to pursue what looks like a philosophical method or technique or an unfailing key to philosophical success. But no such methods or techniques exist: in philosophy methods are unimportant; *any* method is legitimate if it leads to results capable of being rationally discussed. What matters is not methods or techniques but a sensitivity to problems, and a consuming passion for them. . . . But there are others who do not feel this urge, who have no serious and pressing problem but who nevertheless produce exercises in fashionable methods, and for whom philosophy is application . . . rather than search. They are luring philosophy into the bog of pseudo-problems and verbal puzzles; either by offering us pseudo-problems for real ones . . . or by persuading us to concentrate upon the endless and pointless task of unmasking what they rightly or wrongly take for pseudo-problems on 'puzzles' . . . " (p. 72). K. R. Popper, *Conjectures and Refutations, op. cit.*

21. *Ibid.*, chapter 4; see also, K. J. Arrow, *op. cit.*, pp. 26–9, and J. Hicks, *The Crisis in Keynesian Economics* (Oxford, 1974), chapter iii.
22. "There is no logical path", says Einstein, "leading to these . . . laws. They can only be reached by intuition, based upon something like an intellectual love . . . of the objects of experience." Quoted in B. Magee, *op. cit.*, p. 25.
23. See G. Woodcock, *op. cit.*, and *Chairman Mao Talks to the People, op. cit.*
24. "My purpose is to get people to dare to speak out with vigour and invincible force . . . freeing themselves from inhibitions" (p. 123).

    "From ancient times the people who have created new schools of thought have always been young people without great learning. Confucius started at the age of twenty-three; and how much learning did Jesus have? . . ." (p. 20).

    "How can you know more than the peasants?" (p. 21).

    "Those of you who . . . do not allow people to speak, who think you are tigers, and that nobody will dare to touch your arse . . . will fail. People will talk anyway. You think that nobody will really dare to touch the arse of tigers like you? They damn well will" (p. 14).

    All references to *Chairman Mao Talks to the People, op. cit.* See also J. Robinson, *op. cit.*, chapter 11.
25. "We must refuse to be lifted off our feet", said Gandhi. See N. K. Bose, *op. cit.*, p. 119.
26. See J. Robinson, *op. cit.* She writes about the Chinese experience: "Chinese experience has shown what development requires. To get the whole population engaged with goodwill in the economic effort and to organize employment so that all can contribute; to increase productivity in agriculture so that a surplus can be extracted without the need to use brutal methods; to check inequality so as not to waste resources on unnecessary consumption and undermine morale by generating envy; to raise the general level of health and to institute birth control; to build up the basis of heavy industry so as to be able to modernize production as fast as possible, and meanwhile to encourage handicrafts to mechanize themselves by means of intermediate techniques; to spread education and develop self-reliance (at every level from the paddy field to the atomic laboratory) in applying the scientific method of experiment in every activity:" (pp. 111–12).

    "In this, past history was an indispensable support. For three thousand years, the slow turnover of the population, in which class was never based on 'race', has soaked them all in Chinese civilization, and Chinese civilization has always been based upon the conception of correct conduct. ('We may be poor, but we do know right from wrong.') It is much easier to alter the content of correct conduct for people trained in such a view of life than to introduce the concept itself among people imbued with cynicism and grasping competitiveness . . . . The Chinese have set out on the more ambitious course of establishing economic development with a human sense of values" (pp. 103–4).
27. This was the title of Sachin's first *Economic Weekly* editorial.

6. Development Problem, Strategy and Technology Choice: Sarvodaya and Socialist Approaches in India*

MUCH before independence, there were two development ideologies in India—the Sarvodaya one (the word was derived from Ruskin's Unto This Last)[1] represented by Gandhi and the Socialist one with Nehru as its spokesman. The major objective of both was to remove poverty and unemployment through socio-economic development in an environment of freedom and democracy. However, there were major differences between their development strategies and the implicit technology policies.

For Gandhi, the immediate problem was poverty and it had to be tackled *directly* through the *provision of full employment* in traditional sectors—agriculture and cottage industries. The modern sector development was to supplement and reinforce the development of the traditional sector. The emphasis, thus, was on upgrading traditional technology and on *adapting* modern technology in a manner that was consistent with the local situation and the development objectives. The major instruments for the purpose were education and scientific–technological research that was organically related to the identification and solution of concrete socio-economic problems.

Nehru's strategy was large-scale industrialization with emphasis on capital and heavy industry. Cottage industry was to be tolerated with a view to providing employment in the short-run; but the main objective was to develop large-scale modern industries and techniques that would *supplant* the traditional sector. The dominant sector was to be the modern sector, based on modern science and technology. The major instrument visualized was scientific and technological research that gave *mastery* over modern technology. There was no emphasis on *upgrading* of traditional technology nor was there any appreciation of the *problem of adapting* modern technology to the Indian environment. Socio-economic development was to be a planned endeavour with a major role assigned to the State; the objective was to evolve a socialistic pattern of society.

After independence, the dominant ideology has been the socialist one, evolved by Nehru himself, who was the Chairman of the Planning Commission till his death in 1964. However, the Sarvodaya ideology was kept alive out of respect for Gandhi by institutions that were created by the State for the promotion of cottage industry and by the Gandhi followers. The wheel has come full circle in the sense that the present government—the Janata Government—has adopted Gandhi's strategy with emphasis on agriculture and cottage and small industry,[2] for, the problem of poverty and unemployment still remains the major problem after more than twenty-five years of planned development.[3]

* Paper presented at the U.S. Pugwash Committee sponsored *Symposium on Social Values and Technology Choice in an International Context* (Wisconsin: Wingspread, June 1978).

This chapter seeks to trace this evolution and discuss the elements of technology policy that are relevant for India and generally for the less developed countries. In section I, Gandhi's approach is discussed, while Nehru's socialist ideology is presented in section II. Socialist ideology as embodied in the Five Year Plans is the subject of section III. Section V draws attention to the fact that India still has not evolved a viable technology policy as an integral part of development strategy and discusses the nature of relevant technology policy for socio-economic development. Some case studies to illustrate the implications for technology choice of the two approaches are presented in the next chapter.

I. The Sarvodaya Perspective

Gandhi was painfully aware of the degrading dehumanizing poverty of the Indian masses and his principal objective was to create socio-economic conditions that would be consistent with the moral and mental development of each individual and family. He was in search of an "immediate, practicable and permanent" solution to the problem of poverty. This poverty and "enforced idleness" were related and hence *full* employment—work that gave a "living wage"—was to be the basis of his approach. It was not possible to provide a "decent minimum" of living conditions without work and employment and even if it were possible, it would be degrading and demoralizing both for the individual and the society to have parasites—individuals eating without work.[4] "By the sweat of thy brow thou shalt eat thy bread"—this biblical injunction was seen by Gandhi in the Gita which says he who eats without work is a thief. Hence his concept of Bread-Labour.[5] For the full moral and mental development of the individual—for individual was, for Gandhi, "the supreme consideration"—it was essential to find work that gave him opportunity for self-expression and development of creative intelligence; and social relationships would be corrupted to the core if the individual obligation to work were not recognized as a social duty.[6]

Large-scale industries—whether owned by the State or individuals—cannot be developed without wage labour and, for Gandhi, this meant exploitation and lack of freedom. Unless the means of production for basic necessities were owned by families or a cooperative of families, no individual can be really free to mould his life. Hence, agriculture and cottage industry were to be owned and operated by families (without hired labour) or by cooperatives. The village had to be industrialized and resuscitated. This was to be the basis of a just non-violent social order, based on willing cooperation and elimination of social conflict. Conflicts were to be resolved by peaceful and non-violent means—which included civil disobedience and non-cooperation.[7]

Gandhi recognized the need for some large industries. But then, they were to be organically related to the needs and requirements of agriculture and cottage-small industry.[8] This large industry was to be owned and operated by the State; where individuals owned, as a matter of history, such industries, they were to act as trustees. The doctrine of trusteeship was to be enforced by law and if need be by non-violent, non-cooperation on the part of the workers.[9]

The major role of the State was to facilitate the evolution of such a non-violent social order by performing such social tasks as were essential for coordinating and reinforcing the development of "village republics", producing the basic necessities of life—a type of cooperative structure where each family would purchase the necessities that it does not produce from other families, a relationship based on Gandhi's law of Swadshi.[10] Gandhi was vehemently against the "soulless machine" as well as the "soulless state"; both enslave the individual and are not consistent with his Swaraj—self-government that is the basis of a just non-violent social order.[11] The touchstone or criteria for state action, Gandhi provided, in his advice to the Ministers of a state government:

> Whenever you are in doubt, or when the self becomes too much with you, apply the following test. Recall the face of the poorest and the weakest man whom you may have seen, and ask yourself if the step you contemplate is going to be of any use to *him*. Will he gain anything by it? Will it restore him . . . control over his own life and destiny? In other words, will it lead to Swaraj for the hungry and spiritually starving millions? Then you will find your doubts and . . . self melting away.[12]

The major instrument for the purpose of evolving such a social order was, for Gandhi, basic education and adult education. The main purpose of such education was to awaken the individual to "the sense of his dignity and power", make him understand his immediate environment and, develop and sharpen his sense of perception and intelligence to *identify* the collective problems and seek their solution through "scientific inquiry" and intelligent effort.[13] An individual is the product of society and its past; he should, therefore, understand tradition—which is not possible without a certain reverence for the past—his tradition. But he need not be, should not be, a prisoner of the past; he has to develop a critical scientific temper to identify the problems which tradition has created and revolutionize this tradition by adapting it creatively to the changing environment. Education has to develop such creative intelligence to meet life and its problems. "I am all for thorough-going, radical social reordering; but it must be an organic growth, not a violent superimposition", Gandhi said.[14]

His scheme of basic education emphasized learning through a craft. This was the only way to understand environment; further, creative intelligence develops through work by hand and through tackling problems of immediate relevance. Such a system would create a sense of dignity of labour and at the same time would be self-supporting—the financial means to be provided through the sale of the fruits of labour. In the Indian context, such schools to be viable had to be self-supporting.[15]

Such a school system would enable, Gandhi thought, the students to understand their environment—problems of social order and techniques in agriculture, cottage industry, health, sanitation and hygiene, housing and village roads. The crux of technical change for Gandhi was in understanding the relevant problem. Once the problem was identified, the students would experiment to find out its solution—solution that was feasible. Once the problem was understood and if its solution required outside assistance from research laboratories or scientific institutions (anywhere in the world), they would know whom to approach for assistance and how to ask and judge the relevance of the suggested solution. At all stages, the control of their environment would be—should be—in their hands. Such a system of education and research would be, according to Gandhi, "the spearhead of a silent social revolution fraught with the most far-reaching consequences".[16]

For Gandhi, the problem—immediate and demanding action—was to be understood and solved by immediate action. He was not in favour of imprisoning the future in the shackles of a long-term fixed plan; for him, attention was to be focused on the immediate and the urgent. Once that was done with intelligence, the rest would follow. Hence his refrain: "One Step Enough For Me"[17] and "Sufficient unto the day is the evil thereof". Hence his emphasis on creative intelligence: "Swaraj is for the awakened, not for the sleepy and the ignorant." His non-violent movement "is a revolution of thought, of spirit", of awakening each individual to the truth that he or she is "the guardian of his or her self-respect and liberty".

Even during his lifetime, he strived ceaselessly to experiment with changes in technology suited to the Indian conditions. He improved the spinning-wheel, and suggested to those qualified to make further changes in it and make it operate with power. He set up all-India institutes to revive and foster cottage industry. He experimented with the use of human waste as organic manure for agriculture. He made original suggestions for the improvement of sanitation and hygiene and construction of village roads. In health, he suggested and experimented with nature cure. His theory of education was translated in the concept of basic education. In all his endeavours for technological change, his criterion was simple: to devise such techniques and tools which the villagers can make and afford and operate.[18]

For large industry, education and research were to be related to immediate problems and the means were to be provided by the Industry itself.[19] Once the whole effort—in education and scientific-technical research—was directed towards identifying and solving practical problems of immediate relevance, the nation would be able to afford "more and better libraries, more and better laboratories, more and better research institutes. . . . There will be truly original work instead of mere imitation. And the cost would be evenly and justly distributed."[20] The problem in India was immediate and unique: "The solution therefore must be original."[21]

II. The Socialist Perspective

As with Gandhi, Nehru's vision of development policy was formed much before Independence.[22] He was influenced by the Marxian approach to history, Fabian socialism and the Russian experiment in planned development. His conception of socialism, however, had the basic elements of Gandhi's moral approach. Gandhi influenced him in several ways. He approved Gandhi's insistence on purity of means, moral yet critical scientific approach to human problems, concern for the poorest and building a socio-economic order that had its roots in the living elements of Indian tradition and which at the same time promoted world peace and cooperation.[23] Thus a socialist pattern of society was to be evolved through democratic and peaceful means on the basis of, and in tune with, the national genius and cultural heritage.[24]

His major difference with Gandhi was with regard to development strategy. Unlike Gandhi, his approach to the problem of poverty and unemployment was indirect. His immediate concern was to initiate a process of planned large-scale industrialization with emphasis on basic and heavy industry based on modern science and technology; this would provide, according to him, a permanent and enduring solution to the poverty and unemployment problem.

India's poverty and backwardness were due to her failure to adopt modern technology and to change her socio-economic structure in tune with the modern scientific age. Hence a socialistic pattern of society had to be evolved with modern technology. But this was possible only with the growing capacity to (*a*) produce machines that make machines with the adoption of the latest—and hence more efficient—techniques, and (*b*) to make original scientific and technical research.

> The three fundamental requirements of India, if she is to develop industrially and otherwise, are a heavy engineering and machine-making industry, scientific research institutes, and electric power. These must be the foundations of all planning. . . .[25] Again, Political change there must be, but economic change is equally necessary. That change will have to be in the direction of a democratically planned collectivism. . . . A democratic collectivism need not mean an abolition of private property, but it will mean the public ownership of the basic and major industries. It will mean the cooperative or collective control of land. In India especially it will be necessary to have, in addition to the big industries, cooperatively controlled small and village industries.[26]

Unlike Gandhi, full employment was not his immediate objective. One had to strive for maximum employment and for this purpose, cottage and small industry had to be promoted but only as a temporary means to relieve the unemployment problem. The traditional industries and techniques were obsolete and out of date and had to be supplanted by the "big machine". It was the modern sector that had to be developed; the traditional sector had to give way soon.

> Thus an attempt to build up a country's economy largely on the basis of cottage and small-scale industries is doomed to failure. It will not solve the basic problems of the country or maintain freedom, nor will it fit in with the world framework, except as a colonial appendage.
>
> Is it possible to have two entirely different kinds of economy in a country—one based on the big machine and industrialization, and the other mainly on cottage industries? This is hardly conceivable, for one must overcome the other, and there can be little doubt that the big machine will triumph unless it is forcibly prevented from doing so. Thus it is not a mere question of adjustment of the two forms of production and economy. One must be dominating and paramount, *with the other as complimentary to it, fitting in where it can. [Italics added.]* The economy based on the latest technical achievements of the day must necessarily be the dominating one. If technology demands the big machine, as it does today in a large measure, then the big machine with all its implications and consequences must be accepted.

. . . But, in any event, the latest technique has to be followed, and to adhere to out-worn and out-of-date methods of production, except as a temporary and stop-gap measure, is to arrest growth and development.[27]

Thus, in essence, technology for Nehru was a *parameter* and its autonomous development had to dictate the socio-economic structure. There is no appreciation of the role of technological research in *upgrading traditional techniques* nor is there the awareness of the problem of *adapting* modern technology to India's circumstances and environment. In essence, the problem according to Nehru was that of cultivating adequate scientific and technological competence to *master* the latest techniques and to make original research to advance the frontiers of scientific and technological knowledge. Hence his emphasis on capital goods industry and scientific research.[28]

Thus, though Nehru starts like Gandhi with the human problem of poverty and unemployment, his emphasis subtly shifts from this basic problem to the problem of scientific and technological progress—for its own sake. Gandhi's basic teaching appealed to him; as he says: "In two respects the background of his thought had a vague but considerable influence; the fundamental test of everything was how far it benefited the masses, and the means were always important and could not be ignored even though the end in view was right, for the means governed the end and varied it."[29]

Nehru was the Chairman of the National Planning Committee, constituted by the Congress in 1938. This Committee's findings had the stamp of Nehru's vision. As he said: "the National Planning Committee laid the greatest emphasis" on what he called, "the three fundamental requirements", which "must be the foundations of all planning . . ."[30].

III. The Perspective of Five Year Plans

The interrupted work of the National Planning Committee was taken up after Independence by the Planning Commission (constituted in March, 1950). The National Planning Committee had started *its exercise* with the objective of providing *an irreducible minimum standard of living* to each individual and this was based on (*a*) a balanced diet having a calorific value of 2400 to 2800 units for an adult worker, (*b*) 30 yards of clothing per year and (*c*) housing standard of 100 square feet; this was estimated to cost about Rs. 15–25 per capita per month (at 1938 prices) or at present prices about $15–25 per month—a standard to be attained in a decade.[31] It is worth noting that this approach, even as an exercise, was taken up only during the Third Plan (1961–5) when the national minimum income per month per individual was fixed at Rs. 20 per month at 1960–1 prices (or $8 at present prices)—a standard to be attained in fifteen years.[32]

Anyway, the Planning Commission—again with Nehru as its Chairman—by and large adopted Nehru's strategy. "The central objective of planning in India at the present stage is to *initiate a process of development* which will raise living standards and open out to the people new opportunities for a richer and more varied life."[33] *[Italics added.]* As with Nehru, so with the Commission, initiation of a process of development was the principal objective; with Gandhi, what mattered was the immediate objective of removing poverty *through* full employment. Planned development had to concentrate on socio-economic change and technological change. To quote the First Plan document: "The pace of economic development depends on a variety of factors which constitute the psychological and sociological setting within which the economy operates. . . . Basically, development involves securing higher productivity all round and this is a function of the degree of technological advance the community is able to make. The problem is not one merely of *adopting and applying* the process and techniques developed elsewhere, but of developing new techniques suited to local conditions. Modern technology is changing rapidly and no country can hope to maintain a steady pace of advance unless it keeps abreast of current developments."[34] *[Italics added.]* Hence the emphasis on Scientific and Industrial Research to which a whole chapter of the Plan was devoted.

Thus the emphasis was on mastering the latest technology and new research, for which a variety of research institutes were set up during the First Plan period (1951–6).[35] For research results to ripen in actual technical innovations, it was recognized that pilot plant experiments may not suffice and it may be necessary "to install semi-commercial or prototype plants to demonstrate effectively the new processes and their economic possibilities. . . . For this purpose, the establishment of a National Research Development Corporation of India has been proposed . . .". Most of the research activity was to be carried out under the auspices of the Council of Scientific and Industrial Research (CSIR)—originally formed in 1942.[36]

There was no emphasis on the *problem of technological choice or adaptation* and the machinery required for the purpose. There was, in fact, no technology policy.

There was, again, no emphasis on *full* employment as a condition for removing poverty. "Maximum use of idle labour" was mentioned and it was indicated that "For absorbing all, or a large proportion, of the increase in working population each year in non-agricultural occupations, reliance will have to be placed mainly on small-scale and cottage industries involving comparatively small capital investment. If these industries are to afford employment at reasonable rates of wages, their technical efficiency will have to be increased and every effort will have to be made to see that the producer's reward is not intercepted by middlemen. . . . In fact, development is, in a sense, but another name for employment opportunities."[37]

There was some recognition of the problem of upgrading technology in traditional industry. "The research institutions will bring the fruits of research within their reach and enable them to reduce costs and improve the quality of their products. The establishment of these laboratories and institutes is thus complimentary to the objective of promoting the development of small-scale and cottage industries."[38] However, the emphasis was on research and not on appropriate machinery that could make the *search* or identify problems for *research* for appropriate technology suited to solve the actual concrete problems of small industry. There was no technology policy for *upgrading* techniques in traditional industry just as there was none for *adapting* modern technology.

The Second Plan did not add anything of substance to the discussion on technology choice. In fact all the subsequent plans (after the First) did not even discuss the technology question in the first few basic chapters outlining plan objectives and policies; "scientific research" was relegated to a separate chapter, more or less unrelated to the substantive parts of plan policies. And this chapter merely described the structure of the scientific research system and the research problems and results without in any significant way relating them to the actual production or project problems. Scientific research was treated as an *autonomous* activity unrelated to the problems of development.

The significant part of the Second Plan (1957–61) related to the outlining of the strategy of industrial development, based on basic and heavy industry. Its two major objectives were:

(1) "to attain a rapid growth of the national economy by increasing the scope and importance of the public sector and in this way to advance to a socialist pattern of society;
(2) "to develop basic heavy industries for the manufacture of producer goods to strengthen the foundations of economic independence."[39]

Of course, there was emphasis on traditional skills and industries, which were expected to produce consumer goods to the required extent and at the same time serve as a *stop-gap* device to provide *maximum* employment to the poorer section of the people. But there is no discussion of the problem of *upgrading* their technology; after the First Plan, this question is not even posed in any subsequent plan document.

Such, then, was the pattern of development policy; there was place in it for scientific research but the plans lacked a technology policy. The scientific research system and the production system advanced on parallel lines and there was no recognition of the need for a technology policy to relate one to the other.

And so we come to the *abortive* Draft Fifth Plan document (1974–9), which in two crucial respects was a departure from the earlier plans. One related to the central importance of removing poverty. "Removal of poverty and attainment of self-reliance are the two major objectives that the country has set out to accomplish in the Fifth Plan."[40] The other relates to the recognition of the need for a technology policy; "The Science and Technology plan, as an *integral part* of the Fifth Plan, is *one of the major policy instruments* for achieving the objective of self-reliance."[41] [*Italics added.*] After the First Plan, the technology question is posed for the first time in the chapter on plan policies, under the title: *Science and Technology Policy*—a title never before used in the Plan documents.

The Fifth Plan explicitly recognizes the lack of technology policy in the earlier plans. To quote: "More importantly, perhaps, the structuring of the effort has been such that the goals of R & D programmes and projects have, often, not been derived directly from the technological needs of development projects, whether in industry or other areas. At the same time, the scope of 'science planning' has not covered the whole of the 'innovation chain'. As a result, successful research results at the laboratory level have often failed to be linked to such elements as pilot plant work, design engineering, plant erection and commissioning and marketing, which are essential if the nation is to secure real and substantial, social and economic benefits from science and technology. . . . The task involved is really 'planning the promotion of Science and Technology and their application to the Development and Security of the Nation. . . .' What we are primarily interested in, is not a plan merely for education and research in various scientific and technological disciplines but a plan to harness science and technology for achieving the goals and programmes of the Fifth Plan."[42]

The Fifth Plan thus diagnoses the problem—the problem of technology policy, but it does not discuss with sufficient clarity and precision the crucial elements of a sound technology policy. It does not even mention the problem of *upgrading* traditional technology. It does not recognize, for instance, that the three problems—problem of *relevant research,* problem of *adapting* modern technology and the problem of *upgrading* traditional technology—are interrelated and their solution crucially depends on the existence of adequate machinery to identify actual project problems in concrete terms—a machinery that vitally links the production and the technology systems.

IV. Broad Outline of a Technology Policy

That India did not have and still does not have a sound technology policy as an integral and vital part of development strategy is not very surprising. Neither the development economists nor the international development agencies (like the World Bank) have appreciated the crucial role of technology policy—and this in spite of Marx, Schumpeter and Kuznets. The development economists have concentrated on methods and techniques of analysis rather than on the intelligent perception of the process of development and the human problem of poverty. In development policy as in all walks of life what matters is the creative perception of problems; logic and intellect have their role only if they are guided by creative intelligence and perception. Economists can afford to remain imprisoned in certain static moulds and patterns of thought. But such unintelligence would be fatal in policy-makers—and hence development economists; for they have to deal with intelligent action in the present and not with thought which is invariably related to the past—in a world full of uncertainty and complexity.[43]

The less developed countries with all their handicaps of a late start have one critical advantage and that is related to the accumulated and growing scientific and technological knowledge. But to use this knowledge *creatively* for solving their own problems, they need to develop competence in the field of technology choice through an *institutionalized* technology policy. Sophisticated techniques of planning or project evaluation are not—cannot be—a substitute for such a technology policy; the former in fact has relevance *only* with such a policy. What then are the major elements of such a technology policy?

Obviously one has to start with the human problem of poverty as Gandhi did and try to solve it through means (instruments) that are *directly* related to the problem. As Gandhi realized, it is neither practical nor desirable to provide a decent minimum of physical security to each family without providing it with work; that is, employment. So poverty can be removed only through *full* employment—employment of each individual family.

Once one starts from this focal point, and given the natural resources, the problem becomes very *specific* and *concrete:* how to choose organizational forms and technology so as to fully employ the available and growing labour force and at the same time ensure each family initially a decent minimum level of living and later a progressively rising minimum.[44]

Obviously, wherever one wants to go, one has no alternative but to start from where one is. In this context one has to start from the traditional sector with its skills, techniques and organization. In India (and probably in many other less developed countries), this sector employs about 80 per cent of the labour force (60 per cent in agriculture and related activities and 20 per cent in traditional industry like hand-loom, gun-making, rural transport, agriculture, dairy and cattle breeding, forestry, poultry farming, piggeries, fisheries, organic manure, agricultural implements and household utensils and appliances); about 10 per cent is employed in the modern sector and the remaining 10 per cent is actually underemployed or unemployed. With growth of population at the rate of 2.5 per cent per annum, the modern sector, even if it grew at 20 per cent in terms of employment, would not be able to provide employment to the full extent even to the increase in labour force—let alone to the presently unemployed. Thus it is obvious that the traditional sector would have to absorb the currently unemployed as well as a part of the increase in labour force.

Hence, as Gandhi realized, the crucial problem is that of promoting the viable growth of the traditional sector and organically linking the modern sector growth with that of the traditional in a manner that supplements and reinforces the growth and development of the latter. It is not possible to *supplant* the traditional skills and techniques by the modern ones; that cannot solve the poverty problem.

In terms of technology choice, then, there are two problems: problem of *upgrading* the traditional technology and the problem of *adapting and improving* modern technology in a manner that is consistent with the development objectives, changing institutional structure and natural resources. Without such upgrading and such adapting, it is not possible to provide a rising minimum level of living to each family.

For both purposes, it is essential to formulate an appropriate technology policy the main elements of which are discussed in the next chapter.

NOTES

1. See the New Testament: "Take *that* thine *is*, and go thy way: I will give unto this last, even as unto thee." (St. Matthew 20:14.)

   Sarvodayo conveys that the *good of all is served by promoting the good of the poorest—the lowliest and the lost.* See N. K. Bose, *Selections from Gandhi* (Ahmedabad: Navjivan Publishing House, April 1957), pp. 38–41.
2. See C. Singh, *India's Economic Policy: The Gandhian Blueprint* (New Delhi: Vikas Publishing House Private Ltd., 1978).
3. See V. V. Bhatt, *Two Decades of Development: The Indian Experiment* (Bombay: Vora & Co., 1973), chapter 4.
4. See N. K. Bose, *op. cit.* To quote Gandhi: "True to his poetical instinct, the poet (reference is to Tagore) lives for the morrow and would have us do likewise. He presents to our admiring gaze the beautiful picture of the birds early in the morning singing hymns of praise as they soar into the sky. These birds have had their day's food and soared with rested wings, in whose veins new blood had flown during the previous night. But I have had the pain of watching birds who for want of strength could not be coaxed even into a flutter of their wings. The human bird under the Indian sky gets up weaker than when he pretended to retire. For millions it is an eternal vigil or an eternal trance. It is an indescribably painful state which has got to be experienced to

be realized. I have found it impossible to soothe suffering patients with a song from Kabir. The hungry millions ask for one poem—invigorating food. They cannot be given it. They must earn it. And they can earn only by the sweat of their brow."

Again: "Imagine, therefore, what a calamity it must be to have 300 millions unemployed, several millions becoming degraded every day for want of employment, devoid of self-respect, devoid of faith in God. I may as well place before the dog over there the message of God as before those hungry millions who have no lustre in their eyes and whose only God is their bread. I can take before them a message of God only by taking the message of sacred work before them. . . . To them God can only appear as bread and butter."

Further: "My *ahimsa* would not tolerate the idea of giving a free meal to a healthy person who has not worked for it in some honest way and, if I had the power, I would stop every *Sadavrata* where free meals are given. It has degraded the nation and it has encouraged laziness, idleness, hypocrisy and even crime. . . . Do not say you will maintain the poor on charity" (pp. 46–7).

5. *Ibid.*, pp. 48–55.
6. See V. V. Bhatt, "On Development Problem and Strategy", in *Society and Change*, ed. by K. S. Krishnaswami *et al.* (Bombay: Oxford University Press, 1977).
7. G. Woodcock, *Mohandas Gandhi* (New York: The Viking Press, 1971), chapter vii.

See also N. K. Bose, *op. cit.* To quote Gandhi: "My idea of village Swaraj is that it is a complete republic, independent of its neighbours for its vital wants, and yet interdependent for many others in which dependence is a necessity. Thus every village's first concern will be to grow its own food crops and cotton for its cloth. It should have a reserve for its cattle, recreation and play-ground for adults and children. Then if there is more land available, it will grow *useful* money crops, thus excluding *ganja*, tobacco, opium and the like. The village will maintain a village theatre, school and public hall. It will have its own waterworks ensuring clean supply. This can be done through controlled wells and tanks. Education will be compulsory up to the final basic course. As far as possible every activity will be conducted on the cooperative basis. . . . Non-violence with its technique of *Satyagraha* and non-cooperation will be the sanction of the village community. There will be a compulsory service of village guards who will be selected by rotation from the register maintained by the village. The government of the village will be conducted by the *Panchayat* of five persons, annually elected by the adult villagers, male and female, possessing minimum prescribed qualifications . . . here there is perfect democracy based upon individual freedom. The individual is the architect of his own government. . . . He and his village are able to defy the might of a world. For the law governing every villager is that he will suffer death in the defence of his and his village's honour" (pp. 73–4).

See also G. Woodcock, *op. cit.* To quote Gandhi: "In this structure composed of innumerable villages . . . life will not be a pyramid with the apex sustained by the bottom. But it will be an oceanic circle whose centre will be the individual always ready to perish for the village, the latter ready to perish for the circle of villages, till at last the whole becomes one life composed of individuals. . . . The outermost circumference will not wield power to crush the inner circle but will give strength to all within and derive its own strength from it" (p. 94).

8. To quote Gandhi: "If I can convert the country to my point of view, the social order of the future will be based predominantly on the *Charkha* and all it implies. It will include everything that promotes the wellbeing of the villagers. I do visualize electricity, ship-building, ironworks, machine-making and the like existing side by side with village handicrafts. But the order of dependence will be reversed. Hitherto, the industrialization has been so planned as to destroy the villages and the village crafts. *In the State of the future it will subserve the villages and their crafts.* I do not share the socialist belief that centralization of the necessaries of life will conduce to the common welfare, that is, where the centralized industries are planned and owned by the State." Quoted in C. Singh, *op. cit.*, p. 53.
9. To quote Gandhi: "Indeed at the root of this doctrine of equal distribution must lie that of the trusteeship of the wealthy for superfluous wealth possessed by them. For, according to the doctrine, they may not possess a rupee more than their neighbours. How is this to be brought about? Non-violently? Or should the wealthy be dispossessed of their possessions? To do this we would naturally have to resort to violence. This violent action cannot benefit society. Society will be the poorer, for it will lose the gifts of a man who knows how to accumulate wealth. Therefore non-violent way is evidently superior. The rich man will be left in possession of his

wealth, of which he will use what he reasonably requires for his personal needs and will act as a trustee for the remainder to be used for the society. In this argument, honesty on the part of the trustee is assumed."

"If however, in spite of the utmost effort, the rich do not become guardians of the poor in the true sense of the term . . . what is to be done? In trying to find out the solution of this riddle I have lighted on non-violent non-cooperation and civil disobedience as the right and infallible means. The rich cannot accumulate wealth without the cooperation of the poor in society. If this knowledge were to penetrate to and spread amongst the poor, they would become strong and would learn how to free themselves by means of non-violence from the crushing inequalities which have brought them to the verge of starvation . . . all the capitalists will have an opportunity of becoming statutory trustees. But such a statute will not be imposed from above. It will have to come from below." N. K. Bose, *op. cit.*, pp. 78–80.

10. To quote: "The broad definition of Swadeshi is the use of all home-made things to the exclusion of foreign things, in so far as such use is necessary for the protection of home-industry, more especially the industries without which India will become pauperized. . . . But even Swadeshi, like any other good thing, can be ridden to death if it is made a fetish. That is a danger that must be guarded against. To reject foreign manufactures merely because they are foreign, and to go on wasting national time and money in the promotion in one's country of manufactures for which it is not suited would be criminal folly, and a negation of the Swadeshi spirit . . . Swadeshism is not a cult of hatred. It is a doctrine of selfless service, that has its roots in the purest *ahimsa*, i.e., love." N. K. Bose, *op. cit.*, pp. 306–7.
11. To quote: "I look upon an increase in the power of the State with the greatest fear because, although while apparently doing good by minimizing exploitation, it does the greatest harm to mankind by destroying individuality which lies at the root of all progress. . . . The State represents violence in a concentrated and organised form. The individual has a soul, but as the State is a soulless machine, it can never be weaned from violence to which it owes its very existence. . . .

    ". . . It is my firm conviction that if the State suppressed capitalism by violence, it will be caught in the coils of violence itself and fail to develop non-violence at any time. . . . What I would personally prefer, would be, not a centralization of power in the hands of the State but an extension of the sense of trusteeship; as in my opinion, the violence of private ownership is less injurious than the violence of the State. However, if it is unavoidable, I would support a minimum of State-ownership." See N. K. Bose, *op. cit.*, pp. 40–1.
12. Quoted in V. V. Bhatt, "Two Decades of Development", *op. cit.*, p. 1.
13. N. K. Bose, *op. cit.*, pp. 283–98.
14. *Ibid.*, p. 131.
15. See G. Myrdal, *Asian Drama*, vol. iii (New York: The Twentieth Century Fund, 1968), pp. 1655–8. See also V. V. Bhatt, *Education and Economic Development* (Bombay: Vora & Co., 1972), pp. 8–10.
16. See N. K. Bose, *op. cit.*, pp. 291–7.
17. See G. Woodcock, *op. cit.* To quote Woodcock: "The 'one-step-enough-for-me' approach was in complete accordance with the general philosophy of *Satyagraha* and also with the teachings of the Bhagavat Gita as Gandhi interpreted them . . . its exponents developed these principles experimentally in the world of action, where everything is relative and mutable, and in this sense the Gandhian philosophy is one of endless becoming, which makes it—in a somewhat different way from left-wing Marxism—a doctrine of permanent revolution. No society can ever be perfect . . . and for this reason the *Satyagrahi* cannot accept the rigid plans of the Utopian theorist, since he has to be sensitive to the constantly changing demands of human relations, and these assail him, not in the future, but now and here" (pp. 86–7).
18. N. K. Bose, *op. cit.*, pp. 62–89: See also G. Woodcock, *op. cit.*, chapter vii.
19. N. K. Bose, *op. cit.*, pp. 292–8.
20. *Ibid.*, p. 95 and p. 297.
21. *Ibid.*, p. 55.
22. Gandhi's basic ideas on Sarvodaya were formulated as early as 1909; Nehru's as early as 1926. See J. Nehru, *The Discovery of India* (Bombay: Asia Publishing House, 1969).
23. *Ibid.*, pp. 356–65.

24. Nehru used to quote approvingly Gandhi on this. To quote Gandhi: "I do not want my house to be walled in on all sides and my windows to be stuffed. I want the cultures of all lands to be blown about my house as freely as possible. But I refuse to be blown off my feet by any. . . . Mine is not a religion of the prison-house." See N. K. Bose, *op. cit.*, p. 298.
25. Nehru, *op. cit.*, p. 410.
26. *Ibid.*, p. 522.
27. *Ibid.*, pp. 404–9.
28. Apart from scientific research, what Nehru emphasized, as a way of life, was the scientific temper. To quote: "It is the scientific approach, the adventurous and yet critical temper of science, the search for truth and new knowledge, the refusal to accept anything without testing and trial, the capacity to change previous conclusions in the face of new evidence, the reliance on observed fact and not on preconceived theory, the hard discipline of the mind—all this is necessary, not merely for the application of science but for life itself and the solution of its many problems. Too many scientists today, who swear by science, forget all about it outside their particular spheres. The scientific approach and temper are, or should be, a way of life, a process of thinking, a method of acting and associating with our fellowmen. . . . It is the temper of a free man." See J. Nehru, *op. cit.*, p. 512.

    This was precisely the approach of Gandhi; he called his life as "Experiments With Truth". See N. K. Bose, *op. cit.*, pp. vi–x. But Gandhi's emphasis was on intelligence, perception rather than *only* on intellect. See J. Krishnamurti, *The Awakening of Intelligence* (New York: Harper & Row, 1973) on this. To quote: "May we say, thought is barren? . . . which is mechanical and all the rest of it? Thought is a pointer, but without intelligence the pointer has no value . . . so intelligence is necessary. Without it thought has no meaning at all. . . . As we begin to inquire into it, or in inquiring, we come to this source. Is it a perception, an insight, and has that insight nothing whatsoever to do with thought? Is insight the result of thought? The conclusion of an insight is thought, but insight itself is not thought . . .; you come upon it when you see the whole thing. So insight is the perception of the whole . . . the quality of mind that sees the whole is not touched by thought; therefore, there is perception, there is insight" (pp. 520–35).

    Compare Gandhi: "Truly beautiful creation comes when right perception is at work. If these moments are rare in life, they are also rare in art." N. K. Bose, *op. cit.*, p. 304. Again: "In dealing with living entities, the dry syllogistic method leads not only to bad logic but sometimes to fatal logic. For if you miss even a tiny factor—and you never have control over all the factors that enter into dealings with human beings, your conclusion is likely to be wrong. Therefore, you never reach the final truth, you only reach an approximation; and that too if you are extra careful in your dealings." N. K. Bose, *op. cit.*, p. 44.
29. Nehru, *op. cit.*, p. 362.
30. *Ibid.*, p. 410.
31. *Ibid.*, pp. 397–8.
32. See T. N. Srinivasan and P. K. Bardhan (eds.), *Poverty and Income Distribution in India* (Calcutta: Statistical Publishing Society, 1974), pp. 9–39.
33. Planning Commission, Government of India, *The First Five Year Plan* (New Delhi, 1952), p. 7.
34. *Ibid.*, pp. 12–13.
35. *Ibid.*, chapter xxviii.
36. *Ibid.*, p. 418.
37. *Ibid.*, p. 25.
38. *Ibid.*, p. 413.
39. Planning Commission, Government of India, *Papers Relating to the Formulation of The Second Five Year Plan* (New Delhi, 1955), p. 42.
40. Planning Commission, Government of India, *Draft Fifth Five Year Plan—1974–9* (New Delhi, 1974), p. 1.
41. *Ibid.*, p. 18.
42. *Ibid.*, pp. 216–18.
43. See V. V. Bhatt, *On Technology Policy and Its Institutional Frame*, World Development, vol. 3, no. 9 (Sept. 1975), pp. 651–63.
44. On this problem see V. V. Bhatt, *On Development Problem and Strategy, op. cit.*

7. On Technology Policy and its Institutional Frame*

It is indeed amazing but true that the institutionalized profession of economists has, with a few notable exceptions, built dynamic theories of growth in complete disregard of the outstanding significance of technological change—or to use Schumpeter's much more meaningful term, innovation—for the historic process of socio-economic development. It was Marx who perceived more sharply and clearly than anybody else the revolutionary implications of innovation for economic and social change and it was Schumpeter who brought out the significance of the *function* as well as the *ability* related to the introduction of innovations and thus drawing attention to significant aspects of human behaviour in the context of uncertainty.[1] Uncertainty is the challenge which man faces and his response to uncertainty determines the shape of the future. It is only a few who are capable of a creative response to a challenge, the rest merely trying to adapt themselves as best as they can to the changing environment. And it is those few who perform the leadership functions that shape the future. In the socio-economic field, the introduction of innovations constitutes the creative response of the entrepreneurs to the challenge of objective reality with uncertainty as its integral part. Economics and more generally the social sciences have yet to grasp the implications of what Schumpeter termed the creative response to challenge.[2]

Some historians who have studied the facts, without being imprisoned in a theoretical framework irrelevant for understanding historical processes of change, have indeed recognized the obvious and simple fact of the central importance of scientific and technological change in the process of economic development.[3] How this permissive factor interacts with institutional and ideological change in a sort of chain-reaction to generate a total process of change is still little understood. However, what comes out of historical analysis is that, though there may be some degree of universality about technological knowledge—as indeed there must be because of the common inheritance of scientific and technological knowledge—the institutional and ideological counterparts are much more specific to the cultural traits and social structure of the given countries and civilizations.[4]

Since economic theory usually ignores historical time and the process of interaction between technological changes and changes in the socio-economic structure in a world of interdependent countries with unequal bargaining power, access to technological knowledge and development potential, it has not reached the stage of maturity from which policy recommendations can be made. And yet, economists are trying to find the key to development (like the proverbial

* Revised version of the article first published in *World Development*, vol. 3, no. 9 (Sept. 1975). Also in *World Bank Reprint Series*, no. 29.

drunkard) not where it is lost but in an area where the beam of economic theory casts its dim light.[5, 6]

This is the area of multi-sector planning models and cost–benefit analysis of specific projects. For obvious reasons planning models have not been a sure guide to policy problems, though they have provided some insights into certain relationships.[7] And likewise, cost–benefit analysis, though useful for judging in *essentially* static terms the efficiency aspects of specific projects, is not relevant for taking decisions with regard to the central (non-marginal) problems of socio-economic development.[8] Both these approaches can potentially improve the efficiency of the development process only if they are pursued in the light of central decisions relating to the development strategy, of which technology strategy has of *necessity* to be an integral and dominant part.[9, 10]

The principal problem is to generate a process of progressive improvement of the productive power of the existing as well as the new sectors of the economy through appropriate technological changes and such changes in the institutional and ideological framework as are consistent with this process. The beginning, obviously, has to be made with the traditional sectors, skills and occupations and the new sectors have to be organically related to the traditional. The principal instrument for the purpose has to be a technology strategy and an institutional and ideological strategy that can sustain a cumulative self-reinforcing process of resource creation.

The purpose of this chapter is limited to a discussion of only some of the functional/institutional aspects of technology policies. The ways in which the technology problems currently differ from that faced by the nineteenth-century developing countries and the implications of these differences for development strategy are discussed in section I. Section II indicates the major elements of a technology policy and emphasizes the varied role of the Technical Consultancy Service Centres (TCSCs) and the Financial System (FS) in providing essential organic links between Modern Technology and domestic and foreign Technological Research Centres (TRCs) on the one hand and the Production System (PS) on the other. The catalytic leadership function of the FS in such a policy is stressed in section III and how this function has been performed by banks in some countries is indicated in section IV. Some case studies in technology illustrating the primacy of the design-engineering formula are presented in section V.

I. Differential Characteristics of the Technology Problem

The developing countries during the nineteenth century regarded technology advances in the United Kingdom as indicating their development potential which, when contrasted with the actual situation, posed a challenge to which they tried to respond by harnessing technology to the process of development.

> Industrialization always seemed the more promising, the greater the backlog of technological innovations which the backward country could take over from the more advanced country. Borrowed technology, so much and so rightly stressed by *Veblen*, was one of the primary factors assuring a high speed of development in a backward country entering the stage of industrialization[11] . . . it was largely by application of the most modern and

efficient techniques that backward countries could hope to achieve success, particularly if their industrialization proceeded in the face of competition from the advanced country.[12]

This was possible for several reasons. The technological distance between the United Kingdom and the then developing countries was not very significant. For, the cognitive base of technological progress in the United Kingdom was overwhelmingly artisan ingenuity and learning-by-doing experience and its transmittal depended primarily on individual apprenticeship rather than blueprints, technical literature or other formal means of cognitive transfer. Further, both Germany and the United States were ahead of the United Kingdom in terms of adult literacy and were not significantly deficient in scientific cadres.[13]

Under these circumstances adaptation and improvement of borrowed technology did not pose any difficult problem. Quite often, merely imports provided a basis for technology absorption. On the basis of imports of locomotives in the late 1820s and 1830s, it was possible for the United States to copy and improve them and thus "a locomotive-building industry sprang up in the United States almost at once".[14] Despite the ban on British machinery exports, a substantial number of British machines reached the United States to be copied and, more important, modified to suit U.S. requirements. The Singer records reflect a concern about the imitation of Singer sewing machines in western Europe.[15]

In some other cases, informal visits abroad facilitated the international transfer and absorption of technology. On a European trip in 1872 Andrew Carnegie studied the Bessemer steel works, recognized the significance of the new technology, and on his return made plans based on what he had seen in England.[16] Similarly, the hiring of foreign technicians was sometimes adequate for the purpose. In several cases, promising ideas or experimental designs sufficed; the experimental German Otto engine was the basis for the French and American auto designs.[17]

Such instances can be multiplied.[18] But the main point is that, since nineteenth-century technology was based largely not on scientific discovery, but on engineering practice and invention, the absorption of technology created no serious problem, since it was not difficult to learn new engineering practices empirically through trial and error.

There was another factor which facilitated technology absorption without creating a problem of technological unemployment and dualism. The main thrust of technological advance related to the fields of machinery and intermediate goods, rather than to the new types of mass-produced consumer goods. As a result, the international demonstration effect with regard to living styles was negligible, and these styles changed *pari passu* with production changes rather than as a result of consumption changes outpacing the changes in production. Further, the consumption basket of the rich was geared to the quality products of the artisan class; equipment manufacture was still an artisan activity, as was the finishing-touch stage of industrial production. Thus the problem of technological unemployment did not become acute. The traditional and modern sectors grew in a certain organic relationship, the relative contraction in the one being matched by the expansion of the other, while techniques improved in both sectors.[19]

The Japanese case was in essential respects not very different from that of France, Germany or the United States. Japan was probably technologically more backward than Germany or Czarist Russia. Hence the main focus of her attention was on learning to adapt modern technology. Since at that stage the absorption and diffusion of modern technology depended primarily upon design and engineering skills, Japan made a conscious and deliberate effort to develop an industrial design and lab-analytic capacity for adapting modern technologies. Further, the Japanese consumption pattern remained geared to traditional products even till the end of the Second World War; the traditional small-scale industrial sector, as a result, was technologically and organizationally strengthened and became organically related to the modern sector in many ways. The close and intimate contact between the government and Japanese industry enabled the government to direct industrial development along desired lines without the introduction of formal regulatory methods. The typical industrial organization and structure typified by the Saibatsu complexes, closely aligned with the banking system and the government, enabled industry to diversify and grow, as well as to export aggressively, by pooling resources and diffusing risks.[20]

The present-day developing countries, however, face a technology absorption problem which is *qualitatively* different from that faced by the nineteenth-century developing countries. Modern technology has long out-grown the stage when scientist learned from engineering and technological research and hence become immensely complex and knowledge-based, requiring high-level scientific and technological manpower for both its growth and operation. It is capital-scale and skill-intensive and, further, because of economic development and increasing real incomes, it is geared to the production of sophisticated goods and services intended to meet *simultaneously* a wide variety of functional, aesthetic, comfort and status needs and wants.[21]

Thus, both technology as well as consumer products are oriented towards meeting the complex dynamic want-pattern of rich societies and are out of tune with the resource composition and the basic functional want-pattern of the poor countries. The creative absorption of this technology to suit the specific needs of the poor countries requires a high degree of indigenous scientific and technological capability, which these countries lack.

Again, there is an additional factor which operates against any attempt at creative adaptation of modern technology to suit modern as well as traditional sectors. This relates to the international demonstration effect of living styles of rich countries in the context of the wide, and widening, income disparity and technological distance between the rich and poor countries. The modern transport and communication system, of course, has exposed the poor countries to the dazzling glare of the rich-country style of living. But there is a deeper sociological reason for this phenomenon also, and this is related to the intellectual and psychological orientation of the educated and power élites of the poor countries toward the norms and standards of the developed countries, not only in matters of living style but also with regard to scientific, intellectual and educational pursuits, as well as institutional and ideological patterns.

The educated and the power élites in the poor countries have been exposed to the civilization and culture of the rich countries in a variety of ways. This exposure has implanted in these élites a sense of inferiority which they try to overcome by the imitation of that which can be easily imitated—for example, living styles and the outward *forms* of institutions like the banking and educational systems. This rich-country orientation has two effects: the alienation of the élites from the social structure and the masses, combined with exploitation of the latter for the satisfaction of their craving for prestige, defined in terms of the norms and standards of the rich countries. Thus *their* interests and objectives become *national* interests and objectives and the whole system—socio-political–economic—tends to be oriented towards their interests and objectives. In the economic field, the process starts with consumption through imports and later through domestic production of sophisticated consumer goods. The prevailing inequality of incomes and wealth makes this possible and the resulting structure of production and trade—and related structures in other fields—tends to reinforce and perpetuate this initial inequality. This modern structure cannot even potentially meet the functional needs of the rest of the population because of the limitation of resources of all kinds in the context of the requirements of modern technology, and its growth has to be at the cost of the traditional sector, which perforce stagnates. If the population remains stable, this structural feature can be enduring. But the population and labour force outgrow the requirements of the traditional sector. Poverty and various forms of unemployment ensue. Thus, modern technology and the powerful demonstration effect of the rich countries on the élites of the poor, these two factors together, create an economic system which has neither the means nor the incentives for initiating a self-reinforcing process of socio-economic development.

The development strategy for initiating such a process needs to be entirely different. Its starting-point must be the improvement of the technological and organizational base of the traditional sector, the primary requirements for which being design and engineering ability, the type of ability that prevailed in the developing countries of the nineteenth century with regard to the *then* modern technology. The other element of the strategy must concentrate on the growth of the modern sector that subserves the requirements of the traditional sector and is, in its basic design, complementary to traditional-sector development. This requires indigenous scientific and technological capability in order to identify, select, and adapt modern technology to specific needs and to innovate on the basis of the growing body of scientific and technological knowledge.

The other aspects of this strategy relate to such institutional and ideological changes as would promote and reinforce the technological strategy. Very broadly, it implies confidence and pride in initiating a genuine, authentic, original approach to development tasks and problems—in contrast to the present sense of inferiority. It implies the evolution of norms and standards that are relevant for this strategy. Historical experience and the current experience of China indicate that this is unlikely to be possible without isolating the social system from the living styles of the rich countries and yet without *contact* with the living reality of relevant knowledge, particularly in the fields of science and technology. This isolation-yet-contact paradox is vividly illustrated by the historical experience of Japan. The Listian argument for protection, in essence, is an argument for isolation-yet-contact.

Without such a strategy, any attempt to provide major solutions through planning models or cost–benefit analysis (with all the weights of different hues that one can conceive of) is bound to lead to the *evasion* of the problem, which would persist and become progressively intractable to a sane and rational approach. What is amazing is not so much the *naïveté* of the proponents of these approaches but the *naïveté* of those who accept them. Is there a sociological explanation for this desire to create the *illusion* of solving problems, while at the same time evading them? Is it the hold of the past, the vested interests of ideas that can never understand a problem—or, quite simply, a lack of sensitivity and intelligence? Can thought, however profound, ever be intelligent?[22]

II. Development Strategy and Technology Policy

Streeten has posed the problem of technology in terms of two gaps—the communications gap and the suitability gap.[23] These two gaps are not mutually exclusive; both have a common origin—namely, the lack of relevant indigenous scientific and technological capability. However good the channels of communication, one must know what it is that is relevant. And not only that. "Ask and ye shall receive"; but how to know what to ask for? Thus to judge the relevance of what is communicated and to ask for that which is relevant require a certain minimum capability in the technological field. Similarly for the suitability gap, one must first be able to identify the gap to know that which is not suitable and to know, even as a broad idea, the implications of that which may be suitable.[24]

But knowledge in the abstract has no value; it cannot permeate the production process. It has to be embodied in material form such as to be applied in production. The scientific and even technological research that is being done in the developing countries tends to accumulate knowledge, but knowledge that is not immediately applicable and to a large extent irrelevant to the production process. The reason is partly sociological—the imitation psychology of the élite—but partly it is also due to the lack of an integrated institutional structure, which relates the knowledge-gathering process to the knowledge-applications process in an interacting, mutually reinforcing, overall process promoting the knowledge-based expansion of the production system.[25]

What, then, are the elements of such an institutional structure? The first essential is a development strategy translated in terms of specific project or project-complex ideas. One cannot even begin to ask relevant questions without these ideas. If one starts with the traditional sector, one does not have to go abroad to identify the project ideas. For example, take agriculture. The project idea is to make agriculture, and the actual and potential labour force in that sector, productive. One does not want productive agriculture with unproductive labour; one wants to improve the productivity of both. Consolidation of fragmented holdings; land reform; labour-using but more knowledge-intensive techniques; irrigation systems that are consistent with the widespread use of water; marketing, transport, credit and educational systems that are potentially productively usable by the entire agricultural and related sectors, and so on—project-complex ideas are easily identifiable once one starts from a *focal-point*.

It is essential, thus, to identify the concrete ideas relating to the projects or project complexes that have to be undertaken in the light of the development objectives and strategy; for, technology choice problem can arise only after such initial identification. For both the sectors (traditional and modern) this identification process needs to be recognized as a distinct function and institutionalized in, say, Project Identification Centres (PICs).

With such identified project ideas should begin the search for appropriate technology. And this function is of *critical significance* for both the problems—problem of upgrading and the problem of adapting and improving. This is the design-engineering function that needs to be institutionalized in Technical Consultancy Service Centres (TCSCs).

It is the function of such TCSCs to design the machinery, processes and products. It requires knowledge of the initial conditions—of both the production and organizational structures. It requires identification of current knowledge and the current ways in which it can be applied. It requires identification of specific research problems and the ways in which they can be tackled within the country or abroad. And so on. Once one starts experimenting with the design of projects or project-complexes that are to be *implemented*—and this is how the design-engineering function is crucially linked with that of the PICs and the Financial System (FS)—one has set in motion a process of *search* for relevant knowledge as well as relevant *research;* a cumulative process of innovation, a process which is self-reinforcing.

Thus as an integral part of development and technology policies, the LDCs need to develop TCSCs with the capacity (*a*) to identify technological choice problems; (*b*) to *search* for their solutions with the assistance, where necessary, of foreign TCSCs and domestic and foreign Technology Research Centres (TRCs); (*c*) to adapt creatively the suggested solutions to actual project making; (*d*) to *upgrade* technology in the traditional sector (agriculture, and cottage and small industries); (*e*) to identify technological research problems and thus link the TRCs with the productive system. Thus it can function as a vehicle for absorbing and diffusing relevant modern technology, serving as an effective communication link with the foreign as well as the domestic sources of technology. At the same time, it can support and improve machine-building capacities by providing machine industries with designs as well as links with the evolving production structure. In the process, it could generate a wide variety of new project ideas in diverse fields.

Thus such TCSCs are an essential link between Modern Technology and Domestic and Foreign TRCs on the one hand and the Financial System (FS) and the Production System (PS) on the other. Quite a number of countries (like Brazil, Mexico and India) have TRCs but they function in a vacuum and are not in a position to tackle relevant problems of the PS; this has caused both internal and external brain-drain, and irrelevant research. Some countries have tried to evolve TCSCs but have not been able to forge a link between them and the FS and the PS with the result that such TCSCs remain stillborn; some of the small industry service institutions in India and some other countries are of this type. Unless one starts from the *focal-point* of *actual* project ideas—consistent with a country's development strategy—and hence from the PS and the FS, the TCSCs too would function in a vacuum and would become obsolete.

Such TCSCs have to be *functionally* linked with PICs, the FS and the PS; without such an organic functional link, they would become obsolete and operationally irrelevant. Again, they have to be organically linked with the TRCs; without this link, technological research would become irrelevant. A research set-up (TRCs) are essential; but such a set-up can derive its meaning and purpose only if it is related to the design-engineering function which is, in turn, intimately and vitally related to actual projects or project-complexes, which again have to be an integral part of a development strategy.

Strategy; project ideas (PICs); design and engineering (search for appropriate technology—TCSCs); financial system (FS); project implementation (PS); new project ideas—this is one sequence which organically relates one function to the other. The other organically related sequence is: strategy; project ideas (PICs); design-engineering (TCSCs); technological research (TRCs); design-engineering (TCSCs); financial system (FS); project implementation (PS); new project ideas. The third such sequence is: design-engineering (TCSCs); product, process and machine ideas; project ideas; design and engineering (TCSC); financial system (FS); project implementation (PS); new project ideas. The important point to realize, however, is the *central and crucial* significance in these chains of the design and engineering function (TCSCs). The development of the relevant TCSCs is thus a vital part of any development strategy which seeks to improve the technological base of the production process by seeking, receiving, adapting, and improving technological knowledge from whichever source it is available. This is the only way of effectively tackling the communication as well as the suitability gaps to which Streeten refers.[26]

In the field of agriculture, these organic links—project ideas design engineering (extension service); research problems; relevant research; field experiments; new project ideas; design and engineering (extension services)—in a chain process of innovations are fairly well understood and have formed the basis of the Green Revolution. If this revolution has generated inequities in the process, the fault does not lie in this sequence; it reflects a lack of clarity with regard to the development strategy. Why this organically interacting process of technological change has not so far been initiated in fields other than agriculture is an obvious question. Is it the result of ignorance or of national and international vested interests?

What is the role of the international community in general and of the international development institutions in particular in this field? (*a*) They can urge the LDCs to set up PICs, TCSCs and TRCs in relevant fields linked with the FS and the PS, and assist them in the initial stages in a variety of ways. (*b*) For certain complex fields, they can set up regional/international TCSCs. (*c*) They can start on their own international/regional TRCs which should work primarily on research problems identified by the national/regional TCSCs and which should also function as clearing-houses for relevant information for the national TCSCs and the TRCs. It is only thus that national and international efforts can be effectively integrated for solving the urgent and immediate problems of poverty and socio-economic development. The United Nations sponsored World Plan of Action for the Application of Science and Technology to Development[27] is too abstract and too vague and is not organically related to the development process; it may produce some useful results, but on the whole, as it is not integrated with the development process, it is likely to result in the same sort of irrelevant but prestigious pursuits that are the identification marks of the existing scientific institutions in the developing countries.

III. Catalytic Leadership Function of the FS

So far we have identified the technology problem and outlined the institutional structure and functions for a sound technology policy. The next question to be discussed is: which function (institution) should play the *catalytic leadership role* so as to ensure the interaction among functions, specified in the technology policy outline? Since a project cannot be implemented without finance, the vital decision rests with the FS (including the government when it acts as a financier). Hence the leadership function has to be assumed by the FS; and this would be even more so when the FS—like the development banks—has to play a promotional role in the development process. (See Chapter 12.)

Currently, the FS in a large number of LDCs is trying to perform this function by inducing enterprises to make "right" technology choices through its project selection criteria based on social cost–benefit analysis or economic evaluation of projects. However, since the FS tries to evaluate an already formulated project, it obviously cannot affect technology choices, which are made at the project design and formulation stage. (See Chapter 13.) The project formulation task is performed, by and large, by foreign TCSCs or their domestic counterparts for large enterprises; for the small–medium enterprises, the project formulation is based largely on the knowledge acquired by entrepreneurs from machinery suppliers, large enterprises or past experience in the field; here again, the technology choice at one remove is in fact made by the foreign TCSCs or their domestic counterparts. The latter normally do not use accounting prices in their project design work and their choices are largely governed by their experience in the developed countries. This basic limitation of mere economic evaluation of projects is emphasized by Little and Mirrlees in a very illuminating way.[28]

It must be emphasized, as Little and Mirrlees do, that it is not merely a question of the project designer using accounting prices for making technological choices. Even if he did use them, the range of choice is usually limited to actual alternatives already in use in the developed countries, especially with regard to the core processes and products.[29] Of course, this does not mean that there do not exist additional alternative core processes and products even within the range of modern technology. These alternatives, however, can be known only as a result of active search and creative adaptation of the various alternatives, "and in so doing, one ought to go beyond those best-practised technologies on the shelf, giving open-minded consideration to discarded laboratory results, as well as to technologies now considered obsolete by today's major industrial concerns".[30]

Foreign TCSCs or their domestic counterparts would not be inclined for obvious reasons to undertake such processes of search and creative adaptation of modern technology as well as upgrading traditional technology. To induce them to do so would require as Little and Mirrlees recognize, "an informed and critical client, determined to get a plant which will be very profitable". This really means that the FS (development banks) should actively support and/or help promote

TCSCs that have adequate technological competence to ask the right type of questions to all the possible sources of technology—TCSCs, TRCs, and enterprises anywhere in the world—and evaluate the suggested solutions with regard to upgrading of traditional technology and creative adaptation of modern technology. The FS without such domestic TCSCs would not be able to induce and enforce "right" technological choices—the very purpose for which it is using economic evaluation techniques to select projects for financing.

This vital link between the FS and the TCSCs is even more essential in a context where the development banks have to play a promotional role in initiating a viable and widely diffused process of industrialization through the development of small and small to medium enterprises. This small–medium enterprise development is essential for several reasons:[31] to develop latent entrepreneurial and managerial ability on a wide functional and geographical basis; to create employment opportunities on a viable basis for whole families and particularly for workers without much training and literacy in rural and semi-urban areas (to save on overheads and distribution costs); to improve the distribution of wealth and income.

Such small enterprise development requires an institutional machinery (i.e. TCSCs)—linked to the FS (development banks)—for the identification of project ideas, preparation of feasibility studies, making right technological choices, formulation of detailed projects with specification for machines, processes and products and providing assistance in project implementation and operation.[32]

Such TCSCs can help the FS in its promotional role as well as in appraising projects that the FS would get directly from the project promoters. They should be autonomous; the FS should support and/or help promote them but should not interfere in their functioning. Further, the FS should not finance projects, formulated by the TCSCs without an independent evaluation in terms of its social and cost-benefit criteria. Such independent evaluation by the FS serves a very essential function of appraising the soundness of the TCSCs themselves. The latter would have a compulsion to be up to date and alert; for, since the FS personnel would have experience of appraising a wide variety of projects, they would be able to judge effectively the performance with regard to technology choice of the TCSCs. Many government-operated TCSCs like the Indian Small Industry Service Institutes have failed in their main purpose without such a vital link between them and the FS.

Another point also needs to be emphasized. If the TCSCs are, indeed, successful in their functioning, they should be able to enhance the profitability of projects, which obtain their assistance; this is in fact their very purpose. If so, they should be self-supporting in their operations as well as their growth. Hence, they should charge reasonable fees to both the promoters as well as the FS. Free advice is *never* valued and more importantly, those who give free advice tend to become obsolete and irresponsible. Further, the capacity of the TCSCs to generate their own resources is a good index of their fruitfulness and efficiency.

IV. Leadership Role of the FS: Some Examples

A catalytic leadership role of the FS is not a very new phenomenon and it would be useful to indicate how some banks performed this function in different contexts.

This development banking task had been performed earlier during the nineteenth century in the then developing countries of western Europe. Gerschenkron tells us of the "truly momentous role of investment banking of the period for the economic history of France and of large portions of the Continent". The relative shortage of both capital and entrepreneurial talent was made good by the creative response of the banking systems to the challenge of development. "The Continental practices in the field of industrial investment banking must be conceived as specific instruments of industrialization in a backward country", writes Gerschenkron.[33]

> In Germany, the various incompetences of the individual entrepreneurs were offset by the device of splitting the entrepreneurial function: the German investment banks—a powerful invention, comparable in economic effect to that of the steam engine—were in their capital supplying functions a substitute for the insufficiency of the previously created wealth willingly placed at the disposal of entrepreneurs. But they were also a substitute for entrepreneurial deficiencies. From their central vantage points of control, the banks participated actively in shaping the major—and sometimes even not so major—decisions of the individual enterprises. It was they who very often mapped out a firm's path of growth, conceived far-sighted plans, *decided on major technological and locational innovations*, and arranged for mergers and capital increases [*Italics added*].[34]

In those days, the banks could perform the tasks of identification, design and formulation of projects with the available design-engineering talents, supplemented when necessary by foreign talents. Now, with the much greater complexity of these tasks and with the imperative need for domestic technological capability to adapt, modify and improve both traditional and modern technology, the banking system cannot perform these tasks without establishing TCSCs in relevant fields.

The Swedish development banks seem to have perceived the chain relationship with regard to technological advance. High-voltage transmission, an automobile that combines passenger-car styling with the ruggedness needed for poor roads, an aircraft capable of landing and taking off on very short runways—these were some of the technological problems that were identified by bankers. As Drucker reminds us:

> Yet Swedish technological strategy had not been formulated by technologists. It seems to have come mostly from the industrial development bankers who head the country's three large banks. Not one of them is a scientist or an engineer; all of them, however, apparently understand the need for technological strategy that is appropriate to a small country where available resources have to be concentrated on filling gaps in a few areas rather than in providing the main advance. When World War II ended, Sweden was still largely a mining and lumbering economy. Now she has become, in terms of per capita output, Europe's leading industrial economy

and has attained a standard of living second only to that of the United States.[35]

The Industrial Development Bank of India (IDBI) has clearly perceived the need, in the Indian context, of establishing (*a*) relevant TCSCs for performing the various tasks related to project design work, and (*b*) their close and direct links with the banking system so as to enable the latter to perform its promotional role in stimulating a viable yet diffused process of industrialization in the backward parts of the country. As the IDBI report for 1971–2 puts it:

> The IDBI has been keenly aware of the limitations of financial and fiscal incentives in promoting industrial development in backward areas. It has been recognized that it would be essential to undertake considerable amount of project work for the purpose. This work comprises identification of project ideas, preparation of preliminary feasibility studies, search for managerial and entrepreneurial talents, preparation of detailed project reports, managerial technical and financial assistance for project implementation, critical evaluation of projects from the national point of view and finally project supervision.[36]

The IDBI has, since 1970, initiated action in this field by coordinating the functioning of the financial system and by linking this with such TCSCs as are established at its initiative (so far nine have been established). Given dynamic and imaginative leadership, these initiatives are pregnant with great possibilities. The IDBI has got out of the rut of the banking models borrowed from the rich countries.[37]

The IDBI's role in creative adaptation of modern technology can also be illustrated by a concrete case—the case of the Swaraj tractor which is presented in the next chapter. It appears from *a priori* reasoning as well as from this case study that the critical links in the process of creative adaptation of modern technology are the TCSC and the FS; these two provide the *essential links* between the PS on the one hand, and the TRC and modern technology on the other. Without these two functional agencies, the production system and the technological research system are likely to evolve on parallel lines—as it seems to have happened in a number of countries with TRCs.[38]

The vital significance of these links is again borne out by the Korean experience. Korea is one of the few countries which emphasized the relevance of a technology policy.[39] It started in 1966 with a TRC—Korea Institute of Science and Technology (KIST)—which in some respects also performed the role of a TCSC. However, its major emphasis has been on technological research. This resulted in valuable research results. But, KIST *vis-à-vis* its research function had not established the relevant links with the TCSC or the FS. Its research effort, hence, lacked operational relevance.[40] This situation was rectified by the establishment in 1974 of a TCSC—Korea Technology Advancement Corporation (KTAC); KTAC also established links with the FS—Korea Development Finance Corporation (DKFC) and Korea Credit Guarantee Fund (KCGF). As a result, about ten out of the forty research results from KIST have been actually embodied in concrete projects, some of which have been implemented by KTAC itself.[41]

The tasks which the banks in western Europe performed during the nineteenth century and the tasks which the Swedish development banks seem to be performing, and which the IDBI seeks to perform, are the vital tasks of improving the technological base of the economy in the light of the relevant development strategy. These are the tasks which the international banks like the IBRD and regional banks like the Asian Development Bank should perform at the international and regional levels respectively, if their commitment to economic development in the poor countries is a genuine one. The problems relating to the inadequate number of sound projects and the related problem of adapting, modifying and improving modern as well as traditional technology for upgrading the technological base of both modern and traditional sectors so as to eliminate poverty require for their solution the creation of relevant TCSCs and TRCs at national, regional and international levels. The refinement of appraisal procedures and criteria, with shadow prices and weights for all conceivable types of benefits, *without* concentrating on the problems of project design and technology and development strategy, is not only no substitute for these basic tasks but may create a deceptive feeling in the poor countries, as well as in international agencies, that something is being done to eliminate poverty, while in actual fact it would misdirect scarce resources into irrelevant and potentially inefficient fields.

V. Some Case Studies in Technology Choice

The primary of the design-engineering function and the significance of the organic functional sequence discussed in this chapter can be illustrated with some concrete cases. Swaraj tractor case, presented with vivid detail in the next chapter, exemplifies the soundness of this sequence; it also shows how lack of clarity with regard to the technology choice problem led the central government policy-makers (including the *apex* research institution) to distrust indigenous technology effort. The Baby-Food project as well as the Protein Isolate project illustrates again the soundness of the sequence. The Bokaro steel case suggests the implications of the neglect of the crucial function of design and engineering in technology policy as also the power struggle among the élite and its inferiority complex *vis-à-vis* foreign technology.

The other three cases—Bio-gas project, Bharatiya Agro Industries Foundation (BIAF) and the Bamboo Tube Well—illustrate the Gandhian approach; the first two projects were initiated by Gandhian institutions, that have been kept alive and supported by the government partly out of respect for him and partly because of the compulsions of the actual situation. In spite of the large *potential* impact on poverty and employment of these two projects, it is surprising to find that the Fifth Plan hardly mentions them, let alone deriving any lessons with regard to technology policy for the traditional sector. The third shows the significance of Gandhi's strategy of basic education and at the same time the typical attitude of the educated urban élite in the government.

1. Baby-Food Project[42]

Here the obvious project idea was to manufacture baby foods from buffalo milk. The technology available was that of manufacturing baby foods from cow's milk. The multinational companies operated modern technology based on imported materials. A research problem was thus identified in that of reducing the curd tension in buffalo milk to eliminate the digestive difficulties in babies. A national research laboratory worked on this problem and (*a*) discovered a process of curd-reduction, (*b*) found suitable ways of modifying the process technology, and (*c*) suggested certain changes in the existing plant and machinery and operating conditions. This has resulted in a baby food project run by a large cooperative, which has been innovative also in designing effective milk collection centres that have ensured the control of quality at each stage. With the design and research skills built up, improvement and modification of the process continues.

2. Protein Isolate Project[43]

To eliminate protein deficiency, particularly in a vegetarian diet, it was essential to produce vegetable protein-based products from domestic materials. The multinational companies were not attracted by this project idea. A research problem was thus identified and the Central Food Technological Research Institute in India started work on this problem. It developed plant protein foods for human consumption, designed the project and the Indian firm is now manufacturing these products.

3. Bokaro Steel Plant[44]

For reasons of resource endowment and demand pattern, steel production in India was an obvious choice. The Bokaro steel plant was to be the fourth integrated steel plant in the public sector and the sixth in India as a whole. The idea originated in 1955, only a little later than those relating to the first three public-sector steel plants built on a turn-key basis with German, Russian and British assistance respectively.

The Bokaro steel plant, however, was to be built on the basis of Indian design, engineering and construction skills. For the purpose, a deliberate attempt was made to develop Indian design-engineering skills. Dr. Dastur, an Indian by birth and an American citizen, was persuaded by the then Finance Minister, T. T. Krishnamachari, to set up a consulting firm in India in 1954. Thus was set up the steel-consultancy firm, M. N. Dastur & Co. (Dasturco), which was soon to establish an international reputation. This firm was assigned the consulting role for Bokaro at the insistence of the Prime Minister, Jawaharlal Nehru, in 1957.

TABLE 1

	Dasturco	U.S. Steel Corporation
Capacity	1.5 m tons	1.4 m tons
Project cost	$751.47 m	$919.428 m
Foreign exchange cost	$318.48 m	$512.588 m
Date of completion	1969	1971
Foreign experts	30–40	670

The decision to build Bokaro on the basis of Indian design and engineering skills was taken very rationally in the light of past experience with turn-key projects. There were definite advantages in having structural items designed by Indian consultants, who were aware of Indian fabricating needs and limitations. The heavy design features of steel plant equipment, though technically sound, are not necessarily appropriate or economical for Indian conditions, as they have been based in most cases on the codes and practices evolved for specific conditions prevailing in foreign countries. The heavy equipment design, in turn, necessitates heavier structures, foundations, material-handling facilities, etc., which again add to the steel plant costs. There was thus a specific need for an Indian initiative in the development of design norms for its own steel plants.[45]

Dasturco finalized their preliminary report by 1959, which was thoroughly scrutinized by the Technical Committee of Hindustan Steel Ltd. and commended by the Russian and American steel experts who had seen it. In 1962, Dasturco were commissioned to prepare the detailed project report, while at the same time the U.S. Steel Corporation was asked by the U.S. Agency for International Development to make a feasibility study. Both reports were submitted in 1963.

It is interesting to compare the cost and other estimates of the two reports (see Table 1).

In spite of the greater input of capital, foreign skill and foreign exchange in the U.S. Steel Corporation version of the project, its technology was to be inferior; it was of the semi-continuous casting variety, instead of the more advanced and efficient method of continuous casting of flat steel items recommended by Dasturco. Again, the provision of consulting, management and designing fees by the U.S. Steel Corporation was $109.4 million or as much as 15 per cent of the total plant cost estimate.

Since the U.S. negotiations broke off, Dasturco was appointed as consulting engineers for the Bokaro project from April 1974. Meanwhile, the Russians showed willingness to finance Bokaro on a turn-key basis, and submitted their project report in December 1965. Dasturco was kept out of the basic part of the project, but was asked to comment on the Russian report—*within seven weeks*.

Dasturco found that the cost of the project, as estimated by the Russians, could be reduced by Rs. 1,075 million and that the technology could be considerably improved. Dasturco argued for installing large-sized converters for the steel-melting shop on grounds of compelling advantages of economies of scale; this itself would have meant a cost-saving of Rs. 187.2 million. Further, the Soviet technology was found to be obsolete; it did not adopt the continuous casting method, which eliminates the need for a slabbing mill. Again, Dasturco found the provision for the services of foreign consultants and specialists (450 to 500 Soviet experts) to be excessive. They argued that the bulk of the work for which such large amounts were to be paid (including foreign exchange) was essentially local work and could be competently undertaken by the Indian side, which has greater familiarity with Indian conditions and practices, and at a relatively low cost. The Russians accepted a reduction of only Rs. 95 million, as against the total cost reduction suggested by Dasturco of Rs. 1,075 million, from the total estimated project cost of Rs. 7,700 million for four million tons capacity. Again the

Russians stuck to the obsolete technology, even though they recognized the superiority of the technology suggested by Dasturco. The government of India, however, accepted the Russian turn-key project. This is all the more amazing in the light of the fact that the Indians started with a clear vision and had the requisite design and engineering skills—skills which could have reduced the cost of the project, improved upon it and thus set the stage for initiating a process of technological self-reliance in a basic field like steel.

The Indian decision cannot be understood simply in terms of Russian aid. The foreign exchange cost would not have been more than $64 million per year, even with an assumed gestation lag of seven years. This alone would not have been a sufficiently compelling reason for not utilizing the services of Dasturco, for whose extensive services a six-year contract had already been signed. A more plausible reason would seem to have been anxiety on the part of the Ministry of Steel lest Dasturco's increasing influence should have detracted from its own status in the power hierarchy. This power struggle was clothed in arguments of an ideological character—developing public-sector consultancy skills and the like—and the ostensible argument used was the foreign exchange assistance to be obtained from the Russians on Russian terms. Why then did the government of India not function in the country's interests, and why did it succumb to the penny-wise-pound-foolish logic of the Ministry of Steel? Again, why did it not bargain hard with the Russians and emphasize the overriding need to build a steel plant based primarily on Indian design, engineering and construction skills—the concept upon which the Bokaro project idea had been formulated by Prime Minister Jawaharlal Nehru and the purpose for which Dr. Dastur had been encouraged to start a consultancy service in India? Again, the answer, under the circumstances, can only be a lack of clarity with regard to development strategy and the objectives and a sense of inferiority, making for an imitative psychology among the members of the power élite.[46]

4. Bio-gas Project[47]

This case relates to bio-gas projects. (Since cow-dung—gobar—is used as the fermentable material, these projects are called in India gobar-gas projects.) The project idea is to use waste material as fuel in the production of energy as well as fertilizers on each viable small-scale farm. This idea generated research and a classic paper on the fermentation of cellulosic waste was published in 1923 from the Indian Institute of Science, Bangalore. The purpose of this paper was to contribute to the energy problem in India. This was followed by design-engineering work, and designs of various types of small bio-gas plants were accomplished in India. Indian work on the subject was in the forefront until 1952, after which the imitative élite neglected this work in favour of rural electrification on conventional lines and fertilizer production in large naphtha-based plants.

It is a sad commentary on the Indian power élite and its norms and standards; for gobar-gas plants can produce both fertilizers and energy cheaper than the conventional modern technology-based projects, as Table 2 indicates.

TABLE 2. *Implications of production of 230,000 tonnes nitrogen*

	Large-scale coal-based fertilizer plant	Bio-gas fertilizer plant
1. Number of units	1	26,160
2. Capital cost	1,200	1,070
3. Foreign exchange cost	500	Nil
4. Employment	1,000	130,750
5. Energy	About 35 MW consumption	6,350,000 MWh generation

In spite of these obvious advantages, this indigenous technology was neglected until 1970. However, interest in this work was kept alive by the authentic (but powerless) élite groups like the Khadi and Village Industries Commission, the Indian Agricultural Research Institute, and the Gobar-Gas Research Station. As a result, currently twenty different sizes and capacities of gobar-gas plants have been designed and 8000 such plants are in operation. With the oil crisis, this technology has now been recognized and it is planned to build 50,000 such plants in the next few years—an effort which is still much smaller than that which is applied to modern fertilizer plants. At any rate, the design-engineering skills already available have identified several areas for research that can potentially reduce costs still further and link gobar-gas plants organically to agricultural development based on small farms.

5. *Bharatiya Agro Industries Foundation (BAIF)*[48]

India has a large cattle population and dairy as cottage industry is allied to agriculture in relatively fertile areas and is the main means of livelihood in relatively arid states like Rajasthan. Improving the milk-yield of the cattle, thus, has been an urgent problem. The main emphasis till recently was on better feeding and management; however, its cost far exceeded the resulting improvement in milk-yield. It was at this stage that Mr. Manibhai Desai—one of Gandhi's followers—started his experiments with cross-breeding by artificial insemination. He started with the Saurashtrian *Gir* breed of cows and, encouraged by his success, introduced tested exotic cattle for cross-breeding with artificial insemination by frozen semen (now produced locally) with good results.

His Uruli Kanchan (Maharashtra state) foundation—the BAIF—is managing about 500 centres with a capacity to handle 100,000 breedable cows. As a result of the success of the Uruli Kanchan experiment, several dairy breeding centres have been set up in different parts of the country. From available data, it appears that the output capital ratio works out to 1 : 1 and the internal rate of return per year per cow at more than 20 per cent.

6. *The Bamboo-Tube Well*[49]

This is a fascinating story of indigenous technology development by a reasonably educated middle-sized farmer in the Bihar state. As with all farms in this area, irrigation was a problem. And for the new high-yielding varieties of seeds, irrigation was essential. So Mr. Ram Prasad thought of tube-well irrigation and borrowed money for the purpose in July 1968. His failure to obtain iron pipe gave him the idea of using bamboo in place of iron. And thus began his experiment of constructing a bamboo-tube well. He succeeded in this experiment and within less than a month, his bamboo-tube well started functioning. Within the next six months, some farmers took to this technology and by March 1973, more than 33,000 bamboo-tube wells were sunk in ten districts of Bihar.

The cost of such a tube well is only 10 per cent of the cost of sinking an iron-tube well to the same depth.

Of course, Mr. Ram Prasad received a letter of congratulation from the State Ministry for Agriculture in recognition of the worth of his invention. However, the technology policy of the government has taken no note of this indigenous technology; the science and technology élite has not given attention to this as it has not to several such projects. It is surprising that even the economists have not studied such projects.

Traditional industries like hand-loom, gur and rural transport provide the largest employment next to agriculture. It is surprising to find that these industries and their technical structure are not even carefully analysed; obviously, no attention is paid to upgrading their organizational and technical base. The educated élite has not only an urban bias; it has a Western bias; it is mistaking Westernization as modernization. Modernization, as Gandhi and Nehru understood it, implies the use of creative intelligence—not merely intellect—to identify and solve the problems as they emerge. This implies *understanding* the tradition to change it radically from within.

NOTES

1. See J. A. Schumpeter, *Capitalism, Socialism and Democracy,* 3rd ed. (Harper & Row, 1950).
2. See R. V. Clemence (ed.), *Essays of J. A. Schumpeter* (Cambridge, Massachusetts: Addison-Wesley Press, 1951), pp. 216–27.
3. See S. Kuznets, "Modern Economic Growth: Findings and Reflections", *American Economic Review,* vol. 63, no. 3 (June 1973). Kuznets writes (p. 247): "A country's economic growth may be defined as a long-term rise in capacity to supply increasingly diverse economic goods to its population, this growing capacity based on advancing technology and the institutional and ideological elements that it demands. All three components of the definition are important."
4. See A. Gerschenkron, *Economic Backwardness in Historical Perspective* (Cambridge, Massachusetts: Harvard University Press, 1962). Gerschenkron concludes (p. 26): "What makes it so difficult for an advanced country to appraise properly the industrialization policies of its less fortunate brethren is the fact that, in every instance of industrialization, imitation of the evolution in advanced countries appears in combination with different, indigenously determined elements. . . . This is particularly true of the institutional instruments used in carrying out industrial developments and even more so of ideologies which accompany it. What can be derived from a historical review is a strong sense for the significance of the native elements in the industrialization of backward countries."
5. See *Essays of J. A. Schumpeter, op. cit.,* pp. 158–63.
6. See K. J. Arrow, "Limited Knowledge and Economics Analysis", *American Economic Review,* vol. 64, no. 1 (Mar. 1974). See also V. V. Bhatt, "The Sterility of Equilibrium Economics: An Aspect of the Sociology of Science", in A. Mitra (ed.), *Economic Theory and Planning* (Calcutta: Oxford University Press, 1974).
7. See A. Rudra, "Usefulness of Plan Models: an Assessment Based on Indian Experience", in *Economic Theory and Planning, loc. cit.*
8. See B. F. Johnston and P. Kilby, *Agricultural Strategies, Rural–Urban Interactions and the Expansion of*

Income Opportunities (Paris: Development Centre of the Organization for Economic Cooperation and Development, Jan. 1973), chapters i, ii and iii.
9. J. Kornai, *Anti-Equilibrium* (Amsterdam and London: North-Holland, 1971). See also J. Kornai, *Rush versus Harmonic Growth* (Amsterdam and London: North-Holland, 1972). Kornai writes (p. 59): "The substance of development gets lost in a theory which wishes to deem 'optimal' the constancy of structures, the equal rate of growth of all sectors, the invariability over time of input–output combinations. . . . The situation is, however, different with a dynamic model, which intends to describe the path of growth over time. If such a model, by its assumptions, neglects in principle the changes in input structures (e.g., the restratification of the input coefficients of the household sectors, etc.), it has not applied a 'simplification' neglecting secondary interrelations, but has thrown the primary problem itself out of the window." See further, N. Kaldor, "The Irrelevance of Equilibrium Economics", *The Economic Journal,* vol. 82, no. 328 (Dec. 1972).
10. J. Krishnamurti, *The Awakening of Intelligence* (New York: Harper & Row, 1973). To quote (*passim,* pp. 520–35): "May we say, thought is barren? . . . which is mechanical and all the rest of it? Thought is a pointer, but without intelligence the pointer has no value . . . so intelligence is necessary. Without it thought has no meaning at all. . . . As we begin to inquire into it, or in inquiring, we come to this source. Is it a perception, an insight, and has that insight nothing whatsoever to do with thought? Is insight the result of thought? The conclusion of an insight is thought, but insight itself is not thought . . . ; you come upon it when you see the whole thing. So insight is the perception of the whole . . . the quality of mind that sees the whole is not touched by thought; therefore there is perception, there is insight."
11. A. Gerschenkron, *op. cit.,* p. 8.
12. *Ibid.,* p. 9.
13. D. Felix, "Technological Dualism in Late Industrializers: On Theory, History, and Policy", *Journal of Economic History,* vol. xxxiv, no. 1 (Mar. 1974).
14. E. S. Ferguson, "The Steam Engine Before 1830", in M. Krauzberg and C. W. Pursell (eds.), *Technology in Western Civilization* (New York: Oxford University Press, 1967), vol. i, p. 299.
15. M. Wilkins, "The Role of Private Business in the International Diffusion of Technology", *Journal of Economic History,* vol. xxxiv, no. 1 (Mar. 1974).
16. *Ibid.*
17. D. Felix, *op. cit.*
18. See N. Rosenberg, "Economic Development and the Transfer of Technology: Some Historical Perspectives", *Technology and Culture,* vol. xi (July 1970), and W. Woodruff, *The Impact of Western Man* (New York: St. Martin's Press, 1967), chapter 5.
19. D. Felix, *op. cit.*
20. *Ibid.*
21. *Ibid.*
22. See J. Krishnamurti, *op. cit.*
23. P. Streeten, "Technology Gaps Between Rich and Poor Countries", *Scottish Journal of Political Economy,* vol. xix, no. 3 (Nov. 1972).
24. See P. F. Drucker, *Management: Tasks Responsibilities Practices* (New York: Harper & Row, 1973), chapter 38 on "Managerial Communication".
25. See C. Cooper, "Science Policy and Technological Change in Underdeveloped Economies", *World Development,* vol. 2, no. 3 (Mar. 1974).
26. See J. Perrin, "Setting Up 'Engineering' Firms in the Industrializing Countries as Agents for Transferring Know-how", in *Choice and Adaptation of Technology in Developing Countries* (Paris: Development Center of the Organisation for Economic Co-operation and Development, 1974); J. Roberts, "Engineering Consultancy, Industrialization and Development", *Journal of Development Studies,* vol. 9, no. 1 (Oct. 1972); V. V. Bhatt, "Some Aspects of Development Strategy", *Indian Economic Journal,* vol. xiv, no. 8 (Apr.–June 1967).
27. G. B. Gresford and B. H. Chatel, "Science and Technology in the United Nations", *World Development,* vol. 2, no. 1 (Jan. 1974).
28. I. M. D. Little and J. A. Mirrlees, *Manual of Industrial Project Analysis in Developing Countries* (Paris: Development Center of the Organisation for Economic Co-operation and Development, 1968), pp. 64–6.

29. V. V. Bhatt, "Capital Intensity of Industries", *Bulletin of the Oxford University*, vol. 18, no. 2 (1956), pp. 179–94.
30. *Choice and Adaptation of Technology in Developing Countries* (Paris: Development Center of the Organisation for Economic Co-operation and Development, 1974), p. 81.
31. World Bank, *Development Finance Companies* (Washington: Apr. 1976). To quote: "One tendency has been to take a rather conservative view of their role. Such a view has led the DFCs to give more support to the stronger enterprises. . . . Consequently, in its dealings with each DFC, the Bank should encourage the DFC to efforts that would increasingly make it a *catalyst for development*" (p. 8) [*italics added*].
32. World Bank, *Employment and Development of Small Enterprises* (Washington, Feb. 1978). To quote: "A satisfactory arrangement, in the World Bank's limited experience, is a technical assistance agency outside, but closely linked with, the financial intermediary for SSEs; the financial institution would thus act as a sponsor of technical assistance to its clients (actual or prospective) and of its clients to the technical assistance agency. The entity that provides or controls financing seems often to have the most leverage (or catalytic influence) on the other two parties" (p. 40).
33. A. Gerschenkron, *Economic Backwardness in Historical Perspective* (Cambridge, Mass.: Harvard University Press, 1962), p. 12.
34. A. Gerschenkron, *Continuity in History and Other Essays* (Cambridge, Mass.: Harvard University Press, 1968), p. 137. Quite often the problem of creatively adapting the tax and financial technology is not even identified. The Universal Bank in Germany was a creative adaptation of banking technology. To quote Gerschenkron: "In particular, the story of the Credit Mobilier of the brothers Pereire is often regarded as a dramatic but, on the whole, rather insignificant episode. . . . It seems to be much better in accord with the facts to speak of a truly momentous role of investment banking of the period for the economic history of France and of large portions of the Continent. . . . But more important than their slavish imitations was the creative adaptation of the basic idea of the Pereires and its incorporation in the new type of bank, the Universal Bank which, in Germany, along with most other countries on the Continent, became the dominant form of banking. The difference between banks of the credit mobilier type and commercial banks in the advanced industrial country of the time (England) was absolute. Between the English bank essentially designed to serve as a source of short-run capital and a bank designed to finance the long-run investment needs of the economy, there was a complete gulf. The German banks, which may be taken as a paragon of the type of the Universal Bank, successfully combined the basic idea of the credit mobilier with the short-term activities of commercial banks . . . the banks acquired a formidable degree of ascendancy over industrial enterprises, which extended far beyond the sphere of financial control into that of entrepreneurial and managerial decisions", pp. 12–14, in *Economic Backwardness in Historical Perspective, loc. cit.*

    On the role of financial innovations, see V. V. Bhatt, *Interest Rate, Transactions Costs and Financial Innovations* (World Bank: Development Economics Department: Domestic Finance Studies, no. 47, Jan. 1978). Development Banks (or DFCs as they are called) need to adapt creatively the modern technology in Finance if they are to function as catalysts of development—like their counterparts in Europe during the nineteenth century.
35. P. F. Drucker, *The Age of Discontinuity* (London: Pan Books, 1971), p. 71.
36. *Annual Report of the Industrial Development Bank of India, 1971–2* (Bombay, Aug. 1972).
37. V. V. Bhatt, "Industrial Development Bank of India: A Decade of Performance", *Commerce*, Annual Number (Jan. 1975); also in *World Bank Reprint Series*, no. 18.
38. See Baranson and Cooper, *op. cit.* To quote Baranson on the experience in Brazil, Mexico, Colombia and Venezuela: "These programs are generally associated with Latin American Universities and government-sponsored research institutes. . . . These programs have met with varying degrees of success, but their scope has traditionally been limited to topics and areas of scientific investigation and exploratory research. Rarely have the programs concentrated on designing and engineering technologies with immediate and direct application to problems in industrialization" (p. 14).
39. Hyung-Sup Choi, "Adapting Technology—The Korean Case", in *Views of Science, Technology and Development*, edited by E. Rabinowitch and V. V. Rabinowitch (Oxford: Pergamon Press, 1975).

40. Ka-Jong Lee, *Technology Transfer and Developmental Strategies: The Role of Large Firms in Korea* (Ph.D. Thesis, University of Hawaii, Aug. 1977), pp. 53–4.
41. K-TAC, *K-TAC's Role in Commercialisation of New Technology in Korea* (Seoul, 1978).
42. *Source:* H. A. B. Parpia, "Transfer and Adaptation of Western Methods in Agricultural Processing", *World Development,* vol. 2, no. 2 (Feb. 1974).
43. *Ibid.*
44. For details about this project, see P. Desai, *The Bokaro Steel Plant* (Amsterdam and London: North Holland, 1972).
45. See M. N. Dastur, "New Strategy for India's Steel Development", *Economic and Political Weekly,* vol. vii, nos. 31–3, Special Number (1972).
46. Nehru himself was quite conscious of the nature of this imitative psychology of the élite. To quote: "It is not only the Communist Party in India that has failed in this respect. There are others who talk glibly of modernism and modern spirit and the essence of Western culture, and are at the same time ignorant of their own culture. Unlike the Communists, they have no ideal that moves them and no driving force that carries them forward. They take the external forms and outer trappings of the West (and often some of the less desirable features), and imagine that they are in the vanguard of an advancing civilization. Naïve and shallow and yet full of their own conceits, they live, chiefly in a few large cities, an artificial life which has no living contacts with the culture of the East or of the West." See J. Nehru, *The Discovery of India* (Bombay: Asia Publishing House, 1969), p. 517. See also, S. N. Ganguly, *Tradition, Modernity and Development* (New Delhi: The Macmillan Company of India, 1977).
47. For details about the economies and engineering of gobar-gas plants, see (1) C. R. Prasad, K. Krishna Prasad and A. K. V. Reddy, "Bio-Gas Plants: Prospects, Problems and Tasks", *Economic and Political Weekly,* vol. ix, nos. 32–4, Special Number, 1974, and (2) A. K. N. Reddy and K. Krishna Prasad, "Technological Alternatives and the Indian Energy Crisis", *Economic and Political Weekly,* vol. xii, nos. 33 and 34, Special Number (1977).
48. For details, see V. L. Mehta, *Equality Through Trusteeship* (Bombay: Tata McGraw-Hill Publishing Co. Ltd., 1977), chapter viii.
49. For details, see A. J. Dommen, "The Bamboo Tube Well: A Note on an Example of Indigenous Technology", *Economic Development and Cultural Change,* vol. xxiii, no. 3 (Apr. 1975), pp. 483–9.

8. Decision-Making in the Public Sector: A Case Study of Swaraj Tractor*

THE CHARACTERISTIC feature of the development process—both in the developed and developing countries—since World War II is the deliberate assumption by the State of the function of regulating the pace and pattern of socio-economic development.[1] In a large number of the LDCs (less developed countries), the State, in addition, is playing an active role, out of a variety of motives and reasons, in promoting and managing enterprises in the manufacturing sector. The functioning and growth of these enterprises critically depend on the decision-making process in the public sector. It is, therefore, essential to understand this process.

Without a clear insight and understanding of the problem of public sector decision-making, it is hardly possible to suggest any solution or solutions. This process is complex even in the private sector and is inevitably much more complex in the public sector as it is an integral part of the process of socio-economic evolution.[2] However, the decision-making process is somehow not a crucial element in the analytical constructs and techniques developed by the economists—as well as management experts. The static equilibrium theory or the steady-state growth models (which are a relapse into statics,[3] to use Hicks's expressive phrase), or the empirical (even econometric) studies based on the method of comparative statics (the characteristics of different countries at different stages of development); these analytic tools are congenitally incapable of handling the decision-making process and thus inadequate for understanding the vital aspects of the development problem. In economics and management science, the available tools and techniques determine the nature of the problem selected for study; the urgent real life problems require much more thinking and understanding of historical processes of change and are not generally the concern of the economists.[4]

As a result, the suggested solutions for the problems of public sector decision-making are as simple as they are naïve—the government and public enterprises should select an objective function—if there are multiple objectives, they should assign appropriate weights to them: they should have a clear idea of the constraints and choice possibilities: given the objective function, constraints and choice possibilities, they should try to maximize and optimize the objective function. And if they do not do so, their behaviour obviously must be irrational.[5] Indeed very powerful logic but applied to a problem which we do not understand.

And so it is essential to understand the problem—the problem of the agenda of organizations as Arrow[6] puts it. It is not possible to have an in-depth under-

* Published in *Economic and Political Weekly,* vol. xiii, no. 21 (27 May 1978).

standing of the problem on the basis of semi-aggregative data—however amenable they may be to sophisticated econometric techniques. To understand the nuances and facets of decision-making at several levels (institutional and hierarchical), one has to observe the dyamics of an *actual* process. It is for these reasons that one should concentrate initially at any rate on such a case study that could provide an insight into and an understanding of the complexity and multiple dimensions of the problem.

Hence we have deliberately selected this case study of the Swaraj tractor for understanding the problem of decision-making in public manufacturing enterprises in India. This enterprise is modest in its financial and economic dimensions but it has much greater significance from our point of view than any other big enterprise in India; for it illuminates the multiple facets of the problem and makes it possible for us even to draw some general inferences (conjectures) about the behaviour of public enterprises in LDCs.

It would not have been possible to undertake this study but for the assistance of the Industrial Development Bank of India (IDBI). It made available to us several documents—the detailed project report prepared by the technical consultants (Messrs. Suri & Associates), the IDBI project appraisal reports submitted to the *Ad hoc* Committee of Advisers (ASA) as well as its own board of directors and its project supervision reports. In addition, the Punjab Tractors Ltd. (PTL)—firm operating the Swaraj tractor project—made available to us, through the government of India, its progress reports and accounts.[7] Where no references are given, the source of information is IDBI or PTL.

The plan of the chapter is as follows: the introductory section provides some information about the characteristics of the tractor industry in general as well as in India. The narrative on the Swaraj tractor is presented in all its richness in section II. In sections III and IV some problems about the decision process are raised and some conjectures made about public sector behaviour. In the final section, an attempt is made to formulate some explanatory hypotheses about the public sector decision-making process—hypotheses that may have general relevance for the LDCs with mixed economies.

I. Introduction

Before we present the Swaraj tractor case, it is essential to give some background with regard to the tractor industry. In North America, tractors replaced draught animals (usually horses) since 1900 and this substitution process was completed before World War II. In Europe, this substitution occurred during the first decade after the war as small versatile tractors and government support for tractor purchase became widely available.[8]

Most of the technical development of the tractor had taken place by World War II and much of it occurred in the U.S.A. However, the truly revolutionary development of the pre-war period, the "Ferguson System", came not from the U.S.A. but from the U.K. and was introduced in the U.S.A. in 1939. By this time tractor technology was more or less stabilized and there has not been any significant change in this technology. There have been minor additions to the tractor design, like power-steering and automatic transmission. Thus there have been few important patents in the tractor industry since 1939.[9] By comparison with an automobile, a tractor is a simple machine. While a car typically has 15,000 parts, a farm tractor has a mere 2000; of these 1365 are seldom or never actually manufactured by tractor manufacturers.[10] These characteristics of tractor technology and manufacture are worth noting; for they indicate that it should not be difficult for newcomers like LDCs to absorb and master this technology. This point is relevant for the Swaraj tractor case.

There is another characteristic of the tractor industry that is also relevant to note. In the tractor industry there are economies of scale both in production as well as distribution. It has been estimated for the U.S.A. that approximately the same economies of scale, around 20 per cent, would attach to distribution expansion from 20,000 to 90,000 units as would accrue to a production expansion.[11] This is part of the reason why the industry in the non-communist countries is dominated by a few firms, resulting in oligopolistic competition as well as collusion.[12]

In a durable good like a tractor, the farmer essentially buys tractor services and hence is concerned in his purchase decision about after-sales service and parts availability. Farmers' loyalties or preference thus are dealer orientated and sales of tractors thus crucially depend on the quality of distribution and service. As seems to have happened in the U.S.A., this dealership network can reduce competition and work against the interests of the farmers; for farmers generally all over the world have no adequate information to judge the quality of a tractor excepting through the marketing structure. This characteristic of the tractor market suggests the need for public policy in the interests of the farmers—the group in a weak bargaining position *vis-à-vis* the production-distribution system.[13]

This background is essential to understand the Swaraj tractor case in India. Tractor production and imports are controlled and regulated by the government as are all industrial investment and imports. Public sector decision-making, thus, plays a crucial part with regard to the nature and characteristics of industrial evolution. One would expect, therefore, the decision-making organs to be aware of the characteristics of the tractor technology and industry, mentioned earlier.

Farm mechanization in India started only after the war. In 1946–7 there were about 5000 tractors; the number rose sharply to 20,000 in 1956–7 and by 1964–5, where our story begins, there were about 40,000. This was the year when the new agricultural strategy—the so-called green revolution—was formulated. The domestic production of tractors started in 1963–4 with a licensed installed capacity on a two shift basis of 8500 units by two firms—Tractor and Farm Equipment (TAFE) and Eicher Tractors India Ltd. (Eicher), the former with a capacity of 7000 units and the latter with a capacity of 1500 units. TAFE was permitted foreign collaboration with Massey-Ferguson, U.K. in 1961 and Eicher with Eicher of the Federal Republic of Germany in 1961.

As against this domestic capacity, it was estimated that the demand for tractors would increase substantially as a result of the adoption of new agricultural strategy in Punjab, Haryana and western U.P.—the parts of India growing wheat on irrigated land. With large increases in land productivity, farmers were facing a farm power shortage during the peak season; further, and even more important, cost of animal power was rising sharply. The adoption of high-yielding varieties of wheat improved the productivity of land, especially irrigated land. This in turn raised the opportunity cost of using draught animals, as fodder competed for the highly productive irrigated land. Mechanization—task-wise—thus was expected to be an inevitable complement of the green revolution.[14]

However, in view of relatively small holdings—68 per cent of holdings in Punjab were below 9 hectares, accounting for about 20 per cent of the stock of tractors in 1971—the problem which the Planning Commission faced was: what type of tractors would suit the budget and the needs of small–medium farmers.[15]

II. Swaraj Tractor: Decision-Making Process

The story begins in 1965. A new team of members was appointed at the Planning Commission and it was busy formulating the Fourth Five Year Plan. As a part of the Plan, several new projects required assistance—both financial and technical—from Russia. One of them was a 20-h.p. tractor project. The Planning Commission had estimated the demand for tractors to be 40,000 units per year by 1968–9, and of this, half the demand was expected to be for tractors in the hp range of 20 and below. The government of India's delegation, headed by the deputy chairman of the Planning Commission, visited Russia in May 1965 to discuss with the Russian government the nature and magnitude of assistance for this and the other projects. Mr. M. M. Suri, director of the Central Mechanical Engineering Research Institute (CMERI), was one of the members of this delegation.[16]

Origin and Development of Swaraj

The Russians were reluctant to commit themselves to the tractor project. Further, Mr. Suri felt that the project as formulated had excessive foreign exchange content and required a large number of Russian experts. Anyway, since the Russians were unable to assist this project, Mr. Suri suggested to the deputy chairman that CMERI could develop an indigenous tractor design that could be produced without external assistance or even imported parts. The CMERI thus started the work on the new tractor design under the direction of a Committee of Technical Experts (CTE); comprising representatives of the industry, agricultural universities, farmers and the Tractor Training and Testing Station (TTTS) of Budni.

A team of engineers under the direction of Mr. Suri studied in depth the relative merits of the available designs of agricultural tractors, keeping in view the local manufacturing facilities, skills, raw materials and agro-climatic conditions and developed a tractor component by component. Since the availability of standard hydraulics was considered as the key requirement for a good tractor, the CMERI engineers successfully developed an original single lever automatic depth-cum-control hydraulic system, patents for which were accepted in India, the U.K., Japan, West Germany, the U.S.A., France, Poland and Yugoslavia. The first prototype tractor was assembled in November 1967 and was put to extensive endurance tests in CMERI (on specially designed test rigs simulating field conditions), lasting over 1200 hours non-stop running with 10 per cent to 30 per cent overload during the hottest summer months. With the experience gained on this prototype, three more units were assembled in March 1969 for extensive field trials and performance evaluation at the TTTS, Punjab Agricultural University (Ludhiana) and the U.P. Agricultural University (Pant Nagar). As a result of these tests, a number of modifications were incorporated in the hydraulics, steering gear, front axle, engine and its cooling system and the modified tractor was again tested at TTTS in May/June 1971. These tests indicated that its performance was better than most of the imported tractors in the 20–5-h.p. range in regard to drawbar pull and ratio of the drawbar h.p. to the power available at the p.t.o.—which are of primary concern for cultivation. The tractor passed the TTTS test. Thus was born the Swaraj tractor—the product of local technological competence.

The design for Swaraj 20 h.p. was built around the four-stroke, twin cylinder, air-cooled Kirloskar engine, that was being produced in the country. Some of the salient features of the Swaraj were the following.

It has a 20-h.p. diesel engine of French design with a rated speed of 2000 rpm and a compression ratio of 16 : 1. It has a dual range four-speed transmission so as to cover a wide variety of jobs ranging from heavy duty to fast transport, and a provision for an independent p.t.o. which can be engaged or disengaged when the tractor is in motion and can be used as a prime mover for pumps and other similar equipment. Engine cooling is effected by an axial blower and fins provided on the engine cylinder block. Hydraulics with finger-tip control for both positions and draft control of three point linkage is provided for operating the implements. A foot-operated differential lock is provided to improve traction in slippery and muddy spots. It is also provided with adjustable front and rear axles, manual steering and vertical exhaust.

Lack of Sponsorship by Central Government

Thus by 1971, the Swaraj tractor was ripe for commercial production. But the question was: who would adopt this innovation? Earlier, the prototype was constructed with the assistance of a public sector concern, the Mining and Allied Machinery Corporation (MAMC), and it was expected that MAMC would be able to undertake the tractor project with the addition of only some balancing equipment. But in the period of industrial recession in the country (1967–71) the MAMC had incurred financial losses and was not willing to take any additional risk involved in the production of the tractor.

Because of industrial recession and decline in its sales of machine tools, the Hindustan Machine Tools (HMT)—another Central government concern—wanted to diversify its output by going into tractor production.[17] However, it wanted to use its unutilized capacity immediately by first going into assembly of Zeteor tractor parts imported from Czechoslovakia. Further, it thought that Zeteor was a proved production model, while Swaraj was only a prototype. In this decision, it was supported by the National Industrial Development Corporation (NIDC), a consultancy organization sponsored by the Central government.

Thus, at the Central government level, there was no strong support for the

Swaraj. The Planning Commission members were changed by 1969 and the new ones had no particular interest in domestic technological competence. Mr. Suri had left CMERI by 1969. The NIDC and the Council of Scientific and Industrial Research (CSIR) considered Swaraj a risky venture.

State Government Unit Becomes a Promoter

It was at this stage that a state government unit decided to produce the Swaraj tractor. The Punjab State Industrial Development Corporation (PSIDC) was set up in 1966 with the object of promoting medium- and large-scale industries in the state. It had already implemented successfully six industrial projects by 1970: Punjab Prestressed Concrete Works Ltd., Punjab Chemi-plants Ltd., Punjab Footwear Ltd., Punjab Nylo-transmission Ltd., Punjab Saltpetre Refinery Ltd. and Punjab Tanneries Ltd.

The PSIDC had been familiar with the development of the Swaraj tractor; it had observed its field trials in the Punjab and the farmers' favourable response to the Swaraj. Three characteristics of the Swaraj attracted the PSIDC: its indigenous design, its employment potential in the Punjab and its acceptance by the Punjab farmers as a sound dependable tractor. The PSIDC hence obtained an industrial licence to manufacture the Swaraj tractors in 1970.

The PSIDC contacted the CMERI and requested the latter to release the five engineers who had worked on the Swaraj design for its new firm—the Punjab Tractors Ltd. (PTL). Simultaneously, it appointed the consulting firm—Messrs. Suri & Associates, organized by Mr. Suri after he left the CMERI—to prepare a detailed project report and undertake the entire installation and commissioning of the plant along with the company's engineers (the CMERI group). The detailed project report was completed by the middle of 1971. The next problem was: how to finance this project?

Industrial Development Bank of India

The PSIDC and the Punjab Tractors Ltd. approached the Industrial Development Bank of India (IDBI), owned by the central bank of the country—the Reserve Bank of India. The IDBI was set up in 1964 as an apex development bank to promote industrial development—particularly viable projects that cannot obtain financing from the other institutions. Its charter is broad and flexible; it can finance any sound project—irrespective of its ownership, organization and size.

At the time that it was approached by the PSIDC for financial assistance, its top management had changed. This new management had given an assurance to industry that the IDBI would be prepared to finance any sound project that met its selection criteria, irrespective of the assistance required. Its selection criteria related to the project's internal rate of return and exchange rate, the cut-off rates being 15 per cent and Rupees 9.5 to one U.S. dollar.[18] Further, it had taken up active promotional work with regard to the identification of project ideas in backward states, had a firm policy of supporting domestic technical consultancy services and research and had set up its own technical consultancy service—Kerala Industrial and Technical Consultancy Organization (KITCO)—in Kerala to prepare feasibility and detailed project reports and provide technical assistance to small and medium enterprises. The new IDBI management believed that for industrial development, it was essential to develop domestic technological competence in selected areas.[18]

Even with this new IDBI management, the PTL were not completely confident of obtaining financing to the tune of 85–90 per cent of the project cost. The lack of sponsorship by the Central government, and the scepticism about its success expressed by both the CSIR and the NIDC made the PTL somewhat diffident about getting the IDBI support. They, therefore, had suggested only a modest project (capacity output of 5000 tractors in 20–30 h.p. range) with a capital cost of less than Rs. 40 million. They were to buy the Ra-2 engine from another well-established Indian firm, purchase about 80 per cent of total component requirements from established and new firms—largely small-scale engineering firms from Punjab—and concentrate on manufacture of only 15–20 per cent of key components; it was thus that they were able to reduce the project cost to a fairly modest amount.[19]

But the PSIDC was able to contribute only less than 10 per cent of the cost, while the IDBI rule of thumb was that the promoters should finance the project at least to the tune of 15 per cent of the project cost through their own resources. The PSIDC, hence, was willing to take a private firm of civil engineering contractors as a co-promoter on condition that it would provide more than 5 per cent of the required resources. The firm was willing to do so if its representative was made the managing director.

IDBI Appraisal Process

The top management of the IDBI glanced through the detailed project report, prepared by the technical consultants, immediately after it was received in the IDBI. They were impressed by the quality of the report; the IDBI had not received such a high-quality project report from any one of the more than 150 projects that it had financed up to that time. They wanted to satisfy themselves about the commitment to the success of this innovative project by PSIDC, PTL and the technical consultants; for this was to their mind crucial to the success of any project and more particularly for this one. As a result of their discussion with them, they were convinced about the management capacity, technical competence and motivation of the three critical groups.

They were impressed by the following characteristics of this project:

(i) It was based on domestic technology, knowhow and consultancy services and the Swaraj tractor was specially designed to meet the local conditions, had passed the TTTS test and was approved by the farmers; of the existing six producers, the tractor design of only two firms had passed the TTTS test and all of them had obsolete models which were of pre-1965 design of their foreign collaborators and were not specially adapted to local conditions.

(ii) The three groups associated with the project were strongly motivated to make it a success. The PSIDC's reputation depended on farmers' acceptance of the product and the employment effect of the project in Punjab: the technical consultants—in particular Mr. Suri—and the top management team of the PTL had actually identified the problem of tractor design, specially designed the Swaraj tractor over a period of six years and wanted to prove to CSIR, NIDC and the Central government that their design was superior to all the other tractor models produced in India or imported from abroad.

(iii) It would support a large number of engineering ancillary industries in the Punjab—known for its entrepreneurial and mechanical talents—and thus have a large employment impact. In addition, the engine manufacturer was suffering from lack of demand as a result of industrial recession and would now be able to increase his output.

(iv) The project envisaged an efficient distribution and service system, which is crucial from the point of view of the farmers' response; no other existing firm had paid adequate attention to distribution and after-sales service.

(v) It had already started with the establishment of its own tool room to manufacture jigs, fixtures and inspection gauges; this tool room was also to be used for training its personnel, developmental work and research to improve technology and design other tractor models; no existing firm had research and development facilities and none of them had made any conscious effort to improve the design of their models to suit the local conditions.

(vi) About 10,000 tractors in the h.p. range of 20–5 were currently imported, while there was no domestic production of tractors in this range. The demand was expected to grow.

(vii) It was expected to produce and sell Swaraj at a competitive price and, as its capacity expanded, to 12,000 tractors after the initial pilot phase, it would be in a position even to export its tractors abroad.

However, they did not like the idea of a co-promoter; first because the co-promoter did not have particular experience with regard to tractor industry and secondly and crucially because they did not like the idea of the co-promoter's representative becoming a managing director. The success of the project depended on the CMERI assistant director becoming the managing director. They, therefore, assured the PTL that the IDBI would not insist on 15 per cent contribution by the promoters and arrange to finance 85–90 per cent of the project cost in collaboration with the other financial agencies *if* the project met the IDBI selection criteria.

The IDBI project appraisal team then prepared its report within two months. This report was submitted to an *Ad hoc* Committee of Advisers (ACA) for critical examination and, as was the IDBI's practice, invited the ACA to discuss their comments with the project promoters. Such confrontation and dialogue gave the IDBI an additional opportunity to test the managerial and technical competence of the project promoters.[20, 21]

IDBI Approves the Project for Financing

After this exchange, the project promoters left and the IDBI asked the ACA about its views on the project. The ACA approved the project; in their view, it was technically sound and would be able to produce and sell a good quality tractor at competitive prices. However, they felt that it may take longer than expected to complete the project and in any case, in view of its small size—there are economies of scale in the tractor industry—and government control on tractor prices, the project will not be able to have an internal rate of return of 15 per cent—one of the two IDBI selection criteria.

The IDBI then prepared a memorandum for its Board, recommending more than 85 per cent financial assistance (in collaboration with the other financial institutions) for the project: the memorandum argued that the exchange rate criterion was met—the domestic resource cost of saving one U.S. dollar was less than Rs. 9.5—and this showed that the project was efficient. Obviously, an innovative project of this small size would not be able to have an internal rate of return of 15 per cent or more; but this rate was not very much lower than the cut-off rate—it was 13 per cent. The Board approved the project and sanctioned the required financial assistance—partly by way of long-term loan and partly as equity—in February 1972. The technical research for designing this tractor had started only in late 1965 and was completed in May 1970; the PTL was formed in 1970, the project report was completed in September 1971 and was submitted to the IDBI for assistance in November 1971.

Performance of the PTL 1972–7

The construction work as well as the installation of plant and equipment started immediately after the IDBI sanction of financial assistance in March 1972. The performance of the PTL since 1972 has been remarkable with regard to both its cost and time schedules, as well as the manner in which it faced and tackled the problems as they arose:[22]

(i) The project was completed in 105 weeks by the end of March 1974 as was anticipated; the ACA had expressed scepticism about this time schedule.
(ii) The actual project cost was more or less the same as expected—in fact it was somewhat lower—with regard to not only the total cost but also the cost under each head.
(iii) The PTL started manufacturing Swaraj tractor (Swaraj–724) from 1 April 1974 and more or less reached its full capacity output in 1977 again as was anticipated, in spite of raw material shortages, and inflationary pressures and financial stringency.

For the IDBI, this performance was unique. There was hardly any project, financed by the IDBI, that had been completed in time without any cost overrun. Again, there was hardly any project that had reached its capacity output within the planned time frame.

Even the way in which the PTL identified its problems and tackled them reflected top management efficiency. During the first fifteen months (April 1974 to June 1975), as was expected, it suffered from irregular supplies from the ancillaries at rising costs—this was a period of acute inflationary pressures in India. The PTL suffered a cash loss of Rs. 7.8 million as a result.

The top management was aware that it would have to face this problem; the IDBI and the ACA had drawn pointed attention to this aspect of the project. But till November 1973, PTL had no inventories and its relationship with its ancillaries had still not been formalized. At this stage, the PTL could not afford more than one source of supply for each component; the initial production was inevitably limited by the available supplies of components and to develop new sources required intensive technical inputs from the PTL.

Since November 1973, the PTL concentrated on developing multiple sources of supply for each component. It promoted itself new ancillaries near the location of the Swaraj by providing technical assistance to new entrepreneurs. Thus its materials pipeline improved and it was able to increase its output to full capacity level before the end of 1977.

But its production costs rose steadily as input prices rose. Unlike the other manufacturers, its output had no import content; others imported their inputs to the extent of 20–30 per cent of requirements and the prices of imported inputs were significantly lower than those of the domestic inputs. For example, the HMT had started the production of Zeteor 20 by this time with an import content of more than 45 per cent. A Ministry of Finance study indicated that the cost of inputs was lower by about Rs. 4000 per tractor for the Zeteor as compared to that for the Swaraj. Even this figure does not accurately reflect the Zeteor advantage. For Zeteor, all imported inputs did not require further processing as the HMT was largely doing assembly operations. Yet the Swaraj price was comparable to that of the Zeteor; but its margin was much lower—the cost of inputs rose from 77.5 per cent in June 1973 to 93 per cent of ex-factory selling price by March 1975.

Hence, the PTL suggested to the government of India that Swaraj should be exempt from excise duty of 10 per cent (about Rs. 3000 per tractor) to *offset* its higher input prices of domestically bought components. This exemption was granted by the end of 1975 and since then the PTL's financial performance approached the planned level by the middle of 1977—with manufacturing efficiency superior to that of the HMT, producing the Zeteor in the Swaraj h.p. range.

In addition, the PTL took several measures to reduce its costs and diversify its products through an intensive R and D work. It developed a new design (Swaraj-735, 35 h.p.) during 1974–5 and introduced it by the end of 1975—the second year of its operation. For this 35-h.p. tractor the additional costs were only Rs. 2000 per tractor, while the price advantage was of the order of Rs. 4000 per tractor; because of historical reasons, it appears that the farmers regarded a higher price product as a superior product[23] (they were used to the Massey-Ferguson tractor of 35 h.p.—a tractor which had passed the TTTS test and was the most popular tractor since 1961). By 1977, its output composition was 4200 Swaraj-735 and 800 Swaraj-724. It developed a third model—Swaraj Economy—and started its production in 1979; Swaraj Economy is the cheapest tractor in the international free market for equivalent performance and the PTL started exporting it by the end of 1979. No other tractor manufacturer has given such attention to R and D work for product planning—developing new designs and models in response to local conditions and farmers' preferences.[24]

Swaraj has been, as was expected, a successful model judging from the farmers' response. The PTL has been able to sell its entire output; at a point in time orders booked numbered 500 tractors. Its distribution-cum-service system has been superior to that of any other manufacturer in India. It has, however, one handicap. Swaraj was not included as an eligible tractor for the World Bank line of credit, under which finance is provided to farmers at a concessional rate through the Agricultural Refinance and Development Corporation (ARDC); quite surprisingly, this scheme is meant for tractors in the range of 26 h.p. and above and this scheme does not mention Swaraj as a tractor worthy of financial support. Anyway, the PTL has devised appropriate financing schemes with the help of the ARDC.

It is worth mentioning that this new experiment in developing a product based on indigenous technology and know-how won recognition from the central government—*which was not prepared to sponsor the Swaraj project in 1972*; in 1975 the PTL was awarded the National Gold Shield—the country's highest award—for its contribution to the development of indigenous technology, know-how and consultancy services.

III. Problems and Conjectures

Such is the story of the Swaraj tractor. It raises several problems for analytic inquiry—problems relating to the behaviour of various units. In this section we try to examine the problems relating to the Swaraj case proper; in the next section we deal with the problems with regard to the industrial licensing process.

The following questions arise with regard to the Swaraj story:

1. Why did the Central government not sponsor this project?
2. Why did the Punjab government take the risk of undertaking this project? What were the nature and characteristics of its decision-making that accounted for its success?
3. Why was this experiment in the creative adaptation of modern technology fruitful?

Let us proceed to examine these questions and try to draw some inferences (conjectures) about the public sector decision-making process.

Central Government Behaviour

One part of the government—the Planning Commission—took the deliberate decision to develop an indigenous tractor design. The CMERI did successfully evolve the Swaraj tractor; it passed the TTTS test. The HMT—a Central government enterprise—wanted to diversify its output as it was facing the impact of industrial recession on the demand for machine tools; it wanted to undertake a tractor project to use its surplus capacity and thus improve its financial results. At this stage, the NDC considered Swaraj a risky project and advised the HMT to take up the assembly of Zeteor—which had also passed the TTTTS test. This suited the HMT as Swaraj would have involved a gestation lag of two to three years, while the assembly of Zeteor could start immediately. Doubtless, the HMT decision was a rational one from its own point of view. But then the question is: Why did the Central government not sponsor another public sector enterprise to manufacture the Swaraj?

One answer could be that the bureaucrats in Delhi had no technical knowledge about the tractor industry and they probably considered an enterprise based on mere research result as a risky venture. They simply did not want to take this risk. However, this explanation does not seem to be valid. After all, the Central government had adequate technological competence; did it not have CSIR, NIDC and even the CMERI, which had developed Swaraj? And the CMERI personnel were quite confident about the superiority of the Swaraj tractor in the Indian context.

Could it be that the technical personnel in the CSIR and the NIDC and hence the bureaucracy had no confidence or faith not only in the competence of the CMERI personnel but also with regard to indigenous technology and consultancy ability generally? After all, foreigners had experimented with their designs in actual commercial production for a long time and it was much less risky to take their help than to undertake an enterprise on the basis of commercially unproved indigenous know-how.

It appears from the available evidence that such indeed was the response of the Central government scientists, technologists and the bureaucrats. If this be true, how could India ever creatively adapt modern technology to its local conditions? Again, in that case, what could be the rationale of setting up scientific and technological research set-ups as part of the Central government machinery for decision-making in the technological field?

Another explanation could simply be inter-institutional rivalry and jealousy. Mr. Suri, the record shows, was not much liked by the CSIR or NIDC personnel; with the change in the political set-up after 1968, Mr. Suri did resign from the CMERI. By 1971, thus, within the Central government apparatus, there was no leadership—either at the political level or at the technological level—to sponsor an active technology policy that could raise policy issues above the field of interpersonal and inter-institutional rivalries and jealousies.

In this connection, a fact about the World Bank mission is worth mentioning. In 1971, the World Bank sent a mission to study the growth and structure of the tractor industry in India in order to make policy recommendations to the Central government and find out the nature and magnitude of financial assistance that the World Bank should offer. This was the time when the Swaraj model had already evolved and passed the TTTS test and the PTL was organized to implement the Swaraj project. It is surprising to find that the World Bank mission did not contact either the CMERI personnel or the PTL and, in fact, made no reference to the Swaraj project in its report except to mention in a footnote that it was one of the three tractors that had passed the TTTS test. As a result, the World Bank line of credit was not available to farmers purchasing Swaraj, while it was available for the purchase of all domestic tractors in the h.p. range above 25. It is somewhat ironical to find this World Bank study recommending improved product planning to upgrade designs by the domestic producers with the technical assistance of their foreign collaborators. Strange to note is the following recommendation:

"Indigenous capabilities will grow through collaboration agreements but, in addition, firms should initiate cooperative programs with indigenous universities and engineering research centers (such as, for example, the Central Mechanical Engineering Research Institute) aimed at developing tractor features especially suitable for India."[25] Does this require any comment? The question is: Why did the Central government officials keep the World Bank team in the dark about the Swaraj, the CMERI and the PTL? Did one party reinforce the inferiority complex of the other with regard to indigenous technological competence? Why this emphasis on foreign collaboration in a technologically simple product like a tractor? This is a research field in the area of economic sociology.[26]

Decision-Making at the State Level

In spite of the scepticism, for whatever reasons, about the Swaraj project on the part of the various Central government agencies, how did it come to pass that another unit of the government—the Punjab state government—decided to undertake this project in 1970?

The Punjab government and the Punjab farmers were familiar with the whole process of evolution of the Swaraj. After all, the field trials were largely undertaken in the Punjab. The farmers had in a sense become a part of this venture, and they had approved this new product which was expected to save on both capital and operating costs. Further, the Punjabis are proud of their mechanical talents; one of the farmers had in fact successfully done "reverse engineering" (Japanese style) with regard to an East European tractor and had made a similar tractor in his own workshop. (Patent rights violation prevented this farmer from undertaking small-scale production of this tractor.) They were, thus, able to judge Swaraj on its merits and had a certain pride in owning a tractor based on technology and know-how developed in India—and more particularly by the Punjabis. (Mr. Suri happened to be from the Punjab.)

This was one consideration. And the other was the potential employment impact of the tractor project. The Swaraj was to purchase more than 80 per cent of the components from the ancillaries—mostly from the Punjab. And the Punjabis are known for their entrepreneurial and mechanical talents; as a result of which the Punjab has the most thriving small-scale industrial sector in India.

Thus the PSIDC was confident about the farmers' response, the employment impact and as a result the financial success of the project. The PSIDC is an independent agency of the Punjab government with the function of promoting industrial development of the State. It is aware that it can perform this innovating function effectively only if its projects succeed in financial terms. For the Punjab government would not—could not—provide subsidies on a continuing basis; and even if it did, such subsidies would affect its ability to function with a degree of independence and thus its ability to take risks and innovate.

Hard-headed, not romantic, pride in indigenous technology, farmers' response and the potential impact on employment and its own resources—these were the governing factors in the PSIDC's decision to take up this innovative project. For the Central government agencies, Swaraj was an abstraction; it did not have such direct visible impact on them as it had for the Punjab government and its agencies. Only a well thought-out technology policy integrated with the general development strategy of the country could have induced the Central government to sponsor this project; but it did not have such a policy then, nor did it have confidence and pride in domestic technological competence. But the Swaraj success has probably taught some lessons. In 1975 the PTL was awarded the Gold Shield for successfully implementing a project based on domestic technology and know-how by the Central government; this is probably an indication of a new awareness about the role of indigenous technological competence in the development strategy.

How do we account for the remarkable performance of the PTL? The comprehensive and illuminating detailed project report, the timely completion of the construction phase without any cost overrun, the timely realization of capacity output, the ways in which the top management tackled problems as they arose—the problem of sources of supply, and the liquidity and financial problem—and the new models developed through continuing R and D work—all these characteristics of project performance were indeed unique in the financing experience of the IDBI.

The factors which seem to account for this performance are the following:

1. Selection of the project by PSIDC on the basis of its visible and direct potential impact on its financial resources, Punjab farmers and employment in small industries.
2. Selection of technical consultants and top management personnel—persons who were associated with the design of the Swaraj.
3. The powerful *non-economic* motivation of the technical consultants and top management in making a success of the project; the managing director, Mr. Chandra Mohan, was to be paid only a salary fixed on the basis of Central government scales (he was on deputation from the CMERI) and Mr. Suri's fees were much below the fees charged by the other consultants—Indian or foreign.
4. Enlightened development orientation of the IDBI top management and policies; without the IDBI financial assistance and its own motivation to make it a success, the project would not have seen the light of day.

The relationship of these factors with the project comes out clearly in the narrative (section II) of the Swaraj decision-making process; it is not necessary to repeat what has been mentioned there already.

Creative Adaption of Modern Technology

This case has relevance for the decision-making process not only with regard to the Swaraj project but also with regard to the process of creative adaption of modern technology. How do we explain the success of this experiment?

The organic and sequential relationship among the following tasks and functions seem to be the crucial factor.

Identification of a project idea was the critical first stage. This was done by the Planning Commission. The identification of available technological choices for this was the second; this was the function of a Technical Consultancy Service

Centre (TCSC), in this case, the CMERI performed this function. Identification of a research problem by a TCSC, in this case, the CMERI, was the third stage. The research on the problem by a Technological Research Centre (TRC), in this case, the CMERI, and the transmission of this research result to the TCSC, in this case, Messrs. Suri & Associates, was the fourth stage. The detailed project report by the TCSC to the project promoter (PTL) and the financial system (IDBI) was the fifth stage. The association of the TCSC with the top management for project implementation was the final stage.

In this organic sequential relationship, the critical functions were performed by the TCSC and the IDBI—the functions of identifying relevant research problems, embodying the research results meaningfully into a concrete project, and facilitating its implementation. Without the TCSC, neither the relevant research problem nor a concrete project would have been identified; and without the link between the TCSC and the IDBI, the project would not have become an operational project. It appears from *a priori* reasoning as well as from this case study that the critical links in the process of creative adaptation of modern technology are the TCSC and the Financial System (FS); these two provide the essential links between the production system and the technological research system. Without these two functional agencies, the production system and the technological research system are likely to evolve on parallel lines.[27]

IV. Decision Process: Industrial Licensing

In India, the volume and pattern of investment in the manufacturing sector are regulated by the Industrial Licensing System (ILS) in the light of the development objectives and strategy, as worked out by the Planning Commission. In the case of the tractor industry, the actual operation of the ILS raises several questions:[28]

1. After the decision to manufacture tractors was taken (after 1959), why did the ILS issue licences to five units—each to produce on a relatively small scale a distinctive foreign model in the h.p. range above 26?

2. Why did the ILS issue licences and letters of intent to raise capacity much in excess of potential demand for tractors?

3. After the Swaraj model was developed and had passed the TTTS test in 1970, why did the ILS issue licences to manufacture tractor models of foreign designs during 1970–1?

Behaviour of ILS: pre-1965

It is true that the demand for tractors in India was growing, particularly after 1955. However, no agency seems to have examined the question: Was it essential to mechanize agricultural operations when employment was a problem? As it turned out, substitution of tractor for animal power was worthwhile: for timely and dependable results in areas with multiple cropping and because of rising opportunity cost of animal power with sharp increases in land productivity in irrigated areas as a result of the green revolution.[29] Anyway, it is pertinent to note that an agency in charge of regulating industrial development did not raise this basic question before issuing licences to five units by 1965.

There was a growing demand for tractors by the farmers and farmers would not adopt this mechanical device unless it were profitable—such seems to be the logic of the ILS.

Anyway, several further questions arise: in spite of the economies of scale in tractor production and distribution, why did the ILS license five units with relatively small capacities? Why did the ILS not insist that each tractor model should pass the TTTS test before applying for a licence? Why did the ILS not examine the suitability of each tractor design to local conditions and farmers' resources?

The ILS choices were governed by about eleven criteria which the public sector decision-making process had to take into account; briefly these were:[30]

1. Promotion of industrial development.
2. Promotion of a self-reliant and self-generating economy.
3. Preventing concentration of economic power.
4. Ensuring balanced regional development.
5. Setting high welfare standards for labour.
6. Increasing employment opportunities.
7. Strengthening the defence potential of the country.
8. Enlarging the cadre of highly trained engineers and technicians.
9. Setting healthy and clear standards of management.
10. Keeping down prices.
11. Financial viability.

These were the criteria for the public sector projects; for regulating private sector investment, it appears from the operation of the ILS that it chose the first four and the eleventh from this list. The industrial sectors that need to be promoted were, in a sense, indicated by the Planning Commission. Thus the *operating* criteria for the ILS actually were: prevention of concentration of economic power; ensuring balanced regional development and financial viability of the project. It is pertinent to note that there is no mention of the price—quality suitability of the industrial product to be produced and the impact of these characteristics on the Indian consumers, costs of import substitution and industrial exports.

The private firms, it was assumed, would take into account the financial viability of their projects. By this process of elimination, only two criteria of choice effectively remained for the ILS: prevention of concentration of economic power and the promotion of balanced regional development. Both these criteria indicated multiplicity and dispersal of firms and limitation on the size of the production capacity of each unit.

With these two criteria there was a risk: financial viability may not be ensured. The solution was: to issue licences to established well-known firms which could enter into collaboration with established reputable foreign firms. Such firms, it would have been argued, would have adequate management capacity to ensure financial success of their projects. There was thus an obvious bias in the ILS against indigenous technology and know-how, and new entrepreneurs.

Such seems to be the logic governing the behaviour of the ILS. But this logic had the following results by 1971:[31]

(i) Underutilized capacity because of poor management and farmers' rejection of tractor models produced by three out of five firms.
(ii) Complete neglect by the majority of producers of the crucial functions: product engineering and planning, and distribution and after-sales service.
(iii) Lack of resources to expand and diversify tractor output.

Behaviour of ILS: 1970–1

Such was the state of the tractor industry by about 1971. Tractor capacity was underutilized, while imports were substantial (about 40 per cent of total supply). The demand for tractors, however, was expected to grow to about 90,000 by 1973–4; this was the Ministry of Agriculture's estimate. The solution to this problem was to license nine more units and permit six more units (this was the logic of issuing letters of intent) to obtain licences in future if they could finalize their production programmes. The potential capacity of the licensed eleven units was raised to 107,000 tractors; while production in 1971–2 was only 23,469 tractors with imports of 14,000 tractors.

The Ministry of Agriculture had the benefit of other demand estimates: estimates of Indian Society of Agricultural Engineers and Tractor Manufacturers. Both these estimates of demand for 1973–4 were much lower (52,000 and 65,000 respectively) than that of the Ministry of Agriculture. Why did the ILS disregard these estimates?

One reason, of course, was that the Ministry of Agriculture was closer to the ILS and, for the ILS, it was probably natural to trust the Ministry's estimate; after all, both were manned by personnel of the administrative service, which had a common outlook and perspective of approaching economic issues. Further, it is quite likely that the ILS may have taken the view that the Ministry was in possession of data relating to registration for tractors—data which were not available to the outsiders.

But these data were in fact crude; in a controlled system, obviously there were multiple registrations—each farmer registering for several tractor models, in the hope of obtaining whichever was available as early as possible. This obvious fact was disregarded. Further, farmers' demand is a function of tractor prices as well as the nature and terms of credit facilities. These facts, too, were not taken into account.

By 1972, the controlled prices of tractors were raised and the credit facilities became scarce in the light of the anti-inflationary stance of monetary and credit policies. The demand for tractors did get affected; the new revised demand estimates made in 1972 were nearly 50 per cent lower than those made earlier.

The question naturally arises: Why did the ILS not set up a sound machinery for making demand projections? Such a machinery would require a large number of technical experts; after all, the ILS was dealing with a large number of industries and not merely the tractor industry. Besides, such a machinery cannot answer questions without research and research takes time. The decision process cannot wait; its demands were urgent and immediate. But such a machinery could improve the decision process after the initial gestation lag. However, administrative bureaucracy and politicians are not known to take long views; in the long run we are all dead—this Keynesian thought comes naturally to them.

The decisive reason, however, is probably different. After all, if experts are to count, there would be less discretionary power of decision-making with the bureaucracy as well as the politicians. Why give up this power?

Swaraj and the ILS

By 1965 it was known that to suit local conditions the farmers required a tractor in the h.p. range of 20 to 30; such a tractor would mean for the farmers lower capital as well as operating costs. It was because of this reason that Swaraj was developed. By 1970 the Swaraj had passed the TTTS test.

In this context one would have expected the ILS to issue a licence only to such a firm which could produce the Swaraj. Because of economics of scale in production as well as distribution, the choice should have been in favour of a public sector firm; for the private sector the argument of concentration of economic power would apply. Why did the ILS not suggest such a course of action?

Probably, the ILS simply did not know the history of the Swaraj; this information was available elsewhere in the government and there was no communication channel developed for transmission of relevant information to the ILS.[32] And this channel did not develop because the ILS criteria of choice—its agenda[33]—did not require such information. This type of factor was not on the active decision area of the ILS. It is difficult even for a private firm to modify its agenda—taking account of new decision variables—so how much more difficult would it be for the administrative bureaucracy where persons, before they rise to decision-making positions, are already indoctrinated in the virtues of the pre-existing agenda?[34]

Not that the ILS was unaware of the Swaraj; the point is that with the available channels this new fact did not become a "coercive fact" (to use William James's expressive term) for the ILS decision-making process. And so it was disregarded. And after all, even the technical experts in the central government—the CSIR and the NIDC—were sceptical about the potential of the Swaraj; if they had lack of faith or confidence in indigenous technological competence the bureaucracy, with compelling reasons to play safe, had naturally even a greater inferiority complex.

The agenda selected by the ILS—concentration of economic power, regional balance and foreign collaboration—were eminently rational if one viewed it in the context of the political process and the bureaucratic politics. Concentration of economic power and regional balance were the political issues raised by the politicians in a federal democracy. Any decision based on them would be acceptable to the political process; for it is only thus that the political process could impinge on decision-making with regard to technical issues. Thus, this agenda suited both the ministers as well as the bureaucracy; the latter's power and prestige depended on its acceptance of the demands of the political process. And the risk inherent in this agenda was reduced by issuing licences to established firms with foreign collaboration. Thus, this agenda also suited the interests of big business—in India as well as abroad.

There was another merit also. If technical decisions were to be made predominantly on technical grounds, it would be essential to set up an expert machinery for the purpose. Such a machinery, however, would not be set up because of the reasons mentioned earlier in connection with the demand studies. The agenda has the merit that it does not require such expert machinery. For dealing with the minor technical issues that the administrative bureaucracy may not understand, it is possible to have a technical bureaucracy *under* the administrative civil service; this, for obvious reasons, would not attract the right type of talents. Its only advantage is that it can talk the language of the industry as well as of the bureaucracy. But industry would obviously have more expertise than this technical wing; the latter's expertise, whatever it had, would become growingly obsolete. So the technical wing too would accept this agenda. Its technical examination and modification of projects would merely relate to such minor technical changes that can be made, given the constraints of the agenda. This was precisely the role of the Directorate General of Technical Development (DGTD)[35] in the ILS.

Hence the DGTD did not raise the basic issues relating to economies of scale or farmers' preferences. After all, the farmers would know what they wanted and industry would supply a product that the farmers would demand. In the tractor case, it did not occur to the ILS that farmers' preferences are determined by history; in a durable commodity like this, they cannot afford to experiment. So they demand such products of which they are familiar. They would not know the quality of the other alternative products; and quite likely lower-priced product, with which they are not familiar, would be regarded as an inferior product.[36] In a sense, this is what happened. Farmers had become used to 35-h.p. Massey-Ferguson and International Harvester tractors; they were dependable. A cheaper tractor in h.p. range below 30 came to be regarded as an inferior product. It was thus that price difference between 20-h.p. and 30-h.p. tractors was *much* greater than the cost difference. The changeover by the PTL to a 30-h.p. tractor in 1975 was largely because of these reasons; its additional cost was only Rs. 2000 per tractor, while its additional price advantage was Rs. 4000 per tractor. Neither the ILS nor the Ministry of Agriculture considered it essential to provide full information to the farmers on the relative merits of the different tractor models. It is pertinent to note that the ILS did not insist on the TTTS test before issuing a licence nor did it insist on good distribution and after-sales service set-up—key elements for decision-making if the farmers' interests were to be safeguarded.

For some such reasons the ILS did not consider the Swaraj development as a key factor for its licensing policy. But for the CMERI, the PSIDC, Messrs. Suri & Associates and the IDBI, the Swaraj tractor would not have seen the light of day; this success, however, is likely to become a "coercive fact" and has the potential of modifying the "agenda"—the decision criteria of the Central government agencies. Whether this potential would be realized depends on so many complex factors of the socio-political-economic process; one cannot be certain about the direction of change.

V. Decision-making Process: Some General Observations

It seems possible to make some conjectures of general relevance about the problem of public sector decision-making in the developing countries. These conjectures point towards some hypotheses around which it may be possible to formulate a theory of public sector behaviour.

1. Socio-economic development is not an isolated process; it is an integral part of the process of nation building. Most of the developing countries acquired political independence only in the post-war period. These countries are struggling to become nation-states—to evolve a consensus regarding national aims and objectives so that a community can be built; and they are trying to evolve a method of resolving conflict of wills by peaceful and constitutional means. But this effort at nation building does give rise to a variety of tensions and pressures—a conflict among *structural principles* of social fabric. These conflicts are aggravated in a country with a federal democracy and a mixed economy. Anyway, the fact to be recognized is that the two processes—process of nation building and the process of socio-economic development—are interrelated and one affects the other.[37]

2. Such is the context for the decision-making process. Obviously, government cannot be a monolithic structure with a given consistent set of objectives. But this does not imply that each participant in the decision-making process takes irrational decisions. Given his context, he is rational. If the total outcome of the process appears to an outside expert observer as irrational, the reason is not the irrationality of decision-makers but the analyst's incapacity to understand the problem.[38] Because of the nature of the political-bureaucratic structure, the range of choice with regard to objectives has to be, must be, very wide. This range can be narrowed in technical terms if the trade-offs—as the economic jargon puts it—among the given objectives can be settled. But this technical requirement can be in some sense met by developing an *appropriate institutional framework* for decision-making.

3. This choice-range for objectives creates even a wider range of choice for policies and policy instruments (projects) for each decision-making unit. Paradoxically, this fact makes it possible for each decision-making unit to make a choice on the basis of a limited agenda—limited information that is readily available to him—and thus delimits his search for relevant information even from the other parts of the government. The policy decisions or choice of projects in the same broad field may appear to be inconsistent, one with another, to an outsider but may still be based on rational considerations from the point of view of each decision-making unit.

4. In a socio-economic process with these choice characteristics, plurality of decision-making units (Project Promoters, TCSCs and financial institutions) with different agendas seems to be essential.[39] Such plurality makes creative experimentation possible and since the results of such experiments are concrete and easily observable, the information content of the decision-making process would improve and this may tend to narrow the range of choice with regard to both objectives and instruments (projects). Thus a learning process based on experience and experimentation can be set in motion.

5. This study suggests that for effective and efficient choices, it may be advisable to evolve an institutional structure, where actual decisions with regard to projects and policies are made by units, whose growth, development and vitality *critically* depend on the results of choices made.

6. It is possible to improve the decision-making process, as this study indicates, by institutionalizing certain key functions and thus delimiting the range of purely political decision-making. The institutions that seem to be essential are: Project Promoting agencies, Industrial Development Banks, Technical Consultancy Service Centres (TCSCs), and Technological Research Centres (TRCs); each of these institutions should have an identity and a function distinct from the administrative bureaucracy.[40]

7. Such an institutional structure is essential also for the process of creative adaptation of modern technology; from this point of view, the roles of TCSCs and the FS (Industrial Development Banks) are critical—they provide the effective link between the technological research system and the production system.[41]

8. Industrial Licensing System (ILS) is a very blunt policy instrument and is bound to lead to arbitrary decisions and corrupt practices; the magnitude and the complexity of the task of licensing are such that no licensing authority, however competent, can handle it effectively and efficiently. What are indeed required are an efficient *project evaluation machinery* and non-discretionary policy instruments that can promote such industrial development as is consistent with broad development objectives.[42] The project evaluation machinery, to be operationally relevant and effective, should be functionally related with the financing agencies.

9. This study also suggests that implementation and operation of a manufacturing project is likely to be more effective and efficient if its top management is vitally associated with the selection and formulation of the project, which it has to administer, than if it is not.

10. The performance of a public enterprise *crucially* depends on the *quality* and *stability* of the top management and its structure. The selection of top management is the critical decision. The basic functions of the project promoting agencies should relate to (*a*) the wise selection of top management and (*b*) evaluation of its overall performance; for the rest, the top management should have a free hand in taking such decisions as are essential for the effective and efficient functioning of the enterprise and for which it should be held responsible. There should be *agreement* between the project-promoting agencies and the top management with regard to the *overall* performance criteria as well as the structure of rewards and penalties.[43]

11. The advice of outside experts and international agencies can be effective in "improving" the decision-making process only if it is based on a sound understanding of the socio-economic process in a given country. The international agencies and other experts can make a crucial contribution in accelerating the process of change if they helped these countries in evolving a sound institutional structure of the nature indicated earlier. But for this they need to understand the rationality and meaning of this process of change; just to say that it is irrational is not to understand it.[44] What requires understanding is the problem; without this, solutions offered are likely to be solutions to non-problems or pseudo-problems, however sophisticated the language in which they are clothed.

NOTES

1. For the role of the State in economic development, see V. V. Bhatt, *Employment and Capital Formation in Underdeveloped Economies* (Bombay: Orient Longmans, 1960), chapter vi.
2. On the complexity of the motivation pattern and the decision-making process, see (1) R. V. Clemence (ed.), *Essays of J. A. Schumpeter* (Cambridge, Massachusetts: Addison-Wesley Press, 1951), pp. 216–27; (2) K. J. Arrow, *The Limits of Organization* (New York: W. W. Norton & Co., 1974), chapters 3 and 4; (3) J. Kornai, *Anti-Equilibrium* (London: North-Holland, 1971), chapters 7, 11 and 13.
3. J. Hicks, *Economic Perspectives* (Oxford: Clarendon Press, 1977), p. xv.
4. In this connection, see M. Rein and S. H. White, "Can Policy Research Help Policy?", *The Public Interest,* no. 49 (Fall 1977), pp. 119–36. To quote: "The long-standing problem-solving model is in large part a myth. . . . According to the problem-solving model, policy making begins with articulated and self-evident problems, about which it is possible to hypothesize different courses of action and develop goals. But there is actually an earlier stage, often quite extended, during which various indications of stress emerge. . . . There are indications that a problem exists, but as yet no one knows what it is. . . . Problem setting is a form of pattern recognition; it involves finding or imposing an order or structure on incipient events. It is an integral part of the work of the scientist, perhaps the most crucial part, but it has traditionally been the least codified aspect of research in the canons of methodology and 'normal science'. There is, in fact, no orderly and prescribed way of problem setting" (pp. 130–1).

   See also K. R. Popper, *Conjectures and Refutations* (London: Victor Gollancz Ltd., 1964). What Popper says about philosophy is probably true also of social sciences. He says about Philosophy: "Genuine philosophical problems are always rooted in urgent problems outside philosophy, and they die if these roots decay. In their efforts to solve them, philosophers are liable to pursue what looks like a philosophical method or technique or an unfailing key to philosophical success. But no such techniques or methods exist: in philosophy methods are unimportant; any method is legitimate if it leads to results capable of being rationally discussed. What matters is not methods or techniques but a sensitivity to problems, and a consuming passion for them. . . . But there are others who do not feel this urge, who have no serious or pressing problem but who nevertheless produce exercises in fashionable methods, and for whom philosophy is application . . . rather than search. They are luring philosophy into the bog of pseudo-problems and verbal puzzles; either by offering us pseudo-problems for real ones . . . or pursuading us to concentrate upon the endless and pointless task of unmasking what they rightly or wrongly take for pseudo-problems or puzzles . . ." (p. 72).

   The following Nasrudin Mulla story makes the point quite sharply:

   > A man saw Nasrudin searching for something on the ground: "What have you lost, Mulla?", he asked.
   > "My key", said the Mulla.
   > So the man went down on his knees too, and they both looked for it.
   > After a time, the other man asked: "Where exactly did you drop it?"
   > "In my own house."
   > "Then why are you looking here?"
   > "There is more light here than inside my own house."

   See I. Shah, *The Pleasantries of the Incredible Mulla Nasrudin* (New York: E. P. Dutton & Co., 1971).

   On Management Science, see P. F. Drucker, *Management: Tasks, Responsibilities, Practices* (New York: Harper & Row, 1973). Drucker writes: "Throughout the management science—in the literature as well as in the work in progress—the emphasis is on techniques rather than on principles, on mechanics rather than on decisions, on tools rather than on results, and above all, on efficiency of the part rather than on performance of the whole" (p. 509).
5. In this context, see M. Rein and S. H. White, *op. cit.*
6. K. J. Arrow, *op. cit.* Arrow writes: "In classical maximising theory it is implicit that the values of all relevant variables are at all moments under consideration. All variables are therefore *agenda* of the organization, that is, their values have always to be chosen. On the other hand it is a commonplace of everyday observation and of studies of organization that the difficulty of

arranging that a potential decision variable be recognized as such may be much greater than that of choosing a value for it" (p. 47).

On his major theme, he writes: "The theme to be presented is that the combination of uncertainty, indivisibility, and capital intensity associated with information channels and their use imply (*a*) that the actual structure and behaviour of an organization may depend heavily upon random events, in other words on history, and (*b*) the very pursuit of efficiency may lead to rigidity and unresponsiveness to further change" (p. 49).

7. In addition, the author had the benefit of intensive discussions with (*a*) the members of the project appraisal and supervision teams of the IDBI, (*b*) Mr. Suri of Messrs. Suri & Associates, (*c*) Mr. Chandra Mohan, the Managing Director of the PTL and (*d*) the members of the *Ad hoc* Committee of Advisers (ACA) to the IDBI. Of course, the authentic grasp of details and nuances of the project would not have been possible but for the fact that the author happened to be the general manager of the IDBI, when the decision to finance the project was taken.
8. R. T. Kudrle, *Agricultural Tractors: A World Industry Study* (Cambridge, Massachusetts: Ballinger Publishing Co., 1975), p. 3.
9. *Ibid.*, pp. 49 to 53. To quote: "It appears that the improvement in farm machinery before World War II, so much admired by Schumpeter, has continued apace with some types of equipment while tractor design virtually stagnated. Once the Ferguson systems was completely diffused, however, informed opinion has not been able to point to important areas of design neglect . . .; the lack of advance is usually assigned to the rather simple nature of the product and the limited number of areas of possible design improvement. Continuing refinement of the hydraulic system has probably been the single most important area of advance" (p. 203).
10. *Ibid.*, pp. 32–34.
11. *Ibid.*, p. 208.
12. *Ibid.*, pp. 4 to 8.
13. *Ibid.*, chapter 13. To quote: "If the farmer could be made aware by his own organizations of the persistent and substantial discrimination practised against him in the past, it is not unreasonable to assume that he would become at least somewhat annoyed (his Canadian counterparts certainly did!), and the trust which is such a large part of the product differentiation barrier carefully nurtured by the companies over the years would be diminished thereby. A demonstration that fully comparable tractors have been sold for up to two decades in other parts of the world for vastly lower prices than offered to the U.S. farmer should help convince him that a bargain tractor price is something to be carefully considered and not necessarily a sign of inferior design or manufacture" (p. 222).
14. See I. Singh and R. H. Day, "Factor Utilization and Substitution in Economic Development: A Green Revolution Case Study", *The Journal of Development Studies*, vol. ii (Apr. 1975), pp. 155–77.
15. The capital and operating cost of a tractor is a function of its horse-power; these costs are lower for tractors in the h.p. range below 35 than those in the h.p. range above 35. The h.p. requirement depends on the size of the farm, the cost of animal power and labour, and the characteristics of the soil and terrain. In North America and the U.K., in 1970, only 10 per cent of tractors sold were units of less than 35 h.p., while this proportion was 33 per cent in Germany and 23 per cent for Italy. In east European countries and Japan, this proportion is even higher than 50 per cent. See R. T. Kudrle, *op. cit.*, pp. 21–5, 87 and 90.
16. See G. S. Aurora and W. Morehouse, "Dilemma of Technological Choice—The Case of the Small Tractor", *Economic and Political Weekly,* vol. 7, Special Number (1972), pp. 1633–44.
17. See A. Besant and C. Raj, *Public Enterprise Investment Decisions in India* (Bombay: The MacMillan Co. of India, 1977), pp. 115–17.
18. For the evolving role and functions of the IDBI, see *Annual Report of the Industrial Development Bank of India,* 1970–1 and 1971–2 (Bombay, Aug. 1971 and Aug. 1972); V. V. Bhatt, "Industrial Development Bank of India (IDBI): Recent Evolution of its Role and Functions", *PRAJNAN*, vol. 1, no. 3 (July-Sept. 1972). The IDBI was one of the few development banks which had adopted social benefit–cost criteria for project appraisal. Its exchange rate criterion was a simplified version of the Bruno domestic resource cost criterion. See M. Bruno, "The Optimal Selection of Export Promoting and Import Substituting Projects", in the United Nations publication—*Planning the External Sector: Techniques, Problems and Policies* (New York, 1965). At

that time the IDBI was not aware of the much more refined technique evolved by Little and Mirrlees in their *OECD* publication (1968). See also I. M. D. Little and J. A. Mirrlees, *Project Appraisal and Planning* (London: Heinemann, 1974). It is now developing the expertise and information system suited for the adoption of the Little–Mirrlees criteria.

19. For a brief outline of the PTL Swaraj tractor project, see Appendix A, in V. V. Bhatt, *Decision Making in the Public Sector: A Case Study of Swaraj Tractor* (World Bank: Development Economics Department: Domestic Finance Studies No. 48).
20. For details regarding manufacturing firms, capacity output, actual production, tractor prices, and the industrial licences, see *ibid.*, Appendix B—Statement III.
21. For the various demand estimates, see *ibid.*, Appendix B—Statement IV.
22. For the performance indicators of the PTL, see *ibid.*, Appendix A and Appendix B—Statements I and II.
23. The U.S. farmers seem to have behaved in a similar fashion; see R. T. Kudrle, *op. cit.*, chapter 13.
24. In addition, the PTL have initiated research, in collaboration with the Punjab Agricultural University, Ludhiana, on the development of a tractor-drawn paddy transplanter capable of handling six rows of paddy seeding at a time—that is, it could cover 4 acres of transplanting a day. Field trials of the prototype transplanter are completed.
25. World Bank, *Survey of Tractor Manufacturing Industry: India* (Washington: mimeographed, 16 May 1973), p. 23.
26. On economic sociology, see J. A. Schumpeter, *History of Economic Analysis* (London: Oxford University Press, 1954). Schumpeter writes: "To use a felicitous phrase: economic analysis deals with the questions how people behave at any time and what the economic effects are which they produce by so behaving; economic sociology deals with the question how they come to behave as they do" (p. 21).
27. On the role of the ICSC and the FS in technology policy, see V. V. Bhatt, "On Technology Policy and Its Institutional Frame", *World Development*, vol. 3, no. 9 (Sept. 1975), pp. 651–63.
28. See Appendix B—Statements III and IV in the source cited in footnote no. 19, with regard to industrial licences.
29. See I. Singh and R. H. Day, *op. cit.*
30. Government of India, Ministry of Information and Broadcasting, *Toward Prosperity Through Public Sector: Public Sector for Public Good* (Delhi, 1971); see also A. Besant and C. Raj, *Public Enterprise Investment Decisions in India* (Bombay: MacMillan, 1977), pp. 109–11.
31. See Appendix B—Statement III in the source cited in footnote no. 19.
32. See in this connection C. Raj, *op. cit.*, for an illuminating case study with regard to the *Manual of Feasibility Studies*. To quote: ". . . the major guidelines for capital budgeting decisions of public enterprises are contained in a Manual of Feasibility Studies prepared in 1966 by the Committee on Plan Projects of the Planning Commission. . . ."

"The Manual was issued in 1966 and we conducted our interviews in 1970 and 1971. We expected that most of the senior executives of the public enterprises, particularly the senior financial executives, would be very familiar with this Manual. To our great surprise, we realized that many of them had not even heard of the existence of such a Manual. As a means of cross-checking, we often referred to this Manual while conducting programmes on management for senior executives from the public enterprises. Except for a few, on the whole, many of these executives were not aware of this Manual. Responses received to the questionnaire mailed to enterprises were most often categorical that no Manual or guidelines existed for capital budgeting decisions. Due to this consistent response, we decided to raise this issue in the interview we had with the Unit of the Planning Commission which was responsible for the preparation and circulation of the Manual. We were told that more than 1,500 copies of this Manual had been released for use by the various public enterprises. We can only conclude that while a large number of copies of this Manual have been prepared and released by the Committee on Plan Projects of the Planning Commission, neither the existence of this Manual nor its contents are known at this level of executives in the public enterprises. It is likely that the copies of the Manual sent by the Committee on Plan Projects have remained mainly at the level of the administrative ministries and Chairmen/Managing Directors of these enterprises."

". . . However, the initiative and active interest of only one of the members of the Planning

Commission was responsible for the birth of the Manual. Since this particular member of the Planning Commission had a strained relationship with other senior Secretaries of the administrative ministries, and the Finance Ministry, it became necessary to persuade the Deputy Prime Minister, who also happened to be the Minister of Finance, to issue that letter. Here is an instance of personality conflict among the top officials of the Government, which blocks the effective use of a system conceived for the purpose of improving capital budgeting practices and procedures by the administrative ministries. This also demonstrates the resistance of the sub-units of a large organization even to use a control system, designed and developed by another sub-unit of the total system" (pp. 183–4).

33. See K. J. Arrow, *op. cit.*
34. *Ibid.*
35. See C. Raj, *op. cit.*, on the DGTD. To quote: "The Directorate General of Technical Development, which is a part of the Ministry of Industrial Development, is conceived as a body to provide expert advice with regard to industrial development to administrative ministries concerned. . . ."

    "One would expect that such an important organization entrusted with the planning, co-ordination and control of industrial projects in the country would be staffed with the best technical talent available within the country. But, as a matter of fact, the study team of the ARC on personnel administration found that most of the eleven Industrial Advisers and the eighty Development Officers of this organization, either in terms of their education or experience, were not competent to provide technical consultancy services of the highest order to the Government" (pp. 85–7).
36. The U.S. experience is similar. See R. T. Kudrle, *op. cit.*, chapter 13.
37. V. V. Bhatt, "Perspectives on External Assistance", *Economic and Political Weekly*, Annual Number (Feb. 1967).
38. See J. A. Schumpeter, *Capitalism, Socialism and Democracy* (New York: Harper & Row, 3rd ed., 1975). To quote: "It is not a question of rationality versus irrationality. . . . It is the kind and scope of rationality that makes the difference" (p. 196).

    Again, "Rationality of thought and rationality of action are two different things. Rationality of thought does not always guarantee rationality of action. And the latter may be present without any conscious deliberation and irrespective of any ability to formulate the rationale of one's action correctly. The observer, particularly the observer who uses interview and questionnaire methods, often overlooks this and hence acquires an exaggerated idea of the importance of irrationality in behaviour" (p. 259).
39. See P. D. Henderson, "Two British Errors: Their Probable Size and Some Possible Lessons", *Oxford Economic Papers*, vol. 29, no. 2 (July 1977).
40. See J. A. Schumpeter, *Capitalism, Socialism and Democracy*, *loc. cit.* To quote: "This second condition for the success of democracy is that the effective range of political decision should not be extended too far. . . . Democracy does not require that every function of the State be subject to its political method. . . . Thus, almost any type of human affairs may conceivably be made to enter the sphere of the State without becoming part of the material of the competitive struggle for political leadership beyond what is implied in passing the measure that grants the power and sets up the agency to wield it and the contact that is implied in the government's role of general supervisor" (pp. 291–3).

    See also J. Hicks, *op. cit.* What Hicks says about the function of a government bank as a monetary regulator also applies to other fields we are discussing. To quote: "This, perhaps, is a dream; I do not claim to be a judge of political possibilities. But I am not afraid to draw the moral, which emerges rather clearly from the line of thought I have tried to follow out, that the issue with which we have been concerned is political—even constitutional—as well as economic. There is the technical economic problem of the Instrument; but it is tied up with the political problem of how to secure that it is used decisively. This is a problem which Keynesian economics, so it seems to me, has refused to face; while the monetarists, who have seen it, have not faced the political implications. For myself, I would face it. I think we should say that monetary regulation is a major function of Government; but we should emphasize that if it is to be exercised decisively, it needs to be separated, in what is in fact the constitutional sense, from other functions. We need to remember the ancient doctrine of the Separation of Powers.

The judicial function, in well-ordered States, is recognized to be a function of Government, but a function that is better *separated*. So it is with the monetary function" (pp. 132–3).

And so it is, we may add, with the function of promoting and managing industrial enterprises.

See also in connection with the role of the institutional structure and the National Development Bank, V. V. Bhatt, *Structure of Financial Institutions* (Bombay: Vora & Co., 1972).

41. See V. V. Bhatt, "On Technology Policy and Its Institutional Frame", *op. cit.* See also V. V. Bhatt, "Development Banking: Top Management Tasks and Structure", *World Development*, vol. 4, no. 6 (1976), pp. 519–27.
42. See in this connection B. S. Minhas, "Design of Economic Policy and the Phenomenon of Corruption: Some Suggestions for Economic Reform", *Journal of Social and Economic Studies*, vol. iii, no. 2 (Sept. 1975); pp. 271–96.
43. On the importance of the prestige motive and real incomes essential for efficient functioning of the top management, see J. A. Schumpeter, *Capitalism, Socialism and Democracy, loc. cit.*, pp. 207–9. To quote: "We had better recognize from the start that exclusive reliance on a purely altruistic sense of duty is as unrealistic as would be a wholesale denial of its importance and its possibilities. Even if full allowance be made for the various elements that are cognate to sense of duty, such as the satisfaction derived from working and directing, some system of rewards at least in the form of social recognition and prestige would presumably prove advantageous . . . the prestige motive, more than any other, can be molded by simple reconditioning: successful performers may conceivably be satisfied nearly as well with the privilege—if granted with judicious economy—of being allowed to stick a penny stamp on their trousers as they are by receiving a million a year. . . . Why not? Trotsky himself accepted the Order of the Red Flag. . . . Just as race horses and prize bulls are the grateful recipients of attentions which it would be neither rational nor possible to bestow on every horse and bull, so the supernormal human performer has to be accorded preferential treatment if the rules of economic rationality are to prevail. . . . Many incomes high enough to evoke adverse comment do not give their receivers more than the conditions of life and work—distance and freedom from minor worries included—that are sufficient to keep them fit for the kind of thing they are doing. . . . These devices . . . have been greatly developed in Russia. Essentially they amount to a combination of payments in kind with a liberal provision in money for what are supposed to be expenses of the proper discharging of certain duties" (pp. 207–9).
44. See M. Rein and S. H. White, *op. cit.*

    To the problem of public sector decision-making, some simple panaceas are being advocated by economists of the neo-classical tradition as well as the Marxian tradition. The former recommend the abolition of the public sector and the latter, the abolition of the private sector. These panaceas, of course, emerge from the Scriptures and not from the understanding of historical processes of socio-economic change. It does not occur to these interpreters of the Scriptures that there is a problem which needs to be understood: What is the logic and dynamics of the situation that has created mixed economics and, in particular, are responsible for the expanding role of the public sector in the field of industrial development. Of course, to examine this problem requires much more thinking than to churn out solutions to irrelevant problems on the basis of equally irrelevant econometric or theoretical models.

APPENDIX

Comments by Chandra Mohan (Managing Director of the PTL)

Certain Basic Issues

Role of Punjab government/PSIDC

It is not very correct to say that Punjab government went into the Swaraj project with any enthusiasm. The enthusiasm was basically confined to a few individuals. It was these individuals who after detailed discussions with me (at Durgapur) and Mr. M. M. Suri became convinced that the project had a large basic strength. These individuals virtually overstretched themselves into committing the PSIDC into the project. The moment the project came up for specific consideration in the government, serious reservations were expressed both at the political and secretarial levels. These reservations were perhaps also natural; after all, the technology had been discarded by the government of India itself and the commitments of the central government to Indian technology were supposedly far larger than those of the state government, risk-taking capabilities of the Centre were also larger.

In this background the major task for me and the Swaraj supporters was to convince the government step by step to radically alter its thinking.

Inviting G. S. Atwal & Co. to join PTL was a part of the strategy to convince the government of the soundness of the project. This did have the desired effect and the Punjab government did at least take the decision that if PTL could raise the resources from the financial institutions (Rs. 30 million plus), the Punjab government would not mind risking its Rs. 3 million equity. The situation became seriously complicated when IDBI took the decision that G. S. Atwal & Co. had to be dropped and PSIDC equity raised to Rs. 4.5 million. It took nearly one year of hard pursuit to make the Punjab government take this decision.

If I may add, Swaraj/PTL did not come up because of any Institutional support, whether in the Centre or in the State. It survived purely because of certain individuals, who developed strong convictions for the project and the dedicated manner in which the team had inched its way through every hurdle from the beginning in 1965. Fortunately for the project, these individuals did occupy key positions in the relevant decision-making process at every crucial time. Fortunately again these individuals could be approached and convinced by Mr. M. M. Suri and myself. If I were to look back over the twelve years of the project history the number of such individuals would barely exceed a dozen. But this dozen made all the difference.

Now that the project has established itself in every facet, there is all-out support both from the State and central governments.

You would appreciate the reasons for which the financial institutions were kept in the dark was because of all these local problems. You would agree with me that had the financial institutions known, financial clearances would have become almost impossible. Despite all our meticulous pursuit and the speed at which all information was furnished, institutional clearances did take almost 18 months (if one were also to consider the Pre-feasibility Report). Even from the submission of the formal DPR in March 1971, the last institutional clearance came only in June 1972.

Details

Is the making of a tractor a simple technology?

Comparing a car with a tractor at equal levels of sophistication, if I may say so, the tractor is more complicated. In addition to the engine and transmission, a tractor has hydraulic control which is not there in a car. The number of parts are also not far fewer. The only major complication in a car is brought about by the sheet-metal body which is more complicated because of passenger comfort rather than basic utility. The abuse to which a tractor is subject to when compared to a car, also makes design still more difficult. I would therefore say that the technology of a tractor is not as simple as the report makes it out to be.

Economies of scale

This aspect also came up for discussion in a recent meeting convened by UNIDO in Vienna for evolving an approach to the transfer of technology for agricultural machinery to the developing countries.

First and foremost, cost of production is related to design and the methods by which any particular design can be manufactured. Economics of scale can only be related to the scale of production for any particular design and not when different designs are under consideration. Specific examples are given here:

1. Sheet-metal (fenders, bonnet, etc.) of tractors all over the world and more particularly from the developed countries, is so designed that it requires a minimum tooling investment of Rs. 5 million and plant investments of Rs. 10 million. Designs have been developed basically to save labour. On the other hand, Swaraj sheet-metal requires a tooling investment of not more than Rs. 10,000 and it is being made in three small-scale units with investments of around Rs. 100,000 each.
2. The casting-wall thickness for tractors in the developed countries has been so reduced over the years to save material costs that castings can be produced only in foundries with investments larger than Rs. 100 million. On the other hand, Swaraj castings developed specifically for technology levels readily available in India are being made in foundries with capital investments as low as Rs. 500,000.

I am citing these examples just to illustrate the point. Our production costs with these designs are decidedly lower even at low production volumes. I also agree that our own costs would come down if production levels were raised. It will not be correct to compare the economies of scale of production of different designs, again amply proven in India.

A very crucial contribution of indigenous technology is the in-depth flexibility which it provides to the design group to adopt/innovate to bring down the costs while keeping local conditions in view. This flexibility is further increased by their in-depth knowledge of the production processes. We have several times in our own case changed designs of components to cut down capital investment costs. Complementarity of the production group has also shown immense flexibility in selection of machines and stretching them to the limits of their capabilities to conserve capital, a scarce commodity in the developing country. We are perhaps the only unit in the world wherein special purpose machines, which are normally tooled up for the production of one or two components, have been stretched out to handle 4 to 5 components. Our utilization of these very expensive SPMs from the very first day has been near 100 per cent, while all the others will not achieve 100 per cent utilization till they achieve the production levels of 15,000 plus. On the other hand, our SPMs had 100 per cent utilization at production levels of 4000, and as we proceed further to higher production levels, we shall keep on adding SPMs. Capital investments for us will always be made as market demands higher production levels.

Customer preference and education

It would perhaps surprise you that customer preference for brand names, etc., perhaps only exists in the mind of the educated élite. Swaraj, with no established brand name whatsoever, found customer acceptance from the very first day in a market with 10 other well-known international names. It did require intensive marketing, but resistance was in no way near what the élite had forecast. Farmer preference was solely dictated by performance, reliability, servicing and spare parts. We also did have some technical problems when the Swaraj was introduced. With the in-depth knowledge of our R and D, these technical problems were soon overcome. This constant improvement coupled with aggressive marketing has made Swaraj a positive customer preference today. I do not really know whether government can help in customer education. To my mind assignment of the role of customer education to government is hardly feasible in a democracy.

Modest investments

PTL investments were kept modest from two considerations:

1. It was even difficult to raise the modest investment of Rs. 37 million. This itself required 3 years' intense effort, and there were many moments when things looked totally dead.
2. In the detailed analysis of various tractor projects set up in India, it had clearly emerged that reaching productional levels of 5000 is at least two to three years exercise; so why incur interest charges on the investments for higher productional levels? Higher production levels and investments could always follow any expansion.

Air-cooled engine

We did eventually decide to switch to a water-cooled engine, despite proven technological advantages of air-cooled engines. A casual remark of a very senior Punjab government official made us take this decision: "As it is you are trying to market an unknown tractor based on Indian know-how; why open a second front by introducing an air-cooled engine with which our farmers have had bitter experience on some tractors earlier. One front at a time is better strategy."
Some deep thinking convinced me of its irrefutable logic.

Tool room

The biggest strengths which have enabled PTL to weather the dark periods have been:

1. R and D.
2. Tool-design and industrial engineering.
3. Tool-making facilities.

It was these three strengths which made us switch over to the 35 h.p. fast. We are soon coming out with a small economy tractor for the small farmers of the country. R and D on this tractor was started in January 1976 and we should be introducing it commercially before March 1978. Twenty-seven months for design, prototype manufacture, prototype proving, tooling up and commercial manufacture would stand out as a shining performance anywhere in the world. To achieve this time-schedule we resorted to considerable overlapping of all activities, obviously at a certain risk, but this again was a managerial decision. We would have easily met our time-schedule of twenty-four months but for an unfortunate labour strike earlier this year.

World Bank

The World Bank became relevant only in 1974, 1975 and 1976 when a large number of tractors were made available to our farmers at concessional credit under specific World Bank schemes. Despite the best of effort at inclusion in these schemes, we failed in getting the Swaraj included. This did hurt us hard, as 12,000 tractors became eligible for this concessional credit in Punjab and Haryana alone.

Tractor sales of 95 per cent in India are against credit from commercial land mortgage banks. We have been eligible for this finance on the same terms as other tractors. It has taken quite some time to get included in the approved lists of various banks, but slowly and after much effort we have finally obtained recognition. Swaraj today is on the approved list of all the financing agencies in India.

An ironic fact worth mentioning is that Swaraj secured World Bank approval in Afghanistan at its very first international entry early this year—an approval denied to our own country for a number of years.

Swaraj production

Our actual production in 1976–7 (July-June) was 3200. But for the strike it would have been 3800. This year again because of a strike and its aftermath we may not better 4500. Our 1977 Report is enclosed for any detailed information.

Excise duty relief

Excise support was a two-year battle. It was not at all easy to convince the government to take this decision without a precedent. Here again the support of a few individuals finally altered the balance.

Credit financing of tractor sales and ARDC

ARDC finances all commercial banks/land mortgage banks for tractor sales. When we lost the fight for inclusion in the World Bank schemes, we were given an assurance by the Finance Ministry that ARDC would come up for special schemes for financing Swaraj tractors, to give us at least an equal chance to fight. Here again we failed, ARDC's stock answer being how could they single out a specific tractor without inviting public criticism?; they could only develop general schemes for tractorization and it was for us to capture whatever market share we could. Since the fight was becoming prolonged, we ultimately gave up this line, even though some commercial banks were keenly interested in promoting Swaraj.

Gold Shield

I really do not know if the award of a Gold Shield to PTL was a reflection of any changing attitudes or emphasis of the government on self-reliance. This was purely a decision of the award committee, PTL's contribution to import substitution being far too outstanding to be overlooked. PTL's contribution to the total production, based on Indian knowhow last year, was 33 per cent. How could such a contribution be overlooked? Its significance in changing attitudes towards Indian technology in general, however, is totally different.

Technological competence in various institutions

Knowing what various institutions are in some depth, I really do not think that technological capability is the strong point of any. The biggest failing in any developing country is perhaps technological capability or for that matter the capability to even appreciate a technology and its relative merits. Decisions are by and large based on convincing salesmanship, etc.

This inference would perhaps be further strengthened by the fact that even in 1977, the government of India is seriously considering setting up another tractor plant with British Leyland's collaboration. This Rs. 180 million project would involve a lump sum payment of Rs. 7.5 million for technical knowhow, royalties, etc. Such a decision would indeed be ironic, but then every reason is being found to clear this project. Can we really say that the PTL example has made any difference to national thinking and decision-making?

Small-scale industry

It would perhaps be of interest to note that with intensive effort over the last three years, we have been able to develop more than 100 small-scale ancillary suppliers around us, 70 within a radius of 10 km. Their average supplies to us last year were Rs. 100,000 and their average employment is 12. There is hardly any of these units wherein investment exceeds Rs. 200,000, in most it is below Rs. 50,000. In the national perspective of developing small industry and new entrepreneurial talent in modern technology, this is perhaps a no small contribution of PTL.

Selection of a technology group

The actual position was in fact the reverse. It was the team and the consultants which sold the project to the PSIDC and later on forced them through their determination and strategy to go ahead with the project.

Role of the Planning Commission

Here again, if I look back, it was not the Planning Commission which assigned the task to CMERI. It was virtually Mr. Suri who forced the Indian approach on the Planning Commission. With his salesmanship the Planning Commission had little option but to nod yes.

Industrial licensing policies

It has been generally seen in India that licences should be given for capacities way beyond demand projections. This stems from the fact that no detailed assessment is really made of the technological/managerial capabilities of the prospecting parties. Drop-outs are large. This has been amply illustrated in tractors where the following firms given licences in 1971–2 dropped out.

1. United Auto Tractors (Romanian collaboration).
2. Steyr Tractors (Austrian collaboration).
3. Byford Tractors (Japanese collaboration).
4. Perfect Tractors (West German collaboration).

The interest of the promoters primarily lay in selling imported tractors/CKD packs to capitalize on the market boom of 1970–1.

ILS criteria—financial viability

ILS is not bothered about financial viability. This is purely left to the promoters and their financiers. Your experience at the IDBI would perhaps corroborate.

ILS logic—crucial function

Neglect of such crucial functions is perhaps inevitable in a seller's market anywhere in the world. With the changing situation of the Indian market in the last three years it has turned to a completely buyer's market and has made all manufacturers devote attention to these functions.

Indian Society of Industrial Engineers

The correct name is Indian Society of Agricultural Engineers. Tractor manufacturers had developed separate demand projections. Manufacturers have no regular association as such.

Demand projections

Having been involved with tractors for a fair length of time, I feel that it is almost impossible to develop any realistic long-term demand projections in a country like India where economic policies change most frequently. Food prices, bank credit, extension of irrigation, etc., are a large number of variables for a tractor demand. Even when the government commissioned NCAER four years ago to develop realistic demand estimates, projections went astray. In any case, projections were qualified by a whole host of "ifs". Are such projections of any use?

Swaraj and the ILS

At the point of time when Swaraj designs were initiated at CMERI I had analysed that considering the immense popularity of the Massey Ferguson, Swaraj must be fully competitive with MF, if not better.

Now that we have been in the tractor market for some time and know the tractor market better, we are coming out (as mentioned earlier) with the smaller Economy tractor. Present farmer response to the Economy appears overwhelming. Here again, the final proof of the pudding will only lie in its eating. We are approaching the production programme with cautious optimism. According to a global survey conducted by UNIDO three years ago the demand for such a tractor in the developing countries would be of the order of 100,000 by 1980. Whether it really materializes may only be evident once the tractor is launched commercially. As far as I am aware our approach is original and the Swaraj Economy will be the cheapest tractor in the international free market for equivalent performance. After some field experience at home, we hope to make an international launch by the beginning of 1979.

ILS and the Swaraj history

The ILS was completely aware of the Swaraj history because of the fight for more than five years with the government. It was purely a question of a total lack of faith in Indian engineering capabilities. This was even evidenced by the fact that conversion of our letter of intent into a licence took more than two years and any number of doubts had to be cleared. The decision finally swung around in favour of Swaraj again because of one or two individuals.

Pricing and customer preference

I don't think low prices have been taken by the farmers as indicative of inferior performance. The tremendous market which these super cheap Russian tractors enjoyed from 1960 to 1973 and the Eicher in the last three years are a striking proof of this inference.

Swaraj success—a coercive fact

As mentioned earlier actual experience does not substantiate this hope.

PART III. Financial Structure and Policies

9. Some Aspects of Financial Policies and Central Banking in Developing Countries*

ECONOMIC development is not only facilitated but its pace is quickened by the appropriate development of the financial system–structure of financial institutions, instruments and interest rates.[1]

In any strategy of development, therefore, it is essential to emphasize the evolution of a sound and well-integrated financial system from the point of view both of resource mobilization and efficient allocation.[2] In section I of this chapter, an attempt is made to delineate the broad contours of a set of financial policies that seems to be consistent with any sound strategy of development. In section II, the role of Central Banks is emphasized, not only as *promoters* but also as *regulators* of sound integrated financial systems.[3] These two functions are interrelated: the function of Central Banks as regulators is in fact reinforced by their function as promoters.[4]

In spite of the dynamic catalytic role of the banking system in promoting economic development,[5] it is somewhat strange that, at an international level, this role is not sufficiently stressed in providing technical and financial assistance to the developing countries for the purpose of promoting the evolution of sound financial systems. The International Monetary Fund emphasizes the regulatory role of Central Banks only, while the International Bank for Reconstruction and Development lays stress on the development of specialized financial intermediaries only. The result is that a large number of Central Banks have not been appropriately oriented towards development objectives in general, and to the development of sound financial systems in particular. Further, the evolution of specific financial intermediaries takes place in such a way as to promote further fragmentation of the capital market; or at any rate the policy of merely promoting specific financial intermediaries does not stress the need for an integrative mechanism and agency as provided by the existence of a Central Bank.

What needs special emphasis at an international level is the *rationale* and urgency of evolving a sound financial structure through the efficient performance of the twin interrelated functions—as *promoters* and as *regulators* of the financial system—by Central Banks.

I. Some Aspects of Financial Policies

The main object of this section is to show the significance of saving and flow-of-funds analysis as an indicator of a set of financial policies—policies relating to the structure of financial institutions, instruments and interest rates—essential for

* Published in *World Development*, vol. 2, nos. 10–12 (Oct.–Dec. 1974). Also in *World Bank Reprint Series*, no. 21.

resource mobilization and allocation consistent with a country's development objectives.[6]

In a large number of developing countries, the only reliable data available for understanding the trends in the economy and for policy purposes relate to monetary flows and the balance of payments. These data thus assume critical significance. Flow-of-funds data are not available for a large number of countries but are such as can be reliably compiled and presented. The data relating to corporate enterprises and financial intermediaries are available and can be consolidated in the required form with some effort. Similarly, data relating to the government sector and the balance of payments are available and can be presented in flow-of-funds form along with the data for corporate enterprises and financial intermediaries. The data relating to the government sector, corporate enterprise and financial intermediaries can provide the necessary information relating to the transactions of these sectors with the household sector—an omnibus term for the sector comprising all unincorporated enterprises and households. Thus, provided the usefulness of flow-of-funds analysis is recognized, it may not be difficult to collect and process data in this form.

Whatever the development objectives and whatever the nature of planning or programming, it is essential to aim at financial balance. This balance indicates that the investment demand for resources of the deficit sectors is met by the supply of required resources from the surplus sectors. In most of the developing countries, and in the developed countries, the surplus sector is the household sector which provides resources directly, or indirectly through the financial intermediaries, to the government sector as well as to the corporate sector. The other sector which provides resources to these deficit sectors in the developing countries is the external sector through official external assistance and private foreign investment. For the viability of a development programme, it is essential that these resource-flows are consistent with the projected volume and pattern of investment. Further, various policy instruments can be rationally used for attaining financial balance only when the degree and nature of imbalances are clearly known through flow-of-funds analysis. How such analysis can be used as a tool for financial planning is discussed in the next chapter.

A. *Characteristic Features of Saving and Flow of Funds*

Saving and flow-of-funds analysis brings out the crucial importance of household sector saving for financing the saving deficits of the government sector and the private corporate sector. Generally, the latter two are deficit sectors and the only surplus sector is the household sector which finances directly and indirectly, through the financial institutions, a part of the deficits of the other two sectors. The external sector finances the residual deficits.

Table 1, on Sectoral Surpluses and Deficits during 1950–9 in 14 developed countries and 10 developing countries, brings out this fact clearly. In the developing countries, both the government and business sectors have deficits—that is, their total expenditures exceed their incomes, while the household sector shows a surplus and finances, along with the external sector, the deficits of the government and business sectors. In the developed countries, the government sector shows a surplus. However, in the data available, government enterprises are included in the business sector, if these enterprises were shown in the government sector, it is likely that the government sector too would have been a deficit sector.

The second significant implication of the saving and flow-of-funds data is that the saving surplus of the household sector that can be potentially transferred to the other two sectors is represented by the household saving in the form of financial assets. Of course, a part of this surplus returns to the household sector via its borrowing from the financial institutions.

TABLE 1. *Sectoral surpluses and deficits (—), 1950–9*

	Per cent of Gross Domestic Product		
	Developed countries	Less developed countries	All countries
1. Households	6.1	3.5	4.8
2. Enterprises*	–7.6	–4.9	–6.3
3. Government	1.3	–0.7	0.3
4. Rest of the World	–0.1	2.1	1.0

Source: R. W. Goldsmith, *Financial Structure and Development* (Yale, 1969), p. 441.

* Includes government enterprises.

TABLE 2. *Pattern of household saving*

Form of Saving	India (1963–4) (%)	U.S.A. 1909–14 (%)	U.S.A. 1960–4 (%)
1. Financial assets	66.7 (5.5)	98 (8.83)	123 (10.09)
2. Financial liabilities	–16.7 (–1.4)	–46 (–4.17)	–86 (–7.06)
3. Physical assets	50 (4.1)	48 (4.35)	63 (5.17)
4. Total (1+2+3)	100 (8.2)	100 (9.01)	100 (8.20)
5. Percentage share of household saving in national saving	67.2	..	61

Figures in brackets indicate proportion of personal disposable income.

Source: V. V. Bhatt, "Saving and Flow of Funds Analysis: A Tool for Financial Planning in India", *The Review of Income and Wealth* (Mar. 1971). R. W. Goldsmith, "Changes in the Structure of Personal Saving", *Saving in Contemporary Economic Research* (Congress Palace, Brussels, 1965).

Household sector saving is partly in the form of physical assets like residential housing, equipment, and inventories of goods, and partly in the form of financial assets. Saving in the form of physical assets represents household sector investment, which is financed partly by direct saving of the sector and partly by borrowing from the financial institutions.

Table 2 shows the household sector saving pattern for India (1963–4) and for the U.S.A. (1909–14 and 1960–4). It appears from this table that about 50 per cent of household sector saving was in the form of *net* financial assets (net of financial liabilities) in India (1963–4) and the U.S.A. (1909–14). Thus, the household sector transferred half of its saving to the other two sectors.

The U.S.A. data for 1960–4 reveals a picture that is somewhat different and possibly indicates the nature of evolution of the household sector saving pattern for the developing countries. These data show that a dominant part of the saving was in the form of financial assets and that own saving used for direct investment was negligible. Household sector investment was financed completely by borrowing from the financial institutions. There was in fact excess borrowing (that is borrowing exceeded investment in physical assets) which financed the acquisition of consumer durables, which are not included in the data on saving.

B. Desirable Pattern of Household Sector Saving

It is quite likely that in the developing countries, too, saving in the form of financial assets and borrowing from financial institutions would tend to dominate the saving pattern over a period of time. This may happen; however, it should be the aim of financial policies to quicken this process for several reasons.

(i) It is quite likely that the full *potential* saving of the household sector is not mobilized due to the inadequate development of financial institutions and instruments consistent with savers' preferences. In the developing countries, the capital market in the rural and semi-urban areas is highly fragmented. Potential saving in one part cannot easily be transferred to other deficit units. Further, due to inadequate facilities for borrowing on reasonable terms, the potential saving may be inadequate to finance investment required by these units. For both these reasons, this potential saving may prove abortive and be used for consumption.[7]

(ii) The financial institutions finance a very small part of household sector investment. In India, the proportion of investment financed by the financial institutions does not exceed 15 to 20 per cent. A major part of investment is, thus, financed by own saving and borrowing from the surplus units and private moneylenders/indigenous bankers, which constitute the so-called unorganized market for capital funds. Interest rates in this market are very high and range from 20 to 35 per cent per year. These high interest rates have two consequences. Firstly, worthwhile productive projects cannot be implemented at these rates. And secondly, these high rates induce speculative investment—investment in land, real estate, scarce commodities, gold and the like. Thus, on the one hand, potential productive investment is not taken up and, on the other, resources are diverted toward undesirable forms of investment.

(iii) Because of the existence of this unorganized market, government economic policies—credit as well as fiscal policies—are not very effective in influencing the magnitude or the pattern of investment in the household sector.

(iv) Most of the plans in the developing countries require a rapid growth of investment in the government sector and the private corporate sector. This is not possible without an adequate transfer of household saving to these two sectors. Such a transfer can be facilitated only if a major part of household sector saving were in the form of financial assets. In that case, government economic policies could be effective in attaining an efficient allocation of saving among the various sectors of the economy.

C. *Policy Implications*

For evolving an integrated and efficient capital market, it is thus essential to induce the household sector to save a greater part of its surplus in the form of financial assets. The next logical problem is to find out the type of financial instruments that are consistent with the saving preferences of the household sector.

The structure of household sector financial saving is shown in Table 3 for some developed as well as developing countries. This structure reveals that with the evolution of financial institutions, the household sector prefers to hold more than 50 per cent of its financial saving in the form of money and deposits. The second significant preferred asset seems to be claims on social security institutions—life insurance, pension and provident funds and the like. Thus the major part of financial saving seems to be in the form of claims on financial institutions. Excepting in a few countries like Belgium and Malaysia, saving in the form of direct claims on the non-financial sectors is less than 25 per cent of the total financial saving; in the U.S.A. and U.K. it is negligible.

The trend, thus, seems to be towards a financial structure in which indirect financial saving (that is, saving in the form of claims on financial institutions) is gaining at the expense of direct saving (in the form of direct claims on the government and corporate sectors) and in which borrowing is increasing in importance. It seems desirable for the developing countries to assist this trend and concentrate their efforts on bringing about or facilitating those changes in financial structure, and in the laws and regulations which affect it, that will ensure, or at least make more likely, that a predominantly indirect and institutional and largely contractual and compulsory flow of personal saving contributes as much as possible to economic growth.[8] For this purpose, several important changes will be called for in government and business policies from those now accepted in many countries. To give just one example, governments will have to abandon the policy of attempting to bring back, or to create, a broad market for government and corporate securities among *individual buyers.* It does not seem to be essential for developing countries to pass through that phase of the evolution of financial systems through which the developed countries passed several decades back.

TABLE 3. *Structure of household sectors' financial saving*
(in percentages)

	Money		Thrift deposits	Con-tractural saving	Securities: Central govt. bonds	Securities: Other bonds	Securities: Corporate stock	Securities: Total	Others	Total saving
U.S.A. (1960–4)	8	..	52	37	2	4	−3	3	..	100
U.K. (1960–4)	27	..	38	76	12	17	−27	1	−42	100
France (1960–4)	51	..	23	4	..	..	..	18	3	100
Germany (1960–4)	8	..	47	30	12	..	4	16	..	100
Belgium (1959–64)	..	45.7	..	20	..	..	..	33.8	0.4	100
Italy (1964–5)	..	61.7	..	11.5	..	..	..	14.1	12.8	100
Japan (1959–64)	19	..	44	10.0	−1	4	18	21.0	6.0	100
Australia (1957–61)	18	..	33	25	−16	34	5	23	..	100
Greece (1961–5)	..	84.4	..	1.2	..	..	..	14.4	..	100
Korea (1958–9)	38	..	31	1	8	3	13	21	6	100
Malaysia (1955–8)	..	5.6	..	68.9	..	..	..	25.5	..	100
Philippines (1956–60)	23	..	22	38	..	..	..	17	..	100
Sri Lanka (1955–9)	..	45.2	..	43.6	..	..	..	8.1	3.2	100
India (1963–4)	..	53.4	..	27.7	11.0	..	7.9	18.9	..	100

Source: R. W. Goldsmith, *loc, cit.* Organization for Economic Cooperation and Development, *Capital Market Study* (Paris, 1967–8). V. V. Bhatt, "Saving and Flow of Fund Analysis", *Reserve Bank of India Bulletin* (Sept. 1965). "Measures for Mobilising Domestic Saving for Productive Investment", *Economic Bulletin for Asia and the Far East* (Dec. 1962). S. Joshi Madhusudhan, "Financial Institutions and Financial Policy for Economic Development", *Prajnan* (Bombay), vol. i, no. 2 (Apr.–June 1972).

D. Framework for Economic and Financial Policies

To stimulate indirect financial saving, several institutional and policy measures seem to be essential:

(i) Since thrift deposits—saving and fixed deposits—seems to be a preferred asset, the institutional development that should have first priority should be the widening and deepening of the geographical and functional scope of the commercial banking system. This system has already evolved in the developing countries but its scope is largely restricted to urban areas and to the financing of modern enterprises in industry and trade. Instead of creating new institutions, it seems to be more rational and economical to expand the scope of this system through the creation of a nation-wide network of bank branches, and enlarging their functional scope. Such a system need not restrict its role to that of purveying credit and deposit mobilization; it can also provide entrepreneurial and managerial guidance to agriculture and small industry. The functions of such a system are discussed in my book, *Structure of Financial Institutions*.[9]

(ii) Savers are likely to prefer a financial instrument that is simple, convenient and easily intelligible, that does not involve transactions costs and that can be easily and without loss converted into money. Interest-bearing deposits of various maturities do provide such a financial asset. However, to make them attractive to savers, it is essential to devise such deposit schemes as are linked to the basic motives to save. Apart from the link of deposits with saving motives, some deposit schemes should also be linked with certain services desired by savers. Some possible deposit schemes are discussed in my book.[10] Thus the real return on deposits—return inclusive of tangible and intangible benefits other than interest—would be sufficiently attractive to induce savers to prefer this form of financial asset to private lending or other physical assets like gold, real estate, commodity inventories and the like.

(iii) Apart from this, the monetary yield on various types of deposits should be comparable to the yield, exclusive of risk premium, on private lending.[11] The yield on private lending is high but involves a certain degree of risk. If the banks enter the field of lending so far monopolized by private lenders, the interest rate is likely to decline. Taking into account this possible decline in yield on private lending and the risk premium attached to such lending, deposit rates should be so fixed as to be comparable to these adjusted rates on private lending. Interest rates as such may or may not have much impact on total saving, but it certainly has a substantial impact on the pattern of saving. The interest rate structure, then, should be such as to induce savers to keep their saving in the form of bank deposits rather than in the form of private lending, gold, real estate or inventories of commodities.[12]

(iv) Compulsory provident fund schemes have proved attractive in several countries like Malaysia and India. Such schemes should be introduced to cover wage and salary earners in as many sectors as possible. Social security deposits have been a preferred asset in both developed and developing countries as we have discussed earlier. Their full potential should be exploited.

(v) The other asset which savers seem to prefer is insurance policies. Life insurance facilities should be expanded. For farmers, life insurance may not be as attractive as crop insurance; it may be possible to introduce compulsory crop insurance schemes that are attractive to farmers. For these purposes, bank branches can function as agents of insurance companies so as to minimize administrative expenses. Some bank deposit schemes can be linked with life insurance as well as crop insurance.[13]

(vi) To induce a higher rate of overall saving through saving in the form of specified financial assets, it is possible to exempt such saving for the purpose of income tax by permitting such saving to be deducted from taxable income.[14] In a number of countries, provident fund subscriptions and insurance premiums are deductible for the purpose of income tax; the scope of such deduction can be widened by including all financial saving other than that in the form of currency and gold,[15] as suggested in chapter 15.

These policy measures are likely to modify the pattern of household sector saving in favour of financial assets. The saving-investment process thus can be made more efficient than it is. The allocative efficiency of an integrated capital market would be much greater than that of the isolated markets existing at present. Thus, these measures would not only raise the rate of financial saving, but also improve the productivity of investment. Further, it would then be possible to regulate the magnitude and allocation of investment by means of available policy instruments.[16]

II. On Central Banking

There is a significant difference between the role of a Central Bank in a developed country and that in a developing country; and this difference arises from their different stages of development. The monetary and financial system was already well developed when the Central Banks were set up in the developed countries. In the theory and practice of central banking, hence, it is the regulatory role of the Central Bank that is emphasized.[17]

Central banking has to be thought of quite differently in the developing countries where the financial system has yet to evolve to a stage reached in the developed countries. In these countries, the role of the Central Bank cannot be restricted to that of a regulator; for the institutions to be controlled and the credit system to be regulated have still to evolve to necessitate a regulator.[18]

The role of the Central Bank has to be conceived in the context of evolving a sound financial infrastructure conducive to rapid development. It is the Central Bank that has to take the lead in evolving the credit institutions, instruments and yield-structure that are essential for:

(*a*) the efficient mobilization of saving, and
(*b*) the allocation of resources consistent with development objectives.

This developmental function needs to be performed in such a way that the

Central Bank is able to maintain close, continuous and active contact with the credit system so essential for the success of its regulatory function. If such contact were maintained, the ability of the Central Bank to regulate credit would be much greater than it is in a developed country.

A. Promotional Function

In a large number of developing countries, commercial banks have evolved to finance the credit needs of foreign trade, the industrial activities that are ancillary to such trade and the modern industrial structure. However, the credit needs of agriculture, small business and industry and a large number of traditional enterprises are still met by the non-banking traditional institutions like moneylenders. What is required in this set-up is a wider geographical and functional penetration of the banking system. It is the Central Bank that has to take a lead in this matter.[19]

Again, it should be the Central Bank's responsibility to ensure that the evolving banking system is viable, its practices sound and its venturesomeness tempered by wisdom. Regular periodical inspection of banks from this point of view is essential for the sound development of banking. This would inspire confidence in the system. To inspire confidence among savers, some form of deposit insurance would be necessary and to induce the banks to meet the credit needs of agriculture and small enterprises of all types, some credit guarantee organization needs to be developed.

Apart from these devices, it is essential for the Central Bank to do banking business with the banks and the other institutions without inhibitions. Unless the Central Bank becomes not only "central" but also a "bank", its function to supervise and direct the growth of banking would be without adequate sanctions. It should not be merely a lender of last resort; it has to be a lender of early resort and in some cases a lender of primary resort. This need not mean continuous indebtedness; the banks, however, should feel free to approach the Central Bank for help from time to time. Only then would the banks have an incentive to listen to Central Bank advice with respect.[20]

For meeting the long-term credit needs of various sectors for financing investment projects, it is not essential, in principle, to evolve separate institutions like development finance companies. The banks, as the principal mobilizers of saving, should be able to perform this function at least in the initial stages. With their nation-wide branch network, it is the banks which would have close and intimate contact with agriculture and industry and, at the same time, it is they who would be in a better position to meet the term credit needs of these sectors than would a new institution without a branch network and without the banks' resources. For the purpose of division of labour and exploiting the advantages of specialization and scale economies, the banks could develop specialized departments or specialized subsidiaries.[21]

Such an evolution of the banking system has considerable advantages from the point of view of strengthening and fortifying the power of the Central Bank to regulare credit; Central Bank policy instruments to affect the cost as well as availability of credit would be much more effective in influencing not only inventory investment but also fixed investment than in the case where term credit institutions were isolated from the banking system.[22]

B. Regulatory Functions: Limitations

A Central Bank's effectiveness in regulating credit depends upon the geographical and functional scope of the banking system and the extent of the latter's dependence on the Central Bank for assistance.

If the banking system's functions are restricted to meeting the credit needs of only modern industry and trade, a Central Bank's power to regulate credit allocation among the other sectors would be limited, as it has been in many countries. The funds in the so-called unorganized market can be switched from one line to another in search of speculative profits and the Central Bank would not have much control over interest rates or lending patterns. Of course, the overall supply of funds and overall money supply would still be within the powers of the Central Bank to regulate, but the lending pattern and the yield pattern in sectors other than those covered by the banking system would be outside the Central Bank's control. The availability of credit outside the system would affect the Central Bank's control over the modern sector also.

In such a situation, a Central Bank faces a dilemma. Too tight control on the banks may mean starving the modern sector of required credit, while lack of such control would mean supplying resources to the unorganized market, over which the Central Bank has no control. This is, doubtless, one of the reasons why credit-creation by the Central Bank turns out to be excessive in some developing countries.

There is another reason for a similar situation to arise, and that is the excessive reliance of government on Central Bank credit.[23] Being short of resources in relation to mounting needs, governments tend to rely on Central Bank credit to an extent that generates excessive increases in money supply, with inflationary consequences.

In a situation like this, the Central Bank's ability to control and regulate credit again becomes limited. Of course, it can tighten credit and make it costly for the modern private sector; but then this tends to affect output in this sector adversely and thus aggravate inflationary pressures.

C. Regulatory Function: Policy Instruments

A Central Bank's ability to regulate credit depends upon:

(*a*) the extent of reliance of the modern sector on bank credit;
(*b*) the reliance on trade credit from the modern sector of the sectors linked with the modern sector;
(*c*) the dependence of the banks on Central Bank assistance; and
(*d*) the policy instruments available to Central Bank.

In a large number of developing countries, with a rapidly expanding modern sector, the latter does rely on bank credit to a significant extent. Again the modern large enterprises do extend credit to sectors linked with them.

The banks' dependence on Central Bank credit depends on alternative sources of funds. If branches of international banks are dominant, their reliance on the Central Bank may be marginal. If the inflow of banking funds is controlled and the modern sector is rapidly expanding, banks may find their own resources inadequate periodically to meet the credit needs of the modern sector. Again, if the Central Bank has powers to vary the *net* liquidity ratio of banks, it can make the banks marginally dependent on Central Bank credit.

In such a situation, the Central Bank can regulate both the cost and the availability of credit, both to the modern sector and to the sectors linked to it. It can raise the cost of its credit to the banks which, in turn, would raise their rates to their borrowers. The increased cost of borrowing can be made effective by restricting the banks' lending power by raising their *net* liquidity ratios—that is, the ratio of cash and liquid assets, minus Central Bank borrowing, to total deposits.

A Central Bank can also regulate credit to specific sectors by means of selective credit controls operated in the context of overall credit control. Since it has sanctions, it can ask the banks to raise margin requirements as well as the cost of advances to specific sectors which require separate regulation for example, where there is speculative stock building of commodities in short supply.

It can, likewise, encourage banks to lend to specific sectors by linking its own credit to banks with the latters' credit to such sectors.

The traditional central banking instruments like open market operations are unlikely to be successful in view of the narrowness of security markets. Bank rate coupled with powers to vary reserve ratios and net liquidity ratios are likely to be much more effective. Depending on the contact of the Central Bank with the banks and the latters' dependence on it, moral suasion can also be quite effective in regulating the overall volume and structure of credit.

The real limitations on the Central Bank arise as a result of:

(*a*) the excessive reliance of the government on Central Bank credit; and
(*b*) the lack of integration of money and capital markets.

The second limitation would be overcome with the geographical and functional extension of the role of the banking system.[24]

D. Structure of Interest Rates

Central Bank policy with regard to interest rate structure has considerable significance from the points of view of:

(*a*) inducing savers to invest in bank deposits and other financial assets; and
(*b*) bringing about a rational allocation of resources.[25]

Savers can be induced to keep their savings in the form of financial assets if the yield on such assets is comparable to that on physical assets like real estate and gold and commodities, after making allowance for risk premia and transaction costs.

In a climate of reasonable price stability and with such comparable yields on financial assets, it is possible to raise the rate of financial saving and thus bring about greater integration of the money and capital markets.

Again, to achieve a rational allocation of resources, interest costs to borrowers should reflect the relative scarcity of capital. The rate of interest on bank credit, as well as the interest costs of other forms of borrowing, should, therefore, be related to the yield on real investment that is consistent with the attainment of growth targets.

It appears that, in most of the developing countries, the lowest rate—that is the rate on one year's deposits—should not be lower than 6 per cent per year and the annual rate of return on agriculture and industrial projects should not be lower than 15 per cent. The other rates should fall within this range depending on risk premia, transaction costs, marketability and liquidity attached to specific financial instruments. This rate structure should be in *real* terms. On the assumption of *price stability*, the rate structure should be as suggested.

E. *Basic Limitations of Monetary Policy*

Central Banks had effective monetary policies in an environment which now no longer exists—in which governments had, by and large, balanced budgets and exchange rate stability was the primary concern of policy. With other domestic objectives like full employment and development becoming dominant, governments have become aware of the monetary implications of fiscal policy. Monetary policies thus have become secondary to fiscal policies and the latter have proved to lack the flexibility of the former.

On the other hand, with multinational firms and an international banking system, the international monetary system has evolved into a credit system. Now this international credit system is as unstable and fragile as the domestic credit system had earlier become—evolving from a currency system.

For both these reasons, a Central Bank is no longer central; in the domestic sphere, its flexibility is restricted by government fiscal policy and, in the international sphere, by an international credit system. The international system now requires a "central" bank to manage a system that is inherently unstable. But since in the domestic system, governments are not willing to give the power of control to their Central Banks, the question is: how will they entrust the power to regulate the international system to an international central bank? This is the dilemma at present with regard to the international monetary system.[26]

F. *Central Banking in Japan: a Model for Developing Countries*

Monetary policy in Japan has been very effective—and much more so than in any other country during the last two decades. Since the financial structure in the developing countries is likely to evolve on the Japanese lines—and conscious attempts to do so may hasten the process—it is worthwhile to know the factors behind the success of Japanese monetary policy.

A significant factor in Japanese success in this field, as well as in others, is the strong tradition of cooperation between business and government. But this success is *also* due to its financial structure; and it is possible to evolve such a structure in the developing countries.

The rate of household saving in Japan is very high—almost double the rate in the USA, France or Germany. During 1960–9, this saving comprised 19 per cent of disposable income, as against 9.6 per cent in the USA, 10.3 per cent in Germany and 10.0 per cent in France. A much more important factor has been the dominance of financial saving (more than 11 per cent of disposable income) and again the dominance of bank deposits in financial saving (about 80 per cent or more of financial saving being in the form of bank deposits or bank debentures).[27]

Thus saving of the household sector is mobilized primarily by the banks and it is they who finance investment in the economy. Because of the high rate of investment (about 40 per cent of GNP) and its rapid growth, the business sector is able to finance only 46 per cent of investment by ploughing back profits; of the rest, more than 80 per cent is financed by the banks. Straight issues of stock and foreign borrowing are of marginal significance.

The banks—the big city and long-term investment banks—finance mainly large enterprises and their projects, and the large enterprises finance—via trade credit—the small firms. Thus, the small firms too are indirectly financed by the banks.

Banks have even been willing to provide long-term credit by taking big risks involved in low cash ratios, "operations at level of illiquidity that would drive an English or American banker into a state of permanent neurosis".[28] This is made possible by the willingness of the Central Bank to provide credit to banks, which, at the peak of a boom, rises to as high as 10 per cent of the banks' loans and investments.

Government accounts are generally balanced but tend to show a surplus during boom periods, with expenditure lagging behind revenue. This permits the Central Bank to take effective measures to regulate credit in times of emerging payments problems even before the inflationary pressures become serious.

The policy instrument, largely, is credit rationing. Official interest rates are generally inflexible. The Bank of Japan is able not only to ration its own supply of funds to the banking system, but also by other means to exert a strong influence over the expansion of loans and over the credit rationing carried out by the individual banks. In addition to moral suasion, a number of specific devices are used, such as reserve requirements, import deposit requirements, a complicated discount rate structure (with penalty rates partly dependent on the amount of borrowing of the individual bank) and limits set on the loans and investments of each bank.[29]

Because of the Japanese economic and financial structure, the monetary restraint measures work very quickly, with a lag of barely a few months. Inventory investment is the first to be affected, along with imports, spreading from large firms to small firms through the effect on trade credit.

Since the results of monetary restraint are attained quickly, there are generally no longer-term dampening effects on fixed investment and growth. Equally, the elimination of the restrictive measures is also effective in stimulating rapid expansion. Thus, the Central Bank is effective both ways—in curbing booms and in effecting a quick revival of business activity. In no other country has monetary policy been effective in both directions.

The Japanese banking structure, be it noted, can be duplicated easily in developing countries, but on one condition: if the governments are prudent and responsible in the management of the banking system.

NOTES

1. See R. W. Goldsmith, *Financial Structure and Development* (Yale University Press, 1969).
2. See R. I. McKinnon, *Money and Capital in Economic Development* (The Brookings Institution, 1973).
3. See R. S. Sayers, *Central Banking in Underdeveloped Countries* (Cairo, 1956).
4. See J. Hicks, *Capital and Growth* (Oxford, 1965), chapter xxiii, p. 292. Hicks writes: "There is a place for monetary policy . . . it can perform its function more satisfactorily . . . if it is backed by an efficient system of financial intermediaries." See also pp. 290–2.
5. See J. A. Schumpeter, *Business Cycles* (New York, 1939), vol. i, pp. 109–29. See also A. Gerschenkron, *Economic Backwardness in Historical Perspective* (Cambridge, Massachusetts, 1962), pp. 10–15, and R. Cameron *et al.* (eds.), *Banking in the Early Stages of Industrialization: A Study in Comparative Economic History* (Oxford, 1967).
6. For a discussion of saving and flow-of-funds analysis as a technique for financial planning, see V. V. Bhatt, "Saving and Flow-of-Funds Analysis: A Tool for Financial Planning in India", *The Review of Income and Wealth* (Mar. 1971).
7. For the effects of a fragmented capital market and the significance of financial development, see R. I. McKinnon, *Money and Capital in Economic Development* (Washington, D.C.: The Brookings Institution, 1973).
8. See R. W. Goldsmith, "Changes in the Structure of Personal Saving", in *Saving in Contemporary Economic Research* (Congress Palace, Brussels, 1965).
9. V. V. Bhatt, *Structure of Financial Institutions* (Bombay: Vora & Co., 1972).
10. *Ibid.*
11. See D. R. Khatkhate, *Analytic Basis of the Working of Monetary Policy in Less Developed Countries*, IMF Staff Papers (Nov. 1972).
12. See A. G. Chandavarkar, *Some Aspects of Interest Rate Policies in Less Developed Economies: The Experience of Selected Asian Countries*, IMF Staff Papers, vol. xviii (1971).
13. See V. V. Bhatt, *Structure of Financial Institutions* (Bombay: Vora & Co., 1972).
14. See V. V. Bhatt, "Taxation for Economic Development", *Development Digest* (Oct. 1973), and *Economic and Political Weekly* (24 June 1972).
15. See J. A. Schumpeter, *Capitalism, Socialism and Democracy*, 3rd edn. (New York: Harper Torchbooks), pp. 423–4, and R. V. Clemence (ed.), *Essays of J. A. Schumpeter* (Cambridge, Massachusetts, 1951), pp. 245–6 and pp. 302–5.
16. See V. V. Bhatt, "Central Banks: Their Regulatory Functions", *Development Digest* (Apr. 1974), and "Industrial Development Bank of India: Recent Evolution in its Role and Functions", Prajnan (Bombay), vol. i, no. 3 (July–Sept. 1972).
17. J. Hicks, *Critical Essays in Monetary Theory* (London: Oxford University Press, 1967), pp. 158–9.
18. See R. S. Sayers, *Central Banking in Underdeveloped Countries* (Cairo: National Bank of Egypt, 1956).
19. See R. S. Sayers, *op. cit.*, p. 7. Sayers writes: "Another service having immense potentialities . . . is the contribution a Central Bank can make to the growth of a sound structure of commercial banks and other financial institutions . . . but the emphasis in early days must be on the development of a banking system to control. This is not only a logical order; it is also the historical order of events in the underdeveloped country I have most studied: the England of earlier centuries. . . . It must be not only central but also, and very actively, a bank."
20. See R. S. Sayers, *op. cit.*, pp. 13–14.
21. *Ibid.*, pp. 13–15.
22. J. M. Keynes, *The General Theory of Employment, Interest and Money*, First Harbinger Edition (1965), pp. 205–6.
23. T. Hicks, *op. cit.*, pp. 168–71.
24. See R. S. Sayers, *op. cit.*, pp. 19–25. He writes: ". . . central banks, if they are not narrowly conceived, can be a real help to these countries in making economic activity less irregular—but that their power must remain slight if they have to work in a banking vacuum. The

encouragement of the growth of sound commercial banking throughout the economy must always occupy first place on the agenda of a new Central Bank" (p. 24).

25. V. V. Bhatt, *Structure of Financial Institutions* (Bombay: Vora & Co., 1972), chapters 4 and 12. See also J. Hicks, *Capital and Growth* (Oxford University Press, 1965), chapter 23.
26. J. Hicks, *Critical Essays in Monetary Theory*, *loc. cit.* Hicks writes: "The remedy . . . would be an International Central Bank, an International Bank which would underpin the credit structure, but in order to underpin it must have some control over it. That was what Keynes, who understood this international aspect very clearly, wanted to get at Bretton Woods, but all he got was a Currency Board (for it is little more than a Currency Board, being so tied up with rules and regulations)—the IMF. That, we are finding—and Mill could have told us, one hundred and twenty years ago, that it is what we should find—is not enough. But how should the powers, which governments have been unwilling to entrust to their own Central Banks (once they have realized what is involved) be entrusted to an International Bank? That is the dilemma, the old dilemma, to which we have now come back, on the international plane" (pp. 172–3).
27. Organization for Economic Cooperation and Development, *Monetary Policy in Japan* (1973). See also "Key to Success", *The Economist* (27 Jan.–2 Feb. 1973), pp. 41–2.
28. E. Lundberg, *Instability and Economic Growth* (Yale University Press, 1968), p. 334. See also pp. 329–47.
29. E. Lundberg, *op. cit.*, pp. 338–9.

10. Saving and Flow of Funds Analysis: A Tool for Financial Planning in India*

IN THE literature on planning, a good deal of attention is paid to the derivation of investment pattern on the basis of the initial production capacities, the input and capital coefficients, the desired growth rate of consumption and the terminal capital stock. However, it is not sufficiently realized that the investment pattern is also a function of the structure of saving.[1] Quite often, it is assumed that once the total magnitude of investment is based on the overall propensity to save, there would not be any inconsistency between the financial aspects of a plan and its physical aspects. This assumption inevitably leads, when the plan is implemented, to imbalances and inflationary pressures,[2] as indicated in chapter 17.

The reason is that the constraint of the structure of saving on investment pattern is not recognized at the stage of plan formulation. Sector-wise distribution of investment (that is, composition of investment in terms of its ownership—by government sector, corporate sector, household sector, etc.) is one of the important determinants of the investment pattern, that is the functional (industry-wise) distribution of investment. And sector-wise structure of saving determines to a significant extent the sector-wise investment composition. The planned pattern of investment, therefore, has to be consistent with the evolving structure of saving.

The structure of saving has two aspects: one is the sector-wise composition of saving and the other is the pattern of saving of the household sector. The other sectors—government sector and the private corporate sector—are generally deficit sectors, that is, the capital formation in each of these sectors exceeds the sector's own saving. The household sector, on the other hand, is a surplus sector; its saving exceeds its capital formation. It is the surplus saving of the household sector which finances the deficits of the other two sectors, given the sector-wise net inflows from the external sector. The extent to which the household sector finances the deficit of each of these two sectors depends upon its pattern of saving —that is, how its saving is distributed in terms of its claims on the government sector, private corporate sector and the financial institutions.

The sector-wise distribution of saving depends on the income of each sector and its propensity to save. The pattern of household sector's saving depends on household preferences, the structure of interest rates and the structure of financial institutions and instruments. The borrowing of each of the deficit

* Paper presented at the Biennial Meeting of the *International Association for Research in Income and Wealth* held in Nathanya, Israel, in September 1969, and originally published in *The Review of Income and Wealth*, series 17, no. 1 (Mar. 1971).

The Author acknowledges with gratitude the valuable assistance received from Mr. T. R. Venkatachalam of Department of Statistics, Reserve Bank of India, Bombay.

sectors depends on the pattern of household saving and the lending pattern of the financial institutions, for, the household sector lends directly when it purchases claims on the deficit sectors and indirectly when it purchases claims on the financial institutions. In the latter case, what each deficit sector borrows depends upon the pattern of lending of the financial institutions. Thus, it is not possible to determine the overall as well as sector-wise composition of investment and hence the investment pattern without an adequate analysis of the structure of saving and the flow of funds in the base year and the likely changes in this structure during the plan period as a result of changes in fiscal and other policies affecting the structure of financial institutions, instruments, interest rates and overall saving.

This chapter deals with the analysis of the structure of saving and flow-of-funds in India and indicates how such an analysis is actually used for the purpose of financial planning.

The principal sources of data and estimation procedures for deriving this structure are briefly indicated in section I. The evolving structure of saving during the period 1954/5 to 1967/8 is analysed in section II. The flow-of-funds table is presented for the year 1965/6 in section III, while the way in which such flow of funds analysis is used for the purpose of financial planning is indicated in section IV. An attempt is made in section V to formalize the technique of financial planning.

I. Sources of Data and Estimation Procedures

The Indian economy for the purpose of saving and flow of funds analysis is divided into the following sectors:

A. Domestic Non-financial Sector

1. Household sector comprising pure households, non-corporate enterprises in agriculture, trade and industry and private non-profit-making trusts.
2. Private corporate sector comprising all non-financial joint stock companies in the private sector.
3. Government sector comprising central, state and local governments, departmental non-financial enterprises and other non-financial corporate enterprises.
4. Non-credit (private) societies comprising enterprises organized on the cooperative principles.

B. Domestic Financial Sector

(i) *Banking Sector*

5. Reserve Bank of India (Central Bank).
6. Commercial banks.
7. Credit cooperatives.

(ii) *Other Financial Institutions Sector*

8. Term-lending institutions (Industrial Development Bank of India,

Industrial Finance Corporation of India, State financial corporations, Industrial Credit and Investment Corporation of India, Agricultural Refinance Corporation, Unit Trust of India, etc.).

9. Life Insurance Corporation of India (LIC).
10. Provident Funds.

C. External (rest of the world) Sector

The net saving of each of these sectors (excluding the cooperative, household and external sectors) is derived from its current account. The household sector's saving is divided into two parts: Saving in the form of financial assets and saving in the form of physical assets such as residential housing and capital formation in agriculture and non-corporate industry, transport and trade. Its financial saving is derived from changes in its financial assets and liabilities. For this, data available from the balance sheets and capital accounts of other sectors are used. Since the balance sheet data do not in all cases provide sector-wise breakdown of assets and liabilities, additional information on this aspect is collected through various purposive surveys. The changes in holdings of private (both equity and other securities) and government securities are derived on the basis of the total net issue of such claims in each year and the annual changes in the holdings of these claims by other sectors.

The household saving in the form of physical assets is estimated on the basis of data obtained through periodical surveys particularly with regard to rural sector. The estimates of capital formation in non-corporate industry and trade are based on the results obtained from *ad hoc* banking studies. The estimate of urban investment in residential construction is on the basis of the net income originating from this sector and certain assumptions relating to the life of the asset and rate of return.

These estimates of household saving in the form of physical assets represent only broad orders of magnitude and are not as firm and reliable as the estimates of financial saving.

The flow of funds table is constructed on the basis of the balance sheets of financial institutions, the balance sheets and profit and loss accounts of the non-financial private corporate sector (on a sample basis), the financial accounts of the government sector, and statistics of offerings and retirements of securities by their issuers (collected by the government). Some discrepancies do arise as it has been found difficult to obtain a sector-wise breakdown of "other" assets and "other" liabilities of various financial and non-financial institutions; these have been apportioned to various sectors on the basis of informed judgement. A part of these discrepancies is also due to the different methods of valuation adopted by the different sectors with regard to their holding of private and government securities.

Details relating to sources of data and estimation procedures are described in detail in the various articles published in the *Reserve Bank of India Bulletin*.[3] The sources of data used in framing the various estimates are indicated in a summary form in the Appendix.

II. Analysis of the Structure of Saving: 1954/5 to 1967/8

Sector-wise Composition of Saving

Let us now turn to the evolution of the structure of saving during 1954/5 and 1967/8. Table 1 shows the composition—sector-wise—of aggregate net saving for three years—1954/5, 1963/4 and 1967/8. From 1954/5 to 1963/4, overall and sector-wise saving as a proportion of national income show a fluctuating yet rising trend, reaching their peak levels in 1963/4. Thereafter there has been a decline therein largely as a result of the failure of agricultural output to increase at a rate consistent with the growth of the non-agricultural output. The severe consecutive droughts led to large relief expenditures on the part of the government. An attempt at curbing inflationary pressures through reduction in the rate of increase of government capital formation led to excessive under-utilization of productive capacity already created. Further, significant rise in the foodgrain prices led to rise in money wages thus raising production costs in the industrial sector and a reduction in the capacity to save of the urban fixed income groups. Thus, there was a decline in the saving rate (saving as a proportion of national income) of all the sectors, though the sharpest decline was with regard to government-sector saving. The process of recovery of the saving rate has been in evidence in 1968/9 with relative price stability and some recovery of industrial output.

TABLE 1. *Net saving—sector-wise and aggregate*
(Percentage distribution)

	1954/5	1963/4	1967/8[a]
SECTOR			
Government	12.2	26.0	14.0
	(1.0)	(3.1)	(1.1)
Private corporate[b]	6.6	6.8	4.5
	(0.5)	(0.8)	(0.3)
Household	81.2	67.2	81.5
	(6.4)	(7.8)	(6.2)
Aggregate saving	100	100	100
	(7.9)	(11.7)	(7.6)
Aggregate saving as proportion of net capital formation	94.2	80.8	70.2
	(7.9)	(11.7)	(7.6)
Net capital inflow from abroad as proportion of net capital formation	5.8	19.2	29.8[c]
	(0.5)	(2.8)	(3.2)
Aggregate net capital formation	100	100	100
	(814)	(14.5)	(10.8)

[a] Provisional.
[b] Includes also financial institutions and the cooperative sector.
[c] At the new rate of exchange.
Figures in brackets represent proportion (per cent) to national income.

The proportion of net aggregate saving to net national income rose by almost 50 per cent between 1954/5 and 1963/4, rising from 7.9 per cent to 11.7 per cent. Government saving to national income ratio rose three times, while the corresponding ratio for the private corporate sector increased by more than 50 per cent. The rise in the same ratio in respect of the household sector was only marginal—a little more than 20 per cent. As a result, the share of the household sector saving in total saving declined from 81 per cent to about 67 per cent. However, during the subsequent few years, the decline in the government and the corporate sector saving ratios was very sharp, while the ratio for the household sector witnessed modest decline. Consequently, the share of the household sector saving in total saving rose to 81.5 per cent in 1967/8, a share larger than that in 1954/5.

Net capital inflow from abroad as a proportion of national income rose from 0.5 per cent in 1954/5 to 2.8 per cent in 1963/4 and further to 3.2 per cent (at the new exchange rate) in 1967/8. The ratio of net capital formation to net national income, as a result, rose from 8.4 per cent to 14.5 per cent, though it declined in 1967/8 to 10.8 per cent because of a fall in the domestic saving ratio.

Pattern of Household Sector Saving

The marked change which occurred in the saving pattern of household sector was with respect to the progressive rise in the share of saving in the form of financial assets and in the proportion of the household sector's financial liabilities to the sector's total saving (Table 2). These changes reflect the progressive evolution of the financial super-structure in the economy and the rise in what Goldsmith has called the *marginal financial interrelations ratio*.

Among the financial assets, the share of saving in the form of claims on the banking system showed a substantial rise up to 1963/4 at the cost of the shares of the other financial instruments (Table 3). However, after 1963/4, the share of claims on social security institutions rose, while the share of the rest declined somewhat. Over the whole period, the share of saving in the form of direct claims on the government sector and the private corporate sector considerably declined reflecting the growing significance of the financial instruments of the banking system and the social security institutions.

TABLE 2. *Pattern of household saving*

	1954/5 (%)	1963/4 (%)	1967/8[a] (%)
FORM OF SAVING			
A. *Financial assets*	*58.6*	*66.7*	*65.0*
	(3.8)	(5.5)	(4.1)
B. *Financial liabilities*	*−9.0*	*−16.7*	*−14.7*
	(−0.6)	(−1.4)	(−0.9)
C. *Physical assets*	*50.4*	*50.0*	*49.7*
	(3.3)	(4.1)	(3.2)
D. Total (A + B + C)	100	100	100
	(6.5)	(8.2)	(6.4)

[a] Provisional.

Figures in brackets indicate proportion (per cent) to personal disposable income.

III. Saving and Flow of Funds Analysis: 1965/6

The saving and flow of funds table is constructed for the year 1965/6 for all the sectors mentioned in section I. This table is so constructed as could be put to use for the purpose of planning and was actually so used for formulating the financial aspects of the Indian Fourth Plan (1969–74).[4]

The main flow of funds matrix is shown in columns and rows 1 to 11 (Table 4). Each column represents lending by the sector concerned to the other sectors, while each row represents the borrowing by the concerned sector from the other sectors. The column thus represents the marginal financial assets pattern of the concerned sector, while the row represents its marginal financial liabilities pattern. Column 11 represents total domestic borrowing by each sector and row 11 represents total domestic lending by each sector.

TABLE 3. *Pattern of household sector saving in the form of financial assets*
(Percentages)

	1954/5	1963/4	1967/8[a]
FORM OF SAVING			
Financial assets	*100*	*100*	*100*
	(3.8)	(5.5)	(4.1)
1. Currency	23.5	23.5	14.4
	(0.9)	(1.3)	(0.6)
2. Bank deposits	17.5	29.9	35.8
	(0.7)	(1.6)	(1.5)
(1 + 2) *Claims on the banking system*	41.0	53.4	50.2
	(1.6)	(2.9)	(2.1)
3. Life insurance policies	7.6	10.2	12.2
	(0.3)	(0.6)	(0.5)
4. Provident funds	24.0	17.5	22.5
	(0.9)	(1.0)	(0.9)
(3 + 4) *Claims on social security institutions*	31.6	27.7	34.7
	(1.2)	(1.6)	(1.4)
5. Claims on the government sector	16.8	11.0	7.8
	(0.6)	(0.6)	(0.3)
6. Claims on the private corporate sector (including cooperatives)	10.6	7.9	7.3
	(0.4)	(0.4)	(0.3)
(5 + 6) *Claims on government and private corporate sector*	27.4	18.9	15.1
	(1.0)	(1.0)	(0.6)

[a] Provisional.

Figures in brackets represent proportion (per cent) to personal disposable income.

This matrix is partitioned into nine sub-matrices. The left-hand side top matrix of (4 × 4) order represents financial transactions among the non-financial sectors, the left middle matrix of (3 × 4) order represents lending transactions by

TABLE 4. *Matrix of saving and financial flows 1965/6*[a]
(Amount in Rs. crores at current prices; One crore = 10 millions)

From sector	Non-financial sector					Financial sector—banking			
To sector	Household	Private corporation	Government	Non-credit societies	Total borrowing	Reserve Bank of India	Commercial banks	Credit cooperatives	Total borrowing
	1	2	3	4		5	6	7	
1. Household	. .	. .	63.0	16.5	79.5	. .	28.6	120.1	148.7
2. Private corporate	91.7	. .	1.4	. .	93.1	0.9	178.6	. .	179.5
3. Government	107.3[b]	. .	. .	. .	107.3	382.9	139.1	5.8	527.8
4. Non-credit societies	15.6	. .	19.6	. .	35.2	. .	3.9	28.6	32.5
Total lending	214.6	. .	84.0	16.5	315.1	383.8	350.2	154.5	888.5
5. Reserve Bank of India	275.5	. .	. .	. .	275.5	. .	85.9	0.2	86.1
6. Commercial banks	459.3[c]	. .	. .	. .	459.3	. .	. .	0.6	0.6
7. Credit cooperatives	84.7	. .	9.7	9.1	103.5	21.5	4.0	. .	25.5
Total lending	819.5	. .	9.7	9.1	838.3	21.5	89.9	0.8	112.2
8. Term lending institutions	3.1	. .	64.8	. .	67.9	1.9	4.0	. .	5.9
9. Life Insurance Corporation	97.6	. .	. .	. .	97.6	2.0	18.3	. .	20.3
10. Provident funds	102.4	. .	. .	. .	201.4	. .	. .	. .	. .
Total lending	302.1	. .	64.8	. .	366.9	3.9	22.3	. .	26.2
11. Aggregate lending	1336.2	. .	158.5	25.6	1520.3	409.2	462.4	155.3	1026.9
12. External sector	. .	. .	. .	. .	. .	. .	. .	. .	. .
13. Capital formation	541.9	453.8	2015.3	54.3	3065.3	. .	. .	. .	. .
14. Increase in total assets	1878.1	453.8	2173.8	79.9	4585.6	409.2	462.4	155.3	1026.9

From sector / To sector	Financial sector: Other financial institutions: Term lending institutions	Life Insurance Corporation	Provident funds	Total borrowing	Aggregate borrowing	External sector	Own saving	Aggregate resources	Capital formation (aggregate resources aggregate lending)
	8	9	10		11	12	13	14	15
1. Household	7.5	9.9	. .	17.4	245.6	. .	1632.5	1878.1	541.9
2. Private corporate	72.1	22.5	. .	94.6	367.2	0.9	85.7	453.8	543.8
3. Government	. .	112.2	199.5	311.7	946.8	607.2	619.8	2173.8	2015.3
4. Non-credit societies	2.5	6.9	. .	9.4	77.1	. .	2.8	79.9	54.3
Total lending	82.1	151.5	199.5	433.1	1636.7	608.1	2340.8	4585.6	3065.3
5. Reserve Bank of India	. .	. .	. .	. .	361.6	35.4	12.2	409.2	. .
6. Commercial banks	. .	. .	1.9	1.9	461.8	−3.6	4.2	462.4	. .
7. Credit cooperatives	4.3	8.3	. .	12.6	141.6	. .	13.7	155.3	. .
Total lending	4.3	8.3	1.9	14.5	965.0	31.8	30.1	1026.9	. .
8. Term lending institutions	. .	2.5	. .	2.5	76.3	6.1	4.0	86.4	. .
9. Life Insurance Corporation	. .	. .	. .	. .	117.9	−6.7	51.1[d]	162.3	. .
10. Provident funds	. .	. .	. .	. .	201.4	. .	. .	201.4	. .
Total lending	. .	2.5	. .	2.5	395.6	−0.6	55.1	450.1	. .
11. Aggregate lending	86.4	162.3	201.4	450.1	2997.3	639.3	2426.0	6062.6	3065.3
12. External sector	. .	. .	. .	. .	. .	. .	. .	. .	. .
13. Capital formation	. .	. .	. .	. .	3065.3	. .	. .	. .	. .
14. Increase in total assets	86.4	162.3	201.4	450.1	6062.6	. .	. .	. .	. .

[a]Provisional.
[b]After adjustment of Rs. 44.7 crores of disinvestment in government securities by households.
[c]Includes a balancing entry of Rs. 100.2 crores mainly in lieu of branch adjustments (shown on liabilities' side) between Indian offices of banks.
[d]Includes also Rs. 30.7 crores shown as rise in investment reserves and other non-identifiable liabilities of Rs. 19.1 crores.

the non-financial sectors to the banking sector and the left bottom matrix of (3 × 4) order represents lending by the non-financial sectors to the other financial institutions. Since all the non-financial sectors except the household sector are net borrowers, lending by them to the financial sector is netted against their borrowings so that the only sector lending to the financial sector is the household sector. However, since the term lending institutions and cooperatives rely for their resources on the government sector, the latter's lending to these sectors are shown separately.

The middle top sub-matrix of (4 × 3) order represents lending by the banking sector to the non-financial sectors, the middle middle of (3 × 3) order to itself and the middle bottom of (3 × 3) order to the other financial institutions. The right-hand side top, middle and the bottom sub-matrices similarly represent lending by the other financial institutions to the non-financial sector, banking sector and to itself, respectively.

Column 11 represents total domestic borrowing of each sector, column 12, the net inflow of resources from the external sector and column 13, the net saving of each sector. Column 14 represents the total financial resources available to each sector and column 15 represents their net capital formation.

Row 11 represents increase in financial assets of each sector and row 13, the net capital formation in each sector. Row 14 represents the increases in total assets of each sector.

It may be noted that the square block formed by column 11 and row 11 represents both total domestic lending and borrowing in the economy. Similarly, the rectangular block formed by column 14 and row 11 represents the increase in total assets (both physical and financial) in the economy which is equal to the amount indicated in the block formed by column 11—row 14. It may also be noted that total net inflow of resources from the external sector (column 12) plus total saving (column 13) represents net capital formation (column 15 or column 14 minus row 11 or row 14 minus row 11).

The household sector is responsible for more than 50 per cent of aggregate resources, though its capital formation is only 17.7 per cent of the total (Table 5). This is the only surplus sector which is responsible for net lending to all the other sectors.

Since the household sector is the only surplus sector, its pattern of saving determines the transfer of resources from it to the other sectors. This pattern is shown in Table 6; the pattern projected for the Fourth Plan period is also shown. It would be seen from this table that for 1965/6, a little more than one-third of its saving was represented by net capital formation, about half of which was financed by borrowing and the other half by self-financing. Saving in the form of financial assets (gross) represented 80.7 per cent of its saving; only one-sixth of the increase in the financial claims represented claims on the other non-financial sectors, while five-sixths represented claims on the financial institutions. The increase in its claims on the banking sector represented nearly three-fourths of its total claims on the financial sectors.

The dominance of the banking sector is reflected in the financing pattern of the capital formation in the non-financial sectors (Table 7). In 1965/6, nearly 40 per cent of the net capital formation in the private corporate sector was financed by

TABLE 5. *Pattern of saving and net capital formation*

Sector	Actuals: 1965/6 Aggregate resources (%)	Actuals: 1965/6 Net capital formation (%)	Projection: 1969–1974 Aggregate resources (%)	Projection: 1969–1974 Net capital formation (%)
1. Household	52.6	17.7	63.1	36.4
2. Private corporate	2.9	14.8	3.7	14.8
3. Government	21.3	65.7	18.9	47.8
4. Non-credit societies	0.1	1.8	0.1	1.0
5. Reserve Bank of India	0.4	. .	1.7	. .
6. Commercial banks	0.2	. .	0.1	. .
7. Credit cooperatives	0.5	. .	0.3	. .
8. Term-lending institutions	0.1	. .	0.1	. .
9. Life Insurance Corporation of India	. .	. .	. .	. .
10. Providing funds	. .	. .	. .	. .
11. Total domestic resources	*78.1*	*100.0*	*88.0*	*100.0*
12. External (net capital inflow from abroad)	*21.9*	. .	*12.0*	. .
13. Aggregate resources/capital formation	*100.0*	*100.0*	*100.0*	*100.0*

TABLE 6. *Pattern of saving of the household sector*

	Actual pattern: 1965/6 (%)	Projected pattern: 1969–1974 (%)
A. *Change in financial assets*	*80.7*	*56.3*
(i) Claims on private corporate sector	5.9	3.0
(ii) Claims on government sector	7.0	3.4
(iii) Claims on non-credit societies	1.0	0.4
(iv) Claims on Reserve Bank of India	18.0	6.4
(v) Claims on commercial banks	23.5	13.8
(vi) Claims on credit cooperatives	5.5	3.5
(vii) Claims on term-lending institutions	0.2	. .
(viii) Claims on Life Insurance Corporation of India	6.4	9.0
(ix) Claims on provident funds	13.2	16.8
B. *Change in Financial Liabilities*	*16.0*	*14.0*
(i) Borrowings from government sector	4.1	2.0
(ii) Borrowings from non-credit societies	1.1	0.7
(iii) Borrowings from commercial banks	1.9	2.9
(iv) Borrowings from credit cooperatives	7.8	7.6
(v) Borrowings from term-lending institutions	0.5	. .
(vi) Borrowings from Life Insurance Corporation of India	0.6	0.8
C. *Net Capital Formation*	*35.3*	*57.7*
D. *Total Household Saving* (A – B + C)	*100.0*	*100.0*

TABLE 7. *Pattern of financing net capital formation*

	Private (non-financial) corporate sector		Government sector	
	Actuals: 1965/6 (%)	Projection: 1969–74 (%)	Actuals: 1965/6 (%)	Projection: 1969–74 (%)
A. Borrowing from external sources	*80.9*	*69.8*	*39.1*	*37.7*
(i) Household	20.2	12.8	2.2	1.8
(ii) Private corporate sector	. .	. .	−0.1	−0.1
(iii) Government	0.3	0.4	. .	. .
(iv) Non-credit societies	. .	. .	−1.0	−0.5
(v) Reserve Bank of India	0.2	−0.5	19.0	9.4
(vi) Commercial banks	39.3	28.1	6.9	6.6
(vii) Credit cooperatives	. .	. .	−0.2	. .
(viii) Term-lending institutions	15.9	22.1	−3.2	−4.9
(ix) Life Insurance Corporation of India	5.0	6.9	5.6	7.1
(x) Provident funds	. .	. .	9.9	18.3
B. Net.capital inflow from abroad	*0.2*	*5.3*	*30.1*	*22.9*
C. Own Savings	*18.9*	*24.9*	*30.8*	*39.4*
D. Net capital formation	*100.0*	*100.0*	*100.0*	*100.0*

net borrowing from the banking sector, while this proportion was around 26 per cent for the government sector.

From the saving and flow of funds analysis, it is also possible to indicate the extent of development of what Goldsmith calls the financial super-structure.[5] The *new issue ratio* (the ratio of net new issues of non-financial sectors to their capital formation) is 0.53; while the *financial intermediation ratio* (the ratio of new issues of financial instruments to non-financial sectors by financial institutions to new issues by non-financial sectors) is 0.74 and the *layering ratio* (the ratio of total issues of financial instruments by financial institutions to other financial institutions to their issues to non-financial sectors) is 0.13. The marginal financial interrelations ratio is 0.98 (Table 8).

TABLE 8. *Components of financial interrelations ratio*
(Marginal)

	Actuals: 1965/6	Projection: 1969–74
1. Financial interrelations ratio (ratio of increase in financial assets to net capital formation)	0.98	0.84
2. New issue ratio (ratio of net new issues of non-financial units to their capital formation)	0.53	0.43
3. Financial intermediation ratio (ratio of new issues of financial instruments to non-financial units by financial institutions to new issues by non-financial units)	0.74	0.79
4. Layering ratio (ratio of total issues of financial institutions to other financial institutions to their issues to non-financial unit)	0.13	0.21

The *marginal* financial intermediation ratio for India is thus comparable to the average ratio for the U.S.A. and the other developed countries, while the *marginal* layering ratio is a little higher than the *average* ratio in the U.S.A. and some other developed countries. The marginal financial interrelations ratio is also comparable to the *average* ratio in the U.S.A.[6]

IV. Technique of Financial Planning

The main steps in the technique of financial planning as actually used for the work relating to Fourth Plan formulation can be indicated very briefly. The analytic tool for the purpose is the saving and flow of funds table.

The *first* step is to derive sector-wise net saving (column 13) on the basis of the feasible growth rates in net national income and industrial output, given changes in the tax-system and government current expenditures and the average and marginal saving-income ratios of the various non-financial sectors. The saving of the financial sectors can be estimated on the basis of past trends. The net inflows to various sectors from the external sector (column 12) can be taken as exogenously given.

Since the net lending sector is the household sector, the *second* step is to derive its saving pattern on the basis of past trends and expected institutional and policy changes. The figures in column 1 are thus derived.

The *third* step is to derive total lending (row 11) by each sector on the basis of steps 1 and 2 and the exogenously given lending by the government sector to credit cooperatives, term-lending institutions, and the non-financial sectors.

The *fourth* step is to derive sector-wise lending of the financial institutions on the basis of their total lending (step three) and their lending pattern determined on the basis of their past pattern and the expected changes in this pattern—as a result of institutional and policy changes (including interest rate policy changes). The *fifth* step is to derive aggregate resources of each sector (column 14). The *sixth* step is to deduct total lending by each sector (row 11) from the total resources available to each sector (column 14). The final step, *seven*, thus, would indicate the net capital formation of each non-financial sector (column 15)—a pattern which is *consistent* with the saving and flow of funds pattern.

If the *desired* sector-wise composition of investment is different from this pattern, it would be necessary to adopt such policy measures as would change the saving pattern of the household sector and the lending pattern of the financial institutions so as to give the desired sector-wise composition of investment. If such policy measures are not feasible, the desired sector-wise investment pattern would have to be changed to the pattern as emerges from the seven steps indicated. For the Fourth Plan (1969–74) financial planning exercise, it was assumed on the basis of past experience that the gestation lag of investment would be on an average five years so that new investment undertaken during the plan period would have no significant impact on the increase in real national income during the same period.

The feasible growth rate of industrial output (8 per cent) was determined on the basis of productive capacities already built by 1968 and the growth rate of agricultural output (4 per cent) was based on the current and prospective agricul-

TABLE 9. *Matrix of projected saving and financial flows 1969–74*
(Amount in Rs. crores at 1968/9 prices: one crore = 10 millions)

From sector	Non-financial sector					Financial sector—banking			
To sector	Household	Private corporate	Government	Non-credit societies	Total borrowing	Reserve Bank of India	Commercial banks	Credit cooperatives	Total borrowing
	1	2	3	4		5	6	7	
1. Household	..	..	244	80	324	..	344	907	1251
2. Private corporate	360	..	12	..	372	−15	792	..	777
3. Government	410	..	..	..	410	861	600	30	1491
4. Non-credit societies	50	..	45	..	95	..	18	110	128
Total lending	820	..	301	80	1201	846	1754	1047	3647
5. Reserve Bank of India	759	..	..	5	764	..	133	20	153
6. Commercial banks	1651	..	..	4	1655	..	..	30	30
7. Credit cooperatives	425	..	25	35	485	200	155	..	355
Total lending	2835	..	25	44	2904	200	288	50	535
8. Term-lending institutions	10	..	450	..	460	201	28	..	229
9. Life Insurance Corporation	1074	..	..	..	1074	..	..	..	..
10. Provident funds	2010	..	..	..	2010	..	..	..	..
Total lending	3094	..	450	..	3544	201	28	..	229
11. Aggregate lending	6749	..	776	124	7649	1247	2070	1097	4414
12. External sector	..	..	..	..	..	..	..	..	.
13. Capital formation	6921	2816	9097	186	19,020	..	..	..	..
14. Increase in total assets	13,670	2816	9873	310	26,669	1247	2070	1097	4414

From sector / To sector	Financial sector— other financial institutions: Term lending institutions	Life Insurance Corporation	Provident funds	Total borrowing	Aggregate borrowing	External sectors	Own saving	Aggregate resources	Capital formation (aggregate resources aggregate lending)
	8	9	10		11	12	13	14	15
1. Household	10	95	..	105	1680	..	11,990	13,670	6921
2. Private corporate	622	194	..	816	1965	150	701	2816	2818
3. Government	..	643	1665	2308	4209	2080	3584	9873	9097
4. Non-credit societies	15	47	..	62	285	..	25	310	186
Total lending	647	979	1665	3291	8139	2230	16,300	26,669	19,020
5. Reserve Bank of India	..	..	..	..	917	..	330	1247	..
6. Commercial banks	10	9	345	364	2049	..	21	2070	..
7. Credit cooperatives	137	60	..	197	1037	..	60	1097	..
Total lending	147	69	345	561	4003	..	411	4414	..
8. Term-lending institutions	..	29	..	29	718	50	26	794	..
9. Life Insurance Corporation	..	..	..	..	1074	..	3	1077	..
10. Provident funds	..	..	..	..	2010	..	..	2010	..
Total lending	..	29	..	29	3802	50	29	3881	..
11. Aggregate lending	794	1077	2010	3881	15,944	2280	16,740	34,964	19,020
12. External sector	..	..	..	..	..	..	..	..	..
13. Capital formation	..	..	..	..	19,020	..	..	..	..
14. Increases in total assets	794	1077	2010	3881	34,964	..	..	..	..

tural programmes particularly relating to the high-yielding varieties programme. The feasible growth rate of national income (5 per cent) was worked out on the basis of these two growth rates.

The tax-revenue of the government sector was estimated on the basis of the growth rate in non-agricultural output, average tax-income ratio of 12.3 per cent in 1968 and a marginal tax–income ratio of 20 per cent—the ratio realized during the Third Plan period (1961–6) over the previous plan. The main items of non-tax revenue were estimated on the basis of past trends. The net saving of the public sector enterprises was estimated on the basis of the growth in their output and the desired rate of profit on capital employed (with a five-year lag). Current expenditures of the government sector were projected on the basis of the past trends in each category of expenditure. Government sector's net saving was thus derived.

The saving of the private non-financial corporate sector was estimated on the basis of the growth of industrial output, the sector's average saving–income ratio of 33 per cent in 1968 and its marginal saving–income ratio of 55 per cent (actually realized during the Third Plan period) over the Second Plan. The saving of the rest of the corporate sector was derived on the basis of past trends.

The household sector's saving was estimated on the basis of the growth in personal disposable income, the sector's average saving–income ratio of 6.5 per cent in 1968/9 and the observed marginal relationship between saving and income of 12 per cent during the Third Plan period over the Second Plan. The financial saving of the household sector was derived after estimating the saving in the form of each financial asset separately.

On the basis of past relationship, the saving in the form of currency and demand deposits with the banks was assumed to grow at the same rate as personal disposable income. Fixed deposits with the banks were estimated on the basis of a *marginal* ratio of 14 per cent between fixed deposits and personal disposable income (this was the ratio realized in the past several years).

The saving in the form of life insurance policies was estimated on the assumption that the new business of the LIC would grow at an annual rate of 5.5 per cent per annum. With regard to provident funds, subscriptions were assumed to grow at an annual rate of 8.5 per cent, half a per cent more than industrial output to allow for increasing coverage of workers and salary earners under the scheme. The saving in the form of claims on the other financial institutions was estimated on the basis of past trends.

The saving in the form of private shares and securities, company deposits and government securities was assumed to grow at the rate of the personal disposable income on the basis of past trends and expected yield pattern. The net inflow from the external sector to each of the domestic sectors was given exogenously. Accordingly, columns 12 and 13 of the table were filled and also column 1 up to row 11. The government sector lending to the other non-financial institutions were taken as given. The total lending (row 11) by all the sectors was thus determined.

The lending pattern of the financial institutions was then fixed on the basis of the past trend with regard to this pattern and expected changes as a result of institutional and policy measures. For example, the bank's investment in government securities as a proportion of deposits would be less as they are expected to invest relatively more in the bonds of Land Mortgage Banks. Similarly, the investment patterns of the LIC and Provident Funds were likely to change as a result of government policies as well as the new yield structure.

Thus, all the columns from 1 to 11 were filled. The sums of column 11, 12 and 13—each row-wise gave column 14, that is aggregate resources. Then, each sector's lending (row 11) was deducted from its aggregate resources (column 14) to derive net capital formation by each non-financial sector as well as total net capital formation. Sector-wise composition of net investment and total net investment was derived in such a way as was consistent with the evolving saving and the flow of funds structure (Table 9).

V. Formalized Technique of Financial Planning

The technique of financial planning or projections can be formalized on the pattern of the input–output analysis, if the lending coefficients in the table can be taken as fixed. Suppose the problem is to derive an internally consistent sector-wise composition of investment on the basis of a given sector-wise pattern of saving and a sector-wise pattern of net inflow of funds from abroad. This problem can be tackled formally in terms of the flow of funds matrix.

For illustrative purposes, only four non-financial sectors are taken: Government (G), Private Corporate (C), Household (H) and External (E). The financial sectors are: Banking System (B) and Other Financial Institutions (F). The financial flow matrix to be used for the purpose would be given in Table 10 below.

TABLE 10. *Matrix of saving and financial flows*

From sector to sector		H	C	G	B	F	Total borrow-ings	Net saving	E	Total re-sources	Net capital forma-tion
		1	2	3	4	5	6	7	8	9	10
1.	H	..	..	..	L_{BH}	L_{FH}	B_H	S_H	L_{EH}	R_H	C_H
2.	C	L_{HC}	..	..	L_{BC}	L_{FC}	B_C	S_C	L_{EC}	R_C	C_C
3.	G	L_{HG}	..	..	L_{BG}	L_{FG}	B_G	S_G	L_{EG}	R_G	C_G
4.	B	L_{HB}	..	..	..	L_{FB}	B_B	S_B	L_{EB}	R_B	..
5.	F	L_{HF}	..	..	..	..	B_F	S_F	L_{EF}	R_F	..
6. Total lending		L_H	L_C = 0	L_G = 0	L_B = R_B	L_F = R_F	L = B	S	L_E	R	C = S + LE

It is assumed that the household sector is the only net lending sector, while the government and the private corporate sectors are net borrowers. Therefore, lendings by G and C sectors are netted against their borrowing and so columns 2 and 3 remain unfilled.[7] For the B sector, its total lending (L_B) is equal to its total resources (R_B) i.e. what it gets from the H sector (L_{HB}) and the F sector (L_{FB}) *plus* its own Saving (S_B) *plus* inflow of resources from the E sector (L_{EB}); it can be seen that

$$L_B = R_B = L_{HB} + S_B + L_{FB} + L_{EB} \quad (1)$$
$$L_F = R_F = L_{HF} + S_F + L_{EF} \quad (2).$$

Columns 7 and 8 are known. The structure of saving of the H sector is also known in terms of the H sector's saving in the form of financial assets (L_H) and its total saving (S_H). Now, if L_H (column total) is known and L_{Hi}'s (elements of the column—the lending coefficients of the H sector) are taken as fixed, the borrowing of each sector from the H sector is known.

Thus from identity (2) $L_F = R_F$ is known. If the L_{Hi}'s (the lending coefficient of the F sector) are taken as fixed, the borrowing of the other sectors from the F sector, are known. Then L_{FB} is also known and so is $L_B = R_B$ from identity (1). Given the LBi's (the lending coefficients of the B sector), the borrowing of other sector are known. Then L_{FB} is also known and so is $L_B = R_B$ from identity (1). by each sector) and column 9 (total resources of each sector) could be obtained, by subtracting corresponding elements of row 6 (total lending by each sector) from column 9 (total resources of each sector), sector-wise figures of capital formation given in column 10 could be derived. Since $L_B = R_B$ and $L_F = R_F$, for other two financial sectors, no capital formation is shown.

This formalized technique would give valid results only if the lending coefficients can be taken as fixed and known. It would also be useful in cases where the changes in the lending coefficients can be predicted in a more or less direct manner. For the underdeveloped countries, since the financial superstructure is still evolving and the saving structure of the H sector is changing, it would not be possible to use such a formalized technique for the purpose of projection over a five-year period. For these countries, the saving pattern of the H sector and the lending pattern of the financial institutions will have to be projected on the basis of past trends, expected evolution of the structure of financial institutions, instruments and interest rates and policy changes. However, as Divatia rightly mentions, it is possible to evolve an operational mathematical model for short period financial planning.[8] It would certainly be easier to work out the broad implications of alternative assumptions and plans by his technique.

NOTES

1. In the growing literature on planning, it is only at one place that we have found the right emphasis on the integration between financial planning and physical planning. See United Nations, *Problems of Long-Term Economic Projections*, Report by a Group of Experts, New York, 1963, chapter iv. See also B. Hansen, *Long and Short-Term Planning in Underdeveloped Countries* (Amsterdam, 1967), chapter iii. Even in purely theoretical literature, in spite of Keynes, the dichotomy between real and financial analysis still persists.
2. See V. V. Bhatt, "On Inflation and Its Control", a paper presented at the International Economic Association Conference in Kandy (Ceylon) (June 1969).
3. (*a*) "Estimates of Saving in the Indian Economy", *R.B.I. Bulletin* (Mar. 1960); (*b*) "Estimates of Saving and Investment in the Indian Economy, 1950/1 to 1958/9", *R.B.I. Bulletin* (Aug. 1961); (*c*) "Estimates of Saving and Investment in the Indian Economy, 1950/1 to 1962/3", *R.B.I. Bulletin* (Mar. 1965); (*d*) "Financial Flows in the Indian Economy, 1957/8 to 1961/2", *R.B.I.*

Bulletin (Dec. 1964); (*e*) "Financial Flows in the Indian Economy, 1951/2 to 1962/3", *R.B.I. Bulletin* (Mar. 1967).

4. The financial aspects of the Plan as worked out through this technique were changed somewhat in the published version of the Plan, "Fourth Five-Year Plan, 1969–1974—Draft", Planning Commission, Government of India (Mar. 1969).
5. See R. W. Goldsmith, *The Determinants of Financial Structure,* OECD (Paris, 1966).
6. See *ibid.*, pp. 26–30.
7. If, however, it is desired as a matter of government policy to render assistance to any of the sectors, there would be non-zero elements along the column for the G sector. But then the figures of such government lending would be exogenously given.
8. V. V. Divatia, "An Operational Technique for Financial Planning", in *R.B.I. Bulletin* (Bombay, 1969).

APPENDIX

Sources of information used in the construction of sector-wise financial flows in the Indian economy

Sector	*Sources*
1. Reserve Bank of India	1. Weekly statements of affairs of the Reserve Bank of India.
	2. Data on money supply with the public published in the *R.B.I. Bulletin*.
2. Commercial banks	1. Data collected on selected items of assets and liabilities of commercial banks under Section 42 of the Reserve Bank of India Act.
	2. Reserve Bank of India surveys on sector-wise ownership of deposits of commercial banks.
	3. Reserve Bank of India surveys on sector-wise advances by commercial banks.
	4. Survey of bank's investments conducted periodically by the Reserve Bank of India.
	5. Statistical tables relating to banks in India published annually of the Reserve Bank of India.
3. Cooperative sector (banks, credit and non-credit societies)	1. Statistical statement relating to Cooperative Movement in India published annually by the Reserve Bank of India.
	2. Section 42 data for State Cooperative Banks maintaining accounts with Reserve Bank of India published in the *R.B.I. Bulletin*.
	3. A statement "Reserve Bank of India and Agricultural Credit" published in the *Report on Currency and Finance*.
4. Financial corporations	1. Annual reports and accounts of Industrial Finance Corporation of India, State Financial Corporations (including Madras Industrial Investment Corporation), Industrial Development Bank of India, Industrial Credit and Investment Corporation of India, Agricul-

Sector	*Sources*
	tural Refinance Corporation and the Unit Trust of India.
	2. A statement "Reserve Bank of India and Industrial Finance" published in the *R.B.I. Bulletin*.
5. Life insurance	1. Annual reports and accounts of the Life Insurance Corporation of India (the only institution dealing in life business after nationalization in 1956).
	2. Indian Insurance Year Books for years prior to 1956.
6. Provident funds	1. Annual reports on Employees Provident Fund Scheme published by the Provident Fund Commissioner, Government of India.
	2. Reports on working of Coal Mines' Provident Fund Scheme released on annual basis.
	3. Annual reports of Assam Tea Plantations Provident Fund Scheme.
	4. Government budget papers (for figures of State provident funds).
	5. Special returns called for provident fund collections in respect of employees of Financial Corporations.
	6. Own accounts for R.B.I. employees provident funds.
	7. Statement of earnings and expenses received from commercial banks.
	8 *Ad hoc* reports and studies (for provident fund figures in respect of educational institutions trusts, etc.).
7. Non-financial domestic corporate sector	1. Reserve Bank of India's studies on finances of (*a*) public limited companies (medium and large with paid-up capital Rs. 5 lakhs and above), (*b*) public limited companies (small), (*c*) private limited companies, (*d*) branches and subsidiaries of foreign companies operating in India.
	2. Statements issued by the Controller of Capital Issues giving quarterly and annual figures of consents given and capital raised by companies.
	3. Reserve Bank of India's periodical surveys of deposits with non-banking companies.
8. Government sector	1. Economic classification of the Central Government budget.
	2. Budget papers of State Governments and

Sector	*Sources*
	Union Territories and unpublished studies of Ministry of Finance in this regard.
	3. Report on the working of public sector undertakings in India published by Ministry of Finance, Bureau of Public Enterprises.
	4. Reserve Bank of India's studies on finances of government companies.
	5. Reserve Bank of India surveys on borrowings and investments of local authorities.
	6. Reserve Bank of India's annual studies on pattern of ownership of public debt in India.
	7. Statement on small savings collections published in the *R.B.I. Bulletin*.
9. Foreign sector	Surveys and studies undertaken in connection with the compilation of India's balance of payments; for details please refer to Reserve Bank of India's monograph "India's Balance of Payments: 1948/9 to 1961/2".

11. Interest Rate, Transaction Costs and Financial Innovations*

THE FRAGMENTATION of the capital market in the LDCs is generally attributed in the literature to the interest-free policy pursued and it is argued that with a high interest rate, these imperfections would be removed and their saving and investment would be greater than what they are. This diagnosis and this policy advice rest on a theoretical model that is, by and large, irrelevant for analysing the problems of economic evolution. The real question to be posed is: how and through what mechanisms the capital market gets integrated and thus help the process of economic development?

It is not possible to tackle this problem without some understanding of the process of economic evolution and the role of innovations in this process. How financial innovations tend to integrate the capital markets through reduction of transaction costs is discussed in section I. Section II deals with the actual evolution of the credit market in a *specific* rural set-up; it is shown how further development of this market could have favourable impact on saving, investment and output. The final section indicates the nature of financial innovations that are essential for such a development on the basis of an actual case study of a commercial bank.

I. Financial Innovations and Economic Development

Limited Relevance of the Theoretical Model

The theoretical model, on the basis of which advice with regard to development strategy and policy is offered by economists, is in fact not equipped to deal with basic problems of development. It focuses on allocation of *given* resources on the basis of *given* supply and demand schedules and a perfectly competitive market-form—in which the actors or dealers are all alike. The focus, on the other hand, of a theory of economic evolution has to be the question: how and why supply and demand schedules and the market forms change and why behaviour patterns of different actors are not the same. Economic theory does not deal with the process of economic evolution in historic time; hence, however relevant its policy prescriptions may be for certain short-run situations, it is not possible to draw meaningful inferences about development strategy and policy simply on the basis of this short-run static model.[1]

Again, its concept of competition is a mechanistic concept; it does not deal with the essence of competitive behaviour—the powerful motivation to do better than the others in an environment in which the future is unknown. The concept

* Paper presented at the Second International Conference on Rural Finance Research Issues, at Calgary, Alberta, Canada, during 29 Aug.–1 Sept. 1979. Published, in part, in *Development Digest,* vol. xvi, no. 3 (July 1978).

of competitive behaviour to be meaningful implies, as it must, the possibility of attaining monopolistic or semi-monopolistic positions, and at the same time an ever-present threat of competition. The competitive markets of theory rule out competitive behaviour; they assume only *adaptive* responses to changes in socio-economic environment—responses that are prompt and rational and are uniform for all the actors.[2]

Economic evolution cannot take place with such adaptive and uniform responses; if changes in the external environment were the mainsprings of economic evolution, there is nothing much to learn about the relationship of human behaviour with the process of evolution and no policy advice is required from economists. The essence of the processes of evolution in all spheres of human life is, however, the ability to respond creatively to changes in the external environment—the creative response which alters favourably the environment itself.[3] Hence a theory which ignores entrepreneurial behaviour and does not distinguish between adaptive and creative responses to objective opportunity can hardly be relevant for understanding the problems of socio-economic change.

The concepts of evolution, competitive behaviour and creative response to challenges—all these reflect the significance of innovations—changes in production and consumption functions, introduction of new goods and services, changes in organization and market forms. Any theory that deals with the evolutionary processes has thus to concentrate on the impact of innovations on economic evolution. Our theoretical tools are inadequate for the purpose and so is our advice on the basic fundamental problems of development. Since the economists look at reality through their irrelevant theoretical model, their "pungent sense of reality", to use an expression by William James, has become atrophied. They have even lost the ability of direct perception—of intelligently and creatively responding to the challenge of the development problem. Hence there are no innovations[4] in economic theory and economists have become "dentists", to use a phrase by Keynes,[5] much before the age of dentistry has set in.

Finance and Development

It is for some such reason that the economists have hardly been able to appreciate the role of Finance in economic development; in fact the dichotomy of the "real" and "monetary" factors persist in spite of Keynes in the literature. And those who have tried to integrate the two sets of factors have done it on the basis of the same theoretical tool of a competitive market. Capital market is assumed to be perfect; if the resources do not flow where they should, obviously the interest-rate policy—the price policy—must be defective. Once these distortions caused by policy are removed, the imperfection in the market would be eliminated and resources would be allocated "rationally". The basic policy guide-line suggested by this analysis is to have an interest rate that reflects the real scarcity of capital.[6]

Several questions arise in this connection. What is an interest rate? What is capital? Are these two "real" factors or are they "monetary" phenomena? What do we mean by "scarcity of capital"? In spite of Schumpeter, it is not generally appreciated in the literature that both "interest" and "capital" are monetary phenomena and that finance impinges through these two factors on the process of development.[7]

The interest rate (monetary factor) has to bear some relation to the rate of profit (real factor). Unless one assumes away technical change, there is no reason to believe that the rate of profit should be higher in the LDCs than that in the developed countries. If profit rates are not different, why should interest rates be different? Again, why should the profit rate be related to "scarcity" or "abundance" of "capital"? In fact, all these three terms are meaningless. As a matter of history, there has been no trend in the pure interest rate (corrected for price change) in the developed countries for the last two hundred years.[8] Economists need to have a sense of history to understand the process of economic evolution.[9]

The real problem to be examined is quite different. One has to begin the inquiry with the question: why are capital markets imperfect, and how, in spite of the imperfections do they get integrated with economic and financial evolution?

The transaction which takes place in a capital market relates to a relationship *over a period of time* between a lender and a borrower. Hence the product is not merely finance; the nature of the product is also determined by the characteristics of the lender as well as the borrower. Uncertainty is of the essence of any relationship which involves time. Thus, each product is in a sense unique; it is like a custom-made product.

The supply and demand for funds in each of these markets are matched not merely by the interest rate; the terms of lending have variables other than interest rate like margin requirements, repayment terms, security, and compensating balances. Quite often there is no systematic relationship between the terms of lending and the amount to be borrowed.

The crucial non-interest variable which determines the terms of lending to each class of borrower relates to transaction costs—the administrative costs plus the default risk.[10] The fragmentation of the capital market—the phenomena of different markets for different "products"—arises because of the varying transaction costs with respect to the different classes of borrowers. The progressive integration of these separate markets is brought about through financial innovations that tend to reduce these costs. These innovations reduce the costs of lending and borrowing (cost as determined by the terms of lending) and thus bring about shifts in the supply–demand schedules for credit. It is thus that *potential* saving and *potential* investment become actual through the transmission channels provided by the integration of the capital markets.[11]

The principal variable is, of course, the risk; financial innovations tend to reduce risk. But default risk and administrative costs are related; default risk can be reduced by more information which involves administrative costs. Financial innovations tend to reduce *total* transaction costs; they tend to widen and deepen the capital market, and narrow the interest rate differentials.

Nature of Financial Innovations

What, then, has been the nature of the financial innovations during the process of financial evolution?

Historically, it was the trader who extended his business by financial dealings. It is the invention of money that enabled him to make a money loan in place of a goods-loan to another known trader. Here the risk was negligible; for, the trading class evolved certain rules of the game to which the members adhered. But loan to a new trader (not known to him) involved risk—the subjective risk could be very high.[12] But this risk was reduced by the financial innovation of security or guarantee—the bill of exchange with two signatures.[13] These two innovations (the code among merchant bankers and the bill of exchange) did not require the sanction of law. The other innovation (security for the loan) did require legal sanction. Once that was available two kinds of security evolved—the pledge or pawn and the *hypotheca* (of the Roman Law) or the mortgage (of the English Law).[14]

Then followed the innovation of a financial intermediary—namely, the bank. This innovation reduced risk in a number of ways. The bank had economies of scale; hence it could specialize in, and standardize certain types of, financial transactions and thus reduce risk through better expertise. The economies of scale accrued in another way also; its scale enabled it to pool and spread risks—the "Law of Large Numbers", which is the basis of insurance.

This was, however, only a financial intermediation function of the bank. Its capacity to perform this function was greatly enhanced by the innovation of bank-money—its capacity to create credit. It is through this innovation that the banking system helped the process of economic evolution directly as well as indirectly through the provision of finance to other financial intermediaries specializing in forms of financing different from those of the banks. And, of course, the functioning of the government and what Hicks calls "the Administrative Revolution" would not have been possible but for this development.[15]

The bank money and the subsequently related innovations reduced the costs of real transactions and they improved the productivity of balances kept with the banks. The real yield on deposits with the banks improved—the yield which is not reflected in the interest rate on deposits.[16] This revolution in the payments mechanism has been a significant factor in expanding markets for goods and services through reduction in transaction costs. The benefit is not merely the reduction in transaction costs; it also accrues through the reduction in the requirement for money balances for transaction purposes—reflected in the increase in the transaction velocity of money.[17]

However, the banking system became much too specialized; consistent with its origin, it provided credit only for certain types of transactions—like stocks of goods. The credit for other purposes (like housing or plant and equipment) required other specialized agencies like the securities markets, which evolved in the U.K. and the U.S.A. more or less along with the banking system. In countries where the climate was not favourable for these types of credit markets, another financial innovation was introduced—the Universal Bank. After all, the other credit markets in a way developed because the banks lent finance to them through their customers as well as direct purchase of the securities traded in these markets. Why cannot the banks specialize in these functions also? And they did in France and in Germany during the nineteenth century—beginning from the famous *Crédit Mobilier*.[18]

The recent innovation of the Department Store banking[19] in the U.S.A. and the other developed countries has its origin in the concept of the Universal Bank. The economies of specialization do not require separate institutions; they can be exploited by specialization within the banks.[20] The banks have command over financial resources much larger than those with the other institutions; they can easily reap the economies of both scale and various types of specialization.

Nature of Financial Development in LDCs

Should the LDCs pass through the same stages of financial development, through which countries like the U.K. and the U.S.A. passed, or should they creatively adapt the financial innovation of the Universal Bank, or the recent Department Store banking to their specific needs and requirements?

The real problem is that of reducing transaction costs of lending for purposes other than financing of stocks—in Industry and Trade. For example, sectors which require improved access to credit are small enterprises of all types and agriculture. At present, the transaction costs of lending to these sectors is quite high; they are higher than 6 per cent and range between 6 per cent to 20 per cent in different countries. If the financial cost and profit margin are added, the banks cannot afford to lend to these sectors at a cost less than 16–30 per cent. At this cost, there would be no inducement to borrow; for, the expected average rate of profit in these sectors probably does not exceed 15–20 per cent per annum.

Hence the response has been specialized institutions that lend at a loss at subsidized interest rates—the subsidy to the institutions being provided by the government directly or indirectly. But these institutions lack the motivation as well as the means to reduce transaction costs; permanent subsidy cannot be a viable solution.

The banks have the means but lack the motivation. Their Agenda—to use the expressive phase of Arrow[21]—is geared towards financing trade and inventories. They on their own are unlikely to put new items on their Agenda; for, their expertise—the information and communication system—relates to financing trade and inventories and other purposes related to the growth of large-scale industry.

If, however, their Agenda can be changed, it should not be difficult for them to respond creatively through financial innovations to this challenge of financing agriculture and small enterprises. The case study of the Syndicate Bank (section III) shows that this is possible and it also illustrates the nature of financial innovations that would be required to reduce transaction costs. The Lead Bank idea which evolved in India after 1969 should probably be the governing principle for the financial evolution in the LDCs.[22] It is in some sense a creative adaptation of the idea of a Universal Bank in the context of a LDC environment.

II. Evolution of Credit Markets: The Haryana Case

How credit markets evolve with reduction in transaction costs and how they affect real output can be illustrated by the Haryana experience.[23] Haryana has been one of the three states in India which adopted the new high-yielding seeds since 1964 and experienced almost doubling of productivity per acre for wheat in less than a decade.[24]

Traders as Lenders

Before canal irrigation and the green revolution, agricultural credit was provided largely by traders.[25] The latter combined moneylending with trade. Their transaction costs were smaller than any other credit agency for obvious reasons. Since the farmers sold their surplus output to the traders, it was possible for the latter to appraise their "credit-worthiness". Further, the recovery of interest and principal was easier for traders than it would have been for any other agency as it was possible for the latter to deduct what was due to them from the payment for the purchase of agricultural commodities from the farmers. The credit provided was largely what Schumpeter calls consumptive–productive credit[26] required when the the rains failed as also for expenditures on marriage and such other social ceremonies. The effective interest rate was probably higher than 30 per cent per annum—reflecting the average transaction costs exceeding 20 per cent. Of course, it was much higher for small farmers, who did not have much surplus output to sell to the traders.

With this high interest rate, it could be argued that the *existing* trader–moneylenders would face competition from new traders. But this competition was not possible as the transaction costs of the new trader would have been even higher than those of the existing traders; the new trader would lack the expertise built up by the old ones. The effective barrier to competition, thus, is likely to be the differential transaction costs of the *potential* trader–moneylender—which represent his cost of entry into this market.

Technical Change and Credit Market Evolution

With canal irrigation and the high-yielding seeds the situation changed radically. Initially, the medium and large progressive farmers adopted the innovation; but since the innovations were scale-neutral, even some of the small farmers adopted them. The household incomes of the progressive farmers rose by more than 70 per cent and the average propensity to save also rose with incomes. With this development, Haryana experienced a new phenomenon—lending by medium size cultivators to small farmers. This new class of farmer–moneylender has tended to replace the traders in the credit field.

How do we explain this phenomenon?

The cultivators who engage in lending belong to the class of farmers who own 10 to 30 acres. The borrowers are largely small farmers owning land in the size group below 10 acres. The rich farmers (with land more than 30 acres) do not have much surplus to lend as their investment is more or less equal to their saving.

The question, then, is: why do the medium-size farmers lend their surplus instead of using it for productive investment as the large farmers do?

All the farmers use canal irrigation. However, when the rains fail, the canal system of irrigation also fails to deliver the *required* amount of water. Again, for the second crop, the system's supply of water is generally inadequate. The large farmers, therefore, use both canal and tube-well irrigation and thus are able to use high-yielding seeds for both the seasons. The middle farmers, particularly in the *central* and *southern* regions of Haryana, use canal irrigation for one crop only and sow a non-irrigated less remunerative crop for the second season of the crop year. Why do they not invest their savings in tube-well irrigation?

The reason appears to be the high cost of tube-well irrigation. It costs roughly twice as much to sink a tube well in these low ground water areas than it does in the *northern region* of Haryana or in the *Punjab state*. Their own savings are *inadequate* for financing this profitable investment, and in these areas, the institutional credit is not available. The large farmers do invest in tube-well irrigation even in these areas as their savings are adequate for financing this investment. In the Punjab, institutional credit is available to the medium farmers for tube-well irrigation. The institutional credit as a proportion of total credit is much higher in the Punjab than in Haryana as credit institutions are much better developed there than in Haryana.

It is thus that the middle farmers have come to use their surplus for lending to *small farmers*. They have been able to compete effectively with the traders as their terms of lending are more favourable than those of the traders; their interest rate on lending is probably in the range of 15–25 per cent per annum as against the range of 40–50 per cent for the traders for lending to small farmers.

This reduction in the interest rate could have come about as a result of the expansion of the credit market; there was a rightward shift in the small farmer's demand schedule for credit as a result of technical change and the supply schedule shifted rightwards with the emergence of surpluses with the middle farmers, again as a result of technical change. However, this surplus could have been invested in other financial–physical assets by the middle farmers and the small farmers could not have borrowed substantial sums at a cost higher than their expected rate of return. Thus, the critical variable which seems to explain this reduction in interest rate appears to be the lower transaction costs of lending for the new instruments introduced by the middle farmers. This reduction in the transaction costs made it possible for the middle farmers to earn a risk-adjusted yield that probably was higher than that on alternative assets and for the small farmers to borrow at a cost lower than their expected rate of return in agriculture. Thus, there must have been not merely a rightward shift but also a downward shift in the supply schedule for credit.

The reason for this lower interest rate is their smaller transaction costs. The middle farmers are able to appraise the income potential of small farmers much better than the traders. And for this appraisal, they do not need to spend extra time and effort as the traders have to. The small farmer is probably the neighbour of the middle farmer and the two come in easy contact for a variety of common purposes. Both know each other much better than is possible for a non-cultivator to know a cultivator's craft. Again, for recovery of interest and principal, the middle farmer is at an advantage; he does not need to spend any extra time and effort for the purpose. The trader's advantage was his ability to link credit with the purchase of wheat. But middle farmers can also do this in addition to taking the small farmer's land as a security—a security obviously valued much higher by him than by the trader. His ability to store wheat has increased with his income and he need not sell his surplus to the trader only; the trader now is not the only buyer of wheat as the government procurement operations have expanded with the increase in wheat output.

This new and relatively large source of credit has enabled the small farmers to invest in current inputs like fertilizers required for the new seeds and thus turn into progressive farmers. The middle farmers have a new source of income. Thus this evolution of the credit market has helped the process of production and investment; the nature of credit has also changed from purely production/consumption credit to a combination of such credit with investment credit. Even the small farmer's debt to the middle farmer arising out of production/consumption credit does not accumulate at compound interest; because of the possibility of obtaining credit for new inputs like fertilizers and high-yielding seeds, in a *normal* crop year the small farmer's surplus is more than adequate for repaying his debts to the middle farmer—debts contracted during the season when the rains fail. The credit advanced is thus by and large productive credit; this has reduced the risk for both lenders and borrowers and thus expanded the credit market.

Credit Markets and Output

However, even with such evolution of the credit markets, the *full* production potential of agriculture is not realized. For, the middle farmers could invest in tube-well irrigation and thus increase output like the large farmers if credit were available to them to supplement their savings. Again, if additional credit were available to the small farmers, it would be worthwhile for a group of three or four farmers—if not for each single farmer—to invest in tube-well irrigation. Thus both sets of farmers could use high-yielding seeds also for the second crop—for which the canal system does not provide adequate water. Such a development has occurred in the Punjab and it could occur in Haryana, which is more or less similar to the Punjab with regard to the agro-climatic conditions and the innovative characteristics of the farmers. And with appropriate financial instruments, this further development of the ctedit markets may not require, except possibly initially, any outside source of saving.

Nature of Further Evolution of the Credit System: Role of a Lead Bank

It is not difficult to sketch in broad outline the characteristics of this further evolution. There are two to three major all-India banks in Haryana; each one is assigned the responsibility by the Reserve Bank of India for expanding its new work of branches with a view to mobilizing deposit resources as well as providing credit for agriculture and small enterprises. This banking function is thought to be integrated with the function of technical assistance; the lead bank is supposed to coordinate the activities of various technical assistance agencies—and even to create them, if necessary, with the help of the state government—for the purpose of identifying production possibilities and integrating credit with the promotional work. The lead bank thus is assumed to play an active role in exploiting the production–employment potential of the district for which it is assigned the lead bank role.[27]

Such a lead bank, to start with, can offer credit to middle farmers for tube-well irrigation provided they accumulated 25–30 per cent of the cost of investment as fixed deposits, earning an interest rate of 10 per cent per annum. Allowing for the risk premium and other transaction costs with regard to lending by this group of farmers, this interest rate would compare favourably with the rate they earn on lending. Further, their rate of return on investment, facilitated by credit from the bank, would be even higher than what they earn on lending; this is precisely the reason why the large farmers use their savings for productive investment rather than for lending. Thus this type of new deposit instrument tied to borrowing facility would indeed be attractive to the middle farmers.

At the same time, it could take over from the middle farmers the function of lending to the small farmers. This it can do initially with the deposit resources obtained from the middle farmers. This lending too can be tied with deposits; a small farmer can be assured credit in a bad year, provided he accumulated his surplus from a normal year as deposits. The attractive interest rate and the assurance of credit facility could induce the small farmers to save more than they would otherwise do. Credit for fixed investment—like tube-well irrigation—too could be tied with deposits.

The marginal propensity to save of the large farmers seems to be lower than that of the middle farmers. To the extent to which this occurs because of the lack of a suitable financial instrument—without risk and transaction costs—it would be possible for the bank to attract the *potential* surplus of the large farmers in the form of appropriate deposits. For example, the social expenditures of large farmers on occasions like marriage of children are quite high. Further, they invest a larger proportion of their income on children's education. Deposit schemes tied to borrowing facility for these purposes could attract the potential surplus of these farmers into deposits with the bank. Once this instrument becomes popular, it is quite likely that even marriage expenditures—particularly for gifts and dowries—could change their composition; gifts and dowries could be given in the form of deposits rather than in the form of goods.

These new types of deposits linked to lending may suffice after the first few years to meet the credit requirements of the farmers and no injection of external resources may be necessary. In fact, the system could generate resources with increase in incomes for lending to the other sectors of the state-like industry. Surpluses from agriculture thus could be mobilized for financing investment in the non-agricultural sectors.

However, for such an evolution to take place, the transaction costs of lending and borrowing should be lower than what they currently are. The bank should be able to lend at an interest rate of about 12–15 per cent per annum—that is, at a rate lower than that charged by the middle farmer. For this to be possible, its transaction costs should not exceed, say, about 5 per cent. For a bank, it would be possible to realize the economies of scale and spreading of risks. It would have also the backing of the resources mobilized by the bank from all over India; for the lead bank for a district is an all-India bank with lead role in about fifteen to twenty districts. It can also borrow from the Reserve Bank of India. It would not have the type of liquidity constraints from which traders and farmer–money-lenders suffer. But the crucial element is the transaction costs. These have been quite high—in the range of 7–10 per cent. The question is: through what innovations could their costs be reduced? The next section deals with the case of an innovative bank which has been able to reduce these costs.

III. Innovations and Transaction Costs: The Syndicate Experience[28]

Till 1969, the large city-based banks in India concentrated on financing large industry and trade in the urban areas. Their transaction costs for these markets were quite low—well within the range of 1.5 to 2 per cent, which Keynes indicated many years back as the level below which interest rates cannot fall.[29] They did not enter the field of small–medium enterprises in the farm and non-farm sectors. In these markets, their transaction costs would have been very high and at the terms on which they could have lent, it was not possible to widen and deepen these markets.

Characteristics of the Syndicate

For a new bank, it was difficult to compete with these city banks in their markets. It had to enter a new field (a non-competitive field) and this related to small–medium enterprises. This objective opportunity was there but to seize it required an innovative approach to banking—introduction of new "products" and "processes" to reduce transaction costs. And this is precisely what the Syndicate Bank has done since its origin in 1925.

Located in a small town called Manipal (the only bank with a head-office in a rural area) and starting with an initial paid-up capital of only Rs. 8000, its subsequent growth has been remarkable. From a negligible share in banking business till 1950, its share rose to about 1 per cent in 1960 and 4 per cent in 1975. Still, it was unlike the city-based banks particularly till 1969, when it was nationalized along with the other thirteen major banks. In 1968, 32 per cent of its branches were in rural areas; for the entire banking system, the share of rural branches was only 22 per cent. Its loans to agriculture and small enterprises constituted 30 per cent of its total loans; for the other banks, such loans were less than 8 per cent of their total loans. Of its deposit accounts 90 per cent were small accounts (below Rs. 1500) accounting for 50 per cent of its deposits; and 50 per cent of its borrowing accounts related to small–medium enterprises, their share in total borrowing being 30 per cent.

Its average interest rate on loans was not much higher than that of the city banks; in the 1950s and 1960s, it was about 2 percentage points higher than that of the State Bank of India—the largest commercial bank—and from early 1970s, it has been more or less the same as charged by the major city banks. How did it, then, manage to grow so rapidly even with concentration on markets, which the city banks found to be unremunerative? Obviously its transaction costs must have been comparable to the costs of lending to large industry and trade by the city banks.

Transaction Costs and Functional Cost-Structure

We do not have complete data on the cost structure of the city banks. However, the data on establishment expenses are available; establishment expenses include a large part of administrative costs but do not include default risk (bad debt provision). The ratio of establishment expenses to total deposits for the Syndicate was slightly higher than that for the banking system in 1951 and 1961; but since then, this ratio is in fact somewhat lower for the Syndicate than that for the banking system. Quite surprisingly, the Syndicate ratio is comparable to that of the Insured Commercial Banks in the United States.

Much more interesting, however, would be the comparison of the functional cost structure of the Syndicate with the other city banks, who have been financing small–medium enterprises particularly since 1969. However, such data are not available for any bank in any country. Even for the Syndicate, we could obtain such data only for 1975; they were compiled by the Syndicate especially for our purposes. One other major commercial bank located in Bombay could give us these data again only for 1975. The overall transaction costs of the city bank are lower than those for the Syndicate; this was to be expected as this city bank's lending to small enterprises constitutes only 25–30 per cent of its total lending, while the share of small enterprise lending in the total for the Syndicate is about 40 per cent. However, the city bank's costs are *more than three times* those of the Syndicate for lending to agriculture and small enterprises. Again, for deposit mobilization, the Syndicate's administrative costs are *much* lower than those of the city bank. The interest costs of deposits are obviously somewhat lower for the city bank as demand deposits constitute a much higher proportion of its total deposits.

Factors Accounting for Low Transaction Costs

The significant question which arises in this context is: how and through what mechanism the Syndicate has been able to service a large number of small accounts—deposit as well as borrowing accounts—and thus provide credit to the small enterprises at a cost which is much below that of the city banks.

Briefly, it is a new style of banking—an innovative approach to banking—that seems to explain this phenomenon; the creative adaptation of the banking technology to suit local conditions seems to be the crucial factor.

1. NEW ENTREPRENEURS[30]

This adaptation was possible because of the characteristics of the leadership. The promoters came from a lower middle-class background; they belonged to a community which respects learning. None of them came from an industrial house; the city banks were started by promoters who had close links with large industry. Of the three promoters, one was a medical doctor, one an engineer and the third a trader dealing in hand-loom cloth.

All of them were participants in the movement of socio-economic reform, initiated by Mahatma Gandhi. They had a powerful motivation for the socio-economic uplift of the community and the region to which they belonged; hard work, education and thrift—these they considered crucial for socio-economic reform. They had not merely a passion for reform. They had not merely a hard-headed business sense. They had both. And banking was considered by them as an instrument for the purpose; to serve as an effective instrument, it had to be viable and gain vitality for growth.

They were responsible for establishing educational institutions—a school in each village in their district and an educational complex, a type of university centre at Manipal—the villages to which they belonged. The bank management helped the process; but, at the same time, they were conscious of the deposit potential of these institutions. The bank provided employment opportunities for the educated members of the local community; but this helped in having a dependable and dedicated staff. The bank helped the farmers and small enterprises by providing technical assistance; but this enlarged their business. The bank cultivated the habit of thrift in the community through a new deposit scheme—called pigmy deposit; but this enlarged the bank's resources.

2. RECRUITMENT AND PROMOTION POLICIES[31]

The major factor responsible for the relatively high productivity of the staff has been its recruitment policy. It selects relatively unsophisticated persons with local contact and a rural or semi-urban background; and, unlike the city banks, it has preferred again high school graduates to graduates or post-graduates from a university. Their familiarity with the local scene and their contacts enable them to expand Sydnicate business in a variety of ways; they inspire confidence in potential depositors, they are able to appraise well the soundness of projects and the credit-worthiness of borrowers and to assess the business potential of the area in which they function. The information costs thus are reduced; persons without this background would have to collect more information and spend more effort and time in appraising the soundness of borrowers and their schemes.

Since they are high school graduates, they enter the banking business at a fairly young age and thus are more adaptable. Again, since they would not have got such a job in the city banks, they consider themselves fortunate and hence are more dedicated, dependable and disciplined than the graduates. They are prepared to do considerable field-work, which is so essential for attracting, maintaining and supervising small accounts. And, of course, their pay scales are lower than those for the graduates in the city banks; the Syndicate average salary per employee *even now* is 20–30 per cent lower than that in the city banks. And their academic qualifications are adequate for the banking business. Persons with univeristy degrees are, in fact, over-qualified for a large number of jobs in a bank; from the point of view of the institution, such persons are less adaptable, more ambitious and less disciplined than those who have completed high school education.

The promotion policy of the bank is such as to build staff morale and avoid discontent and demoralization. Somewhat on the Japanese style, a person is promoted salary-wise and grade-wise on the basis of seniority, provided there are no consecutive adverse reports on his efficiency. But such a promotion does not mean that he would get a more responsible *functional* assignment. Seniority-wise promotion in a salary grade is divorced from functional promotion. Responsible positions are assigned to bright persons without affecting *adversely* the salary-wise promotion of others and without affecting favourably their own salary grades. Functional promotion thus is a type of reward for the really deserving; he wins recognition for his worth. The others are not discontented as their salary-wise promotions are not affected.

This divorce of functional promotion from seniority-wise promotion in a salary grade helps the bank in selecting persons for senior management positions. For the top few jobs, which are on a pure selection basis, the bank has a choice from among the persons who are really competent—those who are promoted function-wise.

There is another characteristic of the bank's recruitment policy which is worth noting. In cases where it is feasible, the bank recruits married couples. The stability, reliability and dedication of such couples have been significant—more than those of the other employees.

This recruitment and promotion policy is reflected in the productivity of the Syndicate employees. The deposit accounts handled per employee are 287 for the Syndicate, while they are only 120 for the banking system as a whole. Again, the borrowing accounts per employee are 48 for the Syndicate as against only 14 for the banking system. The Syndicate productivity differential as compared with the city banks obviously would be much greater than what is indicated by these figures, for here the comparison is with the *average* for the banking system as a whole. If the wage differential is considered along with the physical productivity differential, the productivity differential in financial terms would indeed be much more significant than the physical productivity differential.

3. TECHNICAL ASSISTANCE

The bank provides technical assistance to farmers as well as small industrialists. It has a special staff for the purpose. The farm representatives are a special cadre of young officers recruited from agricultural universities and specially trained for the banking business. Similarly, for the small industry sector, the bank has a cadre of industrial engineers and technicians.

Each one of these officers looks after several branches—about 5 to 10—depending upon local conditions. The bank's policy of opening branches in clusters in a given region helps it to spread the costs of these special cadres over a number of geographically contiguous branches.

The technical assistance provided, of course, helps the borrowers; but at the same time it enlarges the bank's business and reduces its risk. These special cadres are able to appraise credit proposals in the field—they provide an effective appraisal machinery. But at the same time, their periodical field visits provide an effective machinery for supervision as well as recovery of loans.

4. DECENTRALIZED DECISION-MAKING AND AVOIDANCE OF PAPER WORK

The volume of work involved cannot be effectively handled without decentralized decision-making. The loans to farmers and small enterprises are sanctioned by the branch managers with the advice of the technical cadre; there is no reference to the head office and thus the head office costs for such loans are negligible.

Again, there is much more emphasis on field-work than on desk work, on local decision-making and initiative than on paperwork. The branch and the branch manager are judged on their overall results—the volume of deposits and the magnitude of loans and their recovery; the bank, thus, exercises utmost economy in the sphere of documenting, information and its transmittal to the head office. Such reporting procedures would increase costs and divert the attention of the branch manager from banking business to collecting and documenting such information, which is hardly relevant for decision-making either at the branch level or at the head office level.

Of course, after nationalization in 1969, these information costs have increased because of the Reserve Bank of India directives and requirements. But still, the management is alert to keep them within certain limits. The central banks and the international banks do have a craze for information and demand from the intermediary and final lending agencies type of information which may be enlightening for researchers but is irrelevant for real decision-making; they still have to realize that there are costs involved—sometimes as large as 1–2 per cent of the loan portfolio. Instead of reducing transaction costs, they raise them.[32]

5. INNOVATIVE DEPOSIT SCHEMES

The bank has introduced a variety of innovative deposit schemes linked to motives to save. One recent example is the Farmers' Protection Deposit Scheme. In times of dire necessity arising out of crop failure, the farmer is eligible for a loan equal to double the amount of deposits outstanding in his account. This deposit earns interest at 5 per cent per annum and the loan is at a concessional rate of 9 per cent per annum—repayable over a period of three years. The small farmer does not save normally in the form of a financial asset; interest rate on deposits is not much of an attraction to him particularly when his transaction costs are high. But he can be induced to save in the form of a deposit if it is linked with borrowing at a time of crop failure. In the absence of crop insurance, this is the type of saving which the farmers need.[33]

This principle of linking deposits with lending for a specific purpose has been applied by the bank in several cases. A farmer, for example, would get a loan for the purchase of a pump-set if he has accumulated 25 per cent of the cost as fixed or saving deposits. A small industrialist gets a loan for machinery purchase if he accumulates more than 20 per cent of the cost as deposits. Such schemes help the bank in mobilizing deposits as well as judging the seriousness of purpose of the borrower; at the same time because of the assurance of a loan, the borrower has inducement to save. Without such assurance, in many cases, there would not be saving enough for investment and, hence, there would be a strong temptation to use it up for financing emergencies or social expenditures.

But the one deposit scheme for which the bank is known is the Pigmy Deposit. This was introduced by the bank in 1928 and was part of the crusade of inculcating the habit of thrift among relatively poor people. At the same time, the promoters regarded it as a business opportunity. This opportunity was not seized by the other banks because of the transaction costs involved in collecting small deposits from a large number of relatively uneducated and poor customers.

The Syndicate, however, devised a scheme that proved to be financially profitable for the bank and at the same time attractive to the depositors. The principle of the scheme was simple: it involved door-to-door collection of a given amount of deposits (as low as 25 paise) at stated intervals. Quite a large number of people—workers, petty shopkeepers, vegetable vendors, hawkers, small traders—it was thought, could save these small amounts per day or week or month. But they do not have time to go to a bank and deposit this amount regularly. This *potential* saving was not realized as the poor had no semi-contractual obligation to accumulate. With agents appointed to collect such deposits, this saving capacity and inclination can be tapped.

And, thus, the Syndicate introduced this Pigmy Deposit to be collected periodically from the doorsteps of the saver. The commission rate was linked with the amount of deposits collected and has not exceeded 3 per cent per annum. The interest was 3.13 per cent per annum provided the saver did not withdraw from the scheme for seven years. A depositor saving 0.12 rupees daily could accumulate at the end of the seventh year Rs. 350. Within this period, the saver could borrow from the bank against the security of his deposit.

Such was the original scheme. Its specific features have varied after 1969 but the broad principle still remains the same.

On an average, the total cost to the bank of this long-term deposit has varied between 3 and 5 per cent per annum, significantly lower than the cost of a three- to five-year fixed deposit. Even in 1975, its total cost was only 5.52 per cent as against the cost of fixed deposits at 13 per cent.

The bank was thus able to seize a business opportunity without competition from the other banks till 1960. The Pigmy Deposits constituted 14–15 per cent of total deposits in 1946; this proportion rose to 21 per cent in 1960. Since then, its relative significance has declined with the faster growth of the other deposits and competition of the other banks. Still, even in 1975, these deposits constituted 7–8 per cent of total deposits. In absolute terms, these Pigmy Deposits are currently more than ten times their amount in 1960.

For the saver, such a deposit enabled him to accumulate his small saving into a fairly sizeable figure in seven years. Without this facility, very likely he would not have saved or, at any rate, saved as much. His motivation to save has been to accumulate for emergency or other anticipated expenditures rather than the inducement of earning interest. This deposit thus, has been linked with this type of motive among the relatively poor.[34]

Even the commission paid to the agents has not been a net loss to the bank. The agent has to keep a security deposit with the bank equal to 10 per cent of his commission; this is done to minimize the danger of the agent disappearing with his collection.

Central Bank Response to Syndicate Innovations

The Central Bank (Reserve Bank of India) itself has been innovative in many ways;[35] but with regard to the unconventional practices of the Syndicate, it took a negative attitude. The Syndicate till 1965 was considered as an unsophisticated rural bank and the Central Bank did not like some of its innovations. This is an instance of how central regulatory agencies—particularly when they try to *imitate* rather than adapt the technology of a developed country—come in the way of creative adaptation of modern technology.

1. With regard to the Pigmy Deposits, the Syndicate permitted its own

employees to work as agents during their spare time. For the bank this was one of the ways of reducing its wage costs and increasing its business; for the employee it was an incentive to earn more. But in 1962 the Central Bank found this practice to be objectionable on strict banking principles and prohibited the Syndicate from engaging its own employees as agents.

2. The Syndicate wanted to set up an agricultural demonstration farm in 1964 to enable it to promote the adoption of new high-yielding seeds by the farmers. The Central Bank considered such a venture in technical assistance as not consistent with healthy banking practices. Hence the Syndicate had to think of other ways. It induced the progressive farmers to set up a voluntary organization called Syndicate Agricultural Foundation; the management *in fact* is looked after by the bank—the bank providing financial assistance to the Foundation through annual grants.

3. In 1960 the bank pioneered a unique investment service through its Investors' Agency Department. This service enabled the middle-income group savers to invest in shares of reputable companies. The persons joining the scheme were assured of a return of 9–10 per cent per annum on their saving; the bank in turn invested these sums in shares. This scheme became very popular with middle-income groups in semi-urban areas—persons who were not familiar with the stock market. It was a precursor to the Central Bank sponsored Unit Trust of India. However, this service had to be withdrawn in 1965 as the Central Bank thought it could compete with the Unit Trust of India that was set up in 1964.

It is pertinent to note that since the 1969 nationalization of fourteen major banks, the Central Bank has been inducing the banks to expand their branches in rural areas so as to provide credit to small enterprises in both the farm and non-farm sectors. With this emphasis on the widening and deepening of the geographical and functional scope of the banking system, the Syndicate has recently been regarded by the Central Bank as a Model Bank.

NOTES

1. See J. A. Schumpeter, *Business Cycles*, vol. i (New York: McGraw-Hill Co., Inc., 1939), pp. 98–9; see also J. Hicks, *Economic Perspectives* (Oxford: Oxford University Press, 1977), chapters i and ii; K. J. Arrow, *The Limits of Organisation* (New York: W. W. Norton & Co., 1974), chapters 3 and 4.
2. See J. A. Schumpeter, *Capitalism, Socialism and Democracy* (New York: Harper & Row, 1975). To quote: "The first thing to go is the traditional conception of the *modus operandi* of competition. Economists are at long last emerging from the stage in which price competition was all they saw. As soon as quality competition and sales effort are admitted into the sacred precincts of theory, the price variable is ousted from its dominant position. However, it is still competition within a rigid pattern of invariant conditions, methods of production and forms of industrial organisation in particular that practically monopolises attention. But in capitalist reality as distinguished from its text-book picture, it is not that kind of competition which counts but the competition from the new commodity, the new technology, the new source of supply, the new type of organisation (the large-scale unit of control for instance)—competition which commands a decisive cost or quality advantage and which strikes not at the margins of the profits and the outputs of the existing firms but at their foundations and their very lives. This kind of competition is as much more effective than the other as a bombardment is in comparison with forcing a door, and so much more important that it becomes a matter of comparative indifference whether competition in the ordinary sense functions more or less promptly; the powerful lever that in the long run expands output and brings down prices is in any case made of other stuff" (pp. 84–5).

10. See J. Hicks, *Critical Essays in Monetary Theory, loc. cit.* To quote: "It is implicitly assumed, in Walrasian analysis, that there is no cost (in terms of effort and sacrifice) in the making of transactions: but this, though a fair simplification for many purposes, is hopelessly misleading when our subject is money. . . . There is the same incentive to find ways of reducing transaction costs as of reducing other costs; one way of looking at monetary evolution is to regard it as the development of even more sophisticated ways of reducing transaction costs" (pp. 6–7).
11. See J. Hicks, *Capital and Growth* (Oxford: Clarendon Press, 1965), pp. 289–91. To quote: "The beginning of a process of expansion might occur because of real factors (inventions and the like) raising the real (prospective) rate of profit. But it might also occur because of financial improvements, diminishing the size of our 'gap'; thereby permitting access to funds, for improvements which could have been made earlier, if the necessary funds had been forthcoming. It is not savings only that are required, but a channel of communication between potential savings and potential real investment" (p. 290).
12. On this subjective risk, see J. M. Keynes, *The General Theory of Employment, Interest and Money* (New York: Harcourt, Brace & World, Inc., 1964). To quote: "Two types of risk affect the volume of investment. . . . The first is the entrepreneur's or borrower's risk . . . a second type . . . we may call lender's risk. . . . Now the first type of risk is, in a sense, a real social cost, though susceptible to diminution by averaging as well as by an increased accuracy of foresight. The second, however, is a pure addition to the cost of investment. . . . Moreover, it involves in part a duplication of a proportion of the entrepreneur's risk, which is added twice to the pure rate of interest. . . . For if a venture is a risky one, the borrower will require a wider margin between his expectation of yield and the rate of interest at which he will think it worth his while to borrow; whilst the very same reason will lead the lender to require a wider margin between what he charges and the pure rate of interest in order to induce him to lend. . . . This duplication of allowance for a portion of the risk has not hitherto been emphasised, so far as I am aware; but it may be important in certain circumstances" (pp. 144–5).
13. There is an interesting story about the origin of these two signatures. See E. J. T. Acaster, "Banking With the Labouchères", *The Three Banks Review* (Issue No. 100, Dec. 1973). To quote: "In the 1790s the distinguished Amsterdam banking house of Hope & Company had some business to transact with that rising English banker Sir Francis Baring and entrusted the mission to a young French clerk of the name of Labouchere. During his stay in London the clerk fell in love with Sir Francis' daughter, Dorothy, and asked her father for permission to become engaged. Permission was refused. 'Would it make any difference to your decision if you knew that Mr. Hope was about to take me into partnership?', asked the young man. Sir Francis confirmed that it would.

    "On returning to Holland, therefore, Labouchere mooted with his employer that he should be promoted to the partnership. Unfortunately for the proposer, the idea was not well received. 'Would it make any difference to your decision if you knew that I was engaged to the daughter of Sir Francis Baring?', asked the clerk. 'Well, yes, it would,' admitted Mr. Hope. Then and there the young Pierre César clinched the deal, laying the foundation for his family's fortune by stating his engagement to be a fact, and by the next London mail he was able duly to confirm to Sir Francis that his entrance to the partnership of Hope had become a reality" (p. 29).
14. On financial innovations, see J. Hicks, *A Theory of Economic History* (Oxford: Oxford University Press, 1969), chapters v and vi.
15. See J. A. Schumpeter, *Business Cycles*, vol. i, *loc. cit.*, pp. 111–12. See also Hicks, *Economic Perspectives, loc. cit.*, pp. 78–9. What Schumpeter calls innovations and Hicks calls impulses require credit creation; the latter is, as Schumpeter observes, the "monetary complement of innovation".
16. See B. P. Pesek, "On Post-Robertson Monetary Theory", *Journal of Economic Literature*, vol. xiv, No. 3 (Sept. 1976), pp. 856–81. Pesek also shows how important parts of monetary and banking theory rest on theoretical and empirical assumptions that are indefensible and they lack a sound micro-economic base.

    See also J. Hicks, *The Crisis in Keynesian Economics* (Oxford: The Camelot Press Ltd., 1974), pp. 48–9.
17. See B. P. Pesek, *op. cit.*
18. See A. Gerschenkron, *Economic Backwardness in Historical Perspective* (Cambridge, Mass.: Harvard

University Press, 1962), pp. 11–16. To quote: "In particular, the story of the Crédit Mobilier of the brothers Pereire is often regarded as a dramatic but, on the whole, rather insignificant episode. . . . It seems to be much better in accord with the facts to speak of a truly momentous role of investment banking of the period for the economic history of France and of large portions of the Continent. . . . But more important than their slavish imitations was the creative adaptation of the basic idea of the Pereires and its incorporation in the new type of bank, the Universal Bank which, in Germany, along with most other countries on the Continent, became the dominant form of banking. The difference between banks of the crédit-mobilier type and commercial banks in the advanced industrial country of the time (England) was absolute. Between the English bank essentially designed to serve as a source of short-term capital and a bank designed to finance the long-run investment needs of the economy there was a complete gulf. The German banks, which may be taken as a paragon of the type of the Universal Bank, successfully combined the basic idea of the crédit mobilier with the short-term activities of commercial banks . . . the banks acquired a formidable degree of ascendancy over industrial enterprises, which extended far beyond the sphere of financial control into that of entrepreneurial and managerial decisions" (p. 12–14).

19. See R. W. Goldsmith, "Some Reflections on the Past, Present and Future of Financial Institutions" (Mimeo. 1974). To quote: "There are two tendencies at work here which have already operated since the early history of financial institutions, tendencies which you may call the specialty shop and the department store principle. A specialty shop in finance holds, essentially, one type of financial instrument and raises most of its funds also by one, though a different, instrument. At certain times and certain countries, the one or the other system has prevailed. England was, during most of its modern financial history, a financial specialty shop country, as were the United States. Germany, on the other hand, has always been more of a financial department store country, France being generally in the middle. In the last decade, however, there has been a definite tendency, in virtually all countries, for the department store model of finance to gain, particularly in the field of deposit banking. . . . Finally, something happened during the fifties and the sixties. It probably became obvious to bankers that, if they continued to do business as before, they would continue to lose in importance. This trend soon became worldwide, partly because it is much easier to transfer financial technology from one country to another than to do so in the case of industrial technology. . . . This movement towards financial department store operations is, I think, one of the most important trends to watch in developed countries in the next generation. . . . It has always been present to some extent and is particularly pronounced in less developed countries" (pp. 82–4).

20. See J. Hicks, *Capital and Growth, loc. cit.*, p. 292. Hicks emphasizes the point that the efficiency of a financial system should be judged on the basis of the narrowness of the gap between the lowest and the highest interest rate. The function of the non-bank financial intermediaries is to narrow this gap. But Hicks notes: "An alternative possibility, that the 'contact' (which I have ascribed in the above to financial intermediaries outside the Bank) might sometimes be established by specialised departments within the Bank (or banking system) itself, should not be overlooked. It would certainly need attention in a more extended treatment" (p. 292).

21. See K. J. Arrow, *op. cit.*, pp. 47–57. To quote: "In classical maximising theory it is implicit that the values of relevant variables are at all moments under consideration. All variables are therefore *agenda* of the organisation, that is, their values have always to be chosen. On the other hand, it is a commonplace of every day observation and of studies of organisation that the difficulty of arranging that a potential decision variable be recognised as such may be much greater than that of choosing a value for it" (p. 47).

22. See V. V. Bhatt, *Structure of Financial Institutions* (Bombay: Vora & Co., 1972), chapter i. To quote: "This problem is now being tackled by giving a new radical orientation to the commercial banking system. . . . To provide the agriculture—small industry orientation to the banks' policies, a new and potentially fruitful concept of a lead bank in a district has been evolved. . . . This lead bank scheme is likely to be more effective than a new district bank scheme; for, the lead bank would be much more viable financially because of its nationwide operation and, further, for the same reason, it would have at its disposal much larger resources than a small district bank.

"The main functions of a lead bank would be to: (*a*) identify places in a district for branch expansion; (*b*) prepare a phased program for branch expansion in the district so as to bring banking services within the reach of the entire area; (*c*) estimate the current requirement of credit and prepare a phased program to meet it by supplanting the non-institutional money-lenders type of credit purveyors; (*d*) identify the potential areas of agricultural and small industry development and to induce local entrepreneurs to undertake such development; (*e*) identify the major bottle-necks in the development of the district and induce the appropriate agencies to take remedial action; (*f*) goad the local entrepreneur in agriculture and small industry to improve progressively his productive efficiency; and (*g*) devise such schemes of deposits and financial investments as would prove attractive to the local people and effective for the purpose of mobilising as well as raising the rate of saving in the district.

"The lead bank obviously cannot perform these functions in isolation; it would have to solicit the active support of other banks in the district . . . and other State-level financial institutions as also of the various official and non-official agencies. The role expected of a lead bank is not merely that of purveying credit and deposit mobilisation, it has to provide entrepreneur and managerial guidance to agriculture and small industry" (pp. 16–17).

See also Reserve Bank of India, *Annual Report and Trend and Progress of Banking in India: 1975–76* (Bombay, 1976), pp. 59–60.

23. It is not possible to identify the impact of innovations on the basis of aggregative or semi-aggregative data, however sophisticated the econometric techniques are. See J. A. Schumpeter, *Business Cycles, loc. cit.*, p. 144, and B. P. Pesek, *op. cit.* Hence the emphasis in this article on actual case-studies of financial innovations.
24. Unless otherwise stated, all information with regard to Haryana is taken from G. S. Bhalla, *Changing Agrarian Structure in India* (Delhi: Meenakshi Prakeshan, 1974), and V. V. Bhatt, *Interest Rate, Transactions Costs and Financial Innovations* (World Bank: Domestic Finance Studies No. 47, 1978).
25. See S. Bhalla, "Agricultural Growth: Role of Institutional and Infra-structural Factors", *Economic and Political Weekly*, vol. xii, nos. 45 and 46 (5–12 Nov., 1977), pp. 1898–905.
26. See J. A. Schumpeter, *The Theory of Economic Development, loc. cit.*, p. 103.
27. See V. V. Bhatt, *op. cit.*
28. This section is based on information specially obtained from the Syndicate Bank of India. The latter made available to the author even their confidential data. Again, the author had the benefit of detailed discussions with the top management of the bank. Of course, the grasp of the bank's actual functioning would not have been as sharp and authentic but for the fact that the author happened to be a member of its Board of Directors during 1969–72.

    The document prepared by the bank is published in the Domestic Finance Studies series of the World Bank. See N. K. Thingalaya, *Innovations in Banking: The Syndicate's Experience* (World Bank: Development Economics Department, Domestic Finance Studies, No. 46, 1978). See also V. V. Bhatt, *Rate of Interest, Transaction. Costs and Financial Innovations* (World Bank: Domestic Finance Studies No. 47, 1978).
29. See J. M. Keynes, *op. cit.*, p. 208.
30. For the characteristics of the promoters of the Syndicate Bank, see S. Menefee, *The Pais of Manipal* (New York: Asia Publishing House, 1969).

    See also J. A. Schumpeter, *Business Cycles*, vol. i, *loc. cit.*, pp. 93–7. Syndicate's experience supports Schumpeter's hypothesis that innovation is generally introduced by the rise to leadership of New Men, setting up a New Firm and with New Plant (in this case, a new organisational principle).
31. See V. V. Bhatt, *op. cit.*, chapter 2.
32. See V. V. Bhatt, *Division of Public and Private Finance: Research Program and Its Rationale* (World Bank: Development Economics Department, Domestic Finance Studies, No. 43, 1977), pp. 13–15.
33. See V. V. Bhatt, *Structure of Financial Institutions, loc. cit.*, chapter 4.
34. *Ibid.*, chapter 4.
35. See V. V. Bhatt, *Some Aspects of Financial Policies and Central Banking in Developing Countries* (World Bank: Economic Development Institute, EDI Seminar Paper No. 11, 1974).

12. Development Banking: Top Management Tasks and Structure*

DEVELOPMENT banks are unique financial institutions in developing countries, specializing in the provision of high-risk, long-term financing for the purpose of industrialization. There were only about a dozen viable development banks before 1946; but after the Second World War, the growth of this type of financial institution has been significant. At present, there are about 400 such institutions, of which more than 45 owe their existence and strength to the World Bank.[1]

These banks were expected to provide not only long-term finance but also play a catalytic promotional role—a development role—in setting in motion a viable widely diffused process of industrialization. However, experience so far indicates that they have functioned, with few notable exceptions[2] as passive conservative bankers, supporting financially well-known and well-entrenched business houses rather than as *development banks*.[3] Doubtless they have built up specialized skills and techniques in the field of project appraisal and selection. But even in this field, their criteria for project selection have been more or less the conventional banker's criteria—financial soundness and repaying ability of the project *as well as* the promoter. In brief, though they have functioned as sound *bankers*, they have failed as *development bankers*.[4]

The major reason for this failure seems to be the lack of appreciation by their top managements of their specific tasks in the development context. It is the purpose of this chapter to indicate the nature and structure of these top management tasks. Top management tasks and structure as they relate to development banking are indicated in section I. Communication and information systems are vital to the top management task of effective decision making, and this relationship is discussed in section II.

I. Development Banking: Top Management Tasks

One cannot understand the tasks of management without first analysing the social function which the institution is supposed to perform. Management and the institution managed can be judged only on the basis of their performance with regard to the social need and function, from which the institution derives its social justification. Thus the management problem cannot be understood without the perception of the tasks and functions of management in a social context; for without this context, no institution can survive.[5] So the central focus in any study of management has to be on the tasks of management. It is from these tasks that objectives, strategy and structure are derived; it is not possible to discuss meaningfully the problems related to strategy and structure without first posing the question relating to the social function and tasks of management.

* Published in *World Development*, vol. 4, no. 6 (1976).

Now this social function can never be defined once and for all. The search for the nature and structure of this function has to be a continuing one in a dynamic and interdependent setting of socio-economic change. It is the performance of this evolving social function that determines the survival and growth of an institution; if it fails in this endeavour, its fate is sealed even if it is managed efficiently. For business institutions like development banks, their continuing ability to plough back profits is merely one of the indices of their success in performance; the basic index of their success is the vitality with which they survive and grow.

Both economists and management scientists have not perceived the central function and role of top management as their setting for analysis is essentially a static setting—a setting where things change in systematic known ways or where there is need for mere passive adaptation to exogenous events.[6] The real management problem arises only in a dynamic setting—in a setting where decisions have to be taken for the future which is unknowable and where information even about the present or the past is, in the nature of things, incomplete and imperfect. If the past, present and future were known, there would be no management problem.[7]

In the context of development banking, the question to be raised is: What is the emerging social function of a development bank in a given dynamic social setting? The charter of a development bank can never define the social function once and for all; it is the task of top management to find out the specific implications of this function in the light of the dynamic, changing socio-economic reality. The broad purpose and mission can be easily stated: to serve as a catalyst for generating a viable yet widely diffused process of industrial development in a given country. But the precise social function would depend upon the initial stage of development, the development strategy adopted, the available composition of resources, skills, and manpower, the efficiency with which other institutions are performing functions related to development banking and so on. Top management, thus, needs to have a precise knowledge of all these elements of the socio-economic structure in its dynamic setting. Mere knowledge cannot suffice; it has to evolve organic links with the decision-making process in the institutions, which have an impact on its work, so that its functioning is integrated with that of the related institutions. In this process of interactions, a development bank adapts itself to the other institutions as much as it enforces adaption by the others to its functioning.

Let us take a concrete case. Suppose a development bank is set up in a developing country to provide long-term financial assistance to viable industrial projects. It assumes, to begin with, that project promoters would seek its assistance and that its task is to appraise the soundness of projects and provide such assistance as is really required. The initial task then is: by what criteria should it appraise such projects? Should it look merely to the financial viability of the project and its capacity to repay assistance or should it appraise the project from the point of view of its contribution to the development strategy adopted by the country or, more generally, from the point of view of national advantage? Obviously, a development bank has no *rationale* for its existence unless it looks to national advantage; for its function is not merely banking, but such banking as would promote industrial development. But, then, the problem is how to develop such criteria which reflect national advantage? Obviously, it cannot derive these criteria without reference to the development objectives, strategy and policies of the country. So, it has to have a dialogue with the relevant state agencies for the purpose. But this has to be a real dialogue and not a mere passive adaptation of criteria to what the state agencies may suggest; for a development bank really knows how projects are affected by policies, and it can analyse this concrete evidence to suggest to the relevant agencies how strategy or policies need to be modified in the light of concrete factual evidence. Thus, no criteria for project appraisal can be evolved without this interaction with state agencies, and the bank's own criteria have to be modified in the light of the emerging reality.

The application of whatever criteria that are devised cannot be a mechanical process. For, the criteria may not be appropriate or the contribution of a particular project to some development objectives may not be sharply brought out by the criteria. Or, the contribution of a project to one objective may be so overwhelmingly important that its contribution to other objectives needs to be ignored. The main point is: the appraisal criteria should be such, and should evolve in such a manner that they help in the process of decision making. This implies that the criteria should bring out such implications of a project on the basis of which it is possible to make an informed judgement. Criteria, after all, are tools for decision making; they are not a substitute for decision making.

Decision making, again, is different from decision preparation. The latter process is an *analytic* process of processing meaningfully all relevant information. But decision making is not an analytic process. It is based on the *perception* of the whole problem and not merely on partial fragmentary analysis. This perception, insight, intelligence relate to the total impact of a project—the quantifiable as well as that which is not quantifiable.[8] Obviously, it cannot be governed by mechanical formulae, tools and techniques; if it is so governed, it is the surest index of lack of intelligence and hence lack of ability to take right decisions.[9]

Whatever the decision criteria, if they are not adopted by all financial institutions, a development bank may find that financially viable projects are diverted to other financial institutions, while it is left only with a small number of risky projects. This situation indicates that a development bank simply cannot function in a vacuum and has to have a close relationship with other financial institutions with regard to the selection criteria to be evolved. This relationship is important also for mobilizing resources for the financing of what it considers to be sound projects, but for which it cannot provide adequate assistance.

A development bank, again, is likely to be faced with all or any one of the following problems: (*a*) its appraisal criteria may be sound but it may find that these criteria have not much significance for the appropriate choice of technology or product-mix as most projects are designed by foreign consultants or companies, in the light of technology in use in advanced countries; (*b*) it may find that terms and conditions of foreign technical or financial collaboration are onerous and the negotiating ability of project promoters *vis-à-vis* their foreign partners is not adequate; (*c*) really worthwhile projects are not identified and designed because of lack of entrepreneurial talents in the public as well as the private sector; (*d*) potential entrepreneurs get frustrated as they do not get the required assistance for giving shape to their project ideas; (*e*) projects get concentrated in certain geographical areas or certain fields, as infrastructure facilities including technical and financial assistance are not evenly spread across the country or across different industrial fields.

These are some of the problems with which a development bank is likely to be faced at one time or the other and, if it is to perform its social function, it has to take action towards their solution. This implies that along with financial assistance, a development bank has to be prepared to provide managerial and technical assistance. This really means that it cannot possibly wait for projects to come to it for assistance; it has to *create* projects that are consistent with the overall—explicit or implicit—national development strategy.

If there are institutions in the field of project identification and formulation, it has to develop living contact with them for the solution of some of these problems. If there are none, it has to take the initiative in establishing them in co-operation with the relevant institutions, including stage agencies.

A development bank cannot perform these different tasks unless it is financially viable. It is inherent in its tasks to experiment with innovative ways of fulfilling its social function; and for this purpose, it has to commit key men and resources to new tasks. It cannot do this unless (*a*) it withdraws resources from less vital and increasingly less important tasks—tasks that can well be performed by the other institutions; (*b*) it shares in the profits of really viable and successful projects by devising appropriate flexibility in its terms and conditions governing assistance; (*c*) it attracts new resources from institutions which mobilize savings by designing such financial instruments that would appeal to them; (*d*) it mobilizes resources from state agencies for specific mutually agreed tasks, and (*e*) it attracts foreign resources from other countries and international agencies.

All these are top management functions: (*a*) devising selection criteria; (*b*) interacting with state agencies for modifying development strategy and policies; (*c*) interacting with other financial institutions in the country as well as abroad for mobilizing resources as well as for performing common tasks; (*d*) interacting with institutions in the field of project identification and formulation; (*e*) initiating the establishment of relevant institutions required to provide technical and managerial assistance to entrepreneurs, and establishing organic links with them; (*f*) devising new ways of mobilizing resources; and (*g*) attaining financial viability for creating the right setting for survival and growth.

The performance of these tasks requires a top management team—a task-focused approach to management structure rather than the usual function-focused hierarchical organization approach. It has to be a team with a leader of four to five persons with specific responsibility assigned to each, but yet, working as a team for decision-making. These tasks are so basic and fundamental that this team would not have enough time and energy to devote to them if its members get tied up with operational jobs. Further, they would not be able to take an overall view about the functioning of a development bank if they tie themselves to *specific* operational jobs. Anything that pertains to the performances of the institution as a *whole* and that which others cannot do are their responsibilities.

However, the selection of persons for key management jobs has to be their responsibility; for it is this team which has to create the one that can in time replace it. Otherwise, the institution cannot be perpetuated. For this purpose, they have to be in formal and informal contact with potential and actual managers, devise ways and methods of testing and training them and finally selecting the really best to succeed them in the top management team. A top management team that considers itself indispensable for the institution has really not performed its top management task; such a team needs to be changed by a well-functioning Board, whose only functions can be to (*a*) reinforce top management in its tasks with advice, counselling and review; (*b*) replace the team with a successor team in good time; and, (*c*) perform the ceremonial functions that can project the right public image about the institution. A Board is not a substitute for top management; its functions are similar to those of a constitutional monarch in the United Kingdom.[10]

The top management team cannot function without a secretariat—a secretariat that (*a*) keeps its members informed about the activities of each other; (*b*) identifies and analyses relevant problems for decision making; (*c*) processes information about projects—at the appraisal, decision making and supervision stages—that is relevant for the various tasks of the team; (*d*) suggests new ways of performing conventional tasks or giving up of obsolete tasks, and (*e*) indicates new objectives that are in tune with the long-term growth of the institution. Let us call this secretariat the *Planning and Policy Cell* (PPC). It should be manned by a few professional people (maybe four to five) who should be selected from the operating departments for their competence. They should not be kept for more than five years in PPC; otherwise they would lose touch with reality. After five years, by rotation, they should be sent back to operational departments. PPC can also perform another function; it can be a testing ground for identifying and selecting the potential members of tomorrow's top management team. It would induce the personnel in the operational departments to take an overall view of the functions of the institution as each one would tend to aspire to become a member of the PPC.

Management theory is silent on the function and structure of top management; but in management practice, this was the very first area tackled systematically—long before Frederick W. Taylor tackled organization design in his functional structure. Top management as a function and as a structure was first developed by George Siemens (1839–1901) in Germany between 1870 and 1880, when he designed and built the Deutsche Bank and made it, within a very few years, into Continental Europe's leading and most dynamic financial institution.[11] It was a universal bank, combining commercial banking and development banking functions. These universal banks performed "a momentous role" in German industrialization.[12, 13]

> In Germany, the various incompetencies of the individual entrepreneurs were offset by the device of splitting the entrepreneurial function: the German investment banks—a powerful invention comparable in economic effect to that of the Steam Engine—were in their capital-supplying functions a substitute for the insufficiency of the previously created wealth willingly placed at the disposal of entrepreneurs. But they were also a substitute for entrepreneurial deficiencies. From their central vantage points of control, the banks participated actively in shaping the major, and sometimes even not so major, decisions of the individual enterprises. It was they who very often mapped out a firm's paths of growth, conceived far-sighted plans,

decided on major technological and locational innovations, and arranged for mergers and capital increases.[13]

It is such a universal bank—the ancestor of the modern development banks—that conceived the top management tasks and structure that in many ways are a model for the latter.

II. Managerial Communications and Decision-Making

With all its limitations, there is one fundamental insight underlying management science. It is that an institution or an organization is a system, whose parts are human beings with a variety of skills, knowledge and techniques, who are involved in a joint venture. And the main characteristic of a system is the interdependence of its parts. The primacy attaches to the whole and the parts have to be integrated to form the whole; primary emphasis, thus, has to be on the whole, and the contribution which the parts make to the whole, rather than on the mere technical efficiency of the parts. Technical perfection of a part may sometimes damage the system as a whole. It is a sad irony that in spite of this insight, management science has emphasized the efficiency of the parts—precision of the tools at the expense of the health and performance of the whole.

With this characteristic feature of interdependence, a system cannot function unless the parts move in harmony. This implies communication within the system—each part understanding its relationship with the others and with the whole system. Communication does not mean mere provision of information; it has to be meaningful and relevant information that demands action. Information presupposes communication but there can be communication even without information.[14]

So one must understand what communication means. Communication as an action-oriented system has to convey signals for action, for decision preparation and decision making. Each part has to act—take a decision or communicate the need for decision to other parts or to the centre. So communication has to deal with decisions. These decision signals also perform another function—they function as performance indicators of the part as well as the whole. The test of a good communication system is the economy of information and signals with which it functions.

Communication is an interpersonal phenomenon. Communication does not depend on the communicator; it vitally depends on the recipient, his understanding of the relevance of the information or message conveyed. The recipient will not act unless he understands precisely the full implications of what is conveyed. This understanding, this *perception* of the *meaning* is not a matter of logic nor is it a matter of information. This perception depends on his range of perception and what he expects to perceive.[15] If the information conveyed is not within the recipient's range of perception or his range of expectation, that information has no meaning. Effective communication implies, thus, such communication which the recipient can understand and act upon. Communication has no meaning unless it is related to action—that is, to the perception and motivation of the recipient.

An utterance from the centre has no meaning, however clearly spoken or drafted; for the centre may not understand the perception capacity or motivation of those who have to act.[16] Commands or orders do not improve the understanding or motivation of the recipients. Communication has to start from the recipients—how they understand their problems, how they intend to act or how they want the centre to act. So there has to be listening by the centre to what the recipients want to convey.[17] Communication, thus, has to be upward; it has to start with the recipient rather than the emitter—this is what is implied in the concept of listening. But this listening, too, may not be operational unless it is related to what both the recipients and emitters have in common. The upward communication has to be focused on something that is common to both, and that something is the *objectives*. It is in terms of these objectives that the subordinate should communicate upward what his major contribution should be and for which he should be held accountable. The supervisor may disagree and see the reality differently, but he understands what is conveyed and the subordinate understands why he has to act differently. Thus the perception of both is focused on concrete objectives—objectives that are real to both; hence communication is possible. This is what is meant by *management objectives*.

In a number of development banks, there is a plethora of information upward as well as downward—but no meaningful communication. Let us take the case of projects for which assistance is requested. The *Appraisal Department* may furnish a statement of the various projects for which assistance is sought and classify them into their different stages of appraisal. But such a statement has no meaning for top management; it may just file it even without reading it as this information has no decision signals for top management.

But suppose the *Appraisal Department* has to function within the framework of certain objectives such as: (*a*) no appraisal should take more than two months and, if a project does require more time, specific problems of that project and their possible solutions should be discussed with top management; (*b*) a project with complex technology or uncertain demand for its products should be sent for appraisal to a consultant for a thorough examination within fifteen days after the application is received; (*c*) the specific problems related to a project by a new entrepreneur or in a backward area as well as the proposed solutions should be discussed with top management; (*d*) a viable project requiring larger assistance than what the institution can provide should be sent to top management with concrete suggestions with regard to the possible ways of raising the required finance; (*e*) if a project requires modification to be viable, the possible modifications and the related action programme should be sent to the top management and so on.

If such objectives are laid down, the Appraisal Department would know what is expected of it, the decisions that it has to take and the decisions that it should suggest to the top management. And the information which the top management gets is action-oriented; it suggests the decision problems that it has to face. Thus there is a deadline and a firm commitment to action; and there are precise indicators of performance.

Take the instance of the *Project Supervision Department*, which hardly performs a meaningful function in a number of development banks. The department collects a mass of information, reports and impressions based on personal visits; and yet this information is hardly processed in a form that indicates an action programme. Such information has no meaning either to the Department or to the top management. The objectives need to be of the following type: (*a*) What problems are likely to be faced by specific projects—and what aspects of the projects need close supervision? This along with a proposed action programme should be submitted to the top management immediately after assistance is sanctioned; (*b*) Have these problems arisen? If so, what is the action that is proposed? Does it require top management decision? (*c*) If, during the operational phase, a project is not working at full capacity, what are the problems and what is the suggested solution? (*d*) If a project has failed, why has it failed, can life be put into it and how is this to be done?

In a similar way, there should be clear and precise objectives for the *Legal Section, Project Promotion and Development Department, Research Department and the Finance Department*. For the Legal Section, the objectives can be: (*a*) there should not be a lag of more than fifteen days between the sanction of assistance and the completion of legal formalities; (*b*) if there is likely to be a longer lag, the specific problems, their solutions and the timing should be indicated; (*c*) the norm should be that legal formalities be completed at the same time at which assistance is sanctioned.

Project Promotion and Development Department objectives might be defined in terms of the following questions: (*a*) What are the new project ideas that are consistent with the overall development strategy and what action is proposed for shaping them into implementable projects? (*b*) Who is approached for undertaking identified projects? What specific assistance is needed and what action is required for the provision of such assistance? (*c*) What are the specific problems of entrusting projects to new entrepreneurs or to entrepreneurs in backward areas? How can these problems be solved and what action is required for the purpose?

Research Department objectives can also be framed in terms of questions to be answered. (*a*) What is the development strategy—explicit or implicit—of the country and are actual policies in the industries field consistent with this strategy? If not, what modifications in policies are necessary and what action can be taken? (*b*) How do we devise appraisal criteria, how they enlighten and in what way are likely to conceal significant implications of projects? (*c*) For what projects is it necessary to make an *ex post* evaluation to indicate the soundness of appraisal procedures and criteria, government policies and the institution's policies? (*d*) What new projects can be identified that are related to the projects under implementation or completed and operating projects—new projects that are small and ancillary to large projects or related in any other way? (*e*) What projects can be identified on the basis of trade statistics as viable import-substituting or export-promoting projects? Similarly, Finance Department objectives may be put in the following terms: (*a*) What is the resource picture in the light of actual and potential commitments? (*b*) How should the resource gap be met? What are the new specific ways of raising resources, and what policy changes do they indicate? (*c*) If there is a resource surplus, in what manner should it be deployed to further the interest and objectives of the institution—the overriding objective being the generation of a viable and widely diffused process of industrialization?

Few development banks have a separate Finance Department; it is generally merged with the Accounts Department—and the accountant approach inhibits the exploration of innovative ways of raising resources.[18]

With such key objectives, the communication system can become meaningful and relevant for decision making. Mere perfection of the information system can never be the objective of an action-oriented system. While the pursuit of knowledge is essential for decision making, it has again to be understood that decisions can never be perfect because of uncertainty; and that however superior the information or knowledge, or skills, tools and techniques, they are no substitute for a clear perception of reality, which is complex and constantly changing. Action in the present should never be guided only by the past—that is simply according to skills, knowledge and techniques. But perception of the living reality is not a matter of logic; it is a matter of intelligence—keen sensitivity to men and things, in their measurable and non-measurable aspects, as they interact in the present. Perception, judgement, intelligence differ among different persons and that is why we have good management and bad, in spite of the common inheritance of skills, knowledge, techniques and the rest.[19]

For good and effective major decisions, the requirements are: (*a*) clear understanding of the problem, (*b*) its possible solutions and (*c*) the required action by the relevant group of people in an institution. Quite often, top management may just misunderstand the problem, and its decision, however quick and apparently sound, may be an answer to an irrelevant problem. A decision taken may not be the right decision as the possible alternative courses of action may not have been explored. Again, even if a problem is identified and a decision taken, it may not become immediately effective if the people who have to take action do not understand the problem, its solution and the proposed action.

For major policy decisions—involving innovative departures from the conventional approaches—it may be worthwhile to pose the problem to all relevant departments of the bank. The advantages would be: (*a*) a clear understanding of the problem or the non-problem by the top management as well as the other managerial cadres; (*b*) exploration of alternative solutions and action programmes; (*c*) commitment by the relevant departments to action with all its implications—commitment of key personnel, assignment of responsibilities, performance expectation and its systematic feed-back to top management. With all this preparation for a decision, whatever top management decides is likely to be appropriate and, more important, it is likely to be an *effective* decision in terms of actual action.

Selection of appraisal criteria, new promotional activities, new ways of raising resources, shortening of administrative and other procedural lags, new and more effective ways of project supervision—these are some of the problems which can be tackled in this way. This method ensures good communication and the performance of the system as a whole, as it motivates the entire institution to consider its problems, possible solutions and the action programmes required.

This is the Japanese method of decision making by consensus. This is not consensus as understood in terms of the lowest common denominator. It is really an art of making *effective* decisions. What is important in a Japanese business enterprise is not an answer to a question but the question itself. What they spend much time on is on defining the question—a process in which all managerial and other cadres are involved. The result is that the problem is understood in all its implications and the alternative solutions and action programmes are explored and examined. Once this is done, the decision becomes almost obvious and so does the action programme to the relevant personnel. So that taking a decision and acting on it become two simultaneous processes rather than two distinct stages. Normally, elsewhere a decision is taken and then it has to be "sold" to the people who have to act on it. Hence, the time taken in effective decision making is longer elsewhere than in Japan. Further, in Japan, conflicts are ironed out at the stage of decision making and the entire institution identifies itself with the problem and its solution. This promotes harmony, a sense of participation and hence a sense of identification with the interests and performance of the entire institution.

NOTES

1. J. D. Nyhart and E. F. Janssens, *A Global Directory of Development Finance Institutions in Developing Countries* (Paris: Development Centre of the Organization for Economic Cooperation and Development, 1967).
2. V. V. Bhatt, *Aspects of Functions and Working of Some Development Finance Companies* (Washington: Economic Development Institute, World Bank, 1974) (Mimeo). See also, V. V. Bhatt, "On Technology Policy and its Institutional Frame", *World Development*, vol. 3, no. 9 (Sept. 1975).
3. W. Diamond and R. Gulhati, *Some Reflections on the World Bank's Experience With Development Finance Companies.* Paper presented at an international seminar on development banks under the joint auspices of the Bankers' Training College of the Reserve Bank of India and the Economic Development Institute of the World Bank (Bombay, 1973) (Mimeo).
4. *Ibid.*
5. P. F. Drucker, *Management: Tasks, Responsibilities, Practices* (New York: Harper & Row Publishers, 1973), chapter 4, and pp. 508–10.
6. J. A. Schumpeter, *Business Cycles; Volume I* (New York: McGraw-Hill Co., Inc., 1939). Schumpeter writes: "...The assumption that business behaviour is ideally rational and prompt, and also that in principle it is the same with all firms, works tolerably well only within the precincts of tried experience and familiar motive. It breaks down as soon as we leave those precincts and allow the business community under study to be faced by—not simply new situations, which also occur as soon as external factors unexpectedly intrude but by—new possibilities of business action which are as yet untried and about which the most complex command of routine teaches nothing. Those differences in the behaviour of different people, which within those precincts account for secondary phenomena only, become essential in the sense that they now account for the outstanding features of reality and that a picture drawn on the Walras–Marshallian lines ceases to be true—even in the qualified sense in which it is true of stationary and growing processes: it misses those features, and becomes wrong in the endeavour to account by means of its own analysis for phenomena which the assumptions of that analysis exclude" ... "Those differences belong, as a special case, to the class of facts usually dealt with under the heading of Leadership" (pp. 98–9).
7. K. J. Arrow, "Limited Knowledge and Economics Analysis", *The American Economic Review*, vol. 64, no. 1 (Mar. 1974). Arrow writes: "The uncertainties about economics are rooted in our need for a better understanding of the economics of uncertainty—Even as a graduate student, I was somewhat surprised at the emphasis on static allocative efficiency by market socialists, when the non-existence of markets for future goods under capitalism seemed to me a much more obvious target. ... But he cannot know the future. Hence, unless he deludes himself, he must know that both sets of expectations may be wrong. In short, the absence of the market implies that the optimizer faces a world of uncertainty. ... In fact, of course, the basic economic factors are changing, partly endogenously because of capital accumulation in its most general sense, partly exogenously with predictable and unpredictable changes in technology and tastes; equally if not more important, though, is the fact that the dispersion of

information which is so economical implies that different economic agents do not have access to the same observations. Hence, it is reasonable to infer that they will never come into agreement as to probabilities of future prices. . . . A further implication is that the past influences the future. . . . The past is relevant beause it contains information which changes the image of the future; the probabilities which govern future actions are modified by observations on the past. It follows that present decisions with implications for the future are functions of the past values of variables as well as present values. . . . What still needs to be exploited more, however, is that the inference to the future is necessarily uncertain. . . . A truncated theory of temporary equilibrium in which markets for future goods are replaced by some form of expectations, themselves functions of current prices and quantities, has indeed, been developed, though its empirical content is necessarily meagre if the formation of expectations is left unanalysed".

See also, K. J. Arrow, "On Capitalism and Society", *Business and Society Review*, no. 10 (Summer 1974). Arrow writes: "I've stressed earlier the information element—that links in the chain of communication are in part human. They have to be human because human transducers are incredibly efficient in certain ways, though very inefficient in others. They are relatively poor in arithmetic, but they are very good at integrating disparate pieces of information. There is no likelihood that they will be replaced. So long as they exist, the qualities that make human beings differ from each other and that impede or enhance communication among them will be important. . . . It's also true that when there's flexibility in decision-making, there's power, as well as information transfer. The ability to wield power and the efficiency with which it's harnessed for profitable aims make the difference between successful and unsuccessful firms. They may also determine whether the economy as a whole is more or less efficient."

8. J. A. Schumpeter, *History of Economic Analysis* (London: Oxford University Press, 1954). Schumpeter writes: "Theorists—especially of the planning type—often indulge in the deplorable practice of deriving 'practical' results from a few functional relations between a few economic aggregates in utter disregard of the fact that such analytic set-ups are congenitally incapable of taking account of deeper things, the more subtle relations that cannot be weighed and measured but may be more important to a nation's cultural life than things that can" (pp. 788–9).
9. On the distinction between thought (which is inevitably based on the past—knowledge, skills, techniques, tools) and intelligence (or perception or insight), see J. Krishnamurti, *The Awakening of Intelligence* (New York: Harper & Row Publishers, 1973), pp. 509–38. See also A. Koestler, *The Act of Creation* (New York: A Laurel Edition, 1967), chapter vii. Koestler writes: "Language can become a screen which stands between the thinkers and reality. This is the reason why true creativity often starts when language ends" (p. 177).

   On decision-making see also J. M. Keynes, *The General Theory of Employment, Interest and Money* (New York: A Harbinger Book, Harcourt, Brace and World Inc., 1965). Keynes writes: "The characteristic of human nature that a large proportion of our positive activities depend on spontaneous optimism rather than on a mathematical expectation, whether moral or hedonistic or economic. Most, probably, of our decisions to do something positive, the full consequences of which will be driven out over many days to come, can only be taken as a result of animal spirits—of a spontaneous urge to action rather than inaction, and not as the outcome of a weighted average of quantitative benefits multiplied by quantitative probabilities. . . . Thus if the animal spirits are dimmed and the spontaneous optimism falters, leaving us to depend on nothing but a mathematical expectation, enterprise will fade and die;—though fears of loss may have a basis no more reasonable than hopes of profit had before. . . . We are merely reminding ourselves that human decisions affecting the future, whether personal or political or economic, cannot depend on strict mathematical expectation, since the basis for making such calculations does not exist; and that it is our innate urge to activity which make the wheels go round, our rational selves choosing between the alternatives as best we are able, calculating where we can, but often falling back for our motive on whim or sentiment or chance" (pp. 161–3).
10. See P. F. Drucker, *op. cit.*, chapter 52.
11. *Ibid.*, chapter 49.
12. A. Gerschenkron, *Economic Backwardness in Historical Perspective* (Cambridge, Mass.: Harvard University Press, 1968), p. 12.

13. A. Gerschenkron, *Continuity in History and Other Essays* (Cambridge, Mass.: Harvard University Press, 1968), p. 137.
14. E. J. Hall, *Silent Language* (Garden City, New York: Doubleday, 1959).
15. R. Buckout, "Eyewitness Testimony", *Scientific American*, vol. 231, no. 6 (Dec. 1974).
16. P. F. Drucker, *op. cit.*, chapter 38.
17. E. Mayo, *The Social Problems of an Industrial Civilization* (Boston: Harvard Business School, 1945).
18. P. F. Drucker, *op. cit.*, p. 539. "The justification has been that both deal with money. But, of course, accounting does not deal with money; it deals with figures. The consequence of the traditional approach has been the slighting of financial management" (p. 539).
19. See footnotes 7, 8 and 9.

13. On a Development Bank's Selection Criteria for Industrial Projects*

It is difficult to make any choice without clarity relating to the criteria of choice and the various alternatives from which a choice is to be made. This implies that there should be a meaningful and clear presentation of the alternatives in the light of the choice criteria. The choice criteria depend on the objectives one seeks, and the alternatives depend on the actual information relating to the implications of various feasible courses of action. If the objectives are clearly perceived and are such as can be quantified and combined into a single quantitative measure and if the information relating to all the feasible courses of action is perfect and is such as can be expressed in quantitative terms and hence in terms of the choice criteria, the choice problem indeed would be simple, and the selection process would be mechanical: there would be no managerial problem.

However, reality is different. The objectives may not be clear, and some of them may be such as cannot be quantified and measured; further, the relative significance of the various objectives changes with time and circumstances. In addition, the objectives may not be independent of the extent of information with regard to the alternative courses of action, and this information can never be perfect: not only is the future uncertain and unknowable, but also information relating to the present as well as the past is always incomplete.[1] Thus the decision-making process becomes complex, and the appropriateness of a specific decision depends on the *ability* of decision-making organs to respond creatively to the challenge for action[2] as discussed in the previous chapter.

It is not possible to rely merely on mechanical rules or criteria, techniques or tools, formulae or standards, all of which are related to the past—of which there is no complete understanding—while decision-making has to relate to the present and the unknowable future. At the same time, no decision can be right unless it is based on the full awareness of whatever information is available and whatever criteria of choice seem at the time relevant; again, no decision can be right unless there is a clear perception of the whole situation as it is unfolding and is likely to emerge in the future. So for the right decision—right as it appears at the time, for no decision can be perfect—we require both *analysis of data*, and *perception* of the total *process of change* in the data and its direction.

In this chapter, the problem of selection criteria for industrial projects as it relates to development banks is posed and discussed. In section I, the social objectives that need to be incorporated in the choice criteria are indicated, while the techniques of devising and applying choice criteria of different degrees of refinement are described in section II. The choice criteria that seem to be relevant for a large number of industrial projects likely to be supported by a develop-

* Published in *Economic Development and Cultural Change*, vol. 25, no. 4 (July 1977).

ment bank are indicated in section III. The type of economic analysis that is essential even before attempting the task of economic evaluation is discussed in section IV, and the primary purpose of economic evaluation—providing a development perspective and orientation to development banks—is indicated in section V.

I. Development Objectives and Choice Criteria

The choice criteria of a development bank must indeed have a direct relationship with the development objectives of a country. A development bank cannot act like a normal commercial bank; it has no *raison d'être* for its existence unless it seeks to promote industrial development that is consistent with the country's development objectives. Hence it cannot judge the soundness of a project merely on the basis of its ability to service its debt to the development bank. Doubtless a project should be financially sound in this sense; for without that the development bank itself would not remain a viable institution. But at the same time, a project should be consistent with the development objectives; for without this type of soundness a development bank would not be able to contribute to the development process of the country. If such projects as are sound from *both* these points of view are not available, it is the function of a development bank to take the initiative, in cooperation with other related agencies, in devising changes in institutional and other policies that would (*a*) make economically sound (a term for the soundness of a project from the point of view of development objectives) projects financially viable and (*b*) facilitate the identification and formulation of such projects that are financially as well as economically sound.

But then the question arises. How do we define economic soundness of a project? Obviously it must be related to development objectives; but the question is: What are the development objectives, and which of these objectives are relevant for a development bank?

How do we find out in the first instance the development objectives of a country? Can we take such objectives as are indicated in the development plans or such other government documents as the development objectives of a country? This question is important because some objectives perform, to use Bagehot's expression, a "ceremonial" function while some others perform the "efficient" function. Quite often the declared objectives have merely a ceremonial function, while the efficient objectives are seldom announced and have to be *inferred* from the development strategy and policies that are actually—explicitly or implicitly—formulated by the government. In such a case, the task of a development bank becomes difficult. If the *ceremonial* and *efficient* objectives are different, a development bank can and should point out the difference and indicate, on the basis of concrete evidence at its disposal—the implications of actual industrial projects that are completed or under implementation—the strategy and policies that need to be pursued for the attainment of declared objectives. But if in spite of this evidence the government consciously maintains this difference, a development bank has no alternative but to conduct its operations in terms of the efficient objectives while at the same time continuing to perform the educative function of pinpointing the implications of the actual departure from the ceremonial objectives.

Thus in actual operation what is relevant for a development bank is the development strategy pursued by the government in terms of concrete policies and action programmes.

To discuss in more concrete terms the implications of this divergence between ceremonial and efficient objectives, one might take the case of the objective of social justice. The only effective way of promoting this objective is through productive employment of the available labour force. Since a greater part of this labour force is already "employed" in the traditional sectors—agriculture, rural industries, rural transport, and other related occupations—it is essential to improve progressively the technological base of these traditional sectors in such a manner as to raise labour productivity as well as real incomes of the potentially employable labour force. The development of the "modern" sectors, in this case, has to be consistent with this strategy and actually subserve its objectives. There must be, as indicated in chapters 6 and 7, an organic relationship between the growth of the traditional and modern sectors for ensuring full employment at rising levels of productivity and real incomes.[3]

In a case like this, it is the development strategy and the related policies themselves that seek to promote social justice, and the choice criteria of industrial projects must be such as would ensure the most efficient use and the most efficient way of increasing the supply of scarce resources. The scarcest resources are capital (saving), foreign exchange, and labour with skills of various hues.

But if no attempt is made to improve the technological base of the traditional sectors through an active and relevant technology policy—and this cannot be done by mere imitation of foreign technology—the objective of social justice loses its significance, and any attempt to incorporate it in the choice criteria for industrial projects through assigning different weights to the incomes of different socio-economic groups would merely result in an inefficient process of allocation as well as creation of scarce resources. Social justice, of course, would not be attained, and other development objectives would also remain unfulfilled.

Similarly, let us take the objective of increasing employment and thus improving income distribution through the device of incorporating shadow wages in the choice criteria of industrial projects. This implies a certain technology policy as an integral part of a development strategy. For actually increasing employment through this device, there should be various technological choices available. If technology is imported, there should be an attempt at adapting and modifying this technology to suit the resource structure of the country. This requires the ability to ask meaningful questions of foreign consultants about various technological choices, and this is not possible without a degree of indigenous technological competence in the fields of design and engineering as well as technological research. Without such competence, the actual choices at the project-design stage would be made merely on the basis of technology in use in developed countries, and these choices by and large would be unaffected by the magnitude of shadow wage rates selected for deriving the choice criteria.

On this subject, the observations of Little and Mirrlees are very relevant:

> In other words, a large number of economic choices will have been made

already, either at the level of the initiating department, commission, or other decentralized public authority, or by the designing engineers. . . . Now industrial engineers—good ones, anyway—are economists, but they are not usually the kind of economists who are trained to look at matters from the point of view of the economy as a whole. They will, or should, have profitability very much in mind. But they will, of course, assess profitability in the light of actual prices.

The value of . . . choosing from a list of projects according to a criterion using accounting prices, supposed to reflect real scarcities and benefits better than actual prices, is clearly greatly reduced if each such project has in effect been chosen from a long list of variants by a criterion (profitability) which uses actual prices. For instance, if it is desirable to put stress on employment by using a low accounting price for labour, then clearly this stress should take effect at the level of project design and not merely at the level of final project selection. Indeed, it may be at the former level that a low accounting price for labour would have its main effect. . . .

Of course, the sheer unfamiliarity will make for difficulty at first. . . . Where outside, especially foreign, firms of consultant engineers are involved, the difficulties may be greater. First, their psychological objection to accounting prices may be stronger as a result of private enterprise *laissez-faire* training which does not sufficiently admit the possible divergence of social and private interest. Secondly, they generally have something to sell, which has usually been evolved in the light of actual prices. Designs are not all made afresh, from the bottom up, for the project in hand. . . .

Only very few Western firms appear to have made any effort to adapt their designs to the different scarcities prevailing in developing countries. . . . Sometimes, indeed, the plant which Western engineers design for a developing country is more "modern", i.e., capital intensive, potentially labour saving, than anything that exists in their own country. There are two obstacles to overcoming the problem. The first, and possibly, most important, is often the lack of an informed and critical client, determined to get a plant which will be very profitable. . . .

For the reasons given, it may not be easy to get foreign engineers to adapt. . . . However, it must be admitted, when everything in favour of accounting prices has been said, that communication between . . . departments, etc.: between departmental administrators and engineers and scientists: and between the local client and the foreign firms: is easier in terms of (predicted) actual prices.

For this reason, it is always better to try to make actual prices realistic, whether it be by refraining from malign governmental interference with the price mechanism, or whether it be by benign governmental "doctoring" of the price mechanism. Although this may not always be possible, it is certainly best to keep the use of accounting prices as limited as possible."[4]

What then should one say about such refinement of choice criteria which may make little or no sense to the decision maker on the one hand and to the project designer on the other?

Again, it is not merely a question of the project designer using accounting prices for making technological choices. Even if he does use them, the range of choice is usually limited to actual alternatives already in use in the developed countries, especially with regard to the core processes and products: the choice is wider for processes related to materials handling and other auxiliary operations.[5] Of course this does not mean that there do not exist additional alternative core processes and products even within the range of modern technology.[6] These alternatives, however, can be known only as a result of *active search* through an appropriate method or language which is "intentionally more general than the ones used in engineers' process flow sheets; it is rather similar to the language used in the laboratory stage."[7]

> Identification of alternatives open for choice and possibilities for adaptations would not go very far unless given packages of technology could be broken down into various components or modules; and in so doing, one ought to go beyond those best-practised technologies on the shelf, giving open-minded reconsideration to discarded laboratory results, as well as to technologies now considered obsolete by today's major industrial concerns. Quite a few exercises exist showing that there are in fact hundreds of alternative process design possibilities for a given product line, even in industries with relatively continuous processes. An information-intensive and brain-intensive "unpacking" effort could thus rediscover nearly continuous stretches of the neo-classical economist's isoquant. It appears that the concept of "modules," which facilitates such unpacking and innovative adaptation of industrial technology, deserves further exploration for the benefit of R and D planning and related information service policy on LDCs.[8]

Thus the use of accounting prices would not—cannot—produce the results desired, without an active technology policy to (*a*) upgrade traditional technology and (*b*) adapt modern technology to the resource structure and stage of development of the developing countries. Thus the first priority in any development strategy should be on the development of technological competence for the purpose and not on mere refinement of appraisal criteria for industrial projects; the latter is irrelevant and meaningless without the former.[9]

The use of accounting prices, again, cannot remove "distortions" caused by institutional rigidities. In a backward area, one may take a low shadow wage rate for unskilled labour from the point of view of income-distribution objective; but if the required labour is not actually available because of lack of appropriate changes in agricultural organization or lack of mobility of labour due to institutional factors, the low shadow wage has no meaning, as it would not result in increased employment. Similarly, the use of accounting prices would not produce the desired results, if the financial structure were biased toward urban and metropolitan areas and "modern" industries.[10] Again, without an appropriate development of the infrastructure—transport and marketing, education and health, technical and managerial assistance, credit institutions, and the like—the choices indicated and desired by the use of accounting prices would prove infructuous.[11]

II. Choice Criteria Based on International Prices: Analytic Basis and Techniques

A development bank thus needs to evolve choice criteria consistent with overall development strategy and policies. Since social justice or income-distribution objective can only be attained through an appropriate development strategy, as indicated earlier, the major emphasis of a development bank has to be on the efficient use of scarce resources. For a large number of countries, the scarcest resources relate to saving, foreign exchange, skilled manpower, and entrepreneurial-managerial talents. From an economy's point of view, it is thus essential to concentrate on initiating a process of efficient allocation and *creation* of these scarce resources.[12]

It is quite likely that in the case of countries where the major scarce resources relate to the fields of skilled manpower and entrepreneurial-managerial talents, there may arise a conflict between the requirements of efficient resource *allocation* and efficient resource *creation*. Import controls and high tariff rates are in essence a reflection of this conflict, and since resource creation in these fields is of paramount significance for generating self-sustaining process of development and since it depends critically on on-the-job learning and experience, these external economies of projects need to be taken into account in devising choice criteria. These benefits are real and substantial, even though they may not be quantifiable. However, since a greater part of these benefits are broadly common to all industrial projects, it may not be necessary to take them into account while judging the worthwhileness of a specific project. But there may be particular cases of projects in backward areas or relating to new fields—in terms of technology, product or management—where these benefits may be specific to individual projects, and in such cases they need to be taken into account—of course on the basis of well-informed and sound judgement and not mere wishful thinking and prejudice.

As far as quantifiable costs and benefits are concerned, such costs and benefits as are external to the project but which arise as a result of the project need to be explicitly taken into account. One way, and generally the most effective, of taking them into account is to treat vitally interrelated projects as a single project complex.

A development bank is generally faced with a single project or project complex. It does not have a large number of projects at a time from which it can choose on the basis of its selection criteria. Hence it has to devise criteria on the basis of which it can either accept or reject a single project. This implies that it should have well-formulated cut-off points related to its choice criteria, on the basis of which an accept or reject decision can be based.

In the industrial field, the real choice is beween domestic production and imports. If a product can be imported at a cost lower than that of domestic production, then prima facie it may not be worth producing it at home. The question then is how to compare domestic costs with import costs, particularly when domestic prices are out of line with international prices due to certain economic policies. In this case, the simplest procedure is to express all domestic costs in terms of international prices; since the comparison is in terms of an identical measure or yardstick, it becomes a valid comparison.[13]

Domestic cost can be split into (*a*) cost of tradable goods (and services) and (*b*) cost of non-tradable goods (and services). For tradable goods, it should be possible in principle to obtain the import c.i.f. prices. For inputs that are actually imported, there is no problem; for inputs domestically purchased but tradable, it may not be difficult to obtain import c.i.f. prices, particularly if a country does import these inputs even to some extent. For non-tradable inputs like construction, power, transport, trade, etc., their cost structure can in principle be broken down in terms of cost of tradable inputs and cost of non-tradable inputs like unskilled labour. In principle the only non-tradable inputs would be unskilled labour and raw land; the wage rate for unskilled labour would consist largely of what workers consume, comprising largely tradable goods, and hence can be expressed in terms of international prices. Raw land will have alternative uses, and this opportunity cost of raw land can be translated in terms of international prices through the use of a shadow exchange rate.

For non-tradable inputs, the valuation procedure can be simplified by using appropriate conversion factors; that is, domestic prices can be multiplied by a conversion factor (multiplier) that expresses a general relationship between international prices and domestic costs—a relationship based on a sample study of each sector like construction, power, transport, etc. The use of such conversion factors, if available, would simplify the valuation problem. In cases for which even this is not possible, a shadow exchange rate can be used for the purpose—this in fact reflects a general economy-wide relationship between international and domestic prices.

It may be emphasized that the unit of account can be either local currency or any foreign currency. It would be easier and simpler to use local currency as a unit of account; in this case all international prices can be expressed in local currency through the use of the official exchange rate. This exchange rate has no other significance, and any exchange rate (even other than the official rate) is good enough for the purpose, as long as it is consistently used.

Once the cost and benefit streams are derived in terms of international prices over a period of time—for years inclusive of the gestation lag and project life, a period normally of 20–5 years—the yield of a project can be expressed in terms of its internal rate of return.

This internal rate of return, usually called the economic rate of return, can then be compared with the cut-off rate of return, which for a large number of countries would be within the range of 15–20 per cent per year. The cut-off rate can be determined on the basis of actual experience with regard to industrial projects—a rough average of the rates of return actually realized in the case of existing viable industrial projects. It can also be derived on the basis of the growth target for industrial output and certain assumptions with regard to saving (plow back) in relation to gross benefits. Suppose the target rate for the growth of industrial output is 10 per cent per year and industrial investment constitutes 50 per cent of the gross return (i.e., 50 per cent of the gross return is used for consumption); the rate of return on industrial projects should be 20 per cent.

Let industrial output be expressed as Y, gross returns as P, total capital as K, the proportion of gross returns plowed back into investment as s, investment as I, and rate of growth of industrial output as g. Then $\Delta Y = I.\ Y/K$, where Y/K is the inverse of the capital coefficient. This can be expressed as

$$\Delta Y = sP \cdot \frac{Y}{K},$$

$$\therefore \Delta \frac{Y}{Y} = s \cdot \frac{P}{Y} \cdot \frac{Y}{K},$$

$$\therefore g = sr,$$

where r is the rate of return, P/K. If $s = 0.5$ and $g = 0.10$, $r = 0.10/0.50$ or 20 per cent.

For calculation of this economic rate of return, all taxes and subsidies are ignored, being merely transfer payments; and the financing pattern is also of no significance from the economy's point of view. However, if foreign capital is involved (for financing imports) and this capital is specific to the project (if it is not specific, it should be treated as a cost item, as it is available in principle for other projects also), imports financed by foreign capital should be treated as benefits and the debt-servicing obligations as costs.[14]

III. Feasible and Relevant Choice Criteria

This consistent use of international prices for deriving choice criteria may not be desirable for several reasons:

(*a*) Resource allocation and creation may not turn out to be efficient if the various agencies related to the project—project designer, project promoter, government agencies in charge of various licences like industrial and import licences and taxes and subsidies, other financial institutions—do not use the same set of prices. As argued by Little and Mirrlees, the communication so essential among these various agencies is easier if actual market prices (predicted) are used. That really implies that, if government agencies did use accounting prices, they would have, as a matter of development strategy and actual policies, "doctored" the actual prices in such a manner as to be consistent with accounting prices; if they have not done so, a development bank cannot improve the efficiency of the process of resource allocation and creation by using accounting prices.[15] Of course this does not mean that some sample studies of completed and operating projects by a development bank on these lines would not be useful; in fact it is one of the functions of a development bank to make studies to bring out the implications of actual government strategy and policies and thus to persuade and induce the government to modify its strategy and policies to suit its broad development objectives.

(*b*) Use of international prices involves not only the availability of the required data but also considerable analytic ability and judgement in processing, interpreting, and using them. This type of skilled manpower is scarce, and the appraisal department of a bank may not have it to the extent required. Even if such manpower were available, it is a question whether it cannot be used to better purpose. Further, the margin of error in project evaluation may turn out to be considerable if sophisticated techniques are used unintelligently and on the basis of fragmentary data.

(*c*) If a simpler technique can serve the same purpose of enabling top management to take good decisions, there is no case for perfection of technique as an end in itself. Choice criteria are tools for decision-making and not products in themselves to be perfected.

What are then the conditions which any choice criteria should satisfy? First, they should communicate meaningful information to the decision maker so as to enable him to take a decision. Top management would like the implications of a project with regard to (*a*) its financial soundness; (*b*) its economic rate of return at market prices, which determines the actual outcome with regard to generation of government income, saving, and consumption; and (*c*) the efficiency with which the product is to be produced. Top management would also like such concrete implications of the project on the basis of which it can suggest specific changes in government policies; for it is easier to persuade the government to make specific changes on the basis of concrete evidence than to persuade it to make radical changes on general considerations, which policy-makers may not understand.

For the purpose of indicating the financial soundness of a project, the after-tax rate of return—the financial rate of return—at market prices would be adequate. But this is not the rate of return to the economy as a whole; hence there is a need for calculating the economic rate of return on the basis of market prices. For judging the efficiency of the project, it would suffice to calculate its "exchange rate", that is, the domestic-resource cost per unit of foreign exchange earned or saved for the year in which capacity output is likely to be realized.

In principle, both the time streams of domestic costs and net foreign-exchange earnings can be discounted to the present, and thus the ratio can be calculated on the basis of present values: however, for industrial projects with more or less equal gestation lags and project life, this computation does not seem to be necessary.

Domestic costs for the purpose would comprise interest cost (at the cutoff rate of return) on the capital expenditure on inputs domestically bought, depreciation on this capital cost, cost of domestically purchased current inputs, and cost of labour—skilled and unskilled. These domestic costs should be divided by net foreign-exchange earning/saving (in terms of foreign currency)—that is, the value of the product or products domestically sold at import c.i.f. prices plus exports valued at export f.o.b. prices minus all the foreign-exchange cost items comprising (*a*) interest cost on capital expenditure on imported inputs, (*b*) depreciation on this capital cost, and (*c*) value of imported current inputs at import c.i.f. prices (including import of skilled labour, etc.). All these items should be valued net of taxes and subsidies.

This ratio would indicate the exchange rate of the project or the domestic cost incurred for earning/saving one unit of foreign exchange. The cutoff rate should be the shadow exchange rate, which implies that all projects with an exchange rate equal to or lower than the cutoff rate should be selected.[16]

All these three pieces of information—financial rate of return, economic rate of return, and the exchange rate—are indeed very meaningful for top management. The first relates to *financial soundness*, the second to economic soundness on the basis of *generation of saving*, and the third again to economic soundness based on *competitive efficiency*.

If a project satisfies the economic criteria but is not financially sound, top management has a good specific case to induce the government to modify its tax-subsidy policies so as to make the project financially sound. If it is financially sound but does not meet both the economic criteria, it needs to be examined further or even rejected. If it is financially sound and also meets the criterion related to the economic rate of return but does not satisfy the efficiency test, there is a good case for finding the reasons why it does not meet this test. If on re-examination it is found that the test is not met because the cost of a domestic input is higher than its import c.i.f. price, top management has a good specific suggestion to make to the government with regard to the relaxation of import control on this input. If the government as a result permits even a partial import of this input (not necessarily for this project), this input should be valued at import c.i.f. prices and should be treated as foreign-exchange cost.

Thus *these three criteria* help top management not only in its own decision making but also in persuading the government to make specific changes in policies in terms of a language that the policy-makers are likely to understand. Financial rate of return, economic rate of return, and exchange rate—these are expressions whose content is easily intelligible to top management as well as the government policy-makers.

The shadow exchange rate should be based on actual data relating to viable industrial projects in operation and such changes in government policies as are relevant for this purpose. Of course the shadow exchange rate needs to be changed in the light of the emerging situation and context. Such calculations of the shadow exchange rate would help government policy-makers also in modifying their exchange-rate policies and/or trade policies relating to import control, tariffs, and subsidies.

Available evidence based on the project studies of some development banks indicates that these three criteria provide tests as good in most cases as the economic rate of return based on international prices.[17] Thus a refined analysis may be necessary only in the case of very large and complicated projects—which in any case should be subjected to much deeper analysis than what is implied in these three tests, at the project stage as well as the final project-appraisal stage.

So far the wage rate is taken at its actual market value. Is there a case for a shadow wage rate? Again, the available evidence indicates that this may not make much difference in the case of a large number of projects.[18] However, this evidence relates only to "modern" projects, and development banks by and large have not financed projects related to premodern "traditional" industries like handloom or processing industries related to agriculture and food. Again, they are not financing small-to-medium industries located in rural areas and serving local markets—supplying traditional inputs to agriculture or traditional consumption goods.

If the technological base of the traditional industries is to be upgraded, they require assistance—technical and financial—from development banks.[19] For such enterprises, it is logical to treat shadow wage as zero, as the labour force is *actually* available—is already employed or likely to be employed. For such enterprises, both economic criteria should be derived on the basis of a zero wage rate. This is likely to be consistent with the development strategy and objectives relating to social justice.

For modern industries located in rural areas and serving local markets, the shadow wage rate should be taken at that rate at which labour is likely to be *willing* to be employed (as reflected in the unogenesis labour market) irrespective of whether the actual wage rate is higher than this due to trade-union activity or government legislation. This again accords with development objectives relating to employment and income distribution.

Industrial projects which are to serve nationwide and or international markets are likely to be located in urban metropolitan or port areas. In their case, the social cost of employing labour is in many cases higher than actual wage costs; for the public authorities would have to provide a number of public utilities—water supply, drainage, transport, housing, etc.—to enable the projects to function. Further, the crowding and congestion in metropolitan or port areas have a non-quantifiable but real social cost in terms of potential tensions and conflicts. For these reasons, it does not seem right to assume a shadow wage lower than the actual wage. In any case, a shadow wage for these areas has no meaning for efficient resource allocation and creation, unless the government is likely to provide a subsidy equal to the difference between actual and shadow wage costs. To ask the government to provide this subsidy when in actual fact the government would have to incur considerable expenditure for providing public utilities seems a little odd.

This system of shadow wage rates introduces the necessary bias in favour of traditional and rural industries and at the same time tends to make the modern urban industries internationally competitive without burdening the government with a system of subsidies. In a dualistic economy, the price structure needs to be dualistic also, and this is in accord with a development strategy that emphasizes both growth and social justice.

IV. Economic Analysis Prior to Economic Appraisal

The economic appraisal section (EAS) of the appraisal department of a development bank must necessarily base its appraisal on the detailed project analysis of the soundness of a project—from the points of view of organization, management, and technical and financial soundness—made by the financial appraisal section (FAS). However, the EAS should not accept the FAS analysis without some questioning; the EAS should evolve some general cross-checks with regard to FAS analyses to ensure its soundness. Quite often those who are preoccupied with details miss the overall picture.

The key areas in which general cross-checks are necessary relate to demand estimation, gestation lags, capital and input structure, and the structure of returns. The actual demand estimates should be checked on the basis of the past relationship between the demand for the product and national income or agricultural output or industrial output (whichever is relevant); this overall measure would at least indicate the prima facie plausibility or otherwise of the actual demand estimates. If the actual demand estimates do not tally with such a relationship, one must know why this is not so; if a valid explanation is not available, the demand estimates may need to be worked out afresh.

For a preliminary economic analysis of a project, the project data obtained from the FAS should be processed and presented in a form amenable to economic analysis. Illustratively, they could be presented in the form indicated in Statements A, B, and C in the Appendix: this information should then be converted in terms of ratios indicated in Statement D.

The purpose of Statement D is to compare significant economic relationships related to the project with such relationships in similar projects that have already been implemented or are under implementation (or in similar projects in other countries, preferably in countries at a similar stage of development). Such a comparison would bring out whether the FAS appraisal appears to be prima facie sound: significant divergence would need to be explained by the FAS. If there is no valid explanation for such divergence, the appraisal may have to be done *de novo* by the FAS.

The gestation lag and capital costs of projects are generally underestimated in developing countries.[20] The type of economic analysis indicated here would pinpoint such underestimation and thus induce the FAS to be more "realistic" in its appraisal work.

Such economic analysis implies that the research department of a development bank should make an *ex post* appraisal of the projects already implemented and or collected data on similar projects actually in operation in other countries (preferably developing countries at similar stages of development). Such studies are extremely useful in devising valid criteria and procedures for appraisal work as well as in improving such criteria and procedures on a continuing basis.

This comparative analysis would provide significant information relevant for economic evaluation of the project and hence for decision making. For a large number of small-to-medium-size projects, such economic analysis should suffice for the purpose of economic evaluation and final decision making. The return structure (see Appendix, item D.3) would enable the decision-maker to judge the financial as well as economic soundness of a project.

V. Development Perspective

Economic evaluation of a project is significant in itself: but it is much more significant as a reflection of the development orientation of a development bank. The perspective of a development bank differs from that of an ordinary financial institution: it is a *development* institution, seeking to promote such industrial development as is consistent with overall national development strategy. Economic evaluations of projects as well as *ex post* economic evaluation of completed projects enable it to enter into a dialogue with government and other related agencies about the adequacy and relevance of various policies related to industrial development. This dialogue benefits both parties: government and other agencies can formulate and modify their policies on the basis of specific and concrete evidence, while a development bank can perform its special function in a much more meaningful way that would be possible without such a dialogue.

And what can be the rationale of a *development* bank without this development perspective?

Appendix

Statement A: Structure of Costs (Current Inputs) and Returns

	Year 1	Year 2 . . . Year 20
	D I E[21]	*D I E*
1. Output value		
a. Quantity		
b. Price per unit		
c. Capacity output		
d. *a* as a proportion of *c*		
2. Change in inventory of finished goods		
3. Sales (1–2)		
4. Current inputs (net of indirect taxes)		
a. Material inputs		
b. Power		
c. Steam, fuel and water		
d. Transport		
e. Others		
5. Gross value added (1–4)		
6. Wages and salaries		
a. Number of wage earners		
b. Average wage rate		
c. Total wages		
d. Number of salary earners		
e. Average salary rate		
f. Total salary		
7. Gross profits or surplus (5–6)		
8. Depreciation		
9. Net value added (5–8)		
10. Taxes		
a. Direct		
b. Indirect		
11. Net profits (7–8–10)		
12. Interest charges		
a. On short-term borrowing		
b. On long-term borrowing		
13. Dividend on equity		
14. Retained profits (11–12–13)		
15. Profits to equity holders (13+14)		

Statement B: Capital Structure

	Year 1	Year 2 . . . Year 20
	D I E	*D I E*
1. Capital expenditures (net of indirect taxes)		
a. Land		
b. Building and construction		
c. Machinery and equipment		
d. Others		
2. Inventory (net of indirect taxes)		
a. Stock of materials		
b. Work in progress		
c. Others		
3. Total capital expenditures (net of indirect taxes) (1+2)		
4. Indirect taxes		
5. Total capital expenditure (inclusive of indirect taxes) (3+4)		

Statement C: Cash Flow

	Year 1	Year 2 . . . Year 20
	D I E	*D I E*
1. Social cash flow (A.7–B.3)		
2. Private cash flow (A.7–B.5–A.10)		
3. Borrowing		
a. Short-term		
b. Long-term		
4. Repayment		
a. Short-term loans		
b. Long-term loans		

Statement D: Structure of Capital, Inputs, Returns, and Financing, at Capacity Output

	I Project under Appraisal	II Similar Project: Implemented or under Implementation
1. Capital structure		
a. Capital–capacity output ratio (B.3/A.1.c)		
b. Capital–gross value added ratio (B.3/A.5)		
c. Inventory–capacity output ratio (B.2/A.1.c)		
2. Input structure		
a. Wages–output ratio (A.6.c/A.1.c)		

b. Salaries–output ratio (A.6.f/A.1.c)
c. Materials–output ratio (A.4.a/A.1.c)
d. Power–output ratio (A.4.b/A.1.c)
e. Other services–output ratio (A.4.c+d+e/A.1.c)

3. Return structure
   a. Gross profits to capital (A.7/B.3)
   b. Net profits to capital (A.11/B.5)
   c. Profits to equity holders to equity (A.15/[B.5–C.3])
   d. Interest–borrowing ratio (A.12/C.3)
   e. Ratio of exports+domestic sales–imported current imports to imported plant and equipment (all in terms of foreign exchange at import c.i.f. or export f.o.b. prices, whichever are relevant)
4. Financial structure
   a. Debt service coverage (C.2/[C.4+A.12])
   b. Debt–equity ratio (C.3/[B.5–C.3])
5. Gestation lag
   a. Lag between start of construction and commercial production
   b. Lag between start of construction and capacity output

NOTES

1. K. J. Arrow, "Limited Knowledge and Economic Analysis", *American Economic Review,* vol. 64, no. 1 (1974), pp. 1–10.
2. V. V. Bhatt, "Development Banks: Top Management Tasks and Structure", mimeographed (Washington, D.C.: Economic Development Institute, IBRD, Dec. 1974).
3. V. V. Bhatt, "On Technology Policy and Its Institutional Frame", mimeographed (Washington, D.C.: Economic Development Institute, IBRD, Dec. 1974).
4. I. M. D. Little and J. A. Mirrlees, *Manual of Industrial Project Analysis in Developing Countries* (Paris: Development Centre of the Organization for Economic Cooperation and Development, 1968), vol. 2, pp. 64–6.
5. See V. V. Bhatt, "Capital Intensity of Industries", *Bulletin of the Oxford University,* vol. 18, no. 2 (1956), pp. 179–94: "The substitution of capital by labour, though not very common in the basic technical processes, is fairly common in certain auxiliary operations. ... The most important of these operations seems to be materials-handlings. . . . The underdeveloped economies, it seems, have not been able to develop new technology suited to their own economic conditions. ... The industries of the underdeveloped economies import not only the technology but also the capital goods necessary for that purpose from the developed economies. From the input combinations of the handicraft technology to the input combinations of the modern technology, ... constitutes a big jump and because of the lack of development of any intermediate technology, the industries of the underdeveloped economies face a sharply discontinuous production function, which is continuous only within the ranges permitted by the handicraft technology on the one hand, and the technology of the developed economies on the other, ... taking all the factors into consideration, the capital coefficients

would be on average about the same in both developed and underdeveloped economies" (pp. 184, 191–2). See also V. V. Bhatt, *Employment and Capital Formation in Underdeveloped Economies* (Bombay: Orient Longmans, 1960); D. Morawetz, "Employment Implications of Industrialization in Developing Countries: A Survey", *Economic Journal*, vol. 84, no. 335 (1974), pp. 491–542; and S. N. Acharya, "Fiscal-Financial Intervention, Factor Prices, and Factor Proportions: A Review of Issues", mimeographed (Washington, D.C.: Development Economics Department, IBRD, 1974).

6. V. V. Bhatt, *Employment and Capital Formation.*
7. *Choice and Adaptation of Technology in Developing Countries* (Paris: Development Centre of the Organization for Economic Cooperation and Development, 1974), p. 81.
8. *Ibid.*, p. 17.
9. See J. Kornai, *Rush versus Harmonic Growth* (London: North Holland Publishing Co., 1962). Kornai writes: "Theory gets entangled . . . in the tactical problems of consumption, while the strategy—the Study of fundamental complimentarity of phenomena gets lost" (p. 35). "Far be it from me to deny the possibility of substitution among inputs or that prior signals really exert an effort on those controlling production, save, that the actual role of these phenomena is much more modest and limited than that suggested by traditional production theory. . . . Using the terminology introduced in connection with consumption: the new classical production theory got one-sidedly absorbed with the 'tactical' problems of input combinations. For long-term planning, a theoretical foundation is needed that can be used in formulating the 'strategy' of technical development. . . . The development of production technologies, as well as the improvement in the quality of production or, using another term, both process and production innovation is promoted by research in natural and technical sciences. It is particularly development that is of general importance for every country. Research results may be perhaps taken over from abroad, but 'development' is a non-competitive activity that must be organized by every country itself" (pp. 46–8).
10. V. V. Bhatt, *Structure of Financial Institutions* (Bombay: Vora & Co., 1972).
11. V. V. Bhatt, "Sterility of Equilibrium Economics: An Aspect of Sociology of Science" (Economic Development Institute Seminar Paper No. 9, Washington, D.C., IBRD, 1974).
12. N. Kaldor, "The Irrelevance of Equilibrium Economics". *Economic Journal*, vol. 82, no. 328 (1972), pp. 1237–55. Kaldor writes: "The difficulty with a new start is to pinpoint the critical areas when economic theory went astray. In my own view, it happened when the theory of value took on the centre of the stage—which meant focussing attention on the allocative functions of markets to the exclusion of these *creative* functions—as an instrument for transmitting impulses to economic change" (p. 1240).
13. See M. D. Little and J. A. Mirrlees, chapters 11, 13.
14. Foreign and Commonwealth Office, Overseas Development Administration, *A Guide to Project Appraisal in Developing Countries* (London: Her Majesty's Stationery Office, 1972).
15. A. K. Sen, "Control Areas and Accounting Prices: An Approach to Economic Evaluation", *Economic Journal*, vol. 82, no. 3255, supplement (1972), pp. 486–501. *Guidelines for Project Evaluation*, part 4 (New York: United Nations, 1972).
16. V. V. Bhatt, *Structure of Financial Institutions*, chapters 11, 13. See also M. Bruno, "The Optimal Selection of Export-promoting and Import-substituting Projects", in United Nations, *Planning the External Sector: Techniques, Problems and Policies* (New York: United Nations, 1967); and "Domestic Resource Costs and Effective Protection: Clarification and Synthesis", *Journal of Political Economy*, vol. 80, no. 1 (1972), pp. 16–33; and I. M. D. Little and J. A. Mirrlees, *Project Appraisal and Planning* (London: Heinemann, 1974), chapter 18.
17. "ICICI's Development Impact", vol. 1, part 3, mimeographed (Bombay: Industrial Credit and Investment Corporation, Mar. 1973); also Industrial Development Bank of India, *Annual Report*, 1972–3 (Bombay: IDBI, 1973).
18. "ICICI's Development Impact".
19. V. V. Bhatt, *Development Banks*. See also *Choice and Adaptation of Technology*, p. 126.
20. Industrial Development Bank of India, *Annual Report*, 1971–2 (Bombay: IDBI, 1972).
21. D = domestic market (sales or purchases); I = imports; E = exports.

14. Development Banks in the Financial System*

THE CAPITAL market is—must be—imperfect in the sense in which economists use this term; for it involves a relationship *in time* between the lender and the borrower in the context of uncertainty. However, it does get progressively integrated, widened and deepened with economic and financial evolution. A crucial variable in this context seems to be transaction costs (both administrative costs and default risk). Financial innovations, whether autonomous or policy-induced, reduce these costs and thus lower the costs of lending and borrowing (quite often inadequately represented by the interest rates) and narrow the interest rate differentials among various existing credit instruments. (Of course, a new credit instrument devised for financing an economic activity for which no credit is provided through the *existing* instruments may bear a higher interest rate; but then it has to be compared with "infinite" or "prohibitive" interest on an existing instrument.) This has saving, investment, output and distribution effects,[1] as argued in chapter 11.

The establishment of a development bank in a number of LDCs represents a policy-induced financial innovation. The question to be discussed is whether this innovation has tended to integrate the capital market.

The characteristic features of saving and flow-of-funds in the LDCs are presented in section I. The logic of the innovation of development banking is discussed in section II. The impact of this innovation on capital market integration is analysed in section III. The role of a development bank as a catalyst is indicated in section IV. The critical role of the Central Bank in initiating a process of capital market integration is discussed in the final section.

I. Characteristic Features of Saving and Flow of Funds[2]

Saving and flow-of-funds analysis brings out, as discussed in chapters 9 and 10, the major characteristics of capital market transactions. For this purpose, the economy is divided into four real sectors: Government, Corporate, Household and the Foreign Sector. If detailed data are available, the government sector could be divided into government sector proper and government enterprises, while the household sector could be subdivided into non-corporate farm enterprises, non-corporate non-farm enterprises and the household sector proper. The sub-sectors of the financial sector are the banking system, social security institutions, specialized financial institutions and the securities market; the *financial system* for the present purpose comprises the first three sub-sectors.

* Paper presented at the *Seminar on Development Bank Management*, organized by the World Bank's Economic Development Institute in Washington (February 1979) for the Chief Executives of Development Banks.

Surplus and Deficit Sectors

The government sector and the corporate sector are generally deficit sectors in the sense that their resource requirement for investment exceeds their own saving; their deficits are financed by the household sector and the foreign sector.

Among the domestic sectors, the household sector is the only surplus sector; its saving exceeds its investment and constitutes more than 40 per cent of overall domestic saving. Its surplus finances the deficits of the other two sectors. Its saving is invested partly in physical assets like equipment in non-corporate farm and non-farm enterprises, residential buildings and inventories of goods and partly in the form of financial assets. Of course, there is lending and borrowing by individual units of the sector through what are known as informal credit markets; its borrowing from the financial system is negligible and probably finances about 15–20 per cent of its investment.

Its surplus saving—typically about 50 per cent of its total saving—constitutes financial saving or saving in the form of financial assets. About 80 per cent of this financial saving is usually in the form of currency and deposits and claims on social security institutions like life insurance and provident funds and the remaining 20 per cent is in the form of securities issued by the government and the corporate sectors. Thus the securities market mobilizes only a small part of the household sector's financial saving, the major part being mobilized by the banking system and the social security institutions.

Pattern of Household Sector Financial Saving

It is through the acquisition of financial assets that the household sector finances the deficits of the other two sectors. It directly finances their deficits when it purchases claims (bonds, shares, etc.) of the government and corporate sectors; this is called *direct* financial saving, which is a small part of its total financial saving. It finances these deficits indirectly—the *indirect* financial saving—when it purchases claims on the banking system and the social security institutions, which then finance the resource requirements of the deficit sectors.

It appears from the structure of flow of funds that the household sector prefers to hold its saving in the form of financial assets which (*a*) are relatively liquid in the sense that they can be converted into money either directly or through borrowing against them, (*b*) have low transaction costs, (*c*) are simple, convenient and easily intelligible, and (*d*) earn a *net* real return (not necessarily represented by the interest rate) comparable to that on private lending, which involves very high transaction costs and represents a relatively illiquid form of saving.

To bring about a progressive integration of the capital markets, it seems essential to promote the rate of indirect financial saving of the household sector. In the developed countries like the U.S.A. or Japan, the pattern of the household sector's financial saving has evolved in this direction. In the United States, the major part of the household sector's saving is in the form of financial assets (deposits and claims on social security institutions) and the deficit units of this sector finance their deficits by borrowing from the financial system. In Japan, more than 50 per cent of the household sector's saving and more than 80 per cent of its financial saving are in the form of deposits.

However, mere promotion of indirect financial saving is not enough. By this device it is possible to mobilize saving and improve its allocation pattern. But resource allocation would depend on the *allocation policies* of the banking system and the social security institutions. If they are biased in favour of certain sectors/forms of financing because of their historical evolution as well as their "agenda"[3]—which is a function of their philosophy and the information-communication system evolved for decision-making—the other sectors and projects requiring other types of financing would be discriminated against and capital markets would still remain fragmented.

II. Logic of Development Banking

For historical reasons, the banks in the LDCs are oriented towards financing inventories in urban trade and industry. Economic development, however, requires financing of specific projects—in agriculture, industry and infrastructure facilities—which have a fairly long gestation period and the returns of which are spread over a long period of time. The banks, because of their historical evolution and their "agenda", are not equipped to provide medium to long-term credit required for project financing. Their transaction costs for the purpose are much higher than those for inventory financing *because of lack of expertise*. Hence, even if they did provided long-term finance, they would do so only on terms and conditions—interest, repayment periods and other conditions—that would not be attractive even for otherwise viable projects. (Of course, if the banks were motivated through appropriate policy instruments to extend their "agenda" to include medium to long-term credit instruments, as has happened in some LDCs, they could reduce transaction costs of such lending; in principle, a new *institution* is not essential to perform this function.)

Of course, the banks do finance indirectly fixed investment; by providing working capital finance, they make it possible for enterprises to use their own resources for fixed investment. However, it is only well-established businesses that generate internal resources who can finance fixed investment thus. The new enterprises would not be in a position to finance their fixed investment in this way.

There is thus a gap in the financial structure relating to the provision of medium to long-term finance for new enterprises and this gap is being filled by the development banks. The logic of this innovation of a new financial intermediary can be briefly stated.[4] It relates largely to economies of specialization and scale in the provision of medium to long-term finance for new enterprises. Specialization in the tasks of project appraisal and supervision would reduce the transaction costs of lending and thus lower the cost of borrowing for the enterprises. To be effective, the transaction costs of *lending for fixed investment* should be lower than those of the banks.

How this logic would work out in practice is indicated illustratively in terms of a hypothetical cost-structure in the following paragraphs. The transaction costs, annual interest and annual profit rates are presented as a proportion (per cent) of total assets and on the assumption that the inflation rate is lower than 3 per cent per year. These magnitudes, though illustrative, are based on data of several countries.[5]

The banks' transaction costs *for financing fixed investment* are of the order of 5.5 per cent—comprising 2.5 per cent for *administrative* costs and about 3 per cent for *risk*. Their *cost of funds* is about 6 per cent and if 1.5 per cent *profit margin* is added, they cannot afford to lend at interest rates below 13 per cent for financing fixed investment in new enterprises. The banks' transaction costs of lending for providing *working capital* finances are much lower; administrative costs are of the order of 1 to 2 per cent, and default risk of the order of 0.5 per cent. Thus they do provide working capital finances at an *average* interest rate of about 9 to 10 per cent per annum.

The development banks can reduce their transaction costs in a number of ways—all relating to economies of specialization and scale and spreading of risks. They can recruit staff with expertise in project appraisal and supervision. They can establish links with Technical Consultancy Service Centres (TCSCs) for the purpose of critically examining the complex technical choices relating to a project. Again, they can avail themselves of the services of Management Consultancy Services Centres (MCSCs) for supervising complex and risky projects. They can spread their risks by financing a large number of projects and a wise choice of their portfolio. Thus they can reduce both their subjective as well as their objective risk. Their administrative costs need not be higher than those of the banks—say less than 2 per cent—while they would be able to reduce default risk to 1 per cent as against the banks' 3 per cent. If we add 1 to 1.5 per cent profit margin, the difference between their average lending rate and the average borrowing rate could be about 4 to 4.5 per cent as against the banks' 6.5 per cent for financing fixed investment.

Their actual lending rate would depend on their cost of borrowing. Since the mobilizers of resources are the banks and the social security institutions, the development banks would have to borrow from them. The banks' average cost of funds depends on the maturity pattern of their deposits, the interest rates associated with this pattern, and the administrative costs of mobilizing them. This average cost is unlikely to be less than 5 per cent. With a profit margin of 1.5 per cent, the banks and the social security institutions can afford to lend to the development banks (by way of loans or purchase of their bonds) at a rate of 6.5 to 7 per cent, provided of course that the development banks' securities do not involve much risk. On this basis, the average lending rate of development banks could be 10 to 11 per cent against 13 per cent of the banks.

Thus, this new intermediary specializing in medium to long-term finance can be financially viable and able to grow and diversify its functions if it can lend at 10 to 11 per cent to new enterprises. For this to be possible, the projects to be financed should have an expected internal rate of return exceeding 15 to 16 per cent; for, without a 5 percentage point margin between the expected rate of profit and the cost of borrowing, the enterprise would not be motivated to take the risk of investment. And from the economy's point of view, it is essential to choose only such projects that have an internal rate of return of more than 15 per cent to have a growth rate in industrial output of 8 to 10 per cent (which is the objective of many LDCs).[6] It is assumed, of course, that such projects can be identified and formulated, given an appropriate incentive and institutional structure and that the supply of funds to the banks would be fairly elastic, within a certain range, at the given interest rate.

This logic of development banking does not require the establishment of a separate institution. The same functions can be performed by a specialized department of a commercial bank. If this is possible, the total costs of lending could be further reduced at least by 1 percentage point for several reasons. The commercial banks have a greater familiarity with the enterprises who maintain accounts with them. This additional information could reduce both costs of appraisal as well as supervision. They would be able to pool risks much more than the development banks because of the diversity of their portfolio. Finally, they are in a position to mobilize resources at a cost lower than the development banks.[7]

III. Development Banks: Review of Performance

The development banks—or specialized development banking departments of commercial banks—can, in principle, narrow the interest differentials, as argued in the previous section, and thus bring about a greater degree of capital market integration. The question then is: Have the development banks, in fact, performed this role?

The broad consensus with regard to the performance of the development banks in the LDCs is the following:[8]

(*a*) they have, by and large, provided finance to well-established and well-entrenched business houses;
(*b*) they have failed to play the expected catalytic role of promoting new entrepreneurs and new enterprises;
(*c*) they do not have much impact on the promotion of small–medium enterprises;
(*d*) they have failed to mobilize domestic resources on their own by establishing the necessary links with the banks, the social security institutions and the other financial institutions; and
(*e*) their profit performance on the whole was good till 1973; however, since then, it has not been as good.

Briefly, they have provided finance, by and large, to such enterprises which would have been able to obtain the required finance even from commercial banks. That is, they have not been able to reduce the real resource costs of lending to *new* entrepreneurs. For existing entrepreneurs, they have been able to lend at an interest rate lower than that of the commercial banks, not so much due to their lower real resource costs as due to the supply of funds to them by the government at a subsidized rate.

The major reason for this performance seems to be the interest rate policy of the development banks. Their lending rate has been fixed at around a level which is similar if not lower than the interest rate charged by the commercial banks for *short-term* loans. Their lending rate has been on average 8 to 9 per cent. Given this parameter, it is obvious that they could not have mobilized domestic resources to any sizeable extent from the other financial institutions. Hence, their reliance on government funds and international institutions could not be reduced. Assuming an average cost of funds from these sources of 6 per cent, they had to reduce their transaction costs to about 2 per cent to have a profit margin of at least 1 per cent.

To have their operations at this level of transaction costs, they have to choose such projects that can be financed with minimum of administrative costs and default risk. Obviously, such projects can come only from well-established profit-making business houses which have the resources and expertise to formulate projects in a manner acceptable to the development banks and have adequate assets as collateral.

The result has been that well-established businesses could obtain finance from the development banks at a subsidized rate—this subsidy in effect being provided at the cost of potentially viable new enterprises and of the banks themselves. The other result has been that the development banks could not tap the elastic sources of finance to widen and deepen their operations. In sum, they have neither the means nor the motivation to play an innovative development banking role. *Thus, instead of integrating the capital market, the development banks have tended to fragment it further;* they have not been able to reduce the real resource costs of lending to new enterprises by appropriate financial innovations.

Of course, these banks have performed some vital functions. They have extended the time horizon of the capital market by introducing medium to long-term credit instruments. Further, they have built skills and expertise relating to project evaluation, appraisal and supervision; they have thus improved the selection process for projects and the potential rate of return on assisted projects. Their accumulated experience in medium to long-term financing has had a favourable catalytic impact on the other financial institutions and the securities market. They have, in addition, accumulated data and experience, which are of crucial significance for analysing the impact of government industrial and trade policies and for suggesting, on the basis of such an analysis, modifications in these policies. They have in a sense acquired the "potential" for improving the functioning of the capital market. What is essential now is an incentive structure and a policy framework that will induce them to realize this "potential". Premature withdrawal of support from the government and the international institutions (like the World Bank) would frustrate their efforts in this direction and result in the atrophy of a potentially very effective instrument for industrial development.

IV. Role as a Catalyst

If the top management of a development bank is dynamic, innovative and development-oriented, it would try to influence and modify the aspects of policy environment and framework that are not in tune with its basic objectives. A development bank can serve as a catalyst in several ways in initiating a process of capital market integration.

(*a*) It could make a reasoned case to the policy-making authorities for a change in the interest rate policy. It could point out to them that (i) interest subsidy to well-established business is at the cost of new enterprises; (ii) without this subsidy, its own income would increase and almost 100 per cent of this income would be saved and used for supporting new enterprises; (iii) higher interest costs to enterprises would induce them to mobilize more equity capital; (iv) with the corporate profit tax of about 50 per cent, a 2 to 3 percentage point rise in the interest rate would raise the effective interest rate by only 1 to 1.5 percentage points; and (v) a higher interest rate would induce enterprises to borrow only for their more viable projects. Since a development bank has the required data, it could analyse them to show effectively and in concrete terms to the policy-making authorities the adverse impact of their policies on mobilization and allocation of resources.

(*b*) Even if it were not possible for it to interact effectively with the government or the Central Bank in order to modify the policy framework, it could overcome its adverse impact on its operations and objectives by taking on some commercial banking functions; it could thus mobilize more resources and raise the effective interest rate on lending.

(*c*) If for some reason it cannot assume commercial banking functions also, it could still induce commercial banks to provide a part of the credit for projects that it has appraised and selected for financing; thus, it could mobilize more resources for long-term lending and at the same time raise the effective interest rate. For commercial banks, the transaction costs would be less as their own administrative costs and default risk would be lower for projects which are well appraised by the development banks.

(*d*) Similarly, it could induce the social-security institutions and other such institutions to purchase the bonds/equity of projects that it has selected for financing; of course, this would be possible only if the investment pattern of these institutions is not rigidly controlled.

(*e*) It could reduce its own transaction costs and at the same time improve the project design and formulation for new enterprises by establishing on its own or in participation with the other financial institutions a Technical Consultancy Services Centre (TCSC); such a TCSC would work on business principles by charging appropriate fees for its work to the project promoters. The latter would be willing to pay these fees if they could improve the potential returns on their projects.[9]

(*f*) Similarly, it could reduce its transaction costs relating to project supervision by establishing a Management Consultancy Services Centre (MCSC).

(*g*) With such reduction in transaction costs, it could improve its own profitability and this could make it possible for it to issue its own bonds at attractive interest rates in the securities market and thus mobilize additional resources to some extent.

(*h*) It could serve as a catalyst for the promotion of small enterprises by inducing the promoters of large enterprises, who seek its assistance, to provide management, technical and financial assistance to small enterprises that are ancillary to their own projects; the real problems of ancillary small enterprises relate to marketing, supply of materials and credit and the large enterprises could provide such assistance, which traditionally in Europe and elsewhere was provided by the merchant during the early phases of development. The development bank cannot directly finance small enterprises; its transaction costs would be quite high. But it can finance them indirectly through the large companies.

Some development banks have undertaken some of these functions but a large number of them have not diversified their functions in order to play effectively the role of a development bank.

V. Critical Role of Central Bank

The critical role in initiating a process of capital market integration is ideally that of the Central Bank. The financial structure cannot function well as a system without a leader and a coordinator. This function is best performed by the Central Bank; without this function there is no rationale for its existence.

Unfortunately, the Central Bank in a large number of LDCs emphasizes only its regulatory function. However, in these countries, the role of a Central Bank cannot be restricted merely to that of the regulator; for, the institutions to be controlled and the credit system to be regulated have still to evolve to necessitate a regulator.

A Central Bank in a LDC has first to assume the function of a *promoter* of a sound integrated financial system even to perform effectively its role of a *regulator*.[10] These two functions are interrelated and a Central Bank's function as a regulator is in fact reinforced by its function as a promoter. It is the Central Bank that has to take the lead in evolving credit institutions, instruments and yield-structure that are essential for (*a*) efficient mobilization of saving, and (*b*) allocation and use of resources that are consistent with the basic development objectives. This development function cannot be performed effectively unless the Central Bank is able to maintain close, continuous and active contact with the credit system—the contact which is also essential for the success of its regulatory function.[11] It is thus essential for the Central Bank to do banking business with various parts of the system (including development banks) without inhibitions. Unless the Central Bank becomes not only "central" but also a "bank", it would not have adequate sanctions for performing its functions. It should not be merely a lender of last resort; it has to be a lender of early resort and in some cases a lender of primary resort. This need not mean continuous indebtedness; the financial institutions, however, should feel free to approach the Central Bank for help from time to time. Only then would they have the incentive to listen to the Central Bank's advice with respect.

NOTES

1. See in this connection, V. V. Bhatt, *Interest Rate, Transaction Costs and Financial Innovations* (World Bank: Development Economics Department, Domestic Finance Studies No. 47, 1978).
2. See V. V. Bhatt, *Some Aspects of Financial Policies and Central Banking in Developing Countries* (World Bank: Economic Development Institute, EDI Seminar Paper No. 11, 1974).
3. See K. J. Arrow, *The Limits of Organisation* (New York: W. W. Norton & Co., 1974), pp. 47–9.
4. See J. Hicks, *Capital and Growth* (Oxford: Clarendon Press, 1965), pp. 285–91.
5. See V. V. Bhatt, *Interest Rate, Transaction Costs and Financial Innovations*, *loc. cit.*
6. See V. V. Bhatt, *Aspects of Development Banking Policy* (World Bank: Economic Development Institute: EDI Seminar Paper No. 12, 1975).
7. For the experience of the Development Bank of Singapore in this connection, see V. V. Bhatt, *Division of Public and Private Finance: Research Program and Its Rationale* (World Bank: Development Economics Department, Domestic Finance Studies No. 43, 1977). See also J. Hicks, *op. cit.*

8. See W. Diamond and R. Gulhati, *Some Reflections on the World Bank's Experience With Development Finance Companies* (World Bank: Economic Staff Working Paper No. 145, 1973).
9. See V. V. Bhatt, *Financial Institutions and Technology Policy* (World Bank: Development Economics Department, Domestic Finance Studies No. 54, 1979).
10. See R. S. Sayers, *Central Banking in Underdeveloped Countries* (Cairo: National Bank of Egypt, 1956).
11. V. V. Bhatt, *Financial Policies and Central Banking in Developing Countries*, *loc. cit.*

PART IV. Fiscal and Incomes Policies

15. Taxation and Economic Development*

I PROPOSE to deal in this chapter with three major fields of taxation: (*a*) personal income-tax, (*b*) corporation tax, and (*c*) indirect taxes collected from the domestic manufacturers of products. This discussion would be in general terms in the light of the requirements for economic development in the developing countries. These three taxes for these countries are of major importance from the point of view of both their impact on economic development as well as their contribution to state revenues. As such, their structure and rates need to be devised in such a way as to be consistent with the major policy objectives of the State.

I. Introductory

But before I go over to the discussion of each one of these taxes, I would like to make two observations; the first relates to the nature of stability of the tax structure and the second to the need for adequate open and effective discussion of tax proposals.

For major government policies including tax policy, what is essential is to frame them in the light of the basic requirement of rapid growth with social justice and at the same time to ensure that they are simple and easily intelligible and are not likely to change in an *ad hoc* unprincipled manner. I feel that the tax system is an organic part of the economic system and hence it is essential that there be some certainty and stability about its basic features. A large number of *ad hoc* changes each year creates a climate of uncertainty, which hampers productive effort and diverts valuable scarce resources towards speculative and other undesirable channels as well as in circumventing and forestalling the government measures.

If some stability and certainty with regard to the impact of the tax system on the economy are to be ensured, it is essential, I believe, that tax proposals are formulated in the light of adequate research based on actual experience with regard to the working of the tax system in the country as well as abroad. In some countries, it is the Inland Revenue Board under the Ministry of Finance which is responsible for the implementation of tax laws as well as formulating tax proposals in consultation with some type of Economic Division (called by various names in different countries) in the Ministry of Finance. However, very few countries have a tax research unit in the Board with the result that tax proposals are not formulated rationally.

I think that it would be proper to set up a research cell in the Inland Revenue Board which could be assigned the function of formulating both short-run and long-run tax proposals for public discussion as well as discussion in Parliament.

* Paper presented at a seminar on the subject in Delhi in 1972, and published in *Economic and Political Weekly*, vol. vii, no. 26 (June 1972), and also in *Development Digest*, vol. xi, no. 4 (Oct. 1973).

This Board has actual field experience with regard to the tax system and it would be wise to use this experience for formulating proposals for tax reform. There should be a creative dialogue between the research cell at the Board and the Board's field staff, and the actual proposals for reform of existing taxes or new tax proposals should emanate from the research cell as a result of such a dialogue, which is essential for sound viable and efficient evolution of the tax system. These proposals need to be published so as to stimulate wide constructive public discussion.

From among such proposals, the government should select such proposals as it thinks are worth implementing in a given year. But then, when such proposals are discussed in Parliament, it should be ensured that this discussion is both enlightened and constructive. Under the present system, this is hardly so. I, therefore, believe that in countries with a parliamentary form of government, there is need for a Parliamentary Select Committee to study and report on the tax proposals to Parliament. In the United States, there is such a Congressional Committee. Even this may not serve much useful purpose unless this Select Committee has the right to invite people from the Ministry of Finance, particularly those who may have some share in devising the proposals and those who are likely to have some informed, enlightened views relating to them, as well as those from the public—economists, tax experts as well as laymen—who would be in a position to contribute constructively to the task of evaluation of tax proposals from the point of view of their impact on major socio-economic goals.

With these innovations, I feel that the Select Committee's Report to Parliament would be such as to induce effective and fruitful discussion of the tax proposals in Parliament. The government then would be in a position to choose the final proposals in the light of informed and constructive debate in Parliament. Such wide-ranging effective discussion would ensure the sound functioning of the democratic process and at the same time the selection of tax reforms and proposals that would be appropriate to, and consistent with, the major development objectives.

Let me now pass on to the discussion of the three specific taxes that I mentioned earlier.

II. Personal Income Tax

The personal income tax, I feel, should serve two objectives: (*a*) to promote the incentive to work and save; and (*b*) to make the distribution of consumption more equal.

Progressive and steeply rising tax rates on personal incomes do hamper the incentives to work and save, and in their result are ineffective as they direct personal effort towards activities which can enable the individuals to evade the tax burden. Hence, I suggest that the tax base for personal income tax should not be total income but total income (whether from work or investments) *plus* capital gains, *plus* gifts (including inheritance), *minus net* change in financial assets—that is, change in financial assets minus financial liabilities; the assets to be included should be all financial assets excluding currency holdings and gold. These financial assets comprise bank deposits, small saving instruments, insurance policies, provident funds, and claims on the private sector and the government.

This would be in effect a tax on consumption. With such a tax, the tax rates can be sharply progressive and still the incentive to work and save would not be adversely affected. The demand for social justice would be met as the degree of inequality in consumption can be reduced by means of such a tax. Private fortunes, of course, could be built up but their effect can be offset by a properly coordinated pattern of other direct taxes like an inheritance tax and gift tax.

This reform is administratively quite simple. Even at present, exemptions are given in various countries with regard to some financial assets like provident fund contribution, insurance premium and such other assets. Further, in some countries, interest and dividend incomes are also exempt from tax up to some extent. Instead of this multiplicity and complexity of diverse exemptions, what is suggested is that all savings in financial assets excluding currency and gold be exempted from personal income tax. Obviously, with this reform, no interest or dividend incomes should be tax free. All incomes to the extent to which they are not saved in the form of financial assets (excluding gold and currency) would be taxed.

This reform need not result in any revenue loss for the government. The present tax rates can be revised upwards once the tax base excludes *net* financial saving, so as to result in the same revenue as is obtained at present. If, as a result of this tax reform, financial saving increases at a rate much sharper than it would otherwise have increased, it would more than offset any potential revenue loss. Such, indeed, would be the effect of this measure.

The proposed income-tax reform has several distinct advantages:

(*a*) It would raise the rate of overall saving as a result of the tax exemption for financial saving.

(*b*) It would raise the proportion of financial saving to total saving and thus bring, within the purview of policy-instruments for resources allocation, a larger part of total saving. It may be noted that policy-instruments are available to affect the allocation of only financial saving while physical saving (in the form of houses, other physical assets, etc.) are by and large outside the purview of direct policy instruments.

(*c*) To the extent to which financial saving did not increase, there would be additional tax receipts.

(*d*) Tax receipts could also increase as the proposed tax exemption for financial saving might induce tax evaders to show their correct incomes. Since financial saving would not be taxed, the motive for concealment of incomes could disappear. This itself would be an enormous advantage.

III. Corporate Tax

The tax base for corporation tax in all countries has been profits after providing for depreciation at specified rates. On the false analogy of the progressive income tax on personal incomes, some degree of progression is introduced in some countries in the corporation tax structure. This progression in the corporation tax actually is a tax on efficiency and the tax system, thus, tends to encourage inefficiency in the use of capital resources. Hence, the tax rate on corporate profits should be made uniform and applicable to all companies.

At the same time, the tax base needs to be made uniform for all companies. At present in some countries, there are various types of allowances (other than depreciation provisions) which are tax exempt. Further, there is a tax holiday for new companies on a certain rate of profit for five years. It is difficult to understand this multiplication of incentives. Apart from that, these incentives would have some meaning if they are selectively applied for the promotion of the industries which would not be otherwise started. These incentives, at present, are applied to a large number of industries without much discrimination.

I suggest that such incentives should not be indiscriminately allowed to a large number of companies; they should be very selectively applied to only a few industries which require to be promoted in the national interest and that too only for a stated period of time. Every five years, the industries to be given these incentives should be changed in the context of national priorities.

Further, I have two additional suggestions—one with respect to the tax base and the other with respect to tax incentive for promoting exports, import substitution and productive efficiency.

At present in a large number of countries, the tax base excludes interest payments on borrowed funds. I suggest that this be included in the tax base and the tax rates appropriately lowered so as not to put any additional tax burden on this sector.

Since interest payments are tax exempt, there is a tendency on the part of the corporate sector to rely on borrowed funds to a much greater degree than they otherwise would do. Even parent companies are induced to give loans to subsidiaries rather than make additional subscriptions to the paid-up capital of the latter.

If interest payments on borrowed funds are included in the tax base, the tax system would really become neutral as between sources of funds and there would be to that extent an additional incentive to rely on paid-up capital by issuing additional shares, and borrowed funds would be utilized much more efficiently than at present.

Further, I would like the corporation tax to be used as an instrument to (*a*) promote productive efficiency and (*b*) stimulate both exports and import substitution.

To promote efficiency, I suggest that each percentage point increase in the rate of profit above 20 per cent should mean 1 percentage point decline in the tax rate. The rate of profit should be calculated as a ratio (per cent) of profit (after depreciation) plus interest payments on all borrowings to total capital employed comprising paid-up capital plus all reserves plus all borrowings. A profit rate of 20 per cent is essential, on certain assumptions, if a growth rate of 8–10 per cent in industrial output is to be secured; that is the logic for inducing all firms to realize this rate of profit.

To promote exports and import substitution, I suggest that each percentage point increase in the *net export ratio* should mean 1 percentage point decline in the tax rate. Net export ratio should be defined as the ratio (per cent) of current value of exports minus current value of imports of materials, spare parts and components to current replacement value of imported plant and equipment. Such a link would promote both exports and import substitution and, at the same time, induce efficiency in the use of imported plant and equipment.

These two tax incentives would not only tend to promote productive efficiency of overall investment and investment in imported plant and equipment but would also indicate to the firms rational criteria of project selection. Any decline in tax receipts on these counts would be more than offset by their favourable impact on productive efficiency and on exports and import substitution. With these tax incentives, a large number of complicated measures of uncertain value should be abolished.

IV. Some Commodity Taxes

In developing countries, commodity taxation is of particular significance from the government revenue point of view. Commodity taxes quite often take the form of duties on certain specified commodities; these taxes are collected from the domestic firms producing these products at a specified rate per physical unit of output. This form of taxation would be appropriate in the case of commodities which are standardized and are consumed by a larger number of persons.

However, the other commodities which are subject to such taxes in various countries are more complex and further form only a part of the products which the concerned firms manufacture. In these cases, the administrative and collection machinery has become very complex. The collection costs are considerable; at each factory, there has to be an excise inspector at the gate to watch and supervise the exit of the specific commodities and to be vigilant enough to check whether the taxed commodity is not leaving the factory gate under the name of another non-taxed or low-taxed commodity. Even with these large collection costs, the possibility of evasion is not ruled out as a firm is producing not only the taxed commodity but several others as well. Further, with all these costs, the revenue is by no means substantial and probably, net of collection costs, would be negligible.

I suggest, therefore, that excepting the few standardized commodities and commodities of mass consumption, there should be no such taxes on the other commodities.

Instead, there should be a uniform *ad valorem* tax of the turnover type on all mining and manufacturing establishments on the value of their output. Even at present, some *ad valorem* duties exist in some countries and this principle needs to be generalized for all output other than of the few commodities mentioned. The collection costs would be much smaller as the tax would be on an assessment basis. Further and much more important would be the link established between tax receipts and industrial output and prices; the former would grow at the growth rate of the latter automatically without the need for tinkering with excise duties in each budget as is being done at present.

The next question is: What should be the tax base and what should be the tax rate for this generalized tax? I suggest that the tax base be taken as value of output largely on the ground that it is administratively easier and quicker to collect these data from the existing published sources and no recourse to fresh collection is necessary. The suggested tax base would lead to the so-called "cascade effect". That is, since the material-producing firm will have paid a tax, the firm consuming these commodities would pay a tax on a base which is enlarged as a result of the tax already collected on raw materials. The tax effect thus would discriminate against final goods manufacturing firms, whose raw material costs form a greater proportion of total costs than the rest.

From this point of view, a value added tax would be better than a turnover tax. However, a value added tax is quite complicated and in countries where proper accounts are not kept by industry and trade, it may be difficult to enforce. On the other hand, an excise tax of the type I have suggested is administratively much simpler to enforce as it would be only at the stage of manufacturing and at this stage adequate output data are likely to be available.

However, the so-called "cascade effect" could be minimized by keeping a lower tax rate. Further, the additional "cascade effect" is unlikely to be large as even on the present basis some intermediate goods like cement, iron and steel products, aluminium, paper, tyres and tubes, copper and copper alloys and synthetic and organic dye-stuffs are taxed and some at a fairly high rate. If these duties are abolished and replaced by the new generalized tax, it may turn out that the additional "cascade effect" would be negligible. Since prices have already been adjusted to the present duties, there need not result an additional adjustment in prices. It is glibly assumed that the generalized tax would be passed on to the consumers. If it is not passed on or passed on only partially, the "cascade effect" may be very small. Even if there is some "cascade effect", it would induce economy in the use of materials and capital and this would be worth encouraging.

For export promotion, it would be easier to give remission on tax paid on part of the output exported. A firm exporting, say, 25 per cent of its value of output would not pay tax on this 25 per cent. This tax incentive would be easier and quicker to administer than the drawback provisions existing in some countries at present. If the "cascade effect" is significant (it is unlikely to be so), it may affect adversely exports of products in whose costs raw materials consumption costs are significant. However, this would be offset by the tax incentive with regard to corporation tax suggested earlier. For all these reasons, I propose value of output as the tax base for the proposed generalized excise tax.

What, then, should be the tax rate? For this purpose it would be necessary to work out the proportion of excise duties to the value of mining and manufacturing output (excluding the few commodities mentioned earlier). To keep the revenue at the present level, all that would be necessary is to have a generalized turnover tax equal to this proportion (per cent) on the value of mining and manufacturing output (excluding the few commodities indicated earlier). This rate may be raised marginally for additional revenue purposes.

For export promotion, this tax should be levied only on value of output minus the export value. This tax device would be much simpler than the complicated time-consuming drawback provisions existing at present. From the point of view of administrative convenience and cost as well as the prompt benefit to exporters, the suggested device would be simpler, prompter and more effective than the present provisions.

V. Concluding Observations

I believe that with the suggested tax reforms, the State revenue is likely to increase. What is important, however, to mention is that even if the tax revenue did not increase, there would be an increase in the real resources in the economy and reduction in consumption disparities.

For example, if the additional tax receipts under income tax did not materialize, there would be an equivalent additional increase in net financial saving and reduction in consumption disparities. From the point of view of the economy, additional resources would become available.

To the extent to which the additional tax receipts turned out to be lower than anticipated for corporation tax and generalized turnover tax, there would be a more than offsetting rise in exports, import substitution and productive efficiency. In fact, if the tax receipts proved lower than anticipated, it would mean a substantial increase in domestic and foreign exchange resources, and as a result a higher than anticipated growth rate in national income, investment, exports and import substitution.

Thus, the proposed changes in the tax system would induce either additional tax receipts or additional real resources; in either case, the economy would stand to gain.

16. Guide-lines for Incomes Policy*

A NUMBER of industrially advanced countries have become increasingly aware of the need for a conscious incomes policy for attaining full employment growth with relative price stability and viable balance of payments. In trying to evolve such an incomes policy, it has been now realized that it would have to bring within its purview not only wage and salary incomes but also all other types of incomes. It has become obvious that a policy with such a pervasive impact cannot be evolved and enforced without first attaining the necessary consensus with regard to its objectives and instruments among the various socio-economic groups in the community.

It is somewhat surprising to find that there is hardly any discussion on the relevance of incomes policy for the developing countries, though there is a growing literature on the use of accounting prices and wage rates for the purpose of project selection. In fact, the need for incomes policy is much more urgent in these countries, and particularly the overpopulated developing countries.

With the labour force growing at more than 2.5 per cent per year on top of a considerable backlog of underemployment and unemployment, these countries are faced with an acute employment problem. Because of trade union activity and government legislation, money wage rates are nearly three times the labour productivity and wage rates in the traditional sector; this has two effects. On the one hand, this induces migration of labour from rural to urban areas; and on the other, this makes it difficult to increase employment in the modern sector at the rate required. Open unemployment in urban areas and worsening of the living conditions of small farmers and landless labour in the rural areas are the inevitable consequences of this situation.

If a socially explosive rate of open urban unemployment is to be avoided and the living conditions of the landless rural labour are to be progressively improved to eliminate poverty, it is essential to regulate the level and pace of increase of money wages in the modern sector and at the same time to create conditions for a rapid and accelerating increase in the growth-rate of employment and capital formation. Incomes policy and appropriate policy instruments to implement it, thus, should form an integral part of the development policy framework in the developing countries.

It should be easier to evolve the necessary consensus for such a policy in the developing countries than it would be in the developed countries; for, such a consensus is in any case necessary for formulating and implementing development plans.

* Condensed version of a paper presented at a Seminar on Wage Policy and Wage Determination organized by Centre for Advanced Study in Economics, Department of Economics, University of Bombay, in March 1969, and published in *Economic and Political Weekly*, Special Number (August 1967).

Thus an incomes policy for a developing country with a mixed economy has to be evolved in a wider perspective and would require for its implementation guide-lines and policy instruments different in nature and character from those in a developed country. This chapter discusses the question of guide-lines for such an incomes policy.

I. Role of Incomes Policy

Underdeveloped countries have been engaged in the task of structural transformation of their economies in a planned way so as to attain certain social objectives. These objectives relate to progressive improvement in the living standards of the people through a self-sustaining process of economic development. Progressive improvement in the living standards requires not only an accelerating increase in national income but also its equitable distribution. The objective of raising per capita income levels is generally specified in the plan documents, while the objective of the equitable distribution is just mentioned but is really not translated in terms of any precise measurable index.

Because of this lack of clarity with regard to basic objectives, it becomes difficult to formulate rational economic policies. For internal consistency in the plan as well as policies, it is essential to specify the basic objectives in concrete terms.

The pertinent question which arises in connection with the income distribution objective is whether this objective should be translated in terms of consumption or in terms of income. What seems to be important from the point of view of equity is reduction in the disparity in consumption levels. A certain disparity in the pattern of income distribution may be necessary if incentives to save and work, and hence, growth-rate of income are not to be adversely affected. In fact, an attempt at reduction of income disparities may result in lower consumption levels for the low income groups in absolute terms than the levels that can be reached by maintaining and even widening the initial income disparities. What is required in the context of developing countries is a perceptible rise in the consumption levels of low income groups in absolute and relative terms rather than a reduction in income disparities.

Thus, assuming that investment would not be excessive and given the objectives of planned economic development, the purpose of incomes policy would be (*a*) to prevent the emergence of inflationary pressures, and (*b*) to ensure that the consumption pattern is consistent with the income distribution objective. What, then, should be the guide-lines with regard to the process of income formation? Or to put it differently, what should be the content of an incomes policy?

II. Labour Productivity as a Guide-line not Applicable

In the advanced countries, the major guide-line, which is generally accepted, relates to the increase in the overall labour productivity in the private economy (that is, excluding government services). If all incomes increase at this rate, it is assumed that there would not arise any inflationary pressures. This would be true, however, only under the following assumptions:

(*a*) The present income distribution is more or less acceptable and does not require to be changed.
(*b*) The capital–output ratio would remain constant.
(*c*) The government consumption to income ratio would remain constant.
(*d*) The saving–income ratio would remain constant.
(*e*) There would be a balanced growth of the agricultural and the industrial sectors.
(*f*) There would not be inter-sectoral shifts in the labour force.

Under these assumptions, if all incomes are permitted to rise at the same rate at which overall labour productivity increases, inflationary pressures can be avoided, *provided there is no overall excess demand.*

However, in the developing countries, none of these assumptions holds good. The present distribution of consumption is not acceptable and has to be changed in the light of the development objectives. The marginal capital–output ratio would be higher than the present average ratio as new capital-intensive industries are sought to be developed. The saving–income ratio as well as the government consumption to income ratio has to be raised. It is the essence of economic development to shift labour from low productivity to high productivity sectors.

Under these circumstances, the incomes of the saving and investing classes as well as government taxes should grow at a rate faster than the rate of growth of labour productivity. The income of the non-saving classes should correspondingly increase at a rate lower than the growth rate in labour productivity. Further, to the extent to which labour would shift from low productivity to high productivity occupations, average earnings of labour would rise even without an increase in productivity in the different sectors and hence wage rates should rise even less than what would be indicated by the labour productivity criterion.

III. Planned Increase in per capita Consumption as a Guide-line for Wage Increase

What then is the criterion for the increase in the incomes of the non-saving classes, in which category are included landless labourers, domestic servants, industrial labour and such other wage earning households? In simple terms, for all these classes, their income taken together should not grow at a rate higher than the planned rate of growth of private consumption. This does not mean that all wage rates could rise at this rate. For, even when the wage rates do not rise, total wage incomes could rise if there is a shift of labour from low wage occupations to high wage occupations. In the urban-industrial areas, the proportion of labour in the high productivity sectors would increase with economic development and thus the average wage rate would increase even if productivity in different sectors remained the same. However, this shift probably may be more than offset in the initial stages by a relative increase in the labour force in the lower wage scales as a result of migration of labour from the rural to the urban areas. Thus, the effect of these different types of shifts may cancel out, and the average wage rate may remain constant in the *urban* industrial areas. However, taking both the rural and the urban sectors, the average wage rate would tend to increase. Thus, per capita consumption of the wage-earning classes would increase. Hence, the wage rates in the different occupations can be raised only at a rate which is smaller than the planned rate of increase in per capita private consumption.

There is, however, one further consideration to be taken into account. The urban wage earners do save a part of their incomes in the form of their contribution to the various social security schemes like provident fund scheme, while the rural workers have no such schemes. Hence, though a relative shift of labour from the rural areas to the urban areas would tend to raise the average wage rate, the average rate of consumption per worker may not increase in the same proportion. Further, if the provident fund contribution is raised so as to increase the saving–income ratio of the urban wage earners, the wage rates can be allowed to rise at the rate of increase in per capita private consumption.

In any case, an increase in wage rates above this limit can be viable in terms of the development objectives only if the rate of growth in per capita consumption of the other classes—self-employed farmers, high income salary earners, self-employed businessmen, professional people and other high income non-salary earners—were lower than the planned rate of growth of per capita consumption. This can be done by inducing, in a variety of ways, these classes to save a larger proportion of their incomes than they currently do. But a rise in their saving–income ratio beyond a certain level is unlikely to take place.

The other way in which the growth-rate in the per capita consumption of these classes can be reduced below the expected rate of growth of private consumption is to tax heavily all *functionless* incomes. In this category would come all households receiving incomes–capital gains on the basis of ownership of urban land and such households which come in possession of large fortunes not through their efforts either through work or saving, but entirely on account of gift or inheritance.

IV. Wage Increases and Labour Productivity in Agriculture

Thus the rate of increase in average wage rate can be raised above the planned growth-rate in per capita consumption only to the extent to which the other classes could be induced to save a larger proportion of their income and the functionless incomes could be taxed. However, there would be a limit to the extent to which this can be done. As a guide-line, therefore, it would be desirable to promote the increase in wage rate only to the extent of the planned increase in per capita consumption.

Such a guide-line, of course, assumes that labour productivity in agriculture would increase at an appropriate rate. In the present context, this is a *crucial* assumption. Given the labour force in agriculture and assuming that all increases in labour force would have to be absorbed in non-agricultural occupations, the real wage rate in the non-agricultural sector can increase only if the marketable surplus of food increases at a rate higher than the increase in the total labour force. For marketable surplus to increase, labour productivity in agriculture should increase at a rate significantly higher than the rate of increase in the total labour force. For example, if the labour force increases at 2.5 per cent per year, projected rate of growth of per capita consumption is 2 per cent per year and the expenditure elasticity of the demand for food is 0.6, *labour productivity* in agriculture should rise at 3.7 per cent per annum. Unless such an increase can be brought about, the real wage rate in the non-agricultural sector cannot rise; increase in money wages would be offset by an increase in the prices of foodgrains.

There is another consideration to be taken into account also. If labour productivity in the agricultural sector grows at a rate less than 3.7 per cent per annum, an increase in real wage rate is possible only with considerable unemployment. The already employed labour force would obtain an increase in wage rates; but in that case the additions to labour force cannot be provided with employment in the urban areas. Such unemployment would depress the wage rates particularly in the rural areas, and it is the weaker sections of the community like the landless labourers whose conditions would show deterioration.

Thus there is a vital relationship among the rate of growth of labour productivity in agriculture, the rate of growth of employment and the real wage rate. Any attempt at raising the real wage rates in the non-agricultural sector above the level that can be supported by an increase in labour productivity in agriculture would mean that the economy would not be able to absorb the increases in labour force in productive employment and, in effect, it would mean, by and large, deterioration in the living standards of the landless labourers. Thus the real wage rates in the non-agricultural sector can rise under these conditions only at the cost of the landless labour in the agricultural sector and the unemployed labour elsewhere.

Since it seems to be a basic development objective to improve the living conditions of the weakest sections of the community, the productivity of labour in agriculture should increase at a rate high enough to raise the real wages of the landless labourers and to support productive employment of the rising labour force. The weakest section of the community is landless labour, whose living standards do not seem to have improved over the last fifteen years. If their wage rates and hence consumption are to be raised at a certain rate per annum, it cannot be done unless (*a*) labour productivity in agriculture increases at an appropriate rate, and (*b*) employment opportunities are provided for the increases in labour force. In that case, the rate of growth of the real wage rate in the non-agricultural sector has to bear a certain relationship with the rate of growth of labour productivity in the agricultural sector. All these hold irrespective of the rate of growth of labour productivity in the non-agricultural sector.

V. Structure of Wages and Salaries

These guide-lines are for the rate of growth of the basic wage rate of unskilled labour. The structure of wages in the non-agricultural occupations would bear some relationship to this basic rate. In the productive non-agricultural sector, the structure of wages and salaries would be governed by this basic wage and the relative scarcity of the various types of personnel required. This structure in various industries may need to be rationalized in such a way that for the same occupation the real income should not differ as between industries, or regions, unless there are other compensating factors operating.

The role of the government sector is expanding as it is supposed to play a vital role in the planned process of development. As a result, the government as an employer has to attract and retain an increasing corps of employees with an immensely wide range of occupational skills and abilities. The question, therefore, relating to the wage and salary scales of government employees has become important and some definite guide-lines in this matter need to be thought out.

The foremost consideration in this sector should be the ability of the government to attract the right type of skill and talent to perform the varied functions that the public sector has assumed. It is obvious, therefore, that the wage and salary scales in the government should be comparable to the scales in the private sector for similar types of work and/or similar requirements of skill and talent. This is the principle of "fair comparison" as enunciated by the Royal Commission on the Civil Service (1955) in the U.K. and which forms the basis of the Federal Salary Reform Act, 1962 in the U.S.A. The significance of the comparable principle was stated clearly in President Kennedy's special message to the Congress on Federal Pay Reform. "Adoption of the principle of comparability will assume equity for the Federal employee with his equals throughout the national economy, enable the Government to compete fairly with private firms for qualified personnel, and provide at last a logical and factual standard for setting Federal salaries."

This principle would take full account of national incomes policy, since one of its essential points is that pay in the public services, though it must not be allowed to drop far or for long behind that in good private employment, must not move ahead of it. If it drops behind, it must be brought up. If the public services are to be efficiently manned, incomes policy must include a policy of competitive equality between the public services and private employment with which they compete for recruits. But if pay in private employment does not rise, public service pay, on the principle of fair comparison, should not move at all. It can and, if the public services are to remain efficient, must follow an inflationary spiral if others set one going. But it should never lead the way in a spiral or set one off.

VI. Guide-lines for Non-Wage and Salary Incomes

All classes of people who own property in the form of physical or financial assets derive income in the form of interest, dividends, profits or rent. Since the saving–income ratio has to be raised progressively, the incomes arising from such saving also would increase at a rate higher than national income. Hence, the classes which are able to save would experience a more rapid rise in incomes than the wage and low income salary earners. What has to be ensured, however, is that these classes save such proportion of income and in such forms as are required to attain the plan objectives.

The forms of saving which do not serve any development function are: (*a*) excessive investment in residential construction used for the purposes of conspicuous consumption, (*b*) speculative holding of commodities, (*c*) holding of gold, and (*d*) speculative investment in urban land. If inflationary pressures are generally avoided, speculative holding of commodities would not take place. Excessive investment in residential construction for one's own use would consume scarce resources which could be used for more productive purposes; to restrain such investment, the tax instrument can be appropriately used. The holding of gold has to be discouraged also from the point of view of the foreign exchange leakage that it involves; it is likely that with stable overall prices, and attractive yields on other financial assets, the increase in gold holding for speculative purposes may not arise.

Speculative investment in urban land has become serious in expanding towns and cities. It is undesirable from many points of view. It gives large capital gains to classes which do not perform any productive function at the cost of those who do. It creates inflationary pressures by raising the price–rents of houses and thus helps in aggravating the wage–price spiral. It fosters tax evasion as those who get large speculative gains tend to evade taxes also. These tax-evaded incomes again either tend to be spent on consumption or in other speculative investments and thus the total productive savings of the community get adversely affected.

From all these points of view, it may be desirable to eliminate such speculative incomes by the State, compulsorily acquiring all urban land not effectively used by the owner for any productive purposes. Such a step would at one stroke eliminate functionless incomes as well as a major source of inflationary pressures.

The other functionless incomes arise from gift–inheritance of property. This class of people obtain their incomes neither from their own saving nor work but because of past saving and work of some other individuals. Such gift and inheritance should attract a fairly high progressive tax. It may be argued that such a tax may prove to be a disincentive to save as to be able to bequeath property to one's children is one of the most significant motives to save. However, to the extent to which this is a dominant motive, saving in fact could be larger because of the tax than it otherwise would be. For, to be able to bequeath to one's children property worth a certain value, parents would be induced to save even more than what they would have to without this tax.

VII. Incomes Policy and Rate of Profit

Incomes from the other productive forms of saving would rise as mentioned earlier faster than national income. In fact, the success of the development effort depends on the extent to which they do rise faster than national income as long as the consumption of these classes grows only at a rate lower than or at the rate at which the per capita consumption is projected to rise. If these incomes are sought to be restrained by means of taxes or otherwise, the incentive to work as well as save may be adversely affected. What is necessary is not a restraint on the growth of these incomes but a restraint on consumption out of these incomes.

The rate of profit of a business enterprise, whether corporate or non-corporate, is in one sense an index of the efficiency of the enterprise. Other conditions remaining the same, if an enterprise earns a higher rate of profit than the other enterprises in the same field, it reflects the superior relative efficiency of that enterprise. However, there may arise cases where the enterprise may be a single enterprise and it earns a high rate of profit simply because of its monopolistic position in the market. If such monopolies exist in the field of essential raw materials and consumption goods, their monopolistic pricing may set-off a price–wage or wage–price spiral. Such monopolies would require to be controlled in one way or the other.

The other case may be much more general and relates to the ability of business enterprises to raise prices in the context of an accelerating increase in overall demand. In such a situation, the rate of profit may be maintained or raised by raising product prices and thus setting in motion a price–wage and a wage–price spiral feeding on each other. If wage income rises are regulated, there is no reason why the enterprise should raise prices unless there is an unavoidable increase in some other cost items. If wage incomes are regulated, the overall prices should remain more or less stable though some changes in relative prices as would be necessary for a rational allocation of resources would take place. Therefore, to prevent business enterprises from raising their product prices merely to increase their rate of profit, there should be a careful watch over the factory type of enterprises in the field of certain strategic commodities. Their cost–prices data should be studied and any unjustified rise in prices should be prevented.

Thus what should be sought is not price control as such but some regulation of prices of essential commodities and services, produced by the factory type of business enterprises, to restrain such price increases as are likely to be resorted to mainly for raising the rate of profit. With such regulation of price increases, and with regulated increase in wage and salary incomes, overall prices are likely to remain stable. Any increase in the rate of profit of business enterprises under such circumstances could arise only as a result of technical change and improvement in productive efficiency and would generally be accompanied by some reduction in the prices of their products. Such price reductions should be encouraged as they would be necessary to offset unavoidable price increases in some sectors and further to pass on a part of the benefit of improved efficiency to the consumer. The tax instrument can be used for this purpose.

However, the prices of industrial products would not remain stable if food prices increase relatively to the prices of industrial products. If agricultural productivity increases at an appropriate rate continuously, food prices may not rise. But agricultural output fluctuates and will continue to fluctuate because of the vagaries of monsoon. Hence, in a bad year, food prices would tend to rise and this rise would be aggravated because of the precautionary and speculative demand for food. An energetic buffer-stock policy, therefore, would be necessary if food prices are to be kept stable.

The relative prices of agricultural products have to be determined from the point of view of providing adequate incentive to the farmers to raise agricultural productivity at the required rate. Further, the target for increase in the real wage rate of agricultural labour would also be one of the governing factors for the determination of relative prices. The real wage rate of landless labour should be raised at a faster rate than the real wage rate in the industrial sector for two reasons. Firstly, this is the weakest section of the community and from the point of view of equity, their living conditions need to be improved much more than those of the rest of the community. Secondly, the industrial wage rate is almost three times the wage rate for the landless labour; this disparity is much too great and if continued would tend to promote migration from the rural sector to the urban industrial sector at a rate which cannot be absorbed in productive employment. Thus, open unemployment would rise in the industrial sector and would create grave social and economic problems.

But once these relative prices are determined, policy measures should be effective enough to keep them stable.

If the policy measures to stabilize food prices fail, and food prices do rise, there would be a demand for increase in money wages to neutralize the impact of rise in food prices. This would be a legitimate demand to keep real wages stable. This demand can be successfully resisted by a concensus only if the rise in food prices is expected to be temporary. However, if it is expected to be permanent, the choice would be between allowing money wages to rise and thus to create a wage–price spiral and some machinery for equitable distribution of food at stable prices. A continuous rise in food prices reflects imbalances in the development programme; the attempt therefore should be such as to have a programme which can be supported without a rise in food prices. If they are allowed to rise as a permanent feature of the development process, a wage–price spiral and the resulting socio-economic tensions cannot be avoided.

VIII. Collective Consumption as an Instrument for Reducing Consumption Disparities

The guide-line indicated earlier is that average real wage rate should be allowed to rise only by the planned rise in per capita consumption. The wage rate could rise faster only to the extent to which functionless incomes can be taxed and the consumption of such classes can be prevented from rising. However, these measures would have only a once-for-all impact. From a long-term point of view, the guide-line should be suggested.

However, since the government taxes to national income proportion is to rise progressively, the government would be able to increase the collective consumption of the community. This collective consumption should be directed particularly towards raising the consumption of the weaker sections of the community. Thus, the rate of increase in total consumption of the weaker sections would be higher than that of the better-off sections.

Collective consumption to improve the living standards of the poorer sections should take principally the following forms. Free educational opportunities would improve their productive efficiency and thus would enable them to raise their living standards. Free health services would also likewise improve their productive efficiency. Finally, to enable them to build their own houses, land should be made available to them at nominal cost and such saving institutions and instruments should be created as would induce them to save for building houses for their own use. Unemployment insurance and/or provision of employment opportunities would stabilize their incomes. *All these, of course, can be accom-*

plished only by stages, but a rational perspective plan should be formulated indicating clearly how and in what stages collective consumption would increase and how it would principally be directed towards improving the living conditions of the weak and vulnerable sections of the community. There should be a clear plan of action in this sphere if an income policy is to gain support from the wage-earning classes.

IX. Suggested Guide-line Modified

The suggested guide-line for increase in wage and salary incomes is planned rise in per capita consumption. But the question arises: how could one be sure that the planned rise would materialize? There may be unforeseen developments which may upset the Plan. Further, the Plan itself may not be soundly conceived. Further, adjustment in wage and salary rates on a continuous basis may not be advisable as it might disrupt the economy.

Hence, such revisions should be done once in five years and at the end of each plan. The increase in rates should be equal to half the actual increase in per capita consumption in the Plan just completed plus half the planned increase in per capita consumption in the next Plan. Such a guide-line would take care of uncertainties relating to the Plan. This guide-line can be modified in other future periods in the light of the developing situation.

Such revisions at the end of a Plan are desirable from the point of view of the planning process also. Each Plan can be based on stable wage and salary rates and thus the planning process would not be disrupted as a result of changes in these rates during a Plan period.

X. Summary and Conclusions

This discussion can now be summarized:

1. On basic wage and salary rates, the guide-line should be the *projected* rate of increase in per capita consumption. Any additional rise can take place only to the extent to which the saving classes could be induced to save a larger than normal proportion of their incomes and consumption out of functionless incomes can be restricted. However, there would be a limit to both these and hence as a long-term guide-line only the increase in per capita consumption seems to be valid.

2. The functionless incomes arising from capital gains in speculative transactions in land should be eliminated by *nationalization* of urban land. The functionless incomes arising from inheritance/gift should be taxed at fairly high progressive rates.

3. Price rises and the resulting rise in profit rates arising from exploitation of monopoly position should be restrained. Price rises not justified by cost increases should not be permitted. The relative prices of food and agricultural commodities should be stabilized at an appropriate level.

4. If overall price stability is ensured, the functional incomes arising from saving and property should be allowed to rise faster than national income. However, policy measures should be taken to induce the property-owning and saving classes to save a larger than normal proportion of their incomes.

If these incomes are sought to be restrained, the incentives to work and save would be adversely affected.

5. The wage rate for landless labour should be allowed to rise at a higher rate than industrial wage rate. This can be attained only if (*a*) agricultural productivity rises at an appropriate rate, and (*b*) employment opportunities are provided to the additions to labour force.

6. The living standards of the weak and the vulnerable sections of the community should be raised at a rate higher than the rate of increase of per capita private consumption through the instrument of collective consumption provided by the government. Thus, the disparity in consumption standards would be narrowed. The items to be emphasized in this context are: free educational opportunities and health services, provision of land at nominal prices for the construction of houses for own use and unemployment insurance. All these can be attained only through stages and over a period of time; however, unless a well-conceived action programme in this connection is formulated and implemented, it would be difficult to reach a consensus with regard to incomes policy. Clear purposive action on this front is a prerequisite for reaching a consensus relating to incomes policy.

7. The wage and salary scales of government employees should be determined on the basis of the principle of fair comparison with the private sector employees. If this principle is not followed, public services would not be efficiently manned.

REFERENCES

1. Organisation for Economic Co-operation and Development, *Policies for Prices, Profits and Other Non-Wage Incomes* (1964).
2. Organisation for Economic Co-operation and Development, *Policies for Economic Growth* (1962).
3. United Nations, Economic Commission for Europe, *Incomes Policies in Post-War Europe: A Study of Policies, Growth and Distribution* (1963).
4. F. W. Paish and J. Henney, *Policies for Incomes* (1964).
5. Reserve Bank of India, Steering Group of Incomes, Wages and Prices Policy, *Report on a Framework for Income and Prices Policy* (1967).
6. V. V. Bhatt, "Incomes Policy in Developing Countries", *Economic and Political Weekly*, Special Number (Aug. 1967).

17. On Inflation and its Control*

I. Introductory

The nature of the inflationary process and the policy instruments for its control depend upon the institutional setting of a given country. These would naturally be different in a pure competitive economy from those in an economy with complete centralized planning. The institutional setting that we are concerned with is that of a mixed economy where government expenditures are more or less autonomous and planned, while the economic decisions in the private sector of the economy are governed by the price system as modified by the policy instruments of the government. Of course, in a basic sense one set of decisions is not independent of the other set; the two interact as a result of the interdependence of the two subsystems.

II. Excessive Pressure of Demand

The initiating cause of inflationary pressures in a mixed economy of the type we are discussing is generally the planned spurt in government consumption and capital formation expenditures superimposed on a system in which there is some fluctuating yet overall balance between saving and investment at a certain minimum level.

There are a few characteristics of government expenditure which are significant from the point of view of the inflationary process. A part of this is for improved maintenance of law and order and takes the form of expenditure on wages and salaries and administrative buildings and equipment. Some part is for provision of better health and educational facilities. The other expenditures are largely related to the development of infrastructure facilities like power, transport, irrigation, research institutions, financial institutions, agricultural extension work and the like. There would be some investment in industries like steel which the private sector is unable to develop on its own because of large initial investment and uncertainty of future prospects. Such investment may also be taken up on social or ideological considerations.

Most of the expenditures are productive in one sense or the other, but their gestation lags are significant and they involve lumpy expenditures. As a result there is no prospect of the government realizing profit incomes from its investments for quite a long time.

(1) Inflationary Impact of Excessive Government Expenditure

Such a spurt in government expenditure, then, has direct as well as indirect

* Paper presented at an International Economic Association Conference on Economic Development in South Asia at Kandy, Ceylon, in 1969, and published in *Economic Development in South Asia*, editors: E. A. G. Robinson and M. Kidron (London: MacMillan & Co. Ltd., 1970).

effects on the private subsystem. The government demand for goods and services of all kinds tends to raise the marginal efficiency of investment and thus induces a spurt in private investment. Thus at this stage we have the typical Keynes's Treatise situation of an *ex ante* disequilibrium between desired investment and actual saving. The result is a rise in flexible prices and profit inflation. Some part of the windfall profits would be consumed, some used for speculative investment in commodities and real estate, some part would be saved and some part would be taxed. The price rise and profit inflation would thus have to be equal to a certain multiple of the initial disequilibrium between investment and saving. There is a multiplier here affecting prices and profits.[1]

This intial inflation would be damped at the second stage as a result of some increase in output due to intensive utilization of available productive capacity and increase in capacity due to previous investments. It would be again damped as a result of an import surplus made possible by the use of previously accumulated foreign exchange reserves.

This damping effect may, however, be more than offset by (*a*) a continuing increase in government autonomous investment and its direct effect on private investment; (*b*) an increase in consumption demand resulting from an increase in employment giving rise to induced investment; and (*c*) a rise in money wages and salaries (rigid prices). Once the price rises are expected to continue, the wage and salary-earners would demand a rise in their money incomes to offset the actual decline in their customary standard of consumption. The additional and sometimes independent justification for this demand would be the abnormal increase in profits.

(2) Balance-of-Payments Effect

These inflationary forces would be strengthened by the balance-of-payments effect also. The rise in domestic prices in relation to international prices would serve as a disincentive for exports. On the other hand there would be windfall profits in the import trade. With a fixed exchange rate, the import capacity of the economy would be reduced in relation to its money incomes. In the meantime the previously accumulated foreign exchange reserves also may have been considerably reduced and no further use of these reserves may be possible.

In this situation, external aid may soften the impact of inflationary pressures. However, though some part of it like PL. 480 food aid does have this effect, aid *tied* to fixed investment in specific projects would actually aggravate the pressures, at least initially, by facilitating the desired level of fixed investment, which cannot be undertaken without raising domestic money incomes. These investments would not have been possible but for the availability of specific commodities and services which are not domestically available.

These inflationary pressures may peter out if taxes and profits as a proportion of money incomes rise sufficiently to offset the attempted investment at an *acceptable* level of real wages. But this may take a long time if the profit and income taxes are inadequate or are evaded and there is a continuing rise in luxury consumption and speculative investment as a proportion of profits. But the real danger is that real wages would fall below the acceptable level and the attempt by wage-earners to maintain real wages would create a price–wage spiral. This is the stage at which the Wicksellian cumulative process would operate.

(3) Effect on Money Rate of Interest

So far, however, we have not said anything about the money rate of interest. Would not a rise in the money rate of interest stop this process as in the Wicksell system? Obviously the monetary authorities could raise the money interest rate. Why does this not happen?

The reason is simple. The monetary system has become more or less perfectly elastic not as a result of monetary policy but as a result of fiscal policy. The spurt in government expenditure is itself facilitated by government borrowing from the Central Bank. The bank reserves, as a result, rise; the interest rate does not fall as the increased demand for interest-yielding reserve assets by the banks is matched by increased supply by the government. With a comfortable liquid assets portfolio, the banks are in a position to increase their investment assets and thus meet the demand for loans. Given the money rate of interest, the price rise reduces the real interest rate even to a negative level. The price rise, on the other hand, raises the money rate of profit. This widened gap between the interest rate and the profit rate stimulates the inducement to invest. If this gap is just enough to cover the risk, uncertainty and illiquidity margin required for real investment, the money rate of interest would remain stable.

III. Imbalance between Agriculture and Industry

There is another factor which aggravates the inflationary pressures and which, by itself, is sufficient to cause them even if the overall effective demand were not excessive. And this is the imbalance in a key sector of the economy—between the growth rates of agriculture and industry.[2]

(1) Temporary Imbalance

There are two aspects of this imbalance. One type is purely temporary and arises owing to fluctuations in foodgrain output on account of weather conditions. This may cause a sharp decline in foodgrain output in relation to the demand for food in the industrial sector. The resulting rise in foodgrain prices aggravates the supply–demand imbalance. The farmer may tend to hold larger than normal food stocks from both precautionary and speculative motives. The traders would tend to keep larger reserve assets in the form of food for speculative reasons. And finally consumers in the urban area may tend to raise their precautionary stocks of food. The rise in foodgrain prices would thus be a multiple of the price rise that would have occurred before this shift in supply–demand schedules.

The real wages in the industrial sector tend to fall. The demand for food of wage-earners is related directly to their real incomes, whatever the prices of industrial goods. Thus, though the real wages may be high in terms of industrial products, they decline in terms of foodgrains. The attempt to restore the original level of real consumption of foodgrains would tend to raise prices. The resulting fall in real wages, after a lag, would induce the wage-earners to demand higher money-wages. Industrial costs thus would rise. The supply-induced rise in food prices would cause a cost-induced rise in industrial prices. This price–wage and wage–price spiral may peter out with the next two good harvests. But meanwhile industrial costs may stay put at the new level if the money wages are not flexible downwards or there is no fall in the foodgrain prices.

(2) Long-run Imbalance

This "fluctuation" effect may be strengthened and become permanent if at the same time there is a persistent imbalance between the demand for food in the industrial sector and the marketed surplus of foodgrains by the farm sector. In this case even an occasional good harvest[3] adequate to meet the normal industrial demand for food may not stop even temporarily the price–wage and wage–price spirals. Two consecutive good harvests may stop these spirals temporarily, but they would resume their course again, given the long-run imbalance.

Food imports may damp the spiral effects. But much depends on whether they are adequate and timely. If they are not timely, they would not be able to affect the operation of precautionary and speculative motives for holding food stocks, so that much larger imports would be required. If they are inadequate, these motives would doubtless operate and the spiral effects would continue, though the latter would be less intense than they otherwise would be.

IV. Trade, Exchange and External Assistance Policies

The initial impact of excessive overall demand is obviously on the balance of payments. Imports tend to rise in relation to domestic money incomes; exportable surpluses diminish and the rise in domestic prices in relation to international prices makes it difficult to sustain the original level of exports with a fixed exchange rate. In this situation the balance-of-payments imbalance is sought to be corrected in two ways, both of which tend to aggravate the inflationary pressures caused by excessive overall demand.

(1) Impact of Project Aid

One measure is to obtain external aid. By and large, this aid is tied to fixed investment in specific projects. This type of aid facilitates excessive fixed investment without a corresponding increase in inventory investment. As a result, productive capacity already created tends to be underutilized. This output effect tends to aggravate the inflationary pressures. General-purpose external assistance in this situation could have softened the pressures.

(2) Impact of Import Control through Import Licensing

This effect is strengthened by the nature of direct control on imports through import licensing. In the scheme of import licensing too, preference is by and large given to the imports of machinery and equipment; imports of materials and intermediate goods required for operating increased productive capacity are rationed rather strictly. This has the effect of encouraging fixed investment and limiting the increase in output. The effect of this type of import control is obviously inflationary. The underutilization of productive capacity resulting from import controls is reinforced by a tax system which provides incentives for fixed investment but no incentives for efficient utilization of productive capacity. Credit rationing, sometimes resorted to, also has the effect of accentuating under-utilization of capacity as inventories are largely financed by bank loans.

There is another way in which import controls aggravate inflationary pressures and that is through their effect on functionless profits. With a fixed exchange rate, there occurs a large margin between the costs of imports in domestic currency and their domestic prices. Whoever gets an import licence is thus in a position to obtain a large windfall profit. This leads to a wasteful use of imports accentuating the balance of payments problem. On the other hand the holders of import licences obtain large windfall profits merely through their sale to actual users of imports in the productive process. These profits, which evade taxes, are likely to be spent on luxury consumption goods and thus aggravate the initial inflationary pressures.

Import controls also distort the investment pattern. Import-substitution projects, profitable only at the high level of domestic prices, tend to be encouraged. There is hardly any incentive with a fixed exchange rate for these projects to be planned for tapping the export market; further, their domestic costs are such that it is hardly profitable to export their products. Given the income distribution pattern and the tax system, there is also an incentive for the domestic production of luxury consumption goods. Import controls thus tend to promote an inefficient use of resources on the one hand and diversion of resources for meeting the demand for "non-essential" consumption on the other. Since changes in import control policies create uncertainty, they also tend to promote the precautionary and speculative build-up of inventories of permitted materials.

(3) Structural Payments Problem

Apart from this inflation-induced balance-of-payments problem, the latter could also arise because of structural reasons. For a variety of reasons it may be difficult to convert domestic surpluses of commodities into exports, while imports rise as a result of the need for specific commodities not produced at home. This structural problem is also generally tackled through external assistance and direct import controls of the nature mentioned earlier. Both of them tend to facilitate fixed investment, while limiting strictly the imports of materials and intermediate goods required for utilization of already created productive capacity. There arises, thus, a policy-induced spurt in fixed investment. Initially this may not create an imbalance; fixed investment may be in balance with the propensity to save.

But such a continuing spurt would raise the proportion of fixed investment to national income more than the rise in the saving proportion. And inflationary pressures could result from this cause also. The other effects of import controls would, as discussed earlier, tend to reinforce these pressures.

V. Adjustment Crisis

At some stage, if rapid and accelerating inflation is to be avoided, the process would have to be halted. This happens in a more or less unplanned manner as a result of the reduction in the growth rate or even an absolute reduction of government investment expenditure.

The rise in money wages and salaries increases government consumption expenditure. The tax system may at the same time impinge only on some part of total profits; the functionless profits arising from speculative dealing in commodities, real estate and import licences may evade taxes in one way or the other. The tax receipts as a proportion of profits may thus go down. A sudden drought may involve the government in large relief expenditures. On government fixed investment, profits may not materialize either because of long gestation lags (further lengthened because of the inflationary pressures themselves) and government pricing policies.

In a situation like this, the government may not be able to maintain the growth-rate of its investment without growing budgetary deficits. Desire to curb the inflationary pressures thus may induce the government to reduce its investment expenditure. This will have a direct effect on profits and profit expectations of firms relying on government orders. Hence new investment in this sector may not be attempted. Sudden shrinkage of investment demand will then affect the growth rate of overall demand as well as its expected growth rate. There would thus emerge a situation of abnormal unemployment of productive capacity—a phenomenon of industrial recession. The inflationary pressures would still continue if the basic imbalance between the demand for and supply of foodgrains persist; money wages would rise and there would be a shrinkage of profits, affecting adversely in turn government tax receipts and government investment. There would thus emerge what is currently called an inflationary recession. This is in some ways a Hayek-type crisis.[4]

VI. Control of Inflation

The remedies for inflation would vary with the nature of the initiating causes.

(1) Fiscal Policy

If inflation is caused by excessive pressure of demand, the obvious remedy is to restrict government investment to a level consistent with the propensity to save and a given tax system. Some pressure on demand is of course inevitable in an economy where a spurt in government investment is considered desirable. In a situation of such strain on resources of all kinds, taxes on incomes and profits as well as the other indirect taxes would be partly shifted to consumers and there would be some rise in prices. An adequate tax system, however, would restrict luxury consumption, speculative investments and "non-essential" investments and thus release resources for essential investment. With such a tax system the multiplier effects of a rise in profits on prices could be avoided.

(2) Price and Distribution Controls

It may not be possible, however, in a given situation to devise a "perfect" tax system adequate to affect income distribution in the desired direction and to the desired extent. Some direct controls on prices and distribution of scarce materials may be necessary. These controls uniformly affecting all the sectors of the economy, however, do not always work in the desired direction. Quite often a "black market" develops and scarce materials are passed on from the white to the black market where the prices are much higher than the controlled prices. This has two undesirable effects. One is that producers are unable to raise their prices and profits; profits emerge in the speculative sector so that the capacity of the controlled sector to expand becomes limited. Another effect is the diversion of resources to "non-essential" uses, affecting adversely the planned pattern of investment.

The practicable and effective course appears to be to pre-empt the use of scarce materials and imports for government investments and other "essential" private investments, which are within such effective control of government as to ensure the end-use of these materials and imports. The rest of the domestic output of scarce materials and imports can be sold for other uses at the market prices. The resulting dual price structure would on the one hand enable the producers to enlarge their profits and on the other ensure a rational allocation of resources in the non-controlled sector. With regard to the exchange rate also, there would be a dual price; the fixed exchange rate would apply to competitive exports (largely primary commodities whose prices are determined internationally) and "essential" imports. The market rate will apply to a new non-traditional exports and "non-essential" imports. There would thus emerge an incentive for exports and rational allocation of non-essential imports. The functionless profits on import licences would disappear and would go to provide a subsidy to exporters, whose cost-determined prices are otherwise non-competitive in the international market.

It would facilitate government control on essential imports and competitive exports to the extent to which it is possible to nationalize this trade. This also applies to internal trade in scarce commodities.

With such controls on foreign trade and a dual exchange rate, the balance-of-payments effect of domestic inflationary pressures would not tend to aggravate the latter. On the contrary, such pressures would tend to correct the payments imbalance by a rise in exports; for a rise in import prices would have an automatic impact on the profitability of export trade.

This export "incentive" may also affect the nature and composition of fixed investment and may make it export-oriented. On the other hand, viable import-substituting investment would also be encouraged. These two effects may also tend to correct the long-run payments problem of a structural nature.

(3) Monetary and Credit Policies

Given the excessive government expenditures, monetary and credit policies have a fairly limited role in correcting inflationary pressures. With the price and wage rises, the demand for bank credit would increase and it would be difficult for the banks to resist this pressure for demand for credit[5] without affecting output, particularly when the banks have adequate reserve assets as a result of the nature of financing of government budgetary deficits. Monetary policy cannot be expected to compensate for pressure on demand originating from the government sector. In this situation the direct and immediate impact would be that of fiscal policy and direct controls of the nature discussed earlier.

What monetary policy can be expected to curb is speculative inventory build-up. Even in this case the rise in short-term interest rates may have to be fairly drastic; interest rates, to be effective, must be raised above the expected rate of increase of prices of such commodities. Selective credit control may be of limited effectiveness, for the potential borrowers can resort to other forms of credit. Even if effective with regard to potential borrowers, it cannot prevent the potential lenders from inventory investment.

Even this limited role of monetary policy is likely to be effective only in a situation where inflationary pressures arise primarily as a result of an autonomous increase in speculative inventory build-up. If the origin of such speculation is in sharp fluctuations in the output of agricultural commodities, monetary policy can hardly be effective unless accompanied by appropriate buffer-stock operations.

Apart from this role, the main function of monetary policy should be to maintain an appropriate structure of interest rates. If this structure is unstable, investment decisions are likely to be based more on speculative gains than on prospective yield. As Keynes said, when the capital investment of a country "becomes a by-product of the activity of a casino, the job is likely to be ill-done".[6] For rational investment decisions, then, the structure of interest rates should be fairly stable.[7]

The maximum interest rate in that case cannot exceed the expected rate of profit on marginal investment. What this rate of profit should be is governed by the desired growth rate of income. Given the distribution of income and the saving propensities, the rate of profit should exceed the growth rate by a certain margin. Again, to provide sufficient inducement to invest, the rate of interest at which the firms borrow money should be lower than the rate of profit to cover the risk, uncertainty and illiquidity margins. Thus between the lowest interest rate on bank deposits and the rate of profit, the other interest rates would be determined in the light of the given structure of financial intermediaries.[8] Since in a developing economy the banking habit has to be fostered (to secure greater mobility of funds and greater control over their allocation), the rate on deposits has to be higher than the marginal convenience of holding currency as a reserve asset.

(4) Policies for Correcting Food Imbalance

These fiscal and monetary measures and the direct price and allocation controls would suffice in controlling inflation only if there is no imbalance between the supply of and demand for foodgrains. This imbalance itself is sufficient to create inflationary pressures and is not amenable to correction through the measures so far discussed. For temporary imbalances of this nature, the only reliable policy is to operate a buffer-stock policy of compensate for output fluctuations. For a longer-run imbalance, there should be adequate provision of food imports or food rationing or policy measures to secure an adequate growth rate in food output. If persistent food imports and food rationing are not feasible (the former would strain the foreign exchange resources and the latter may not be socially tolerated), the only course open is to have such policy measures affecting incentives, technology, units of cultivation, food procurement and investment composition as are adequate for ensuring a growth rate in food output consistent with the acceptable growth in real wages.[9] Fiscal and monetary policies cannot correct such inflationary pressures; they would merely create uncertainty in the other sectors, affecting adversely the investment and production climate.

(5) General Case for Reserves of Resources

The case for buffer-stocks of food is in fact a part of the more general case for adequate reserves—cushions—in the economy. It is necessary to keep buffer-stocks of foreign exchange and scarce commodities vulnerable to shocks as also of reserve assets with the banking system to enable the economy to withstand shocks. Any economy, whether planned or unplanned, is liable to shocks as a result of the occurrence of unexpected events. Monetary and fiscal measures or even direct controls in this situation cannot ensure smooth adjustment of the economy to such shocks; they are likely to create uncertainty and imbalances. Reserves of critical resources in such cases can be used as short-run stabilizers and could make the adjustment process smoother.[10] Foreign exchange reserves are of particular significance as they represent a very pliable and versatile form of reserves.

VII. Inflationary Pressures and the Planning Process—I

There is one aspect of excessive investment which is worth noting and that is related to the planning process. Quite often, at the plan stage, some balance between planned investment and saving is struck. Yet when the plan is implemented, there emerges a saving–investment imbalance. The reason is lack of awareness of the functional relationship between money incomes and the saving pattern of the community on the one hand and between output and inventories on the other.

The saving rate of the household sector (other than the government and private corporate sectors) is hardly a guide for determining the investment levels in the other two sectors. It is necessary to know the structure of the household saving. Quite a substantial part of this saving is in the form of physical assets like housing, investment in non-corporate industry and agriculture, and trade inventories. The rest is in terms of financial assets. What is significant from the point of view of the other two sectors is the household saving in the form of financial assets. For it is thus that its saving is transferred to the other sectors for meeting their deficits. Given the structure of financial institutions, instruments and the interest rate, the saving pattern is governed largely by the preference system of the households. These functional relationships are ignored (partly owing to lack of data) and it is arbitrarily assumed that since the household sector is likely to save a certain proportion of its income, this saving would be available to offset the planned investments in the other two sectors. This leads to excessive planned investment in the government and the private corporate sectors resulting in inflationary pressures.

Another aspect of the same phenomenon is underestimation of the requirement of inventories for the full utilization of available productive capacities.[11] This leads to excessive emphasis on fixed investment. The inflationary pressures so generated are then aggravated by a policy of import controls which give preference to imports of capital goods. There thus arises a scarcity of materials causing underutilization of productive capacities and a slower (than what would otherwise be possible) growth of real income and exports.

VIII. Inflationary Pressures and the Planning Process—II

The structure of household saving is important from another point of view also. The households do keep a certain part of their saving in the form of money (currency and bank deposits). This is largely kept for transactions and precautionary motives. The demand for money for transactions motives depends largely on the time structure of incomes and expenditures and the rate of monetization of the part of output earlier exchanged on a barter basis. This demand itself is likely to grow at a rate higher than the growth rate of personal disposable income.

Quite apart from this, with the growth of money incomes of lower-middle and middle income groups, a greater part of their saving is likely to be of a precautionary nature and would be kept in the form of more or less liquid assets which have no transaction costs and are readily realizable without any capital loss. Such assets by and large comprise currency and bank deposits, in view of the lack of other assets which can serve the desired purpose. Further, since they would have to accumulate enough funds even for acquiring investment assets, there would also be a demand for money as a running asset for their investment operations. Since these incomes grow faster than the overall income, the demand for money as a reserve asset is also likely to grow faster than income. This is a demand for money which, as Hicks has noted, is likely to be insensitive to changes in yield expectations.[12] With the high income groups, money may be a luxury asset and may have an income elasticity of more than 1. Further, in a growing economy, businesses and households would tend to keep a larger than normal part of their saving in money form so as to be able to seize investment opportunities as and when they materialize.

Given, therefore, an initial balanced structure of assets with the households and business, the demand for money is likely to grow considerably faster than the increase in real income. If the interest-rate structure is to be stable, the reserve assets including money have to be created at a rate consistent with the preference of savers.

That monetary system, then, has to be elastic enough for the purpose. That means that the Central Bank assets have to be increased appropriately, assuming that there are no excess reserves with the commercial banks. The Central Bank can do this by the purchase of government bonds or foreign exchange assets and by granting loans to commercial banks. Assuming that foreign exchange assets are unlikely to change significantly, the Central Bank can directly purchase government bonds. In effect, there would be credit creation in favour of the government, which can be used for financing its capital expenditure. This credit creation, in turn, would tend to raise the reserve assets of the banks and their lending power.

Thus a part of the saving of the community can be *directly* mobilized to offset government expenditure. Given the growth-rate of national income, the desirable structure of interest rates, the structure of financial institutions and instruments, and the saving propensity and structure of the households, the saving which can be so mobilized can be estimated. And if the credit creation by the Central Bank in favour of the government is restricted to this limit, and if the wage goods supply–demand balance is maintained, the inflationary pressures are unlikely to be generated.

It is due to the lack of proper appreciation of these factors at the planning stage that budgetary deficits to be financed by Central Bank credit creation turn out to be excessive, resulting in excessive pressure on demand.

IX. Some Conclusions

It may be useful to summarize briefly the major findings of this chapter at this stage. Their relevance to the inflationary process in India is indicated in the Appendix.

One of the basic causes of inflation is, of course, excessive government fixed investment in relation to the propensity to save and the given tax system (section II). The monetary complement of this phenomenon is excessive credit creation, particularly by the Central Bank in favour of the government. This overall imbalance is partly deliberately created. But partly it is also the result of errors at the planning stage (sections VII and VIII). Given the structure of financial institutions, instruments and interest rates, the structure of household saving is determined by the preferences of the households. If the structure of saving so determined is not consistent with the investment plans in the government and the private corporate sectors, the result could be excessive investment as well as excessive credit creation. This consistency requirement is not satisfied at the planning stage owing to lack of data as well as the lack of awareness of this constraint. The resulting price rise initially brings about profit inflation, and consumption out of profits raises the value of the price multiplier. What makes the inflationary process self-reinforcing is the induced productive and speculative investment in the private sector and the rise in money wages, after a lag, demanded by the wage-earners to offset the decline in real wages.

These domestic pressures are softened initially by a spurt in imports of all kinds. The export surpluses and competitiveness as well as foreign exchange reserves diminish and a payments problem emerges. This problem is tackled by means of a policy of import controls, while maintaining a fixed exchange rate. These measures aggravate the inflationary pressures by creating (*a*) functionless profits in import trade, (*b*) underutilization of productive capacity as a result of foreign exchange allocation for capital goods in preference to materials, and (*c*) incentives and pressures for inefficient use of resources and their diversion to meeting "non-essential" needs. External aid tied to capital-goods imports hardly enables the country to meet its requirements of imported materials.

A structural payments problem is also tackled in a similar way, and this tends to reinforce or even to create inflationary pressures (section IV).

The inflationary effects of excessive government investment are aggravated, with a temporary or permanent imbalance between food demand and supply. This imbalance itself can create an inflationary price–wage and wage–price spiral. With the rise in food prices, there emerges a speculative and precautionary demand for food stocks and this aggravates the original imbalance. The wage-earners' efforts to maintain their real consumption of food tend to raise money wages which in turn raise industrial costs (section II).

Inflationary pressures resulting from excessive investment can be controlled directly and effectively only by fiscal measures. However, an attempt to realize as large a spurt in government investment as may be feasible and even the adoption of appropriate tax measures are likely to create some price rise, and in a situation like this some direct controls on prices and allocation of scarce materials and imports would be necessary to realize the planned investment and output targets. For the effectiveness of these controls as well as for facilitating rational allocation of resources, they need to be accompanied by a dual price system. With regard to the exchange rate, this would mean the policy of a dual exchange rate.

A temporary food imbalance can be corrected only by an effective buffer-stock policy. A long-run imbalance has to be corrected either by a policy of food rationing, possibly accompanied by food imports, or by securing the desired growth in food output.

Any economy, planned or unplanned, is liable to some sudden shocks as a result of unexpected events. For smooth and steady development, these shocks need to be absorbed by adequate reserves of foreign exchange and commodities vulnerable to shocks. Even the monetary system needs to have adequate reserve assets for effective monetary management in such situations.

Monetary and credit policies can at the most tend to correct inflationary pressures brought about by an autonomous speculative demand for inventory investment. In other situations they cannot be expected to compensate for the effects of excessive fixed investment or food imbalance (section VI).

Without such a policy-mix any inflationary process tends to be cumulative, and at some stage, when this becomes socially intolerable, government investment tends to be reduced. The direct and indirect effects of this reduction on the private sector tend to magnify the underutilization of productive capacity. At the same time if the food imbalance persists, inflationary pressures continue, creating a phenomenon of inflationary recession (section V).

NOTES

1. See Sir J. Hicks, "A Note on the Treatise", in his *Critical Essays in Monetary Theory* (Oxford, 1967), pp. 196–8.
2. See N. Kaldor, "Monetary Policy, Economic Stability and Growth", in his *Essays on Economic Policy*, vol. i (London, 1964), pp. 142–3.
3. See N. Kaldor, "Economic Problems of Chile", in *Essays on Economic Policy*, vol. ii.
4. See Sir J. Hicks, "The Hayek Story", in *Critical Essays in Monetary Theory*, pp. 212–13.

5. See N. Kaldor, "Economic Problem of Chile", in *Essays on Economic Policy*, vol. ii, pp. 270–3.
6. See J. M. Keynes, *The General Theory of Employment, Interest and Money* (London, 1936), chapter 12.
7. See N. Kaldor, "Monetary Policy, Economic Stability and Growth", in *Essays on Economic Policy*, vol. i, pp. 135–7.
8. See Sir J. Hicks, *Capital and Growth* (Oxford, 1965), chapter 23.
9. See V. V. Bhatt, "Some Aspects of Development Strategy", *Indian Economic Journal* (Apr.–June 1967).
10. Sir J. Hicks, *Critical Essays in Monetary Theory*, pp. 187–7, 202.
11. See A. K. Sen, "Working Capital in the Indian Economy: A Conceptual Framework and Some Estimates", in *Pricing and Fiscal Policies*, edited by P. N. Rosenstein-Rodan (London, 1964). See also R. K. Hazari, *Industrial Planning and Licensing Policy* (Delhi, 1967).
12. See Sir J. Hicks, *Critical Essays in Monetary Theory*, p. 68. See also J. M. Keynes, *A Treatise on Money*, vol. i (London, 1935), pp. 34–6.

APPENDIX

The Indian Experience

This is precisely what happened in the Indian case after 1965–6, at the end of a decade of persistent and accelerating inflationary pressures.

The inflationary pressures in India during 1956–7 to 1960–1 arose largely from an attempted spurt in government expenditure generally and particularly in government investment.[1] The food sector was in overall balance.[2] But temporary fluctuations in foodgrains were not offset by an appropriate buffer stock policy, and hence this imbalance tended to reinforce the inflationary pressures.[3]

However, a liberal import policy in the initial years absorbed a part of the shock. It was only after 1957–8 that a drastic reduction in foreign exchange reserves resulted in stricter import controls. But then there were PL.480 food imports. Further, the price-rise expectations were not firmly held, with the result that though real wages fell, money wages did not rise at the same rate at which the cost of living index rose.[4] The share of profit-type incomes in the total rose[5] as a result of the profit inflation and tended to raise the saving–income as well as the tax–income ratio.[6] The luxury consumption and speculative investments financed out of profits did rise but were still gathering momentum. The effects of strict import licensing were already emerging.

The wholesale price index rose during this period at an average annual rate of 6 per cent. But a substantial part of this rise was due to the price rise of agricultural commodities and was partly a corrective for an earlier abnormal fall in their prices.

1960–1 was a year of good harvests when food availability exceeded the demand for food, and this was followed by another good year. Further, the share of government expenditure in the total national expenditure was kept in the previous two years at a level lower than reached earlier. The inflationary pressures were thus fairly mild during 1961–2 and 1962–3.[7]

But after 1962–3 there was again another fairly large spurt in government expenditure both on account of defence and investment. The tax–income ratio was raised but was hardly adequate for the purpose. Further, since 1961–2 there emerged a long-run food imbalance which was only partly offset by large food imports.[8] Money wages became progressively tied to the cost of living index and industrial costs rose. The system of import licensing became progressively rigid and insensitive to the demand for imported materials and had the effects discussed earlier.[9] The growth-rate of national income was just maintained at the level reached in the earlier years till 1964–5, but became negative in 1965–6. There was, as a result, an accelerating price rise. Monetary measures were tried to curb these pressures on prices during these years[10] but did not have much effect.

From 1965 to 1966 government investment was reduced and this in turn affected private investment and industrial output. The degree of underutilization of productive capacity rose sharply, the employment situation deteriorated and the investment climate worsened. Still, the sharp downward fluctuation in foodgrain output in 1965–6 and 1966–7 gave life to the inflationary spiral.[11] It was only in 1968–9 that two good consecutive harvests and larger food imports softened the spiral effects. There is now some degree of stability in food prices but at a reduced rate of investment and a high degree of underutilization of productive capacity in the industrial sector.

Even with this inflationary process, the economy did experience a fairly impressive growth during the entire period since 1950–1, when the planning experiment was initiated. The trend growth rate of national income was around 4 per cent per annum, while the growth rates in foodgrain output, total agricultural output and industrial output were 2.4 per cent, 2.6 per cent and 7.1 per cent respectively.[12] The pace of development potential was about 7–8 per cent per annum.[13] The saving–income ratio rose to a peak of 11–12 per cent in 1963–4 from an initial level of 6–7 per cent, while investment–income ratio rose to a peak level of 14–15 per cent in 1963–4; these rates, however, have declined since 1965–6.

Though per capita income rose, real wages and wage-type incomes per person hardly rose and may even have declined. Profit-type incomes rose as a proportion of national income and so did luxury consumption and speculative investments.[14] If the suggested policy-mix were adopted, it is likely that growth would have been more rapid, the rise in real wages more substantial and the growth process smoother. It may as well be, however, that the political and social constraints were such that a structural change could be initiated and rational policies evolved only through a process of inflation and creation of crisis-like situations.

NOTES TO APPENDIX

1. For basic statistics relating to output, sector-wise investment, government expenditure, taxes and balance of payments up to 1967–8, see Government of India, Planning Commission, Perspective Planning Division, *Economic Recovery* (Oct. 1967, New Delhi), mimeographed.
2. See A. Rudra, *Relative Rates of Growth: Agriculture and Industry* (Bombay, 1967), chapter 8. See also T. K. Velayudham, "Price Trends during the Three Plan Periods", *Reserve Bank of India Bulletin* (June 1967).
3. See V. V. Bhatt, "Savings and Capital Formation", and D. R. Khatkhate, "The Impact of Inflation on India's Economic Development", *Economic Development and Cultural Change*, part i (Apr. 1959).
4. See H. B. Shivamaggi, "Trends in Money and Real Wages in India", *Reserve Bank of India Bulletin* (Apr. 1964).
5. With regard to profit inflation and increase in income inequality in the urban sector, see P. D. Ojha and V. V. Bhatt, "Distribution of Income in the Indian Economy", *Reserve Bank of India Bulletin* (Sept. 1962).

6. For the extent of tax evasion, see P. D. Ojha and V. V. Bhatt, "Some Aspects of Income Distribution in India", *Bulletin of the Oxford University Institute of Statistics*, vol. vi, no. 3 (1964).
7. For overall and also sector and commodity-wise price behaviour, see T. K. Velayudham, *op. cit.*
8. See S. S. Madalgi, "Foodgrains Demand Projection: 1964/5 to 1975/6", *Reserve Bank of India Bulletin* (Jan. 1967).
9. For the impact of import licensing and fixed exchange rate, see B. R. Shenoy, *Indian Economic Policy* (Bombay, 1968). On the effects of inflationary pressures, fixed exchange rate and trade policies on exports, see M. Singh, *India's Export Trends* (Oxford, 1964). See also Panchamukhi, "Import Dependence and Production Efficiency", *Economic and Political Weekly*, Annual Number (Jan. 1969).
10. On the evolution of monetary and credit policies, see V. G. Pendharkar and M. Narasimham, "Recent Evolution of Monetary Policy in India", *Reserve Bank of India Bulletin* (Apr. 1966).
11. See M. Narasimham, "India: Inflationary Recession", *Bankers' Magazine* (Mar. 1968). See also "On Recent Recessionary Trends in Organised Industry", *Reserve Bank of India Bulletin* (July 1968).
12. For trend rates of growth, see V. V. Bhatt, "Agriculture in the Fourth Plan", *Economic and Political Weekly* (26 Oct. 1968).
13. On the concept and measurement of pace of development, see V. V. Divatia and V. V. Bhatt, "On Measuring the Pace of Development", *Reserve Bank of India Bulletin* (Apr. 1968).
14. For the effect of import controls and profit inflation on luxury consumption, see V. V. Desai, "Import Substitution and Growth of Consumer Industries", *Economic and Political Weekly*, (Mar. 1969); see also B. R. Hazari, "Non-Essential Consumption", *Economic and Political Weekly* (29 Mar. 1969).

18. Centre-States Financial Relations in the Context of Planned Development*

IN A FEDERAL form of government, the right to levy certain taxes by the Centre (federal government) and the States (State governments) as well as the right to share the proceeds of certain central taxes are governed by the form of the constitution adopted. However, even in the older federations like the United States, these inter-governmental financial problems are still live problems and are not settled once and for all.[1] More serious problems arise with regard to the rights of different governments to raise loans and the rights and duties in respect of planning and economic development. These problems did not arise when the older federations like the United States of America were formed as economic development was not then a national objective.[2] However, for the new federations like India, Nigeria and Brazil, the problem of planned economic development is vital and hence what Lady Hicks calls the capital account problems,[3] require urgent solution in the light of the objectives of the planned process of development.

Since the growth-responsive taxes can be largely levied only by the Centre and since the Centre has the dominant right to borrow in the domestic market as well as from abroad, a greater part of the financial resources accrues to the Centre. At the same time, a large segment of the development plan has to be implemented by and through the States.[4] Adequate planning and implementation at the State level thus require strengthening of their financial position in a manner that would evoke a creative response by the States to the challenging problems of development, which largely arise at the State level.

India has been a pioneer in Federal and State planning since 1950, and her experience in this field would doubtless be useful to the other new federations. It is the purpose of this chapter to indicate the broad lines on which Federal–States financial relations have evolved in India (section I), to discuss briefly rational principles of allocation (section II), to suggest a new institutional device for the rational use of borrowed resources by the Federal government and the States (section III), and finally to indicate the broad principle according to which such problems need to be tackled in a country with a democratic framework of government (section IV). Some of the suggestions may have some relevance to the problems of the older federations also in the context of their search for "major new fiscal coordination devices".[5]

I. Evolving Pattern of Centre-States Financial Relations

The Indian Union comprises seventeen States of varying size and at different

* Written in collaboration with Dr. Deena R. Khatkhate of the International Monetary Fund and published in *World Development*, vol. 6, no. 6 (June 1978).

stages of socio-economic development and their relations with the Centre are governed by the Constitution of India[6] which came into force in 1950. The process of planned development was initiated in 1951 with the formulation of the First Five-Year Plan (1951–2 to 1955–6; year: April to March).

Since the major elastic sources of tax revenue were allocated to the Central (Federal) government, the Constitution of India did acknowledge that the resources of the State governments would prove inadequate for the discharge of their functions. Accordingly, it provided for the obligatory sharing of income-tax receipts (Article 270) and permissive sharing of excise duties (Article 272) between the Centre and the State and grants-in-aid of the revenue to the States (Article 275). Articles 268 and 269 mention items of taxes which are to be allocated completely to the States, whether collected by the Centre or the States.

The Constitution, however, did not indicate either the *total share* of the States of the *allocation principles* with regard to income tax, excise duty or grants-in-aid. These were to be decided by the Finance Commission[7] to be appointed under Article 280. Thus, the total share of the States as well as its allocation among them has been governed by the periodical awards of the Finance Commissions.

(a) Finance Commission Assistance

With regard to tax sharing, it is likely that the intention of the framers of the Constitution was to specify the share of each State on the basis of what it could have collected, had it been in a position to levy that tax. In actual practice, it has been difficult to apply this principle either to income tax or excise duties. Under income tax, it is not possible to determine the magnitude of income assessable to tax of local origin. Similarly in the case of excise duties, it has not been possible to base the share of each State on the basis of consumption of commodities on which excise duties are levied.

As a result, income tax has been shared 80 per cent on the basis of population and only 20 per cent on the basis of collection, while excise duties have been shared 80 per cent on the basis of population and only 20 per cent on the basis of relative backwardness in terms of the recommendations of the Fourth Finance Commission.

Again, the total share of the State in each of the two taxes has been decided on a very *ad hoc* basis; the Fourth Finance Commission recommended 75 per cent share in income tax and 20 per cent in the excise duties.

With regard to grants-in-aid also, though the Finance Commission was expected by the Constitution to frame principles of allocation, no principles have been evolved and grants are recommended by and large on the basis of revenue deficits of the States.

However, since then, the Fifth Finance Commission has submitted its report (July 1969).[8] The Fifth Finance Commission has maintained the States' share at 75 and 20 per cent respectively, with regard to income tax and excise duties. It has, however, enlarged the divisible pool by including *advance* income tax payments under divisible income tax and *special* excise duties under divisible excise duties.

The share of each State in income tax on the basis of population is raised from 80 to 90 per cent (the Second Finance Commission had recommended this weight to population), while the remaining 10 per cent is based on assessments instead of collections. The criteria for the distribution of excise duties remain the same as given by the Fourth Finance Commission; however, social and economic backwardness is defined in more concrete terms than was done earlier. With regard to grants-in-aid, the Fifth Finance Commision has emphasized, as did the Second Finance Commission, broad fiscal needs as the governing criterion in place of just budgetary needs. Like the earlier Finance Commission, the Fifth Finance Commission has also examined in detail the projections with regard to the revenue and non-Plan expenditure items of the States. In the case of some States, it has recommended increases in expenditure on social services like education. It has also made some broad recommendations with regard to tax policy. However, no objective operational precise criteria of allocation have been evolved even by the Fifth Finance Commission. Again, Plan expenditure and the Plan assistance under Article 282 have continued to remain outside the purview of the Finance Commission.

Thus, in spite of the work of five Finance Commissions, no definite rational principles have been evolved to determine (a) the total share of the States in the Centre's tax resources, and (b) the relative share of each State. This indeed is a very unsatisfactory state of affairs and provides scope each time that a Finance Commission is appointed, for a variety of pressures and pulls to modify the awards of the previous Finance Commission. Such a situation could result in resource transfers that may prove detrimental to national interests as well as to the interests of some States. There is, thus, an urgent need to frame rational principles of allocation of resources—from the Centre to the States as a group as well as among the States.

(b) Planning Commission Assistance

In addition to such assistance to the States by the Centre, Article 282 of the Constitution provides for grants by the Centre to the States "for any public purpose". With the constitution of the Planning Commission, the latter invoked this Article of the Constitution for making grants to the States for Plan purposes. The grants by the Centre to the States under this Article are determined by the Planning Commission on the basis of the Plan expenditure by the States and their additional mobilization efforts; the grants-in-aid, as determined by the Finance Commission, are largely based on non-Plan expenditure of the States and their current receipts on the basis of existing taxes and tax rates.

Further, Article 239 of the Constitution provided for loan assistance by the Centre to the States; the Article states: "The Government of India may . . . make loans to any State . . .". This is thus a permissive provision and not an obligation on the part of the Centre.

However, considerable loan assistance to the States by the Centre is being provided under this Article on the basis determined by the Planning Commission.

Both the grants and the loans provided by the Centre to the States under Articles 282 and 293 are determined by the Planning Commission on the basis of the over-all Plans of both the Centre and the States. So far, however, neither the total share of the States nor the allocation among them was decided on any rational principles.[9]

Apart from there being no objective criteria to determine the allocation of Centre's Plan assistance, the nature of this assistance was such as to create inflexibility in its use and inequity in allocation.

> Hitherto the Plan schemes under different heads of development had their own patterns of assistance and the States could draw their grants or loans accordingly. Outlays under certain heads of developments as also some of the specified schemes were earmarked and could not be diverted to other heads of developments or schemes. This involved procedure of estimation, intimation and payment of Central assistance led to a complicated system of accounting and delays in final financial adjustments. Another feature of this system was that comparatively more advanced States were able to obtain a larger proportion of Central assistance in the form of grants even though the total quantum of assistance from the Centre was less in comparison with the less advanced States as they could adopt, in view of their revenue position being comfortable, such schemes as would attract large amounts of grant. In order to simplify the procedure for release of Central assistance, to avoid adoption of standard schemes unsuited to local conditions and needs as well as to ensure equity among States in regard to the grant assistance for the Plan, it has been decided that in future there will be no *schematic* patterns of assistance. Central assistance will not be related to any specific scheme or programme under the State Plans but would be given to the States through block grants and block loans. Each State will get a fixed proportion (30 per cent) of Central assistance in the form of grant and the balance (70 per cent) by way of loans. In order to ensure that the overall priorities of the Plan are adhered to, outlays under certain heads or sub-heads of developments and specified schemes will, however, be earmarked and will not be diverted to other heads of development.[10]

The share of each State in Central assistance is now determined (since 1969–70) on the basis of a rational objective formula evolved by the Committee of the Chief Minister of the States—a committee appointed by the National Development Council, which is the highest decision-making body with regard to Plan policies and which has as its members Ministers from the Centre as well as the States. The accepted formula is:

> after providing for the requirements of the States of Assam, Nagaland, and Jammu and Kashmir (the three border as well as backward States), the Central assistance to the remaining States for the Fourth Plan be distributed to the extent of 60 per cent on the basis of their population, 10 per cent on their *per capita* income if below the national average, and 10 per cent on the basis of tax effort in relation to *per capita* income, and that another 10 per cent be allotted in proportion to the commitments in respect of major continuing irrigation and power projects. The remaining 10 per cent it was decided, should be distributed among the States so as to assist them in tackling certain special problems, like those relating to the metropolitan areas, floods, chronically drought-affected areas and tribal areas.[11]

The *total* share of the States for the Fourth Plan, however, has been decided in a somewhat arbitrary manner at Rs. 35 billion for the five-year period.

(c) Central Assistance: Magnitude and Allocation

It is worthwhile to have some idea of the magnitude of Central assistance to the States in different forms. Table 1 presents the total assistance in the form of tax-shares and grants to the States as a proportion of the Centre's current receipts and also as a proportion of States' current expenditure; it shows loan assistance as a proportion of total capital receipts of the Centre and also as a proportion of total capital expenditure of the States. Table 2 shows the pattern of Central assistance to the States. The relative significance of Central assistance for each State is shown in the Appendix Table, while the share of each State in Central assistance is presented in Table 3.

TABLE 1. *Central assistance to States*
(per cent)

	A	B	A	B
	Proportion of current receipts of the Centre	Proportion of current expenditure of the States	Proportion of current receipts of the Centre	Proportion of current expenditure of the States
(i) Tax-sharing	15.7	17.1	15.8	18.9
(ii) Grants-in-aid	3.2	3.5	4.4	5.3
1. Finance Commission assistance (i + ii)	18.9	20.6	20.2	24.2
2. Planning Commission grants	6.8	7.4	4.0	4.8
1 + 2	25.7	28.0	24.2	29.0
3. Planning Commission loans*	24.2	37.0	22.4	30.5
4. Tax-sharing plus all grants and loans†	25.9	31.4	23.5	29.6

* Loans under A are given as a proportion of Centre's capital receipts and under B as a proportion of States' capital expenditure.

† Total Assistance (4) under A is given as a proportion of Centre's current and capital expenditure.

II. Allocation Criteria for Financial Assistance

(a) Criteria for Distinguishing the Roles of the Two Commissions

It is pertinent to draw attention to a development in the field of Centre–States relations that is against the spirit of the Constitutional provisions. The Constitution required all *normal* Centre–States financial relations on current account to be subject to the recommendations of a non-political independent body like the Finance Commission and envisaged only emergency grants under Article 282 to be provided to the States at the discretion of the Central government. However, after the appointment of the Planning Commission and the beginning of the era of economic development under Five-Year Plans, Article 282 grants have become a regular and an equally significant feature of the Centre–States financial relations. This development has introduced a political element in financial relationships, which the Constitution intended to be settled in a non-political environment.

Further, the basis on which Central grants are determined by the two Commissions is different. The Finance Commission takes into account non-Plan expenditure and current receipts with existing taxes and tax rates, while the Planning Commission's basis is Plan expenditure and the proposed changes in taxes and tax rates. Since States have to submit the required data to the two Commissions at different times and since the Central assistance by each is determined on different considerations, there has been some manipulation of data presented by each State to the two Commissions and the two sets of data are not consistent. Such manipulation of data is possible also because it is very difficult in practice to make a distinction between Plan and non-Plan expenditure. This distinction is spurious and in fact not relevant.

TABLE 2. *Pattern of Central assistance*
(per cent)

	1961–2	1968–9
A. *Finance Commission*	41.1	50.8
(*a*) Tax-share	34.1	39.8
(*b*) Grants	7.0	11.0
B. *Planning Commission*	58.9	49.2
(*a*) Grants	14.8	10.1
(*b*) Loans	44.1	39.1
C. *Total*	100.0	100.0

For these reasons, it does not seem rational to treat the Planning Commission grants on a different footing. The Article 282 grants should really become a part of *normal* grants-in-aid provided under Article 275 and should be governed by the recommendations of the Finance Commission. Grants under Article 282 were meant to be discretionary and the Constitution made this provision for emergency cases like drought, famine and other such natural and man-made calamities.

If this is done, there would emerge a valid distinction between current account transfers and capital account transfers; the current account transfers would be determined by the Finance Commission and the capital account transfers by the Planning Commission.

With regard to the current account transfers, the distinction between tax-sharing and grants has become increasingly unreal. For, in actual practice, the dominant criteria used for the purpose are the same in both the cases and relate to population, tax effort, relative backwardness and the like. Since both tax-sharing and grants have to be governed by more or less the same considerations, it should be possible to evolve rational criteria of allocation applicable to the *total* current resources transfer from the Centre to the States. Further, since the Planning Commission criteria also relate to more or less the same considerations which are taken into account by the Finance Commission, it would be rational to use a common set of criteria for the allocation of current as well as capital resources.

TABLE 3. *Allocation formula for Centre's assistance 1969–70*

States	Weights under the proposed criteria: Population	Average *per capita* revenue expenditure	Average *per capita* social expenditure	Tax revenue expenditure ratio	Total share	Fifth Finance Commission weights 1969–74*	Planning Commission weights 1969–74†
(1)	(2)	(3)	(4)	(5)	(6)	(7)	(8)
Andhar Pradesh	2.5	2.5	1.6	1.4	8.0	8.1	6.9
Assam	0.9	..	..	..	0.9	4.7	6.3
Bihar	3.2	14.3	4.2	..	21.7	9.7	9.8
Gujarat	1.4	..	..	3.8	5.2	4.3	4.6
Haryana	0.5	..	..	6.4	6.9	1.4	2.3
Jammu & Kashmir	0.2	..	..	..	0.2	2.6	4.2
Kerala	1.2	..	..	..	1.2	4.7	5.1
Madhya Pradesh	2.3	3.5	..	0.2	6.0	6.5	7.6
Maharashtra	2.8	..	..	5.3	8.1	9.2	7.1
Mysore	1.7	..	..	2.3	4.0	4.7	5.0
Orissa	1.2	..	1.3	..	2.5	6.1	4.6
Punjab	0.8	..	..	5.4	6.2	2.1	2.9
Rajasthan	1.4	..	..	..	1.4	5.3	6.3
Tamil Nadu	2.3	..	..	3.5	5.8	7.1	5.8
Uttar Pradesh	5.2	9.7	2.9	..	17.8	14.7	15.2
West Bengal	2.4	..	..	1.7	4.1	8.9	6.4
Total Weight	30.0	30.0	10.0	30.0	100.0	100.0	100.0

* Excluding share of grant in lieu of tax on railway passenger fares; excluding Nagaland.
† Excluding Nagaland.

(b) Rational Allocation Criteria

(I) TOTAL SHARE OF THE STATES

The first question which arises in this context is with regard to the criteria for determining the *total share* of the States in the current as well as the capital receipts of the Centre.[12]

With regard to the current account transfer, the total assistance to the States under tax-shares as well as grants by both the Commissions form about 50 per cent of the total receipts of the Centre with regard to the income tax and the excise duty (including additional and other special excise duties). Since these two tax sources are growth-responsive and since they are specifically mentioned in the Constitution, it would be desirable to fix the total share of the States with respect to these two taxes only. The proportion of these taxes to be transferred to the States may be fixed at the present level of about 50 per cent. The development function of the States with regard to law and order, education, health, housing, agriculture, industry and power are growing quite rapidly and for planned development in various spheres, a greater part of the responsibilities inevitably rest with the States. Their resources are inadequate for properly discharging these vital functions. For this reason, 50 per cent sharing appears to be an equitable formula for the purpose. Anyway, once some formula of this nature is devised, there would emerge some objective criteria and reasonable certainty with regard to the current account transfer to the States.

Similarly, rational objective criteria can be devised with regard to the total share of the States in the total *domestic* borrowing of both the Central and State governments. At present, each State has its own borrowing programme in addition to what it receives from the Centre by way of loan assistance. Domestic borrowing by the Centre as well as the States is mainly from institutional sources like the banking system, the Life Insurance Corporation and the Employees' Provident Fund. These institutions have to lend to the governments statutorily a certain fixed proportion of their liabilities and hence the total resources that can be borrowed by the Centre and the States are determined more or less by Statute. In these circumstances, the share in the total resources of each State is determined at present somewhat arbitrarily by the Reserve Bank in India in consultation with the Central government.

Borrowing from these institutional sources should then be centralized for the purpose of rational allocation. In such total borrowing, the total share of States (comprising States' direct borrowing as well as the Central loans to the States) has been, on an average, about 55 per cent for the last few years. It would be better to fix this share at some reasonable level so as to inspire confidence in the States with regard to the rationality as well as the certainty in relation to the determination of their total share. To begin with, in view of past experience, this share can be put at, say, 55 per cent.

(II) SHARE OF EACH STATE

This next question would be with regard to the rational criteria of allocation of central assistance among the States.[13] The present criteria give undue emphasis to the population basis for assistance. On the other hand, the weight assigned to equity and efficiency considerations is quite small even in the new formula devised by the National Development Council. The population criterion is a neutral criterion and does not serve the equity objective. Further, apart from equity, there need to be built-in incentives in the assistance formula for better tax effort and economy in expenditure by the States.

Thus, in addition to a neutral criterion like population, the allocation formula should give equal emphasis to equity and efficiency considerations. The following formula is devised in such a way as to take into account all these relevant considerations.

1. Thirty per cent of the total assistance should be given on a neutral criterion like population. This criterion is neutral as a very populous State could be either rich or poor.

2. Another 30 per cent should be shared on the basis of *per capita* revenue expenditure; all States with *per capita* revenue expenditure below the average *per capita* revenue expenditure for all States would get a share on the basis of the extent to which its *per capita* revenue expenditure is below the national average. All States with above average *per capita* expenditure would not be eligible for this share. This criterion subserves the equity principle as it would tend to equalize average *per capita* revenue expenditure in all States.

3. There would be an additional equity criterion. Ten per cent of assistance should be shared on the basis of *per capita* social expenditure comprising expenditure on education and health only. The sharing formula should be similar to the one under (2). The criteria (2) and (3) thus effectively serve the equity principle.

4. Finally, there has to be a criterion which rewards tax effort by the States. The assistance formula, hence, should have a built-in incentive for the States to improve their tax effort. Since their tax effort has to be judged in the light of their revenue expenditures, the criterion should be related to the ratio of taxes (excluding tax devolution from the Centre) to revenue expenditure. States with this ratio below the average ratio for all the States should not be eligible for this part of the assistance. States with above the average ratio would receive assistance and the extent of assistance to each State would be related to the extent of difference between the State ratio and the average ratio.

Such a criterion would serve as an incentive for the States to raise their tax effort as well as to economize on their current expenditure. The significant feature of the suggested criterion is that it would serve as an incentive for both these; for, the ratio could be raised by improved tax effort as well as economy in expenditure.

The proposed criteria depend on data relating to population and government budgets only. These data are firmer and more reliable than any other set of data. If the criteria are based on data with regard to *per capita* income or some composite index of economic backwardness, they would give rise to needless controversy as the data on which they would be based are neither firm nor reliable. The proposed criteria have an advantage over any other set of criteria such as the NDC criteria, as they are based on firm and reliable data.

Table 3 shows the weights to be given to each State under each criterion and the share of each State in the total assistance for the year 1969–70. The weights actually given by the Finance Commission as well as the Planning Commission are also shown in Table 3.

These weights could be fixed on the basis of average data for the last three years. That is, the weights for the next year should be fixed on the basis of data for the previous three years. Each year the weights should be revised and the share of each State determined afresh.

It would be seen from the table that the proposed criteria raise the shares of backward States like Bihar and Uttar Pradesh and at the same time raise the shares of some prosperous States also like Punjab as compared to the shares assigned by the two Commissions. This itself is an indication that both equity and efficiency considerations are given weights more appropriate than under the *ad hoc* formula of either the Finance Commission or the Planning Commission.

III. Institutional Machinery for Loan Assistance: Proposal for a National Development Bank

Even with these rational objective criteria, there is a further problem to be tackled. The current account transfer would be automatic in terms of the criteria suggested; it would be within the discretion of the States to use it for their normal functions relating to general administration, law and order, education, health, housing and such other services. However, the capital account assistance cannot be made automatic without defeating the very purpose of planned development. The capital account assistance is meant to finance sound and economically viable projects as are consistent with Plan priorities and objectives. Hence, though the shares of the Centre and the States would be determined in terms of the criteria suggested, the actual disbursement of this assistance should be governed on the basis of a rational appraisal and selection of well worked-out projects. If either the Centre or a State is unable to formulate sound projects, it should not obtain its share automatically; in such a case, the unused portion of its assistance should be diverted to financing sound projects in the States, which are in a position to present well worked-out projects which are viable and sound.

For this purpose, it would be necessary to create appropriate institutional machinery. What is suggested is a National Development Bank (NDB).[14]

It is this Bank which should have the sole right to borrow in the domestic as well as the foreign market. The Centre and the States would give up the right to borrow in the domestic as well as the external market. Thus, the Bank would be in a position to centralize all the resources which the Centre and the States obtain at present by means of borrowing from the financial institutions, corporate sector and the household sector in the domestic market and from foreign governments and international agencies. The securities of the Bank would be guaranteed by the Centre as well as the States.

The Bank would determine the share of the Centre as well as of each of the States in the resources on the basis of the criteria already discussed. However it would not automatically disburse this assistance to either the Centre or to any State. The actual disbursement would depend on its rational objective examination of the projects in the light of the Plan priorities and objectives. The funds of the Bank, thus, will not be rigidly earmarked for the Centre or any State; if either the Centre or any State is unable to present sound projects, the resulting surplus funds would be diverted for use in such States which have formulated sound schemes which can be approved by the Bank.

Further, the Bank would not give assistance to the Centre or the States directly. It would provide loan assistance only to statutory corporations and companies in the public sector. This would mean that all government enterprises in the fields of transport, power, mining and manufacturing industries, irrigation, housing, etc., should be organized as corporations and/or companies.

Three additional considerations should be kept in view. First, this Bank would give only loan assistance and not grants. Second, the assistance that it may provide to either a Central agency or a State agency should be governed by the condition that such an agency should foot the bill in financing a project up to a stipulated proportion of the total cost of the project; this condition is necessary in order to induce the Centre as well as the State agency to run its existing enterprises efficiently and plough back its surpluses for financing new projects. Third, there would be a need to introduce "soft" type of loans as is done by the International Development Association—an affiliate of the World Bank; such loans would mainly be for financing infrastructural projects like irrigation, transport and housing, where the social rate of return is higher than the private return. The softness of loans would be in the form of liberal conditions governing the repayment schedule or the rate of interest charged or both.

The broad sectoral as well as regional pattern of assistance would be determined by the Planning Commission. However, the assistance for individual projects—whether State or Central—would be left to the discretion of the Bank and would depend on the rational appraisal of the planned projects and their actual implementation.

For this purpose, the Development Bank should have adequate trained staff to appraise projects as well as to supervise the performance of selected projects. At present, there is some such staff in the various States as well as in the Central Ministries which could be transferred to this Bank. Further, the Bank can avail itself of the services of technical consultants in India as well as abroad. This would enable the country to pool its technical talents at one place in order to utilize it most effectively. As the Bank evolves, it could provide technical and managerial assistance to the various enterprises and even assist them in designing and formulating projects. In various fields, it can maintain a list of technical consultancy services available in India and abroad; and in cases where its own staff is inadequate, it could arrange the required assistance from these consultants. It should maintain live contact with technological research institutes in India as well as abroad; and in the light of this contact, it should be in a position to suggest appropriate technological modifications in projects that come to it for assistance. Further, it should be in a position to refer technological problems for their solution to research agencies in India as well as abroad. It should, in fact, be in a position to direct technological research in India towards the solution of current problems.

Such a Development Bank would improve the Plan implementation process in several ways:

(1) The selection of projects would be done on the basis of rational criteria, evolved on the basis of Plan objectives.
(2) The Bank would be able to identify the causes of delays and waste in the implementation of projects and render useful technical assistance to remove the deficiencies in the process.
(3) In view of delays in the implementation of some projects, the Bank would be in a position to switch over resources from such projects to other worthwhile projects and thus ensure optimum and effective utilization of its resources.
(4) The Bank would induce the public sector enterprises to formulate and implement projects in a business-like way.
(5) The location of projects would not become political issues but would be judged on the basis of rational criteria.

(6) The scarce technical, managerial and research talents would be used most effectively.
(7) The mobilization of financial resources would be done on sound business principles.
(8) Foreign governments and international agencies would be willing to extend assistance to the Bank run on business principles and thus the 'political element' in such assistance would be minimized.
(9) The terms and conditions for external assistance would be negotiated in a business-like way and would not become a political issue to the extent to which it does at present.

By centralizing these functions in the Bank, it would be possible to evolve a sound investment programme and ensure an optimum and effective use of resources. This would minimize the play of the irrational and arbitrary elements in the development process, and the administrative and political organs of the government would be able to perform their respective functions more efficiently than at present, once the specialized technical functions are taken away from them. Thus, there would be considerable gain in efficiency and, in consequence, the functioning of a democratic process would be facilitated.

IV. Delimiting the Range of Effective Political Decisions

The proposals with regard to the rational allocation of financial resources as between the Centre and the States and again among the States, as well as the proposal for a National Development Bank, are made in the light of a principle which seems to be of paramount importance for the efficient functioning of the democratic method in the context of the requirements of a planned process of development. This principle is of general applicability in all countries with a democratic form of government, where socio-economic development has become a national objective to be attained by means of appropriate State policies.

This principle relates to the proper demarcation of the fields of decision-making. There are certain fields in which decisions have to be primarily *political* decisions. These fields relate to the basic aims and objectives of planned development and the machinery for attaining these aims and objectives. However, once the aims and objectives have been specified and the machinery decided upon, the rest of the decision-making process should be governed by purely rational business-like considerations with the role of the State restricted to that of a general supervisor. If the effective range of political decisions is not properly delimited, it is quite likely that in a democracy with an increasing role of the State, decisions would turn out to be irrational from the point of view of the basic aims and objectives. Democracy does not require that every function of the State be subject to its political method. Thus almost any type of human affairs may conceivably be made to enter the sphere of the State without becoming part of the material of the competitive struggle for political leadership, beyond what is implied in passing the measure that grants the power and sets up the agency to wield it and the control that is implied in the government's role of general supervisor.[15]

NOTES

1. See W. W. Heller, *New Dimensions of Political Economy* (Harvard University Press, 1966). Mr. Heller argues for a new look at the Federal–State fiscal relationship in the United States and makes some specific suggestions for the allocation of federal tax revenue.
2. In the older federations, uncontrolled borrowing by the States gave rise to repeated trouble and led to the virtual bankruptcy of certain States. This was especially true in Australia. As a result of this experience, most of the older federations have now evolved orderly devices and practical methods of coordination. Australia has, for some decades, employed the services of an independent Loans Board on which both the Commonwealth and State governments are represented. See U. K. Hicks, *Development Finance* (Oxford, 1965), chapter 6.
3. See U. K. Hicks, *op. cit.*, pp. 110–11. Lady Hicks writes: "But planning for economic development, and particularly the construction and finance of fixed capital formation, presents problems in federal finance that are essentially new. India has been a pioneer in Federal and State planning since 1950. Other developing countries have all enthusiastically followed suit. ... In this field the older federations have much less experience to offer than in respect of borrowing policy and debt service, since they were already largely developed by the time that planning became feasible."
4. Mr. Heller notes: "Or to put it bluntly, the Federal Government simply cannot carry out large segments of its responsibilities at all—or at all efficiently—without strengthening the States and localities. A very large part of what we do through government is done through State and local units. ... But the States and localities are still the most essential part of a mechanism for feeding ideas up the line and having them come back down with money attached." See W. W. Heller, *op. cit.*, pp. 121–4.
5. See W. W. Heller, *op. cit.*, p. 117.
6. Government of India, Law Ministry, *The Constitution of India* (Delhi, 1965).
7. For a critical study of the Federal–State fiscal and financial relations in India, see D. T. Lakdawala, *Union–State Financial Relations* (Bombay, 1967). Mr. Lakdawala writes: "The role of the Indian Finance Commission is unique in many ways. It is one of the few Commissions provided in the Constitution. It has no parallel in established federal constitutions. The only close substitute is the Australian Commonwealth Grants Commission which examines the pleas of the claimant States for assistance. It has, however, no powers to suggest changes in tax-sharing nor the basis for distribution *inter se*" (pp. 47–8). See also, Government of India, Administrative Reforms Commission, *Report of the Study Team on Financial Administration* (Delhi, May 1967).
8. *Report of the Fifth Finance Commission* (New Delhi, 1969).
9. See A. H. Hanson, *The Process of Planning—A Study of India's Five-Year Plan: 1950–64* (Oxford, 1968). Hanson writes: "... the principles on which Central assistance to State Plans is allocated have never been made clear. ... At present no one knows, and even if the (Planning) Commission has all this worked out, no one is likely to be told, at least just yet" (p. 321).
10. Government of India, Planning Commission, *Fourth Five-Year Plan 1969–74* (New Delhi), pp. 54–5.
11. *Ibid.*, p. 54–5.
12. The problem of current account transfer from the Federal government to the States in the United States is being discussed currently and several criteria have been suggested. There seems to be some agreement with regard to the linking of the total share of the States to the Federal personal income-tax base; the allocation of such assistance to the States, it is suggested, should be based primarily on the basis of population with some adjustment for relative revenue effort and some equalization adjustment. See in this connection, M. L. Weidenbaum and R. L. Joss, "Alternative Approaches to Revenue Sharing: A Description and Framework for Evaluation", *National Tax Journal* (Mar. 1970).
13. In this connection see V. V. Bhatt, "On the Magnitude and Allocation of Federal Assistance to the States in India: Some Rational Criteria", *Public Finance*, vol. 24, no. 4 (1969).
14. See in this connection, Government of India, Administrative Reforms Commission, *Report of the Study Team on Financial Administration* (Delhi, 1967), pp. 345–402.
15. See J. A. Schumpeter, *Capitalism, Socialism and Democracy* (New York: 2nd edn., 1942), pp. 291–5.

Schumpeter writes: "The second condition for the success of democracy is that the effective range of political decision should not be extended too far. . . . As a third condition, democratic government in modern industrial society must be able to command, for all purposes the sphere of public activity is to include—no matter whether this be much or little—the services of a well-trained bureaucracy of good standing and tradition, endowed with a strong sense of duty and a no less strong *esprit de corps*" (pp. 291–3).

APPENDIX

APPENDIX TABLE. *Relative significance of central assistance to the States*

States	Grants* as a proportion of current expenditure		Loans† as a proportion of capital expenditure		Grants plus loans as a proportion of total current and capital expenditure	
	1961–2	1968–9‡	1961–2	1968–9‡	1961–2	1968–9‡
Andhra Pradesh	29.2	26.9	29.0	33.1	29.2	29.1
Assam	30.2	39.9	32.6	44.4	31.1	41.5
Bihar	37.8	35.6	41.9	42.2	39.4	38.2
Gujarat	34.8	25.3	47.6	37.1	39.2	29.4
Haryana	. .	20.4	. .	29.8	. .	24.2
Jammu & Kashmir	41.7	37.7	45.1	68.9	43.3	47.9
Kerala	22.2	35.4	35.9	45.3	27.1	38.3
Madhya Pradesh	28.2	22.5	58.3	48.5	38.1	31.3
Maharashtra	18.0	22.7	29.7	17.4	21.4	20.7
Mysore	29.4	32.5	38.9	23.3	33.6	28.5
Orissa	24.3	46.1	62.3	32.0	34.7	41.0
Punjab	29.9§	17.0	25.2§	19.5	27.8§	20.4§
Rajasthan	38.5	23.4	32.2	37.0	30.5	29.3
Tamil Nadu	22.2	26.7	30.0	12.7	24.9	20.7
Utter Pradesh	32.0	33.5	43.7	26.9	36.1	30.8
West Bengal	26.9	22.9	30.5	37.6	28.1	27.2

Sources: The ratios have been worked out on the basis of the data available from: (*a*) Government of India, Report of the Finance Commission, 1969; (*b*) Government of India, Planning Commission; and (*c*) State Budgets.

Notes: * Grants include tax-share plus grants by both the Finance Commission and the Planning Commission.

† Loans comprise Plan loans as determined by the Planning Commission.

‡ Revised estimate.

§ Punjab and Haryana.

POSTSCRIPT

This paper was published in 1978. Since then, the Seventh Finance Commission's report has been published. Even this Commission has maintained separate *allocation criteria* for income tax and excise duties. Of course, they have raised the share of States in income tax from 80 to 85 per cent and in excise duties from 20 to 40 per cent, thus raising the overall share of the States in the two taxes taken together well above 55 per cent. The allocation criteria for income tax are not changed. But the allocation criteria for excise duties are related to poverty and poverty-related variables and State Domestic Product. The basic data and techniques relating to these criteria, however, are *not reliable*. Even with these criteria, the shares of the poorest States, like U.P. and Bihar, are lower than those based on our criteria. Further, the Commission has not included any criterion which provides an incentive to the States to increase their tax-effort and/or economize on their expenditures. The merit of our criteria is that they are based on *firm* and *reliable* data and take into account both equity and efficiency considerations. In this connection see V. M. Dandekar, "Below the Poverty Line", *Economic and Political Weekly*, vol. xiv, nos. 7 and 8, Annual Number (1979). Dandekar writes: "There is a larger question involved: how much academic sophistication to permit in operative decisions of government? On closer examination, it is found that most often neither the underlying concept such as poverty nor the data such as coming from the National Sample Survey can bear much of the academic sophistication in which academicians often indulge. Nevertheless, such sophistication is legitimate in academic exercises which in their nature are exploratory. But it is clearly dangerous when academicians enter the field of operative decision-making without realizing the exploratory and speculative character of much of their past academic work. . . . With increasing computer facility, the danger today is real. In the particular case, we should be grateful that the exercise was simple and the error could be easily seen" (p. 286).

PART V. International Aspects of Development Strategy

19. International Monetary Reform: A New Proposal*

WITH such a large number of proposals for international monetary reform, it is with some trepidation that one ventures to add one more. However, I put forward this proposal in the belief that it is an operational proposal in the sense that it tries to supplement and not to supplant the existing international financial framework and seeks to improve the working of the international monetary system in two important ways.

It provides an internationally acceptable rule of thumb for increasing international liquidity. Professor Triffin's proposal leaves the expansion of international liquidity to the discretion of the reformed IMF and this may not be acceptable to sovereign countries, while the proposals of Stamp and Bernstein and the French collective reserve unit (CRU) proposal provide a very arbitrary rule. The basic idea behind the proposal of Professors Hart, Kaldor and Tinbergen is in some respects similar to mine but it does not seem to be operational for the reason that it involves avoidable costs and complexity in the working of an international monetary system. My rule of thumb has the merit, like Stamp's proposal, of taking into account the needs of the developing countries.

The other way in which my proposal would improve the working of the international monetary system is by providing a mechanism for expanding international liquidity *in such a way as to broaden the existing "key-currency" system. This would work by strengthening the system while permitting exchange rate variation in a "key-currency" country for the improvement of its payments position.* This mechanism has the virtue that it can work not only with my rule of thumb but also with any other universally acceptable rule of thumb. It is possible to accept *the mechanism* even if the rule of thumb is *not* acceptable. In fact, the proposed rule of thumb and mechanism for varying the volume of international liquidity can be treated as two independent proposals.

The Problem of International Liquidity

Because international trade is expanding, it has been argued that international liquidity should increase at an appropriate rate to facilitate the trade expansion. In principle, there should not be any need for an increase in international liquidity if the payments adjustment mechanisms of all countries are working smoothly. However, since all countries—developed and developing—have other paramount social objectives which cannot be sacrificed for the purpose of payments-adjustment there arises an increasing rigidity in payments-adjustment mechanisms and, hence, growing surpluses and deficits in the payments positions

* First published in *The Bankers' Magazine* (London, June 1966).

of various countries. International liquidity should therefore increase at a rate necessary for the finance of these growing payments imbalances so that *time can be provided* to the deficit countries to make whatever structural changes are necessary in their economies in order to correct their payment imbalances. Adjustment can then take place in a manner which is not inconsistent with the adjusting countries' own paramount objectives of maintaining full employment and/or economic expansion and which does not affect other economies adversely.

How then can we provide for this increase in international liquidity? This problem has arisen now because the existing gold-exchange standard ensures growth in international liquidity only at the rate at which increases in gold output are absorbed in monetary stocks. Reserves in the form of currencies will not increase once the payments deficits of the "key-currency" countries (the U.S.A. and the U.K.) are corrected; if however these deficits are not corrected, then the "key-currencies" must become weaker and a general rush to convert them into gold may well cause the collapse of the system.

Gold and International Liquidity

One way out of these difficulties would be to pre-empt the increase in the output of gold for use only as monetary stock. The increase in gold output (excluding the U.S.S.R. during the period 1950–62) was of the order of U.S. $13·2 thousand million, while the increase in "visible" gold stock of monetary authorities amounted to only $6·4 thousand million.[1] An international agreement could be arrived at by means of which the gold-producing countries were allowed to sell gold only to the IMF, which could later sell gold to monetary authorities.[2] The sale of gold to private parties would then only be allowed for approved industrial purposes through the central banks.

If the use of gold could be thus restricted to monetary reserves by international agreement, it would also help some of the developing countries like India to tackle the problem of gold smuggling, which probably is of the order of Rs. 400 million (£30 million) per year. This amount of foreign exchange, which now escapes the exchange-control authorities in a variety of ways, could then be used for more productive purposes. Further, if one of the speculative assets, which absorb current savings in the developing countries, were to be eliminated, these savings might seek other more productive avenues.

But even these measures would only bring about a once-and-for-all increase in gold reserves and arrange for their annual increase at the rate of annual gold production. This rate of increase would doubtless be inadequate from the viewpoint of international liquidity.

Revaluation of the price of gold has been suggested. However, its acceptability is dubious since it would provide a continuous gain only to the gold-producing countries and a once-and-for-all gain only to the gold-holding countries. Further, if this measure aroused expectations of a further rise in gold price, it would be difficult to prevent gold from being absorbed by private speculators. Finally, it seems difficult to justify a measure which would encourage the use of scarce resources for the production of a commodity which after all has no use value.

Search for An Alternative Universally Acceptable Rule of Thumb

As this analysis shows we must devise other ways of increasing international liquidity. One alternative suggested is credit creation by an international authority like the IMF. But the essence of any such proposals is to endow the IMF with the power to create credit at its discretion. Sovereign countries may well feel uneasy at proposals to give such discretionary power to the IMF for this would inevitably restrict the use of their own discretionary powers to manage their currencies.[3]

The alternative, then, is to devise a universally acceptable rule of thumb for the purpose of credit creation. Hitherto the use of gold automatically provided a universally accepted rule of thumb. Now it has to be replaced by some other rule.

This rule has to be such that the resulting credit creation provides not only some degree of stability in the world economy but also promotes trade through a fuller realization of its growth potential, while at the same time providing the necessary increase in international liquidity.

The vital yet vulnerable sector where incomes need to be stabilized is the sector of primary products. The price mechanism does not work smoothly in this sector. When the prices tend to decline, factors cannot shift easily from this sector to the manufacturing sector because of the dominance of fixed specific factors. Hence the common response is to increase output in order to maintain income levels. In many of the primary producing and developing countries, there are, in the short run, no employment outlets in the manufacturing sector. In addition the predominance of the family type of organization encourages the tendency to respond to price declines by increases in output.

In a situation like this, what is necessary is not to *reduce* the primary products output but to *raise* the growth rate in the manufacturing sector. For a relative excess of primary products output indicates that the growth potential of the world economy is not fully utilized. The manufacturing sector, however, does not respond to this situation in the expected way. In principle, when the primary product prices tend to decline, the real incomes in the manufacturing sector should tend to increase and this should provide an incentive to increase manufacturing output. But this does not happen as effective demand of the primary producing sector for manufactured products declines, as incomes in this sector are dominated by prices. Further, money wages in the manufacturing sector are rather rigid. They do not decline with the decline in primary goods prices. Hence the decline in the profits of the manufacturing sector as a result of a fall in effective demand is not offset by a fall in money wages. Moreover, in the developing countries, the considerable fluctuations in incomes experienced in the primary producing sector result in an uncertain demand for manufactured products and thus fluctuating and uncertain demand does not itself provide adequate incentives for investment in the manufacturing sector. Further, since their exports are dominated by primary products, the developing countries' capacity to invest by importing technology and equipment for their manufacturing sectors also tends to fall. The decline in the effective demand of the primary producing sectors is of course accentuated if investment in these sectors also tends to decline, since this investment consists largely of purchases of capital and intermediate goods.

The primary producing sector can be turned from a passive to an active sector if there is some mechanism to ensure stability in its income. If this condition could be met, effective demand for manufactured products could be maintained and even increased and a more favourable climate could be created for the required structural transformation in the developing countries.

This could be done for the primary products sector as a whole (and at the level of the world economy) by linking the changes in international liquidity to changes in the outputs of primary products in relation to the outputs of manufactured products. This is the basic idea behind the proposal for an international commodity reserve currency of Professors Hart, Kaldor and Tinbergen.[4] However, their proposal is probably too radical and complicated as well as administratively cumbersome and costly.[5]

International Monetary Reform: A Proposal

The basic idea in my proposal is to link price compensation to the primary goods exporting countries with the creation of international credit; this creation of international credit does not require the replacement of the present "key-currency" system but only its broadening in such a way as to reduce, if not eliminate, its present instability.

For *each* country, the primary export products should be identified. The price of this composite export should then be fixed within a certain range for, say, the next five years on the basis of the average prices during a previous period of, say, five years. Once the minimum and maximum prices are determined, any decline below the minimum prices should be fully compensated by the creation of credit by the IMF and any rise above the maximum prices should lead to a reduction of credit. Such a scheme would stabilize the export value of primary goods as a whole within a certain range and thus promote income stability in this sector.

The maximum and minimum prices of a *composite* export commodity for each country should be revised once in five years so that they may be consistent with the basic forces of international supply and demand. Further, the maximum and minimum prices of a composite commodity for each country would be fixed for a period of five years for determining the extent of price compensation for each country only so that the latter's export income from primary commodities may be stabilized. However, the actual prices of individual commodities would be governed by the basic market forces; the resource allocation thus would not be distorted. In the case of a decline in the price of a composite commodity for a given country below the fixed minimum price, in the first instance, it is the government of the country which would get the compensation; how to use the amount of compensation which it receives for strengthening the primary sectors would be left to the discretion of the government concerned. The latter would be expected to use it to bring about an optimum allocation of the resources of the country. In the reverse case, when the price of a composite export commodity rises above the fixed maximum price, it is the government of the country which would have to make payment in the first instance to the IMF; how it would distribute this burden by means of the tax machinery among the primary producing sectors of the country would again be left to the discretion of the government.

How should international credit be created? At the international level, the present gold-exchange standard would continue to operate. However, no country would be permitted to hold *gold* exceeding a certain proportion of its *gross* foreign exchange reserves. This proportion would be fixed in the light of the present gold holdings of different countries and probable increase in the gold output; this proportion should be modified at the interval of, say, five years in the light of changes in international liquidity. Further, the IMF quotas would remain and would be modified every five years in the light of the emerging situation. On top of this structure there would be a mechanism to increase international liquidity *in the form of short-term liabilities of the countries with convertible currencies*.

Suppose for a given country, the price of the composite primary goods "export" declines below the minimum price. This price fall would be fully compensated[6] by providing this country with convertible currencies. Which convertible currencies and in what combination would they be provided?

This would be decided on the basis of partly the *net* foreign exchange reserves (gold+foreign exchange deposits+reserve positions in the IMF minus short-term foreign exchange liabilities) at the *end* of a year and partly the *change* in the net foreign exchange reserves *during* a year of each country with a convertible currency. Half of the total compensation to be provided to a given country would be distributed among the different convertible currencies in such a way that the share in the resulting increase in the total short-term liabilities of each country with a convertible currency and *positive net foreign exchange reserves* would be the same as its share in the *total* net foreign exchange reserves of all the countries with a convertible currency and with *positive net foreign exchange reserves*. Thus, the increase in short-term liabilities of the convertible currency countries would be equitably distributed and the share of the countries with large net foreign exchange reserves would be higher than the share of the countries with low net foreign exchange reserves. This would correct any tendency toward an uneven and unbalanced distribution of net foreign exchange reserves among the convertible currency countries.

The other half of the total compensation should be distributed among the different convertible currencies on the basis of the *change in the net foreign exchange reserves of these countries during a year*. In this case, the increase in the short-term liabilities of each convertible currency country would be equal to half the total amount of compensation to be paid to a given country multiplied with the ratio of the *increase* in its net foreign exchange reserves during a given year to the total increase in the net foreign exchange reserves of the convertible currency countries *with a positive change in their net foreign exchange reserves during the given year*. In this case, the short-term liabilities of countries with a strong payments position would increase more than those of the countries with a weak payments position. How this scheme would operate is illustrated in the last section.

Such a broadening of the "key-currency" system would reduce the likelihood of speculative capital movements and thus make it simpler for a "key-currency" country to change its exchange rate if its relative payments position indicated the need for such a measure. Among the developed countries, the burden of adjustment in the event of a fundamental disequilibrium in their payments positions would thus be shared by both the surplus and deficit countries. In addition changes in exchange rates, if they become necessary, could be made without weakening their respective international monetary positions. Such changes in exchange rates would be further facilitated if the convertible currency country provided a gold guarantee with regard to its short-term liabilities *at the time of the change in its exchange rate*. The burden of such a gold guarantee would not be excessive as a weak country would not be adding to its short-term liabilities at the same rate at which the strong countries would be doing. This would be different from the present gold-exchange standard, which operates in such a way that international liquidity is provided by weakening a "key-currency".

In the event of a rise in the price of the composite primary "export" of a given country above the maximum, the country concerned would give up its additional export income and this would go to liquidate the short-term liabilities of the convertible currency countries.

Of the total proposed reduction in the short-term liabilities of the convertible currencies, one half would be based on their net foreign exchange reserves positions. In the first instance, the short-term liabilities of convertible currency countries *with negative net foreign exchange reserves* would be liquidated; the share in the reduction of short-term liabilities of each convertible currency country *with a negative net foreign exchange reserves position* would be equal to the ratio of its *negative net foreign exchange reserves to the total negative net foreign exchange reserves of all convertible currency countries with negative net foreign exchange reserves*. After the negative net foreign exchange reserves positions are liquidated, the remaining reduction in the short-term liabilities would be distributed among the convertible currency countries in such a way that the share in this reduction of short-term liabilities of each convertible currency country would be *inversely* related to its share in the net foreign exchange reserves of all convertible currency countries.

The other half of the total proposed reduction in the short-term liabilities of the convertible currency countries would be distributed among them in such a way that the share in this reduction of short-term liabilities of each convertible currency country *experiencing* a decline in its net foreign exchange reserves during a year would be equal to the ratio of the decline in its net foreign exchange reserves to the total decline in the net foreign exchange reserves of all convertible currency countries *experiencing such a decline during a given year*. If the actual reduction in the short-term liabilities is less than the proposed reduction, the balance would be distributed among the convertible currency countries in such a way that the share of each in this reduction is *inversely* related to its share in the total increase in the net foreign exchange reserves of all the convertible currency countries. Such a reduction in the short-term liabilities of the convertible currency countries would strengthen the relative position of the weaker countries in this group *vis-à-vis* the stronger.

This scheme thus would tend to stabilize incomes derived from the primary-goods exports of different countries so long as such incomes fluctuate directly as a result of international demand factors. If they fluctuated as a result of supply factors, prices would be stabilized but incomes would not be stabilized. For example, a drought or such other natural calamity may tend to restrict the supply of a primary product from a given country and thus tend to raise its price. In such a case, its export income would fall as a result of price stabilization. In this case, there would be a case for providing a more or less automatic resort to its drawing rights at the IMF on the lines suggested by Sir Roy Harrod[7] and for additional external assistance. The purpose of credit creation at an international level is to offset the working of adverse demand factors at a global level rather than to provide assistance in cases where there are supply difficulties.

Merits of This Proposal

Let us then summarize the advantages of IMF reform on the lines suggested:

(1) It would create the least disturbance to existing institutions and practices. The present gold-exchange standard would continue, and so would the IMF system. The IMF quotas would be periodically revised and more automatic and liberal drawing rights against the quotas would be permitted. But the gold holdings of each individual country would be restricted to a certain proportion of its gross foreign exchange resources and this proportion would be modified in the light of the trends in international liquidity.

(2) The creation of credit would tend to stabilize the prices and incomes of the primary producing sectors in as much as they are affected by demand factors. This would make it simpler for the manufacturing sectors to exploit its full growth potentialities.

(3) Since the developing countries are, by and large, primary producing countries, their export incomes would be stabilized and this would provide an appropriate international financial setting for their industrialization. Further, the price compensation provided in the event of a price fall can be utilized for the purpose of their structural transformation.

(4) The instability of the present gold-exchange standard would be removed as the "key-currency" system would be broadened in such a way that the creation of credit as well as its contraction would be related to the relative strength of each convertible currency country rather than to its relative weakness as under the present system.

(5) As a result of (4) and a gold guarantee with regard to short-term liabilities, it would be easier for a "key-currency" country to change its exchange rate when its payments position required it than it is under the present system. Exchange adjustments could be further facilitated if the member countries were allowed to use their drawing rights in a more or less automatic and liberal manner by the IMF.

(6) When there is overall inflationary pressure in the world economy, international liquidity would contract and overall inflationary pressure would be countered by the creation of liquidity.

(7) The changes in international liquidity would thus be regulated not at the discretion of the IMF but according to a rule of thumb. Sovereign countries would be free to pursue their internal policies in the light of their own objectives.

NOTES

1. B.I.S. *Annual Report* and N. Kaldor, "The Problem of International Liquidity", *Bulletin of the Oxford University Institute of Economics and Statistics* (Aug. 1964).

2. See C. P. Kindleberger, "The Prospects for International Liquidity and the Future Evolution of the International Payments System" in Sir R. Harrod (ed.), *International Trade Theory in a Developing World* (New York, 1963).
3. For a systematic and lucid analysis and summary of the different proposals for international monetary reform, see F. Machlup, "Plans for the Reform of the International Monetary System", *Special Papers in International Economics,* no. 3 (Princeton, 1962). See also *The Economist* (29 May–4 June 1965), p. 1065.
4. See A. G. Hart, N. Kaldor and J. Tinbergen, "The Case for an International Commodity Reserve Currency", *Trade and Development,* vol. iii (New York: UNO, 1964).
5. Since the commodity stocks will have to be turned over regularly in order to avoid spoilage, gross purchases would have to be much larger than the net additions required. These gross purchases would form a substantial proportion of the total world trade in these commodities. Thus, apart from the complexity of managing such purchases, this would give enormous power to the International Monetary Authority. Further, the costs of storage and proper maintenance of stocks may come to about $18,000–20,000 million even in the initial years. Thus, from the point of view of management as well as costs, the proposed international commodity reserve currency seems to be unworkable. See in this connection, H. C. Grubel, "The Case Against an International Commodity Reserve Currency", *Oxford Economic Papers* (Mar. 1965).
6. See, in this connection, J. E. Meade, "International Commodity Agreements", *Trade and Development,* vol. iii (New York: UNO, 1964), pp. 451–8.
7. Sir Roy's proposal is to transform existing drawing rights at the IMF into unconditional deposits usable without any conditions, freely transferable into any other currency but not into gold. These deposits can be periodically changed in the light of the developing international payments situation. See Sir R. Harrod, *Reforming the World's Money* (London: Macmillan, 1965).

APPENDIX

Suppose the compensation to be paid to the primary producing countries at the end of 1964 amounted to $1000 million. $500 million of this would be paid by the convertible-currency countries with their short-term liabilities in amounts based on *their net foreign exchange reserves position at the end of* 1964; the other $500 million would be paid by them in amounts based on *the increase in their net foreign exchange reserves during* 1964.

It will be seen from the table that the increase in the short-term liabilities of the U.S.A. is negligible, while there is no increase in the short-term liabilities of the U.K. and Japan. The largest increases in the short-term liabilities are with respect to France, Germany, Italy and Netherlands, the countries with the largest net foreign exchange reserves and strong payments positions. The impact of compensation payments in evening out the net foreign exchange reserves positions can be seen from the last two columns.

In the event of a rise in the price of a composite "export" of a given country above its fixed maximum price, the country concerned will have to pay the IMF, which would reduce the short-term liabilities of the convertible currency countries. Suppose the total reduction of short-term liabilities to be made amounted to $1000 million at the end of 1964. In this case, on the basis of *the negative net foreign exchange reserves,* $500 million worth of short-term liabilities of the convertible currency countries would be reduced; this would mean a reduction in the short-term liabilities of only the U.K. and Japan. The remaining reduction of $500 million of short-term liabilities would be distributed among the U.S.A, the U.K, Belgium, Canada and Japan on the basis of the share of each

See also P. J. McNulty, "Economic Theory and the Meaning of Competition", *The Quarterly Journal of Economics* (Nov. 1968).

The concept of competitive efficiency or of the optimum conditions again is not adequate to judge the results of evolutionary processes. On this, see J. A. Schumpeter, *Capitalism, Socialism and Democracy, loc. cit.* To quote: "First, since we are dealing with a process whose every element takes considerable time in revealing its true features and ultimate effects, there is no point in appraising the performance of that process *ex visu* of a given point of time; we must judge its performance over time, as it unfolds through decades or centuries. A system—any system, economic or other—that at *every* given point of time fully utilises its possibilities to the best advantage may yet in the long run be inferior to a system that does so at *no* given point of time, because the latter's failure to do so may be a condition for the level or speed of long-run performance" (p. 83).

See also K. J. Arrow, *op. cit.*, "The theme to be presented is that the combination of uncertainty, indivisibility, and capital intensity associated with information channels and their use imply (*a*) that the actual structure and behaviour of an organisation may depend heavily upon random events, in other words on history, and (*b*) the very pursuit of efficiency may lead to rigidity and unresponsiveness to further change" (p. 49).

3. See J. A. Schumpeter, "The Creative Response in Economic History", *Essays of J. A. Schumpeter*, edited by R. V. Clemence (Cambridge, Mass: Addison-Wesley Press, Inc., 1951).

   See also J. A. Schumpeter, *Business Cycles*, vol. i, *loc. cit.* To quote: "And this is equivalent to saying that the assumption that business behaviour is ideally rational and prompt, and also that in principle it is the same with all firms, works tolerably well only within the precincts of tried experience and familiar motive. It breaks down as soon as we leave those precincts and allow the business community under study to be faced by—not simply new situations, which also occur as soon as external factors unexpectedly intrude but by—new possibilities of business action which are as yet untried and about which the most complete command of routine teaches nothing. Those differences* in the behaviour of different people which within those precincts account for secondary phenomena only, become essential in the sense that they now account for the outstanding features of reality and that a picture drawn on the Walras–Marshalliam lines ceases to be true—even in the qualified sense in which it is true of stationary and growing processes: it misses those features, and becomes wrong in the endeavour to account by means of its own analysis for phenomena which the assumptions of that analysis exclude" (pp. 98–9).

   * "Those differences belong, as a special case, to the class of facts usually dealt with under the heading of Leadership" (p. 98).

4. Economists' analytic framework is congenitally incapable of handling the impact of *new* commodities—the vital fact about evolutionary processes. See Hicks, *op. cit.*, pp. 192–5.
5. J. M. Keynes, *Essays in Persuasion* (New York: W. W. Norton & Co., Inc., 1963), p. 373.
6. See R. I. McKinnon, *Money and Capital in Economic Development* (The Brookings Institution, 1973).
7. See J. A. Schumpeter, *Business Cycles*, vol. i, *loc. cit.*, pp. 123–30.
8. See J. A. Schumpeter, *The Theory of Economic Development* (Oxford: Oxford University Press, 1974). To quote: "There is nothing in our theory to support the old view—which with many people from the classical economists onwards has acquired the force of a dogma—that interest must of necessity display a secular tendency to fall. It may be shown, however, that the impression to that effect, which seems so strongly to suggest itself, is largely due to the element of risk, which accounts for medieval figures; and that the *real* rate of interest does not display any clear secular trend . . ." (p. 210).

   See also J. Hicks, *Critical Essays in Monetary Theory* (Oxford: Clarendon Press, 1967), chapter 5; "The Yield on Consols".

9. See J. A. Schumpeter, *History of Economic Analysis* (London: Oxford University Press, 1959). To quote: "Nobody can hope to understand the economic phenomena of any, including the present, epoch who has not an adequate command of historical *facts* and an adequate amount of historical *sense* or of what may be described as *historical experience* . . . the fact that most of the fundamental errors currently committed in economic analysis are due to lack of historical experience more often than to any other shortcoming of the economist's equipment" (pp. 12–13).

Example of working of the scheme

Country	Net foreign exchange reserves (end 1964)		Change in net foreign exchange reserves (end 1964 over end 1963)		Increase in short-term liabilities as a result of compensation payments			Net foreign exchange reserves *after* compensation payments (end 1964)	Change in net foreign exchange reserves *after* compensation payments (end 1964 over end 1963)
		Per cent of total positive reserves		Per cent of total positive changes	Based on reserves (end 1964)	Based on change in reserves (end 1964 over end 1963)	Total		
	[$ million]	(%)	[$ million]	(%)	($ million)	($ million)	($ million)	($ million)	($ million)
U.S.A.	762	3·04	−731	. .	15·20	. .	15·20	746·80	746·20
U.K.	−6562	. .	−873	. .	. .	. .	. .	−6562·00	−873·00
Austria	1148	4·58	+ 40	1·78	22·90	8·90	31·80	1116·20	+ 8·20
Belgium	912	3·64	− 2	. .	17·20	. .	17·20	894·80	− 19·20
Denmark	625	2·49	+168	7·46	12·45	37·30	49·75	575·25	+118·25
France	5643	22·50	+805	35·76	112·50	178·80	291·30	5351·70	+513·70
Germany	5730	22·85	+ 7	0·31	113·25	1·55	114·80	5615·20	−107·80
Italy	1573	6·27	+705	31·32	31·35	156·60	187·95	1385·05	+517·05
Netherlands	2349	9·37	+247	10·97	46·85	54·85	101·70	2247·30	+145·30
Norway	387	1·54	+ 33	1·47	7·70	7·35	15·05	371·95	+ 17·95
Sweden	953	3·80	+201	8·93	19·00	44·65	63·65	889·35	+137·35
Switzerland	3123	12·45	+ 45	2·00	62·25	10·00	72·25	3050·75	− 27·25
Canada	1871	7·46	− 94	. .	37·30	. .	37·30	1833·70	−131·30
Japan	−784	. .	−671	. .	. .	. .	. .	−784·00	−671·00
Totals	25,076*		2,251†		500‡	500	1,000‡		

* Total of *positive* reserves. † Total of *positive* reserve changes. ‡ Total 2·05 less than this amount due to rounding errors.

The table shows the net foreign exchange reserves positions at the end of 1964 and the changes in the net foreign exchange reserves during 1964 (difference between 1964 end position and the 1963 end position) of fourteen countries classified as industrial countries in the IMF's International Financial Statistics. The gross foreign exchange reserves include gold, reserve positions in the Fund and foreign exchange; they are taken from the table on Total Reserves (IFS, December, 1965, p. 15). The short-term liabilities are taken from the country tables in the IFS and include all short-term liabilities (including dollar liabilities reported by U.S.) mentioned under International Liquidity; these figures probably are not as reliable as the figures for gross foreign exchange reserves.

country in the total decline of net foreign exchange reserves of these five countries. The *total* reduction of the short-term liabilities of the U.K. would amount to $635 million.

20. A Payments Union for Developing Countries*

THIS chapter deals with clearing and payments arrangements among developing countries as means of facilitating trade liberalization and accelerated economic development. It is divided into three parts. Section I deals with the need for a universal Payments Union comprising, in principle, all developing countries' regional and subregional unions. It is argued in this part that unless the developing countries agree among themselves to take decisive, concerted self-help measures to expand their intra-group trade with a view to overcoming the foreign exchange bottleneck to the pace of their economic development, their case for assistance by the developed countries and international agencies in the field of trade and aid would appear much less convincing than it is.

In section II, a scheme for a universal Payments Union is proposed. This proposal seeks to provide merely a framework for actual discussion and negotiation among developing countries. The necessary details can be worked out only after there is general agreement with regard to the desirability of setting up of such a union and an appropriate number of countries agree to initiate this process.

A summary of the main points is given in the final section.

I

The consensus that has emerged from the various UNCTAD Conferences and the deliberations of various expert groups is that trade expansion among developing countries has to be viewed as an instrument for accelerating the pace of economic development and this can be facilitated by appropriate clearing and payments arrangements. Thus, in principle, the need for import substitution in the developing countries as a group through intra-group trade expansion and a payments arrangement to facilitate such trade expansion is recognized both at the expert level as well as at the political level.[1, 2, 3,]

As is now generally recognized, it is not possible for the developing countries individually to overcome the balance-of-payments constraint on their development through an industrialization process aimed at substituting domestic production for imports. Such measures have in fact intensified this constraint by inducing a higher growth in imports relatively to exports. The only viable long-term solution is to expand exports conmensurate with rising import requirements.

Such export expansion is not feasible unless the developing countries are able to produce industrial goods on terms, both with regard to price and quality, that can stand competition in international markets with similar products from the developed countries. This implies that the individual developing countries should

* Published in *Economic and Political Weekly*, Annual Number (Jan. 1969).

be in a position to reap the full benefits of specialization and economies of scale with regard to the industries that they set up. This is possible only if each such industry is assured a large enough market for its products.

The dilemma then with which the developing countries are faced is this. Their industrial exports should increase at an adequate rate if the industrialization process is to be viable. These exports are not feasible unless they can reap the full economies of specialization and scale. However, they cannot avail of these economies unless there are more or less assured export markets. A way out of this dilemma is to have a cooperative solution among the developing countries by means of which they agree to promote trade among themselves by adopting complementary production programmes.

Under the present circumstances, a complete harmonization of development plans is neither technically nor politically feasible. An advance can be made in this direction by coordination of plans in specific sectors only among small groups of countries. However, it is feasible to adopt agreed measures of trade liberalization and expansion so as to induce complementarity in the development process among the developing countries. This is the rationale for international cooperation in the trade field.

In principle, it is possible to expand trade among the developing countries in a reciprocally balanced way, so that no payments problem arises in the process. However, in actual practice, it is unlikely that the process of trade liberalization and expansion could be so perfectly synchronized. There would be inevitable delays in the expansion of industrial capacity so that the countries experiencing such delays would not be able to take prompt advantage of the trading opportunities offered by other countries. Thus transitional payments problems are bound to arise. Unless these payments problems are softened by appropriate credit extension, the purpose of trade liberalization and expansion would be thwarted. Mutual credit extension thus should form an integral part of the measures for trade liberalization and expansion. A Payments Union with credit facilities would not only facilitate trade liberalization and expansion but by its very existence would also serve as an inducement for the adoption of trade promotion measures. The consensus reached so far with regard to the need for a Payments Union rests thus on a sound logical basis.

The Payments Unions which are thought of at present are largely at subregional and regional levels. It is quite natural that such countries should get together and devise schemes of trade expansion and payments arrangements as are linked together through some consultative or cooperative machinery which, for historical and geographical reasons, has developed on a subregional and regional level. Such attempts should be actively supported by the UNCTAD as they represent gradual evolutionary steps toward world-wide cooperation in the development process.

Case for World-Wide Union

However, these subregional and regional schemes would naturally tend to discriminate against the non-member developing countries. Of course, some such discrimination is inherent in these schemes, as they represent forms of cooperation more intensive than are feasible in schemes of a universal nature. This discrimination, however, can be minimized and the benefits of these schemes can be progressively universalized if these schemes are operated within the framework of a world-wide scheme of trade expansion and payments arrangements for the developing countries.

There is, thus, need for a Payments Union, membership of which should be open to any developing country and subregional and regional unions. It should be obligatory on the part of the members to adopt agreed measures of trade liberalization and expansion if they are to avail themselves of the credit facilities of the Union. The very purpose of a Payments Union would be defeated if it is not linked with a well-phased-out programme of trade liberalization and expansion. It may not be possible for all the countries to join such a Union right at the time of its establishment. For one reason or the other, some countries would take time before they are convinced of the effectiveness of a Payments Union and are able to seize the opportunities for trade expansion generated as a result of the setting up of such a union. The significant thing, however, is to keep its membership open to all developing countries and to all subregional or regional payments unions.

Conditions of Success

The Union, itself, could be set up if ten or eleven countries, with significant potentialities of intra-group trade expansion, are willing to become the founder members of the Union. These would be the countries which have reached a certain comparable stage of development and which do experience, with some intensity, the balance-of-payments constraint on their further development. Further, it would be desirable to have fairly good representation of the various geographical regions in order to give the union an interregional or universal character. Of the eleven countries, at least three should be from each of the main geographical regions—Latin America, Asia and Africa. Purely illustratively, the following countries are suggested as the possible founder members of the union: Mexico, Argentina, Brazil, India, Pakistan, Ceylon, Uganda, Kenya, Libya, Yugoslavia and United Arab Republic. The Central American Clearing House or the proposed full-fledged clearing house in the Latin American Free Trade Area or any other subregional or regional union should be accepted as a member.

The opportunities for trade expansion of the developing countries would be greater if some developed countries participated in this Union as associate members on condition that they would accord in their markets preferences to industrial exports from developing member countries on a non-reciprocal basis. Subject to this condition, therefore, the developed countries should be accepted as associate members of the union.

Another condition could be that a developed country, desirous of becoming an associate member, should agree, in principle, to provide *net* external assistance to developing countries to the extent of at least 1 per cent of its GNP. Net external assistance should mean gross assistance in all forms with a maturity of more than five years minus all debt-servicing obligations of the developing countries.

These are the two significant contributions which the UNCTAD is persuading the developed countries to make towards viable development of developing countries. By formalizing these two demands the Union would provide some effective machinery for their acceptance by the developed countries. Once some developed countries accept these conditions, the process could gain momentum.

The first UNCTAD Conference represented a signal achievement for the developing countries inasmuch as it reflected the unity of their aims and objectives and indicated the various cooperative institutional and policy measures that are necessary at an international level to attain a process of self-sustaining growth. The subsequent UNCTAD Conferences should have taken some concrete measures to promote trade and particularly exports of the developing countries. However, no concrete proposals for action has emerged so far.

The UNCTAD would be justified in persuading the developed countries to grant financial assistance and take other appropriate measures to increase their imports of primary commodities as well as industrial products from the developing countries. However, all these demands would carry weight only to the extent to which the developing countries are prepared to adopt the various self-help measures required for the purpose. From this point of view, setting up of a Payments Union linked with an appropriate machinery for progressive trade liberalization and expansion should be given the highest priority by the UNCTAD.

The crux of the problem, therefore, would be that of devising a workable operational scheme for payments arrangements linked with trade expansion among the developing countries. The UNCTAD should actively promote, through an appropriate machinery, the adoption of acceptable schemes at subregional and regional levels. At the same time, the UNCTAD should ensure that the discrimination inherent in these schemes against the non-member developing countries is minimized and the benefits of such schemes are progressively universalized. The attempt, therefore, should be to promote subregional and regional schemes in the framework of a universal scheme which would, in principle, comprise all the developing countries and their subregional and regional schemes.

II

The suggested payments union would be open to all developing countries and subregional–regional unions, provided they accept the agreed code for trade liberalization and expansion. However, since all countries may not join it at the start, it would have to be set up initially by the countries which realize its need for mutual trade expansion.

The terms and conditions governing the credit facilities in such a Union can be worked out in detail only by discussion and negotiation among the founder members of the Union. Further, since this is a new experiment and since, in the nature of things, it would be difficult to predict the precise outcome, these terms and conditions would have to be sufficiently flexible and adaptable to the developing situation. At this stage, all that is possible is to indicate the broad framework for such a Union.

Since credit facilities would be related to the intra-group surpluses and deficits of the member countries, the Union would have to assume the clearing function.

The Union would deal exclusively with the member Central banks rather than with commercial banks or the public. Private traders would continue to operate with their own commercial banks and the latter would clear with their Central bank only those operations which cannot be cleared directly among them through the market.

Each Central bank would deposit with the Union the member currencies sold to it by its traders or commercial banks; its clearing account with the Union would be credited by this amount. It would draw on this account for the purchase of member currencies required for sale to its own traders and bankers. The Union would also debit each Central bank's account for any amount of its currency deposited with it by the other members, and credit it for any amount of its currency purchased from it by the other members.

All intra-group payments transactions, subject to each member country's exchange control regulations, would have to pass through the Union. The purpose of the Union would be defeated if the members are allowed the discretion of using or not using the clearing facilities for particular transactions. Since all intra-group payments transactions would have to pass through the Union's Clearing House, each member country would have to set up exchange control machinery for the purpose of distinguishing intra-group from extra-group transactions.

Two Distinct Advantages

Such multilateral settlement of surpluses and deficits of member countries would have two distinct advantages. First, intra-group trade would expand to the extent to which this multilateral settlement would replace the existing bilateral agreements involving settlement in inconvertible currencies. Second, this would economize on the use of foreign exchange reserves as only *net* surpluses and deficits would have to be settled by means of the use of foreign exchange reserves and that too only to the extent to which they exceed the credit facilities visualized by the Union. The saving in terms of foreign exchange could be considerable as the transaction costs in terms of convertible currencies on compensable trade and credit-financed trade would be avoided.

Intra-group trade among the developing countries was of the order of $6 billion in 1960.[4] Assuming that half of this trade is compensable (this proportion for the developing ECAFE countries is even higher) and further assuming that transaction costs amount to only one-half of 1 per cent, the total saving in terms of convertible currencies as a result of multilateral clearing arrangements could be of the order of $15 million per year. This figure is mentioned just to indicate the order of magnitude of saving in transaction costs. Further, the use of foreign exchange reserves of the order of $200–300 million could be avoided even with multilateral clearing arrangements without credit facilities, on the assumptions that clearing would involve monthly settlements and that the average lag between the conclusion of a commercial transaction and the receipt of the goods would be one month.

The net surpluses and deficits of member countries would have to be ascertained and settled periodically. In the EPU there were monthly settlements. The shorter the settlement period, the greater would be the operational costs of the Union. In order to save on transaction costs it would be desirable to have quarterly settlements with fixed ceilings on credit–debit positions of individual members—the ceilings to be fixed on the basis of the credit facilities envisaged.

For settling intra-group transactions of member countries each quarter, the Union would grant credit to the deficit countries and the surplus countries, in turn, would grant credit to the Union. On what principles should these credit facilities be determined?

The initial question that arises in this context is: should the Union relate its credit to the *total* intra-group deficit of a member or should it relate it only to the *incremental* deficit? Conversely, should a member relate its credit to the Union on the basis of its *total* intra-group surplus or should it relate it to its *incremental* surplus?

This question has to be settled in terms of the basic objectives of the Union. In order to relax the balance-of-payments constraint on economic development, the developing countries need to increase their intra-group as well as extra-group exports. The Union is an instrument for increasing intra-group trade. However, if its operation affects adversely developing countries' exports to the developed countries, it would defeat the main purpose of this device.

If the Union aimed at reciprocally balanced intra-group payments positions of the member countries, it could succeed either by diverting the exports of the developing countries to the developed countries toward intra-group exports or by reducing total intra-group trade. In either case, the basic purpose of the Union would not be served as the allocation of resources would not be based on rational considerations. Further, it would lead to such anomalous situations as where a poor country having a surplus with the Union but with a deficit with the developed countries would have to extend credit to the Union.

The way out is to relate credit facilities to either overall payments positions of members or to incremental intra-group payment positions. If credit is linked to overall payments positions, the Union would not be effective in its main purpose of increasing intra-group trade. Besides, credit facilities linked to overall payments positions are available through the International Monetary Fund. No purpose is served by duplicating the IMF machinery by creating a miniature IMF.

To attain the main purpose of the Union, therefore, its credit facilities should be linked to *incremental* intra-group payment positions of its members. This could be done by the establishment of a series of "initial positions" corresponding to the anticipated intra-group structural surpluses or deficits of particular countries. Such "initial positions" could be fixed, in the first instance, on the basis of the previous three years' intra-groups structural surpluses and deficits. For example, if a member had a structural intra-group deficit of $100 million in the past three years it would get credit only if its deficit exceeded $100 million; similarly a surplus country would grant credit to the Union only if the intra-group surplus exceeded its structural intra-group surplus during the past three years. These "initial positions" should be revised every three years so as to accommodate changes in the trade structure of the member countries. The objective of the Union, thus, would be to secure not an overall intra-group balance but balance only with regard to incremental trade.

Automatic Credits

The next question is whether credit facilities should be automatic or discretionary. Discretionary credit would involve an examination and assessment of the policies of a deficit country. Such discretionary provisions would be cumbersome and costly. On the other hand, a country would be inclined to liberalize and expand its trade with the member countries only if it is certain of obtaining credit facilities from the Union in the event of a resulting payments deficit. "... the more certain a country is of access to credit facilities, the more inclined it will be to risk the balance-of-payments consequences of reducing restrictions on imports from other members of the group."[5] As long as there are other provisions to prevent *persistent* surpluses and deficits, the Union's credit facilities should be automatic.

Since the objective of the Union is to expand intra-group trade, the credit extension to the Union by each member should be related to its intra-group exports in a base period (say, the past three years). Each year, a member country should agree to grant credit to the Union to the extent of 10 per cent of its average intra-group exports during the past three years. The absolute credit extension by each member, thus, would be determined each year afresh.

The borrowing right of each member should correspondingly be related to its intra-group imports.

On the basis of 1960 data for developing countries, their intra-group exports amounted to about $6 billion.[6] The total credit extension visualized would thus amount to about $600 million to begin with if all developing countries joined the Union. This is by no means an ambitious figure.

Terms of Credit

To induce developing countries to expand their exports to developed countries, a part of these credit facilities can be linked to hard currency settlement. For example, a deficit country could be granted full credit if its deficit is within the first half of its borrowing rights; while if its deficit exceeded this limit, it would be made to settle half of this excess in terms of convertible currencies. Similarly a surplus country would grant full credit to the Union up to half of its credit quota and for its surplus exceeding this limit, it would be paid half of the excess in terms of convertible currencies by the Union. Apart from inducing developing countries to expand their exports to developed countries, such provisions would also make surplus countries willing to grant credit and at the same time would induce deficit countries to adopt sound financial policies.

Surpluses and deficits in excess of the quotas would, of course, be settled in convertible currencies.

The creditor countries would naturally expect interest earnings on their credits comparable to what they would have obtained, had they accumulated reserves in the form of convertible currencies, say sterling or dollar. Interest charges on debit balances could be higher by one-eighth to one-quarter per cent so as to enable the Union to meet its operating expenses.

Since the objective of the Union is to attain reciprocally balanced positions with regard to incremental trade, credit and debit positions should not persist for more than five years. If they do, it would indicate that the member countries are either not liberalizing trade on the agreed basis or are unable to seize the trade opportunities in time. To induce them to correct their persistent creditor–debtor positions, the interest paid by the Union should be reduced on persistent creditor positions after three years by 1 percentage point and interest charged on persistent debtor positions should be raised by 1 percentage point.

Further, credit and debit balances with the Union persisting for more than five years should be amortized by a series of transfers of reserve assets among the member countries. The terms and conditions governing this amortization should be flexible and the governing council of the Union should take into account individual circumstances in determining the amortization schedule. *Discretionary* credits could be granted at this stage on the basis of examination and assessment of the member country's payments position and policies. Similarly, provision could be made for discretionary credits to the Union by persistent surplus countries.

To make this scheme of credit facilities acceptable to member creditor countries, it should not involve any exchange risk and there should be sufficiently strong guarantees against default. All accounts, therefore, should be denominated in U.S. dollars of a given gold value. A common unit of account would facilitate computations with regard to rights and obligations of countries having multiple currency practices. Of course, to the extent to which multiple currency practices are discriminatory as among member countries, they would violate the spirit of trade liberalization and expansion measures. The machinery set up for the purpose of trade liberalization should ensure that such practices are non-discriminatory as far as member countries are concerned.

All members should be required to channel through the Union's clearing all payments to a defaulting member until such default is fully covered and met. This would provide an exceptionally strong guarantee against default.

The Union could work without any working balances in convertible currencies if intra-group surpluses and deficits were to be evenly distributed among member countries. However, there could arise situations where there may be a convergence of many countries' deficits upon a few surplus countries only. In such a situation, the borrowing rights of the deficit countries could exceed the credit commitments of the surplus countries.

To meet such a situation, the Union would require some working balances in convertible currencies. These working balances should be provided by each member country agreeing to deposit with the Union 5 per cent of its gross foreign exchange reserves in the form of convertible currencies (excluding gold). This would be only a deposit which can be drawn upon by the member country in proportion to its use of its other reserves. Thus for all practical purposes, this deposit would form part of the member country's reserves and would be as liquid as its other reserves. Because of the exchange guarantee envisaged, this deposit would not involve even as much risk as is inherent in the reserves being kept in the form of convertible currencies.

No Serious Risk

The working balances of the Union, thus, would change from year to year and would increase as long as the reserve gains of some member countries exceed the reserve losses of other members. In any event, since developing countries would be maintaining certain minimum reserves in convertible currencies for meeting extraordinary payments problems, the Union's working balances would not decline below a certain level.

Member countries face no serious risk or inconvenience in agreeing to this commitment. Their deposits would earn as much interest as their deposits in the U.K. or the U.S.A. And, further, they would not face even as much exchange risk as they do on their deposits in the U.K. or U.S.A. because of the strong guarantees against exchange risk and default mentioned earlier. Such deposit commitment does not involve any cost to the member countries as would arise if they had to make a once-and-for-all subscription to the Union's funds.

The question, then, is: would the working balances so constituted be adequate?

Foreign exchange reserves in the form of convertible currencies (excluding gold) of the seventy-seven UNCTAD developing countries amounted to \$6769 million by the end of 1966.[7] If they agreed to deposit 5 per cent of these reserves as deposits with the Union, the Union's resources would be about \$340 million. The Union's convertible currency resources thus would be more than one-half of the total credit facilities (about \$600 million) envisaged, if all developing countries joined the Union, while the actual need may not exceed \$100 million. Dollars 340 million worth of resources, thus, should be adequate for the immediate future.

Drawing Rights with IMF

In future if the foreign exchange reserves of developing countries did not grow apace with their trade and particularly intra-group trade, the Union's resources may have to be strengthened in other ways. To meet such an eventuality, it is suggested that the IMF should accept the Union as a member and accord it appropriate drawing rights. Since the Union would be tending to promote a system of freer and multilateral trade and payments and induce rates of growth of trade and output higher than could be otherwise attained, it really would be trying to attain the basic objectives of the IMF. From this point of view, the IMF should explicitly support the establishment of such a Union and accord it adequate drawing rights and facilities for stand-by credits.

Once the Union gets enough experience and members inspire confidence among one another, the deposit commitment of members could be increased from 5 per cent of their gross foreign exchange reserves to 10 per cent and even further. And these additional resources can be used for the purpose of short-term investment in the member countries by the Union. Developing countries do at present invest in developed countries where they keep their reserves in the form of convertible currencies; it is a case of poor countries giving assistance to the rich. Since the rationale of accumulating foreign exchange reserves is investment in other countries, there is no reason why developing countries should not lend—they cannot help lending, in any case—these resources to member countries through the Union. With the guarantees envisaged and with the provision that only 50 per cent of the Union's resources would be invested in convertible currencies, there is no risk or inconvenience to member countries as their deposits with the Union would be as liquid as, and safer than, their convertible currency reserves.

Such a scheme would have several advantages:

(*a*) the Union would be in a position to grant short-term discretionary credit to member countries for meeting their deficits with developed countries;

(*b*) as a result, there would be saving in transaction costs involved in frequent and large foreign exchange transactions reversible within a short period of time;

(*c*) with resources in convertible currencies larger than any country could afford to hold, the Union would be able to invest them in longer-term deposits and investments than is now possible for each country acting separately. Thus the earnings from these reserves would be larger and developing countries as a group would be a net gainer in terms of convertible currencies; and

(*d*) since a part of the Union's resources would be invested in member countries, the rates of capital formation and growth would be higher in developing countries than they otherwise would be.

Superiority Over Reserves Fund

In the Report of the Group of Experts on "Payments Arrangements among Developing Countries for Trade Expansion",[8] the majority view has been in favour of a simple reserve fund, comprising only convertible currencies; this fund would grant discretionary credit in convertible currencies to a member on the basis of its overall payments position rather than on the basis of its payments position with the members.

We agree with the minority view that such a simple reserves fund would not be adequate for the purpose of trade liberalization and expansion within the group. It would merely duplicate the function of the IMF on a smaller scale. Since the credit facility would be discretionary and not automatic, the member countries would not be induced to use them. Further, since the fund would comprise only convertible currencies, the size of the fund would not be adequate for the purpose in view. The argument that trade patterns may be distorted resulting in misallocation of resources if the emphasis is on balance at the group level is not valid, as the Export Group itself realizes, for a Payments Union which links credit facilities to incremental trade within the group. The proposed provisions relating to credit facilities, further, provide adequate incentives for promoting extra-group trade also.

The proposed Union can work only on the basis of appropriate cooperation among member Central banks. Since the Union would be operated through Central banks, it would be worthwhile for the Central banks of the countries desiring to set up such a Union to initiate discussion on the subject. Such Central bank initiative has a further advantage that the whole discussion would remain at a technical level. With initiative taken at the governmental level, political factors may dominate.

III

1. It has been recognized both at the expert as well as political level that expansion of trade among developing countries has to be viewed as an instrument for accelerating their pace of economic development and that appropriate payments arrangement among developing countries would facilitate the required trade expansion.

2. The UNCTAD could justifiably ask for technical and financial assistance for the purpose from developed countries and international agencies.

3. In particular, GATT and IMF should make explicit statements supporting measures by developing countries for intra-group trade liberalization and expansion and for setting up subregional, regional and extra-regional payments arrangements.

4. The main task of UNCTAD, however, would be to stimulate efforts towards the establishment of subregional and regional trade-and-payments arrangements in a framework which would minimize the discriminatory effects of such groupings on non-member developing countries.

5. Such a framework can be provided by a Payments Union in which membership would be open to all developing countries and subregional and regional unions and which would be linked with agreed trade liberalization and expansion measures by member countries. Such a move would stimulate trade within the entire group of developing countries.

6. To start with, this Union should have at least three countries as members from each region—Asia, Africa and Latin America. Existing or proposed subregional or regional unions can become members of the Union.

7. Such developed countries as agree to the following conditions could participate in the Union as associate members:

(*a*) they should give trade preferences to industrial exports from developing countries in their markets on a non-reciprocal basis;
(*b*) they should agree to provide annually 1 per cent of their GNP as *net* external assistance to developing countries.

8. Clearing arrangements with regard to all payments transactions subject to exchange control regulations of member countries on a multilateral basis would reduce the transaction costs in convertible currencies of their trade and thus result in net saving of real resources. The unit of account could be the U.S. dollar of a given gold value.

9. Credit facilities should be automatic and should relate only to incremental trade of member countries within the Union. For this purpose, countries with structural surpluses and deficits should be assigned appropriate "initial positions" based on last three years' experience and these "positions" should be periodically revised. Thus, no distortion in trade patterns would result from the setting up of this Union.

10. Terms and conditions governing credit facilities should be such as to

stimulate intra-group trade without discriminating against trade of member countries with developed countries.

11. Countries having a deficit would get automatically from the Union credit up to 10 per cent of their intra-group imports in the past three years; however, excepting the first credit tranche, in the other tranche 50 per cent of the deficits would have to be settled in hard currencies. The interest rate would rise with the duration of outstanding debt, and persistent credit and debit balances for more than five years would be amortized by transfer of reserve assets among the member countries.

12. These provisions would provide incentives for correcting payments problems within the group; they would also provide an incentive to increase exports to developed countries.

13. Credit facilities would be available to member countries only if they adopt agreed measures of trade liberalization and expansion.

14. Surplus countries would grant credit to the Union up to 10 per cent of their exports in the past three years: excepting their first tranche credit, they would be paid 50 per cent in convertible currencies by the Union. The interest on outstanding credit balances would decline with increase in duration of such balances. Surplus countries would thus have an incentive to correct their payments surpluses.

15. All accounts with the Union would be denominated in U.S. dollar of a given gold value. Further, all members would be required to channel through the Union all payments to a defaulting member until such default is fully covered and met.

16. Thus there would not be any exchange risk for the members and at the same time there would be exceptionally strong guarantee against default.

17. There would arise occasions where the payment by the Union to the surplus countries would exceed its receipts from the deficit countries. For this purpose, the Union would require adequate working balances.

18. Such working balances should be provided by each member agreeing to deposit 5 per cent of its gross foreign exchange reserves (excluding gold) with the Union. Such deposits would for all practical purposes form part of the reserves of the member countries and would be available for meeting payments deficits in proportion to their use of their other reserves. The member countries would face no serious risk or inconvenience because of the exchange guarantee and strong guarantee against default. These deposits would be more riskless than the member countries reserves in the form of convertible currencies.

19. To meet situations where the reserves of the Union would be inadequate to meet its liabilities, the Union should be accorded membership status and drawing rights by the IMF.

20. The Union, after some experience is gained and mutual confidence among members is established, could raise the deposit obligations of members from 5 per cent of their gross convertible currency reserves to 10 per cent and use these additional resources for short-term investment in member countries instead of lending them to developed countries.

21. The initiative for setting up this Union should be taken by the Central banks of countries desirous of joining it. Initial discussion can start in a small

group of ten or eleven Central bankers. This would ensure that the discussion would remain on a technical level. And, in any case, the Union can operate only in cooperation and consultation with the member Central banks.

NOTES

1. *United Nations Conference on Trade and Development*, vol. i (New York, 1964), p. 31.
2. Report of the Expert Committee on Trade Expansion and Economic Cooperation among Developing Countries (TD/B/68).
3. UNCTAD, Report of the Group of Experts on Payments Arrangements among Developing Countries for Trade Expansion, TD–66–2357 (July 1966), chapter v.
4. *United Nations Conference on Trade and Development*, vol. vi, part i, pp. 97–9.
5. United Nations, TD/B/68, *op. cit.*, para. 61.
6. *United Nations Conference on Trade and Development*, vol. vi, part i (New York, 1964), pp. 97–9.
7. IMF, *International Financial Statistics.*
8. United Nations, TD–66–2357, *op. cit.*

21. Perspectives on External Assistance

THE ROLE of external assistance in the context of the evolving trends in the world political economy is little appreciated either in the developed or the developing countries. Whatever the motivations, attitudes and volitions of different countries and in spite of the conflicts which loom so large on the horizon, it appears that there are two significant trends asserting and unfolding themselves in the world at present. There is a trend towards building of an international community; the different countries, rich and poor, are struggling to evolve a consensus regarding the aims and objectives of an international community and a method of changing these aims and objectives by consent rather than by force. As an integral part of this process of international community building is the process of nation building going on in the developing countries, many of which acquired political independence only in the post-war period. These countries are struggling to become nation-states. They are striving to evolve a consensus regarding national aims and objectives so that a community can be built; and they are trying to evolve a method of resolving conflict of wills by peaceful and constitutional means. This effort at nation building does give rise to a variety of tensions, pressures and even violence; but in the ultimate analysis, this effort is a prerequisite to any advance on the front of economic and social development.

External assistance and, in fact, all types of mutual assistance in the field of ideas as well as techniques have to be viewed as instruments for accelerating these two interrelated processes—the process of building an international community and the process of nation building in the developing countries. If this role of external assistance is recognized, these two processes would be accelerated and there would emerge a viable international community as well as viable constituent units of this community—the two essential prerequisites to a process of steady and peaceful socio-economic and cultural development.

Failure to appreciate these trends has led, at present, and particularly since 1962, to a growing feeling of frustration in the developed as well as the developing countries with regard to the role of external assistance. The developed countries have started questioning the role of external assistance in accelerating economic development in the developing countries and the developing countries also feel a sense of frustration as they have not been able to attain the stage of self-sustaining growth as early as they had expected. This widespread frustration is largely due to the failure of both sets of countries to view the role of external assistance in the perspective of the objective trends and in a rational time-perspective with regard to the development process in a peaceful and stable environment.

* Paper originally presented at a United Nations sponsored seminar in Japan in May 1966, and published in *Economic and Political Weekly,* Annual Number (Feb. 1967).

An instrument can be effectively wielded only if the goals to be attained and the process of attaining them are clearly perceived. It is the lack of such perception which is responsible for the poor handling of this otherwise effective instrument. As I shall argue in this chapter, the process of socio-economic development has to be viewed as an integral part of the process of nation building and the time horizon for both these processes to work themselves out would be quite long. If this time perspective is kept in mind, it has significant implications with regard to the nature, magnitude and forms of external assistance viewed as an instrument for accelerating the pace of the interrelated processes of international community building, nation building and economic development. Since external assistance is an instrument for attaining certain ends, its effectiveness has to be judged by certain rational criteria which need to be evolved for a rational distribution of external assistance. Finally, if external assistance is to generate a viable growth process in the developing countries, it has to be coupled with active assistance in the field of export promotion.

I. Problem in Time Perspective

As it has been argued already, the process of economic development cannot take roots in the developing countries without nation building. This process of nation building can take various forms. The conflict of wills in these countries can be resolved by force. This presupposes, in the modern context, a well-organized disciplined party imposing its will on the people by force. This has happened in some countries and could happen in some other countries. But this way of nation building can be ruled out as undesirable both from the point of view of the citizens of a developing country as well as from the point of view of the international community. In fact, the success of external assistance should be judged by the extent to which it helps the developing countries in the task of nation building without the use of force.

The other way of resolving the conflict of wills is to develop a consensus with regard to the aims and objectives of the community and a method of changing them by consent of the members of the community. Whatever form this process may take in specific situations, this is essentially a democratic process and external assistance should try to accelerate this process. This means that external assistance sometimes would be used for the purpose of keeping the diverse elements of a country together rather than strictly for the purpose of economic development, narrowly conceived. For example, a project in a certain region of a developed country may not be the best from the economic point of view but it may have to be implemented with a view to keeping that region satisfied and thus evolving a consensus. What might appear as unproductive or wasteful use of resources to an aid-giving country may actually be the best way of promoting a process of nation building and thus a viable process of socio-economic development.

Further, it has to be realized that most of the countries attained independence with high expectations regarding the possibility of improving their living standards. As a result, different social and regional groups are exerting pressures for having a larger share of national income. For the sake of holding the community together, these egalitarian pressures would have to be recognized and to some extent satisfied in the process of economic development. However, this would mean that the capacity to save of the developing countries would not increase at the rate at which it could have increased without these pressures; external assistance requirements thus would be larger. If external assistance is viewed in this light, its magnitude may have to be greater, its duration much longer and its terms more flexible than what would be considered as reasonable from a strictly economic, and hence partial, view of the process.

Apart from this socio-political reason, even from the strict economic point of view, the time horizon for external assistance policies would have to be much longer than is commonly realized. The attainment of viability in the economic process would depend upon the minimum social goals which ought to be attained if the processes of nation building and economic development are to be generated and accelerated in a stable, peaceful and democratic environment and the speed with which the required resources can be generated by the country concerned. To simplify the problem, let us express the social goals in terms of national income and the required means in terms of the capacity to save and export of the developing countries.

Even to keep living standards at the present level, national income has to grow at the rate of population growth, which is about 2.5 to 3 per cent per annum in the developing countries.[1] A further at least 2 per cent per annum growth would be necessary in the consumption standards to provide the required incentive to carry out the transformation referred to above. Overall consumption, thus, should grow at least at 4.5 to 5 per cent per annum. For attaining self-sustaining growth in about twenty years, this would probably require an income growth of 6.5 to 7 per cent per annum[2] and may require an annual *net* investment–income ratio of about 23 to 24 per cent.

Even the minimum growth target of 5 to 6 per cent per annum as accepted by the United Nations would require a net investment–income ratio of about 17 to 21 per cent. Their *net* saving–income ratio probably varies from 5 to 10 per cent and probably on an average would be around 7.5 per cent.[3] The minimum *net* inflow of external resources the developing market economies may require, for a 5 to 6 per cent per annum growth rate, may be of the order of 15 to 21 billion dollars, assuming their net national income to be about 160 million dollars at *1960 prices*[4] and further assuming that their terms of trade would remain constant and the additional external resources for meeting the obligations relating to the servicing of their debt would be provided. This would come to 1.6 to 2.2 per cent of the 1960 gross domestic product of the developed market economies.[5] Assuming that the marginal *net* saving–income ratio in the developing countries would be at least 20 per cent, the required *net* inflow of resources would decline progressively over time and would become negligible in about twenty years' time. The *net* inflow of resources during a *period of two decades* that would be required by the developing countries would thus be only 0.8 per cent[6] of the gross domestic product of the developed market economies assuming that the latter grows at 4 per cent per annum during the period.

But even these rough calculations are based on the assumption that the real bottleneck in growth is domestic saving, and that the balance of payments would adjust itself over time. This assumption would be valid only if it would be possible for the developing countries to increase their exports at the appropriate rate. It has been estimated that a 5 per cent per annum rate of growth would require a 6 per cent per annum increase in imports, while the growth-rate of exports of primary products may rise from the present 3 per cent per annum rate to about 3.8 per cent rate by 1980, excluding petroleum exports and assuming that the terms of trade would not deteriorate.[7] If these trends continue, there would arise a foreign exchange bottleneck, though the saving bottleneck may not be operative. Under these circumstances, either continuing external assistance would be necessary or the growth target would not be realized. The only practical alternative is to increase the exports of industrial products. Thus for a viable development process, though external assistance is necessary, it cannot be a substitute for export expansion; but in this case, it may take a longer time for the attainment of self-sustained growth and it is necessary to keep in mind this time perspective.

Kaldor has estimated that with a 5 per cent growth-rate per annum and assuming that exports of the developing countries of primary products rise at 3 per cent per annum to the developed market economies and at 9 per cent per annum to the centrally planned economies, and that exports of manufactured goods increase at 10 per cent per annum, while imports grow at 6 per cent per annum, the balance-of-payment gap of these countries as a proportion of imports would diminish after 1990 and would diminish even in absolute terms after 2000. Their cumulative deficit in the balance of payments, excluding debt-repayment and interest payments on future external assistance, over a period of forty years would be equal to 0.8 per cent of the GNP of the developed countries, assuming that the latter would grow at 4 per cent per year.[8] These are all very rough calculations but they do indicate the necessary time perspective for tackling the development problem as well as the structural changes that would be necessary in the world economy.

II. Implications for Aid Policies

Though the quantum of external assistance to the developing countries from the developed countries has significantly increased since 1955,[9] as yet no uniform criteria have been evolved for the purpose. Different developed countries have different criteria; historical–political relationships tend to be the governing factors and even the mode of assistance is governed more by *ad hoc* factors than the real needs of the developing countries.[10] Further, since 1961, the magnitude of external assistance has not increased and the net assistance available for imports has actually declined as a result of the rising burden of servicing debt.

What is necessary to realize is that economic development of the developing countries is likely to be a fairly long-drawn-out process and that their need for extraordinary assistance is likely to continue for the *next forty years*. Even within this time period, the viability and speed of this process would depend on the long-term development strategy of each developing country and to what extent this is supported by external assistance and the evolving international framework relating to trade and finance.

To the extent to which it can be assumed that the marginal propensity to save as well as to export of the developing countries cannot increase till a certain development stage is reached and thereafter would depend on the rate at which growth takes place, the need for external assistance may be the greatest during the next two decades or so. On the other hand, the quantum as well as the forms of assistance would differ from country to country. In some countries, the absorptive capacity may be large, and greater capital assistance may serve the purpose of accelerating growth. In some others, absorptive capacity may have to be built up predominantly by technical assistance and their immediate need for capital assistance may not be as large as in the case of the former countries.

This means that external assistance requirement in the sense of *net* flow of resources to the developing countries[11] may be a stable proportion, say about 1 per cent of the GNP, of the developed countries *for the next forty years or so*. This proportion has to be decided at an international level; but it appears that less than 1 per cent may prove inadequate and may merely prolong the period of development. In any case, there has to be an international recognition of the need for this order of assistance for the next forty years or so; otherwise the aid policies would be too much governed by *ad hoc* temporary factors and may lead to a sense of frustration both in the developed and the developing countries.

This time perspective is also essential from the point of view of the terms and conditions governing external assistance. Short repayment schedules and high interest charges would merely tend to raise the figures of gross external assistance, assuming, of course, that the development process would be long drawn out and that the developed countries accept it as a political objective to facilitate viable growth in the developing countries.[12] On these assumptions, it would be politically much more feasible to keep in view the *net* inflow of resources required by the developing countries. This would mean that for the next forty years or so there should be a waiver on interest and debt repayment or, to the extent that these debt-servicing obligations are found to be necessary, they should be linked to the increase in trade among the developing countries, as suggested later.

Again if this time-perspective is kept in view, external assistance should be assured to a developing country on a continuing basis for the period necessary. Any uncertainty in this matter would upset their planning and development process and raise the final costs of development. Such would also be the case if assistance is tied to projects and no free assistance is provided for other purposes. Such project-tied assistance distorts the development pattern in favour of projects requiring direct external assistance while other more worthwhile projects may be ignored. Further, such assistance also distorts the investment process in favour of fixed investment, while other import needs necessary for operating investment projects are not met. Further, the use of abundant factors in a country like labour, local raw materials and indigenous capital goods may be discouraged as their indirect import requirements may not be met. All these distortions can be avoided if assistance is related to the requirements as worked out in the development plan of a country and further, if it is given to a substantial extent in the form of free foreign exchange resources; in this case, readjustment of a plan in the light of the developing situation can be rationally done and would not have to necessarily favour the projects for which external assistance is obtained. The magnitude as well as forms of external assistance, then, should be related to the development strategy and plan of each developing country.

III. External Assistance for Export Promotion

The growth process in the developing countries can be viable in the long run only if their capacity to export industrial goods is matched with their import requirements. It is increasingly recognized that even with an optimum choice of industries, it would not be possible for the industrial exports of the developing countries to be competitive in the international markets in the initial stages. The developing countries doubtless have an advantage of borrowed technology; but they have still to learn to adapt it to their own environment and develop the labour, technical and managerial skills required for the use of this technology. Further, by the development of an appropriate socio-economic infrastructure, the economic environment has to be made favourable for technical change. This learning process would inevitably take some time and doubtless much more time and resources would be necessary for the purpose than was necessary during the nineteenth century, since the technological distance to be covered is much greater. This learning process, once completed, would lead to increasing returns to factor inputs. Thus, the long-run social costs of industrialization would be much less than the immediate private costs.

This divergence between social and private costs is in fact the classical argument for protection since the days of Friedrich List. This protection, however, traditionally meant only tariff protection and that too restricted to a few selected industries. This, however, is too narrow a conception of protection. When a pervasive structural transformation is required, the price-mechanism does not reflect true social costs in any sector and hence this divergence between social and private costs affects all the sectors of an economy. Further, the nature of protection has to be related to the nature of structural transformation. Japan is a classic case, where, till 1898, protection was given not by tariffs but in other ways. As was the case in Japan and as it is the case with the developing countries, what is necessary is to reduce the prices of manufactured goods in relation to the prices of primary goods; for, primary goods prices are internationally determined and hence have to be competitive, while the prices of manufactured goods are high due to high costs during the learning process in the developing countries and thus are not competitive in the export markets. What is necessary, therefore, is not tariff protection, which does not reduce prices, but protection of the infant industrial export sectors through subsidies.

Even if the developing countries try to increase their industrial exports by an appropriate industrialization strategy and a subsidy to industrial exports, this policy would not succeed if the developed countries continue to protect their domestic markets against imports from the developing countries. Of course, it is true that if the developing countries succeed in increasing their industrial exports to the developed countries, the latter would have to adapt their domestic output structure to this development as has now become obvious in the case of the textile industries in the U.K. and the U.S.A. But these structural adjustments are relatively minor compared with the major structural transformation required in the developing countries. And in fact such structural adjustments are being made more or less continually as a result of technical change. Hence the developed countries do not require the type of protection which is necessary in the developing countries. With economic expansion and full employment policies, these structural adjustments would be easier to carry out especially as they would tend to raise real incomes in the developed economies.

Further, if the developed countries give preferential treatment to industrial imports from the developing countries, as a matter of deliberate policy, the adjustment process can be planned and effectively carried out. This is what seems to be happening in the trade of the developing countries *vis-à-vis* Russia. Both parties are enabled, thus, to adapt their output patterns to the developing trade pattern. The simplest and most effective way of giving preferential treatment would be to remove all import quotas and duties relating to the industrial goods of the developing countries. This would amount to one-way free trade between the developed and the developing countries. Once the need for protection is recognized for the developing countries during their learning period, free trade on the part of the developed countries should also be recognized as the counterpart of the same policy.

Apart from this, the developed countries can help the industrialization process in the developing countries by facilitating trade in industrial products among the developing countries. This can be done in a variety of ways.

1. Much of the external assistance provided by the developed countries to the developing countries is tied to purchases in the aid-giving countries because of balance-of-payments considerations. If such tied aid continues to be provided, there is no reason why the use of such aid for purchases in the developing countries should not be permitted. If, say, the U.S.A. provides aid to Thailand, the latter may not be permitted to make purchases in, say, Western Germany as the U.S.A. payments balance with Western Germany may be adverse; but the U.S.A. could permit Thailand to make purchases from Pakistan. With growing industrialization, it may be possible for some developing countries to meet the requirements of industrial goods of some other developing countries. The U.S.A. already permits such purchases under development grants.

2. The other suggestion is with regard to linking of debt repayment with industrial exports.[13]

Some developing countries have already accumulated foreign debts to such an extent that their debt-servicing obligations constitute a significant proportion of their exports.[14] For some of these countries, consolidation of a number of short- or medium-term debts and the extension of the average repayment period for the external debt as a whole would be necessary. But apart from this aspect of the problem, as long as external assistance has to be repaid and interest is charged on that, this would be a burden on the balance of payments of the developing countries. This can be lessened if external debt servicing itself can be linked with additional industrial exports.

This can be done in the following way. The total interest and amortization payment on external debt to be made by a developing country can be given over as external assistance by the donor country to another developing country and the latter country's purchases should be tied to the industrial goods of the repaying developing country. Suppose India has to pay $10 million as interest and amortization to the U.S.A. in a particular year. Suppose the U.S.A. has decided to give assistance of the value of $100 million to Ceylon in that year. The U.S.A., in that case, could give assistance of $90 million in terms of U.S. dollars and $10 million in terms of Indian rupees to Ceylon. India, in that case, would provide industrial goods worth $10 million to Ceylon and thus would meet the debt servicing obligation to the U.S.A. Ceylon now would be indebted to the U.S.A. for the amount of $100 million; but Ceylon too can likewise meet its debt-servicing obligations to the U.S.A. by supplying industrial goods to another developing country against a part of U.S. assistance to that country. This process could go on till the developing countries taken together are in a position to liquidate their debt to the developed countries by an appropriate increase in their capacity to export to the developed countries.

The same objective can be attained by another institutional device also. Suppose there are three regional development banks, one for each of the developing regions: Latin America, Africa and Asia. The interest and amortization payments on external debt by a developing country can be made to the regional development bank in terms of its own currency. The developing country would thus liquidate its debt-servicing liability to the donor country and it is the development bank which now would be indebted to the donor developed country. The development bank then would lend this money to the countries of the region or to the other regional banks. The development bank may insist on a part of the interest and amortization charges on its own loan to be made by the debtor countries in a convertible currency; this proportion may be progressively increased over a period of forty years, depending on the rate of increase in the exports of the developing countries to the developed countries, so that at the end of this long period, it may be able to liquidate its debt to the developed donor countries. Thus the regional development bank would get the funds that the developing countries are not in a position to provide; and the active and purposeful functioning of the development banks would lead to more effective coordination of industrial projects among the developing countries through an expansion of trade among themselves than would be possible by regional customs unions which may face several political and administrative problems.

From the point of view of the developed countries, such a scheme does not increase their burden. Let us assume that they would increase the *new flow of resources* to the developing countries from the present level[15] to 1 per cent of their gross domestic product and maintain it at that level for four decades or so. On this assumption, it does not make any difference with regard to the burden on the developed countries whether the interest and amortization payments are made directly to them or are passed on as assistance to the other developing countries. If the developing countries make the payments directly to the developed countries, the gross flow of aid will have to be higher by the amount of the payments in order to maintain net aid at a given level. The political advantage of the suggested scheme to the developed countries is that their new assistance each year would be exactly equal to the net flow of resources to be maintained towards the developing countries; the figures of gross assistance, then, need not look larger than what they actually are and this may facilitate their acceptance by the legislatures of the developed countries. Further, this scheme will enable the developing countries to increase their capacity to export and thus will also enable them to liquidate their debts finally to the developed countries in a shorter period than would be otherwise possible.

Such a scheme would facilitate the increase in trade in industrial goods among the developing countries. Their need is not only to make their industrial exports competitive but also to establish external markets for their goods. With a dual exchange-rate system, their industrial exports could become competitive. And the more difficult process of acquiring external markets for their industrial goods can be facilitated by this form of making interest and amortization payments. And once the developing countries get interested in such trade among themselves in industrial goods, this itself would provide a stimulus for appropriate coordination of their industrialization strategies. Such international specialization as would emerge from expanding trade would enable them to make their exports competitive in terms of price as well as quality in the markets of the developed countries also.

IV. Concluding Observations

Economic development of the poor countries is not merely an economic process but is an integral part of a wider social process of nation building. The development process therefore has to be judged in this wider perspective. Further, it has also to be realized that this process of nation building is interrelated with the process of evolving an international community.

External assistance should in fact be viewed as an instrument to facilitate and accelerate the pace of these processes in a peaceful, stable and democratic environment. Obviously, therefore, external assistance policies should be framed and implemented in this wider context.

Further, even the process of structural transformation which development implies would inevitably be a long-drawn-out process. To change over from a state of relatively static technology complex to one of continuous technical change involves a fairly time-consuming process of learning, absorbing and evolving the necessary skills, technical know-how, attitudes and behaviour patterns; it takes time to evolve an institutional framework necessary for absorbing and stimulating technical change. It may thus take a generation or two before the industrialization process can become viable and self-sustaining in these countries.

It is in this time perspective that external assistance policies should be evolved. The developing countries are likely to need external assistance for the next thirty to forty years. For such assistance to be effective in enabling them to generate a viable development process, it should be assured for a long enough period so that it can be effectively integrated with their development strategies and its terms and conditions should be fixed in the light of this objective of generating self-sustained growth in the developing countries. The United Nations Development Programme can play a vital role in developing appropriate machinery for assisting the developing countries not only in the field of formulating plans and strategies but also in the fields of project formulation and evaluation, technological research and manpower planning. Such assistance by the United Nations would ensure the soundness of plans and projects. External assistance policies then can be evolved on the basis of objective criteria and the developed countries would have adequate assurance of proper utilization of this assistance.

The ultimate viability of the growth process in the developing countries would depend on their success in promoting industrial exports. Their efforts in this field would be facilitated if the developed countries assist them in this process by (*a*) carrying out the mutually advantageous structural transformation in their own economies; (*b*) giving preferential treatment to their imports of industrial goods from developing countries; (*c*) linking interest and amortization receipts on their external assistance to trade in industrial goods among the developing countries; and, (*d*) permitting purchases by developing countries getting tied aid from the other developing countries.

NOTES

1. United Nations, *World Economic Survey 1963* (New York, 1964). See part i, "Trade and Development: Trends, Needs and Policies", p. 26. The average annual rate of growth of population in the developing countries is assumed to be 2.4 per cent during 1960–70.
2. The annual growth rate of their gross domestic product during 1950–60 was 4.4 per cent. See *World Economic Survey 1963* (New York, 1964), p. 19.
3. *Ibid.,* pp. 37, 227 and 236.
4. *Ibid.,* pp. 19 and 37.
5. *Ibid.,* p. 19.
6. During 1960–2, the annual average net flow of long-term capital and official donations from the developed market economies to the developing countries was of the order of 6 billion dollars. The interest and dividend payments on external capital by the developing countries were probably of the order of 2 billion dollars. Thus in 1960, the net flow of resources from the developed market economies to the developing countries constituted less than 0.5 per cent of the gross domestic product of the developed market economies. See United Nations, *op. cit.*, pp. 19, 227 and 236.

   Further, the proportion would be even lower if the real burden of this external assistance is calculated. For example, the "grant" element of a loan would be equal to the face value of the loan minus the discounted present value of future amortization and interest payments. Further, the PL 480 food aid should be valued at prices that would have ruled in world markets if the shipments had been sold rather than at the prevailing prices. If both these factors are taken into account, the estimated real cost of aid commitments by the OECD members comes to 4.2 billion dollars as against a net flow of official resources of the order of 6.3 billion dollars in 1963. See, in this connection, *Re-appraisals of Foreign Aid Policies*, by G. Ohlin (OECD Development Centre, Paris, 1959), chapter v. See also "The Cost of Foreign Aid", by J. A. Pincus in the *Review of Economics and Statistics* (Nov. 1963).
7. See United Nations, *op. cit.*, chapter 3; and N. Kaldor, "Dual Exchange Rates and Economic Development" in *Economic Bulletin for Latin America* (Nov. 1964).
8. N. Kaldor, *op. cit.* See in this connection, United Nations Asian Institute for Economic Development and Planning, V. V. Bhatt and N. A. Khan, *A Framework for Planned Economic Development of Lower Mekong Basin Countries* (Bangkok, 1966); for attaining viable growth, it is estimated in this study, on the basis of certain assumptions, that the Lower Mekong Basin countries would take about thirty years, provided they get external assistance of about $25 billion during this period.
9. The net flow of long-term capital and official donations from the developed market economies to the developing market economies increased from an annual average of $2.6 billion during 1951–5 to $6 billion during 1960–2. The centrally planned economies gave commitments of

external assistance worth $2.3 billion before 1960 to the developing countries; in 1962, their commitment was of the order of $429 million. See United Nations, *World Economic Survey* (1963), *loc. cit.*, pp. 227 and 273. Currently, external assistance has stagnated more or less at the level of $6 billion; the net flow of resources to developing countries is less than half this ratio.

10. The patterns of per capita assistance received so far by the developing countries from the developed market economies do not bear any close relationship to the needs of each country. The quantum of assistance seems to be determined by a complex of motives and is governed by historical–political relationships. See G. Ohlin, *op. cit.*, chapters ii and v.
11. Net flow of resources is defined as gross assistance less amortization and interest payments.
12. If net flow of resources to the developing countries is to grow, say, at 5 per cent per annum, and this is to be met by loans at 5 per cent with a maturity of twenty years, gross lending would grow progressively and will be about six times the net flow of resources in the thirtieth year. Thus, if the net flow of resources to the developing countries is to be maintained at, say, 1 per cent of the GNP of the developed countries, the gross lending by the latter would progressively rise to 5–6 per cent of their GNP if loans are at 5 per cent interest rate with a maturity of twenty years. If interest and debt-repayment are to be re-financed, as they would have to be if the net flow of resources is to be maintained at a certain rate to the developing countries, for the donor countries as a whole the question of the terms of aid is in the long run a choice between a large gross flow of loans with a substantial reflow and a smaller flow of grants or softer aid, with the same net effect on the balance of payments. See in this connection, G. Ohlin, *op. cit.*, chapter v.
13. See D. R. Khatkhate, "Debt-Servicing as an Aid to Promotion of Trade of Developing Countries" in *Oxford Economic Papers* (July 1966).
14. The outstanding external public and publicly guaranteed debt of developing countries amounted to over 24 billion dollars at the end of 1962. The servicing of that debt involves annual payments of some 900 million dollars for interest and 2.1 billion dollars on account of amortization. The total debt service burden of 3 billion dollars was equivalent to over 10 per cent of their export receipts in 1962. If income payments on private foreign investment are included, the total burden would be about 12–15 per cent of their export receipts. Further, according to a survey of the IBRD, thirteen developing countries, which account for close to half of the total outstanding debt, will be repaying over the next five years two-fifths or more of their public external debt. In addition to "long-term" debt, that is, debt repayable over periods exceeding one year, the developing countries have also large outstanding short-term liabilities, which must be settled within a year. See United Nations, *World Economic Survey, 1963, loc. cit.*, pp. 254–7.
15. The net flow of long-term capital and official donations from the developed market economies to the developing market economies was of the order of $6 billion per year during 1960–62. The annual interest, dividend payments and capital exports by the developing countries probably amounted to about $4–5 billion. Thus the net flow of resources to the developing countries was of the order of $1–2 billion only. See United Nations, *World Economic Survey, 1963*, pp. 227–8 and 254–7.

Author Index

Subject Index